Adulthood

Sheba → bskemp@mail.uh.edu   713 772 7717
                             832 577 2696
Amy Insall ainsall@yahoo.com 713 702 4063
Laura lofan hellokitty1979@msn.com 713 921-0744
AISHA ZAHIA JEREMYANDAISHA@aol.com

Essays by

Erik H. Erikson

Herant A. Katchadourian

Robert N. Bellah

William J. Bouwsma

Ira M. Lapidus

Tu Wei-ming

Thomas P. Rohlen

Susanne Hoeber Rudolph
and Lloyd I. Rudolph

Martin E. Malia

Winthrop D. Jordan

Tamara K. Hareven

Robert Coles

Wallace Stegner

Kenneth S. Lynn

Joseph Goldstein

Adulthood

Edited by ERIK H. ERIKSON

W · W · NORTON & COMPANY
New York · London

W. W. Norton & Company, Inc., 500 Fifth Avenue, New York, N.Y. 10110

Library of Congress Cataloging in Publication Data
Main entry under title:
Adulthood.
  Bibliography: p.
  Includes index.
  1. Adulthood.   2. Developmental psychology.
3. Cross-cultural studies.   I. Erikson, Erik
Homburger, 1902–
BF724.5.A35   1978   155.6   77–16659

ISBN 0-393-09086-8 pbk.

8 9 0

Contents

Preface to the Issue "Adulthood"

THE WORD "ADULTHOOD" figures rarely in the scientific literature of our time; it has none of the concreteness that attaches to terms such as "childhood" or "adolescence," and indeed seems almost a catch-all category for everything that happens to the individual human being after a specific chronological age—whether eighteen, twenty-one, or some other. Since the concepts of "childhood" and "adolescence" are themselves of relatively recent invention—Philippe Ariès reminding us in his *L'Enfant et la vie familiale sous l'ancien régime* (1960), translated into English as *Centuries of Childhood: A Social History of Family Life* (1962), that the idea of childhood did not even exist in medieval society and that our present "obsession" with it is related to certain specific modern societal needs—it is well to ask whether a comparable "obsession" may not soon show itself with respect to the next stage of the human life cycle. To suggest that we may be entering the "century of the adult," and to realize that this is not simply a function of changing demographic trends in advanced industrial societies and that it need not lead to a diminished interest in childhood, is the principal justification for the publication of this volume.

Adults in contemporary society are still generally viewed in too undifferentiated a manner; all too little thought is given to the ways in which they differ from one another or from children. Despite the growth of interest in the human life cycle, we still know far too little about the "stages" of adult life, not nearly enough about the transition from adolescence to adulthood, and surprisingly little about middle age, let alone senescence. We are insufficiently informed about how concepts of adulthood have changed over time, about how adult behavior is culturally conditioned, about the relevance of work, leisure, and family to adulthood. If adult status represented nothing but a chronological fact—the achieving of maturity in the eyes of the law—there would be no reason to explore its character further. But because the chronological concept of adulthood is useful only in quite limited contexts, telling us almost nothing about the affective life of individuals, very little about the ways in which men and women relate to one another both in the family and in other social groups, and still less about how all this may differ even among societies that appear to be superficially alike, more substantial inquiry is called for.

The archives for the study of adulthood still wait to be created. As will become obvious even from this volume, the materials for such study are abundant and varied. Whether the data are psychoanalytic, medical, literary, or religious, whether they are contained in moral and religious precepts, expressing normative values not necessarily realized, or in a historic record, revealing practices common to a specific people at a particular time, whether in a film, a diary, or a great literary work that waits to be interpreted, the problem is to develop analytic procedures that will make the study of "adulthood" as common as the study of "childhood." Indeed, the greatest need may be to relate the two.

Erik H. Erikson opens this discussion of adulthood by using Ingmar Bergman's film *Wild Strawberries* to illustrate his concept of the life cycle and the generational cycle. Building on ideas that he first adumbrated in his Jefferson Lectures, where he discussed some of the spatial and temporal aspects of being "grown up," Erikson interprets the extraordinary symbolism, verbal and visual, that Bergman introduces to illuminate his major propositions about the life cycle. The journey of an aging Swedish physician, Dr. Isak Borg, on his way to receive an honorary degree, is seen by Erikson to be "a pantheistic reunification with nature, a Christian pilgrimage to salvation—and, indeed, a modern self-analysis." In his confrontation with himself, through his memories, through others, and through his experience on that memorable day, Dr. Borg's adult life is given wholly new meaning, only vaguely hinted at in the first frames of the film. Erikson reminds us of our larger purposes in this volume when he writes: "Only the century of the child has made us study childhood and, indeed, youth, not only as the causal precursors of adulthood as it was and is, but also as a potential promise for what adulthood may yet become." In Erikson's essay, adulthood and old age are viewed in a context that makes them something more than the later stages of the human life cycle, separated off from the others.

Herant Katchadourian, in considering the biological transition from adolescence to adulthood—what he defines as the successful completion of puberty—insists that the process is "subject to a large number of genetic and environmental influences, including familial and possibly racial factors, and the effects of seasons, perhaps of climate, definitely of nutrition, illness, and emotional state." The "biological clocks" that indicate reproductive maturity reveal very little about the individual's capacity to cope with the social demands of adulthood in contemporary society. Katchadourian writes, "One possible though partial explanation for the current plague of psychosomatic ailments and stressful lives is that the culturally set pace of life in industrialized societies is frequently out of phase with its basic metabolic rhythms."

Those who planned this volume agreed that it would be useful to consider how concepts of adulthood have changed over time and how various civilizations and religions have defined maturity. Robert Bellah, in considering what is implied in the distinction between the *vita activa* and the *vita contemplativa*, shows their origins to be biologically based notions of activity and rest common to many archaic and primitive peoples, but taking on wholly new dimensions as philosophical constructs in the writings of Plato and Aristotle. In the East, in Buddhism and Confucianism, analogous transformations occurred. Bellah's principal interest, however, is to show how the Greek idea, modified and altered by Philo, Origen, and Augustine, and further transformed by Renaissance "civic humanism" culminating in the work of Machiavelli, took on even more radical forms in the writings of Thomas Hobbes. Bellah considers the role of modern science in rejecting Aristotelian views and in imposing a preference for action over contemplation. That the victory of the *vita activa* has not been complete, however, Bellah suggests, is demonstrated in the careers and intellectual preferences of men like Jefferson and Lincoln.

William Bouwsma, in writing about Christianity, distinguishes between "historical Christianity," which he defines as the record of Christian civilization, and "normative Christianity," which he defines as an ideal type, providing Christianity with whatever identity it may properly claim. It is "normative Christianity" that has particular interest for Bouwsma. In his view, Christianity's "conception of full adulthood" is nothing less than "total conformity to the manhood of Christ." Because this is an unachievable goal, man's duty lies in persistently and conscientiously proceeding toward it. The Christian life is seen as one of "indefinite growth"; the Christian is viewed as a pilgrim. The idea, Bouwsma explains, is replete with paradox, but it depends ultimately on the individual growing in community with others.

Ira Lapidus, in writing about Islam, concentrates on the Sunni tradition, the most important of the Muslim belief systems. Religious fulfillment, Lapidus explains, is to be found in the world of everyday reality; to grow in self-awareness is one of the Muslim's chief purposes in life. In considering the lives and teachings of al-Ghazali and Ibn Khaldun, Lapidus stresses the importance of the process of personal maturation for both these leading Muslim figures. As Lapidus explains, "In the Muslim view religious maturity is the integration of the individual with the norms of his religion and culture. . . . It is inner peace expressed and achieved through living in the world in accord with the revealed reality."

Confucianism, as described by Tu Wei-ming, is "not so much a state of attainment as a process of becoming." Tu explains the importance of the Way, which he calls a "root metaphor or basic analogy" that "depends as much upon a sense of inner direction as upon a prior knowledge of the established social norms." In each stage of life, the individual must be on guard against certain specific hazards; in each stage, he must be incited by equally specific possibilities. The paths of self-realization are various, and Confucius' life does not provide the one and only norm. As the author explains, "Actually the Master never instructed his students to follow him in order to find the Way. Instead, he inspired them to pursue the Way by realizing humanity—or adulthood, if you will—in themselves."

If these articles on adulthood and religion serve to indicate something of the ideals that various religious traditions have enunciated, it is important also to consider how the cultures within which these religions operated have conceived of this stage in the life cycle. The Japanese, according to Thomas Rohlen, have "an acute awareness of aging"; they live in a world very preoccupied with the change of seasons and of years. Rohlen believes that the Japanese interest in "character improvement" comes very close to being a national religion. The concern with personal cultivation, while very real, cannot be presented as an absolute which is unchanging and unrelated to the political and social events that have affected Japan. In recapitulating, necessarily briefly, the history of the last century in that country, Rohlen seeks to suggest how Japanese spiritualism has fared in different circumstances and what its present condition may be said to be.

Susanne and Lloyd Rudolph refrained from writing about adulthood per se in India, regarding it as a meaningless concept for Indian culture. Instead they considered one form of adulthood as it existed around 1900 within a single extended family of the ruling class in Rajputana. Their source, the diary of a Rajput nobleman named Amar

Singh, gives a picture of adult life very different from what is commonly found in the nuclear families of Europe or America. The importance of corporate identity is stressed; so, also, is the authority of elders, although it would at the same time be a mistake to talk of "gerontocratic omnipotence." The benefits and the costs to the individual of the extended-family system are weighed by the authors, and many of the conventional explanations of the differences between extended and nuclear families are denied. The authors write, "In arguing this way, we do not mean to suggest that becoming an adult in an extended family is just like becoming an adult in a nuclear family, but we do find that it is not so different, not so dichotomous, not so mirror-like, as much of the literature dealing with it depicts it to be."

Martin Malia, in writing about Leo Tolstoi, Tsarist Russia, adulthood, and the Russian family, gives this theme yet another dimension. Interested in documenting Tolstoi's preoccupation with an ethic of social concern within the context of a larger Russian literary tradition, Malia's purpose is to show how Tolstoi's great early works, including *War and Peace* and *Anna Karenina*, reveal a continuing exploration of the search for maturity and offer a coherent and appealing picture of what may be called the "normal" human life cycle. After 1880, Tolstoi is no longer satisfied with these "normal" descriptions of life, and in his post-"conversion" phase he writes in a very different vein. It is easy to ascribe this change purely to personal factors in Tolstoi's life, but Malia is clearly unwilling to leave the matter there. He believes that it is difficult "to win through to the self-determination of 'adulthood' and maturity in any age or any society," but that it has "clearly been more difficult to do so in modern Russia than anywhere else in the European world." His essay is in great part an exploration of why this has been so.

Winthrop Jordan suggests why the very notion of adulthood was unknown in the eighteenth and early nineteenth centuries, and why it was only in the twentieth century that the term came to have some meaning in the United States. Altered social conditions, drawing largely on the consequences of industrialization, made the distinctions between men and women less conspicuous, while establishing barriers to the employment of the young. As Jordan writes, ". . . work, or 'career,' began to lose its linkage with sex just at the time when the age of 'getting a job' was rising considerably. There was an increasingly solid social base for thinking of the late teens as an age when people of both sexes entered a distinct new phase of their lives, one which would last until it came to an abrupt halt, not so frequently as before by death but by mandatory retirement."

This is a theme that Tamara Hareven develops in very considerable detail. Her interest is to explore how in the late nineteenth century the aged came increasingly to be seen in the United States as weak and obsolescent; old age itself came to be viewed as a major social problem. Hareven speaks of the "growing segregation of different stages of life," of the changes in family structure and function, of the growth of privatism and individualism, all of which influenced the ways in which the aged were, and are, treated and regarded. In the end, the problems of the aged may be only the most acute manifestations of problems that are general to the society, experienced by others also, but particularly painful to those who are thought to be useless.

The centrality of work—the role of work in giving the individual a sense of his or her own worth—emphasized by Hareven is also developed by Robert Coles and Wallace Stegner. Without pretending to have found the "representative" American worker, Coles suggests that to be "grown-up" in the world of working men and women means to be "responsible, hard-working, dedicated, and, not least, self-sacrificing without demonstrations of self-pity." He sees Freud's emphasis on love and worth "as the normal aims of mature men and women [coming] very close to approximating what ordinary people say about themselves when they try to gauge their 'success.'" Unemployment is not simply an economic scourge; it is a psychic wound—a loss of self-respect.

Wallace Stegner writes that "more people than would probably admit it find in work the scaffolding that holds up the adult life." Even those "papered-over puritans" who choose to flee industrial civilization are almost always looking for the kind of autonomy in their work that artists and writers are thought to enjoy. Stegner describes how a writer's life is lived in fact, and what the decline in his creative powers does to his view of himself as an adult.

Kenneth Lynn approaches the subject historically and writes about how major American writers have represented adulthood in their books. He asks why so many American nineteenth-century novels have ended up on the shelves of children, and finds the answer in the psychic immaturity of the novelists themselves, who failed to treat many of the more important aspects of adult life, including that of adult sexuality. The heroes of these works typically resolve their problems by running away, "taking to the sea or withdrawing into gloomy mansions or high-walled castles or disappearing into the forest." Lynn finds the explanation for this escapism in the unwillingness of nineteenth-century American civilization more generally to face reality. The tendency has not totally vanished even in the twentieth century where much of American fiction appeals chiefly to the adolescent mentality, rather than speaking to the adult condition.

Joseph Goldstein considers the ways in which American law perceives the adult. He notes that American secular law rarely uses the term "adult" except to distinguish such a person from a child, nor does it impose moral or ethical standards for adulthood, though it may set minimum standards below which no adult may go without incurring certain penalties. Goldstein then examines "the interrelated processes in secular law for determining what persons are to be recognized as adults and within what boundaries such persons are to be free of coercive state intervention to pursue their own individual notions of adulthood."

This book owes a great deal to Erik H. Erikson, who conceived the idea for such a volume, pressed for it with the editors of *Daedalus*, and recognized very early the advantages of engaging authors from a great variety of disciplines and professions. In meetings, both formal and informal, held in various places in the United States, Erikson provided not only the focus for the discussion but also the intellectual inspiration for many of its more important features. Our debt to Erik Erikson is very substantial; we are pleased to acknowledge it.

So, also, we wish to thank the Ford Foundation for its generous support of this study. The Center for Advanced Study in the Behavioral Sciences in Palo Alto made its superb facilities available to us for one of our most important conferences. We recollect that occasion with great pleasure.

Stephen R. Graubard

ERIK H. ERIKSON

Reflections on Dr. Borg's Life Cycle

I. "Wild Strawberries"

1. THE PROLOGUE

INGMAR BERGMAN'S MOTION PICTURE *Wild Strawberries* records an old Swedish doctor's journey by car from his place of retirement to the city of Lund. There, in the ancient cathedral, Dr. Isak Borg is to receive the highest honor of his profession, a Jubilee Doctorate marking fifty years of meritorious service. But this journey by car on marked roads through familiar territory also becomes a symbolic pilgrimage back into his childhood and deep into his unknown self. For the doctor has been dreaming strangely of late. "It is as if I'm trying to say something to myself which I don't want to hear when I'm awake"—so he says during the course of the day to his companion on the ride, his daughter-in-law Marianne, who (for reasons of her own) does her best to confront him in their conversations with a number of disturbing, but at the end liberating, truths both about himself and about the Borgs generally. At the end of the day, the ceremonial honor bestowed on him seems almost unreal or, at any rate, transcended by a certain simple depth of wisdom that he has gained—and by a decision through which he and his immediate family find themselves firmly and subtly united.

I shall use Bergman's screenplay in order to present a conception of the life cycle and of the generational cycle which I find admirably illuminated in it and illuminated, for once, in a memoir which begins with the end—that is, it demonstrates how a significant moment in old age reaches back through a man's unresolved adulthood to the dim beginnings of his awareness as a child. To use the screenplay, however, means to retell it in my own words, which is already a first step in interpretation. But it also allows me to select quotations from Bergman's text and to describe his imagery, both of which are apt to get lost in the somewhat cumbersome experience of most non-Swedish audiences who must read the captions and ignore the foreign dialogue, as they attempt to view the picture in all its detail.

The prologue of the screenplay begins with a scene depicting the old doctor noting down the events and the reflections of that memorable day. Sitting at his massive desk, on which we see family pictures and writing utensils in faultless array, the white-haired, slightly stooped but solid old man with a square, handsomely aged face introduces himself as Dr. Isak Borg, age seventy-six, a Swede, and, of course, a

1

Lutheran (for "a mighty fortress," in Swedish, is *an vaeldig borg*). He has outlived nine brothers and sisters and has been widowed for many years. He is the father of one married but childless son, also a doctor, who, in fact, lives and teaches at Lund. Borg says of himself in a voice both pedantic and somewhat querulous, as if somebody had accused him of something:

> At the age of seventy-six, I feel that I'm much too old to lie to myself. But of course I can't be too sure. My complacent attitude toward my own truthfulness could be dishonesty in disguise, although I don't quite know what I might want to hide. Nevertheless, if for some reason I would have to evaluate myself, I am sure that I would do so without shame or concern for my reputation. But if I should be asked to express an opinion about someone else, I would be considerably more cautious. There is the greatest danger in passing such judgment. In all probability one is guilty of errors, exaggerations, even tremendous lies. Rather than commit such follies, I remain silent.
>
> ... As a result, I have of my own free will withdrawn almost completely from society, because one's relationship with other people consists mainly of discussing and evaluating one's neighbor's conduct. Therefore I have found myself rather alone in my old age. This is not a regret but a statement of fact. All I ask of life is to be left alone and to have the opportunity to devote myself to the few things which continue to interest me, however superficial they may be.[1]

Incidentally, at the doctor's feet, as he writes at his desk, is a Great Dane bitch, to all generous appearances a recent mother. Knowing Bergman, we realize this must be symbolic of a major theme to come. In the meantime, we note in Borg's opening statement a strange half-awareness that he can maintain a certain strained integrity only by withdrawing ("of my own free will") from sociability and attending to his own restricted sphere of interests. It is fascinating how, from the beginning, Bergman the director reveals in small visual and auditory hints a "classical" case of compulsive character: here, it is the old man's defensive voice and his punctilious manners that indicate with how much self-restriction he has paid for that seeming autonomy of proud withdrawal. It is, indeed, as if in the journey to come we were to be led from the compulsive "rituals" of a lonely old man, through some everyday ritualizations of his culture, to a grand ritual which both seals and permits a transcendence of his over-defined professional existence.

2. My Task

Before I continue to record Bergman's pictorialization of Dr. Borg's self-reflections and to reflect on them in turn, let me acknowledge a few unsolvable aspects of my task—and explain why I nevertheless persist in it. The occasional and cryptic use of psychoanalytic jargon by some of the less heartwarming figures in Bergman's casts of characters both acknowledges and wards off his obvious knowledge of depth psychology, Jungian and Freudian. In the foreword to the screenplays, he in fact refers to a textbook on the psychology of personality by Eiono Kaila, which he says was a tremendous experience for him: "His thesis that man lives strictly according to his needs— negative and positive—was shattering to me, but terribly true. And I built on this ground."[2] It is not my intention, however, to search the reflections conceived by this playwright to have been recorded by his "hero" regarding himself and other personages, encountered or remembered, for indices of what may have been conscious or unconscious to whom. As Bergman said, he "built on that ground," and a master's building has its own laws of solid construction and transcendent beauty. It is his art alone that permits him to depict a variety of persons of different ages in acute life crises in a sequence of short scenes which typify the whole course of their lives so vividly that we viewers are sure we have "met" them—both on the screen and in ourselves. That these persons are also linked with each other in an intricate network of archetypal symbolism is intrinsic to the artist's medium. One can, of course, elect to show in all detail the superb use of that medium[3] and to show, say, how the director uses an intricate composition of facial expressions and postures, of landscapes and seaviews, of roads, streets, and buildings in line with a symbolism that makes the journey at the same time a pantheistic reunification with nature, a Christian pilgrimage to salvation—and, indeed, a modern self-analysis. Or one could show, as I shall indicate, that what is pictured here is imbued, as well, with the inner logic of Freud's discoveries of the repressed unconscious, a logic equally indispensible for the foundation of such work. But the building itself is held together (perhaps more than any other Bergman play) by a pervasive realism, a tender earthiness in all its characters, and a sometimes ironical appreciation of their existence at their age in that spot on earth in that period of cultural and historical determination. It is this that makes them prototypical for human beings in other times and places and thus existential in the most concrete sense of the word.

As for psychoanalytic symbolism, the imagery does not, in fact, use the symbols indicative of the repressed unconscious (or does so only in well defined moments), but rather those denoting a tacit knowledge of the dimensions of existence that dwell in our preconscious and that we can become aware of in all its simplicity and depth in special moments, whether brought about by the "natural" crises of life, or by a meaningful confrontation with a significant person, or, indeed, by fitting ceremonies. As we shall see, all three conditions come together in Dr. Borg's journey: old age, confrontation, ceremonial. The result is that of a transcendent simplicity rather than a mystical rapture or an intellectual reconstruction. I am reminded here of what a minister friend recently said to a man who had felt induced to participate in the Eucharist, but could not explain to his skeptical wife what had "happened." What, he asked of my friend, should he tell her? "Tell her," he said, "that you ate bread and drank wine."

Only the rarest rituals convey this kind of truth, but works of art are bridges to them. I found in this screenplay an incomparable representation of the wholeness of the human life cycle—stage by stage and generation by generation—which again and again was also conveyed to my students, and which I now feel I should spell out for this new generation of adults who (after all we have learned about childhood and youth) feel impelled to comprehend, not without some reluctance and distaste, what adulthood and old age are really all about.

Now, my choice of this movie, year after year, in my undergraduate course on "The Human Life Cycle" at Harvard, has of course also earned me some more or less friendly suspicions from my students. Some said I looked like Dr. Borg, for which my thanks, although who *could* look like Victor Sjoestroem? Or did I, with my background, *wish* I had become just such a doctor? Now, there is a "connection" between the movie and my childhood, for Lund lies on the Ore Sund, on the Danish side of which (only twenty miles away) I spent the sunniest summers of my early years visiting my uncles' country houses and being taken for boat rides. But when it comes to some students' further queries whether such affinities might not be the reason for my seeing such a detailed resemblance between this movie and my views of the human life cycle, I can only register such suspicion as an essential aspect of any conception of the whole of life: for can our concepts and can our terms ever transcend the observations and values that are part of our own limited existence—and of the illustrations we chose? Nevertheless, it so happens that this screenplay is a good one, as well as the only one of its kind and, furthermore, that it would well lend itself to a social critique demarcating what is universal in it and what hopelessly culture- and class-bound.

I will, then, proceed, after a summary of each major scene, to offer my terms for the psychosocial stages and crises encountered, and I will even capitalize them in order to point up the scheme to be accounted for systematically in the second part of this paper.

3. THE DREAM

Over the years, my students nicknamed my course on "The Human Life Cycle" "From Womb to Tomb" (or "From Bust to Dust"). It was, therefore, of some ironic significance that this screenplay opens with a view, as it were, from tomb to womb, or more exactly, from the coffin to the cradle. It begins with a dream in which the doctor comes face to face with his own corpse. This dream is the psychic background for the day's events; we shall learn only later what—besides the dreamer's age—was the dream's own "cause."

In the dream memoir we see Borg briskly, if on not too firm legs, pursuing his "usual morning stroll" through some familiar but now, indeed, very empty streets, their façades shining in the northern summer's morning light. The "silence was absolute," and his footsteps echoed rhythmically. Over a store, apparently shared by a watchmaker and an optometrist, there hung a large clock by which he usually set his own watch for the exact time. But now it had no hands, and two large eyes-with-eyeglasses that hang beneath it appear to have been bloodied. The doctor pulled out his own watch: it, too, was without hands, and when he held it to his ear, he heard, instead, his own heart beat wildly. But, ah, there *was* somebody standing there in all the emptiness: a man with a felt hat, his back to Borg. On being eagerly touched, the man turned. He had "no face," and promptly collapsed. On the sidewalk lay only a heap of clothes with some liquid oozing out of them: the person was gone.

Up the empty street now came the sound of trotting hoofs as church bells began to toll. An ornate hearse appeared. As it passed, one of the wheels got stuck on a lamp post, broke off, and struck a church wall right behind the doctor. The hearse began to sway, somewhat like a cradle, with an eery creaking sound strangely reminiscent of a tortured birth cry. A coffin, splintered, lay on the ground, and from it a corpse reached out for the doctor. It had, in fact, the doctor's face "smiling scornfully." The dreamer awakened.

Let us see: Footsteps that echo; bells that toll; a clock that ticks but does not tell time; a heart that thumps and pounds. It may be that, thus enumerated, the symbolism might seem almost trite. But there is the overall imagery and, of course, a sequence of utterly convincing close-ups of the old man's facial expression, ranging from outright fear to the daily dread known to all old people: when will it all suddenly stop. And then there is an inkling of a personal, a neurotic, anxiety revealed only in the imagery. The text says that the other man's, the double's, face was "empty." Yet, his appearance shows thin lips tightly drawn down and eyelids pressed hard together: tight-sphinc-tered, then, and caricaturing a retentive personality—holding and keeping out. That other person, that double, collapses and spills his lifeblood in the gutter—a theme to be repeated that day in a number of wasteful and destructive "spillings."

Awakened, the dreamer, as if to ban a curse with a formula, pronounces: "My name is Isak Borg. I am still alive. I am seventy-six years old. I really feel quite well." The viewer's first impression is that the dream tries to tell the dreamer—is it "merely" because of his advancing age or in view of the approaching "crowning" event in his life, or for some other reason?—that he must not permit his official and so isolated self to beckon him into the grave. Perhaps he must as yet learn to die?

Let me, at this point, briefly and didactically introduce some capitalized terms for the last crisis of the Life Cycle. In my publications on the subject,[4] I have postulated a dialectic struggle in old age between a search for Integrity and a sense of Despair and *Disgust* (or *Disdain*). These contraries, in dynamic balance, are essential to a final human strength: Wisdom. While, at this point, I will not try to explain or defend these terms, they should denote to the reader some of the qualities of Borg's inner, as well as social, discord and suggest that such qualities can be present, in some simple form, in any old person. If I also assume that these qualities have precursors in earlier crises throughout the life cycle, "crisis" at any age does not necessarily connote a threat of catastrophe but rather a turning point, a crucial period of increased vulnerability and heightened potential. "Cycle," in turn, is meant to convey the double tendency of individual life to "round itself out" as a coherent experience and to form a link in the chain of generations from which it receives and to which it contributes both strength and fateful discord.

It will take Dr. Borg's whole journey (and this whole paper) to come to a closer formulation of the old-age crisis in the light of the whole course of life.

4. THE DECISION

It is three o'clock in the morning, a Swedish summer dawn, and Borg suddenly knows what he must do: he must go to Lund by car rather than, as planned, by air-plane. We learn only gradually that this is, indeed, a fateful decision, for the fourteen hours required for the trip also allow for a number of half-planned, half-improvised events. But we know immediately that such autonomy itself is utterly surprising; for in a scene both humorous and pathetic, it becomes clear that the widower lives in some antagonistic interdependence with a very bosomy and very possessive housekeeper named Agda. She has been with the family for forty years, many of them with him alone. She is his age, but (typically?) he refers to her as "an old woman." Awakened by Borg (his nightclothes in disarray), she can only ask, "Are you sick, Professor?" Hearing his decision, she is upset and hurt: he is destroying, she says, the most solemn day of *her* life. Whereupon he mumbles that they are not married, and she praises God for it. But she gets up, dramatically packs his clothes, and sulkily serves breakfast, anticipating with some disgust that she must fly ahead alone to get things ready in Lund.

But then a houseguest appears, awakened by the old couple's bickering. She is a beautiful, clear-eyed, strong-faced young woman in a dressing gown: Marianne, son Evald's wife. She has been visiting and now asks whether she can accompany the doctor to Lund. Thus, truly, the scene is set for the most significant of a number of masterly encounters. For as they leave the big city and drive into the countryside, Bergman makes the most of the alternative possibilities of the perspectives provided by the automobile. We first see the car from the air, moving with other tiny vehicles on a central urban traffic circle, choosing their destined exit. Then, focusing on the car's interior, we see the rest of the world move by. Both driver and passenger can look ahead at near and distant goals or inward into the sequence of their thoughts; they can throw sideward glances away from each other, or look at each other with rare, sudden, and necessarily fleeting visual engagements. Whoever is driving can glance at the rear-view mirror and see what is approaching or perceive the faces of whoever happens to be in the back seat. This moving stage also permits dozing off—and dreaming! Thus, Bergman civilizes the mechanical range of a car's interior for his own story-telling purposes. Let me list the scenes that follow and then characterize some in my terms.

First, as Borg drives along dreamily (maybe thinking of his dream), he is obviously made uncomfortable by the young woman's presence. Marianne, with a determination born of some circumstance that for a while remains a secret, decides to confront him with his discomfort: one cannot help thinking of Cordelia, driving Lear's despair to the surface. It all begins—as it will later end—with small, even petty, items which yet betray basic attitudes. She, nervous, wants to smoke, he stops her, nastily. She says the weather is nice, he predicts a storm. Suddenly, she asks him his "real" age—for no "real" reason. But under the impact of his dream, he knows that she, too, wonders when he will die. Pettily, still, he thinks of the money her husband owes him, pleads principle: "a bargain is a bargain." Evald, he is sure, understands this, for they are "alike," as she, indeed, admits they are. Then the bombshell: "But he also hates you." An indescribable horror appears on his face, but he keeps calm. Asked why she doesn't like him, she elaborates on the fact that she has now stayed with him a month with the "idiotic idea" that he may help Evald and her, but that he had refused adamantly to hear about their marital trouble, suggesting that maybe she needs a quack or a minister. He is half amused, half shocked to hear some of the uglier things he has said. She concludes that she does not dislike him, but "I feel sorry for you." Second look of terror, startled to the core. But they both maintain amenities—even some amusement.

The issue is joined. And the interplay (one could speak of the interlocking) between his dreams and her behavior leads to surprising acts on his part. First, he, of all people, wants to tell her his dream. She claims no interest. But there soon comes a chance to involve her in his life: arriving at a side road, he swings the car into it, to lead her down to a house by the sea where he had spent much of his childhood and youth.

But before we attend to that sunny scenery and to the wealth of reveries which are about to emerge, I must confess one of those "clinical" impressions which seemed to explain why the old man and the young woman, at that time, experience one another as living in an increasingly tense polarity. If it is true (the text does not confirm it) that in Borg's dream the noise made by the broken-down hearse, as it sways like a cradle, eerily reflects the crying of a newborn, then the old doctor's medical intuition may well have told him that the reason for proud Marianne's seeking help from him is that she is pregnant, and that his reaction to pregnancy is, to say the least, deeply ambivalent (see the Great Dane bitch). But if this is so, the issue that is joined is Marianne's concern over harboring a new Borg and the old man's sudden awareness that he who is close to death must yet learn to affirm life. This assumption is necessary to recognize Marianne's (and, as we shall see, her husband's) aggravated life crisis as being what I have called the psychosocial crisis of *Generativity versus Stagnation*[5] *or Self-Absorption*. Generativity includes, in its wider sense, the mature drive to generate and regenerate products and ideas; but the birth cry emanating from the hearse begs us on this day of professional triumph to consider generativity in its procreative essence. For each such crisis I have postulated an emergent "virtue," in the sense of a vital strength necessary for the life cycle as well as for the cycle of generations. Wisdom is the virtue of the last crisis; Care, for the mature stage of adulthood. In that mature stage, fate, as well as the life lived so far, decides whom and what one is committed to take care of so as to assure the next generation's life and strength. But where Disdain is the destructive counterpart to Wisdom, I would nominate *Rejectivity* as the counterpart to Care. And I suggest that it is this rejective trend which Marianne recognizes as an all-too-well-rationalized developmental defect in Dr. Borg—and a generational one in the Borgs. In her, a strong ethical determination seems to have been awakened that the future must not be forfeited to what is dead in the Borgs' past, even as Borg's old-age struggle against despair makes him comprehend that what he has become must not be all that he is and must not be all that he leaves behind. To paraphrase William James, he must find behind his relatively peaceful and yet disdainful isolation not only his "murdered self" but also his murderous one, so he may find his living and life-giving self.

5. THE STRAWBERRY PATCH

They are driving down the side road to a point where they can see the old summer house. The façade of the house first looks like that tightly closed face of the dream's alter ego: it "slept behind closed doors and drawn blinds." Marianne, in fact, calls it "a ridiculous old house," and she decides to take a quick dip in the sea, leaving Borg to his reveries. In a dreamlike fashion, he knows where to go: to the strawberry patch. He sits down in the grass and slowly eats some strawberries "one by one," almost ritually, as if they had a consciousness-expanding power. And, indeed, he now hears somebody play a piano, and suddenly the house appears transformed. The façade comes alive, "the sun glittered on the open windows," and the place seems to be "bursting with life," although no one is in sight as yet.

Then, he sees her: his "first love," his cousin Sara, as she had been (now nearly sixty years ago), a blond, "light-hearted young woman" kneeling in the patch in a "sunyellow cotton dress." She is gathering strawberries into a small basket. He calls, she does not hear. Then his elder brother Sigfrid appears in a college student's white cap, self-assured to the point of sassiness. He wants to make love to her, and, over her weakening protests that she is engaged to Isak and that he, Sigfrid, is of all the Borg brothers the most "awful . . . unbearable . . . stupid . . . idiotic . . . ridiculous . . . cocky," he embraces her with a passionate kiss which she reciprocates. Then she falls weeping to the ground, the strawberries are spilled, and a red spot appears on her dress: he has, she cries, turned her into a "bad woman, at least nearly." She is a fallen woman, then, and one senses that this whole earthy scene, beyond its precious gaiety and its symbolic reference to defloration, points to something primeval, some garden, long forfeited by Isak.

Borg continues to "dream": a breakfast gong sounds, a flag is raised (the flag of Swedish-Norwegian unity, to be exact), and a crowd of brothers, sisters, and cousins converge on the house. The festivity is presided over by a dictatorial aunt. The center of attention is nearly deaf Uncle Aron, whose birthday it is. "The only ones missing were Father, Mother, and I," says Borg significantly. Somebody announces that Isak is out fishing with his father—"a message," Borg later notes, at which he felt "a secret and completely inexplicable happiness," wondering at the same time what he should do in this "new old world which I was suddenly given the opportunity to visit." It is impossible to describe the noisy and gay, intimate and yet also somewhat grating, birthday scene that follows. As old man Borg appears to watch his childhood milieu, it becomes clear that he had always felt like an isolated onlooker in all that gaiety and activity which, to a withdrawn and sensitive boy, must have seemed marked by some overpopulation. A series of skirmishes are fought between the authoritarian aunt and a succession of healthy, boisterous children who protest their right to be. At the end, it is Sara who takes the brunt of all the impertinent vitality, for two unspeakable twin sisters in braids who always chant in unison announce that they saw Sara and Sigfrid kiss in the patch. Sara runs out of the room onto the veranda. There, she tearfully confesses to her older cousin Charlotta how much she loves Isak, but that he (who will kiss her only in the dark) is simply too mysterious a man for her: so "enormously refined" and sensitive, so "extremely intellectual," and so moralistically aloof.

And now I should, because I said I would, relate the brief but obviously central scene of the spilled wild strawberries to one of the stages of life. It is that of young adulthood, with its manifold playful intimacies which must mature into a quality of Intimacy—in friendship, in erotic life, and in work. The related danger is some form of Isolation—and it becomes immediately probable that it was when he lost Sara to Sigfrid that something in Isak turned away from women and that he remained not only wanting in Love—the strength of this stage—but, again, possessed of a pervasive Exclusivity. There is, in fact, a symbolic hint pointing way back in Isak's life, for, in the Bible, Sara was Isak's mother; and we realize that Isak had known his mother as a very young woman. Is Sara's name an allusion to the fact that she had been old when young, or that he had lost his young mother, too, to another man? The breakfast scene seems to affirm this in the noisiest way possible, for six brothers and sisters were born during Isak's childhood; it seems also to illustrate the ruthless politics of a large and, in summer, extended family. As the aunt calls for order, respect, and propriety, each youngster in his or her way fights for survival. And it becomes all the more painfully clear that Isak's way of autonomy had been gifted isolation—and so, perhaps, had his father's been. At any rate, they went fishing together—sharing, maybe, a certain exclusiveness from the family.

Didactically speaking, this childhood scene would permit us, step by step, to sketch the way in which, in comparison to the others, Isak resolved his childhood crises by acquiring some specialized strengths that would later serve him well in a professional career in his cultural setting, but for which he would have to pay with a certain compulsive self-restriction that began to possess him early. If it is his central lifelong endeavor which is to be crowned that day, so are all the unresolved early and later crises to be faced along the way.

We almost forgot Uncle Aron: he is a man in his second childhood, prepared for *his* special day by some secret libation—also witnessed and announced by the twins. He is sung to lustily, as Isak will be later in the day, although Aron is nearly deaf: these familial ritualizations prepare us for the more ironic aspects of the coming ceremony. Maybe being like Uncle Aron could save one much existential trouble—and some bad dreams? In the meantime, the silly twins seem to have prepared us for another and more weighty double appearance—a second Sara.

6. PASSENGERS

As Isak Borg, overwhelmed by his reveries, sits by the patch and only slowly comes to with a strong feeling of emptiness and sadness, a most real, blond, and tanned young girl, as if jumping down from a tree, awakens him fully. Obviously a member of Sweden's contemporary *jeunesse d'orée*, she is dressed in shorts and is sucking on an unlit pipe. "Is this your shack?," she inquires, and presently asks whether the "jalopy" by the house is his. Instead of being shocked, however, he is amused, for the girl looks like a reborn Sara (and is played by the same actress, now with a pageboy haircut). And her name *is* Sara. She is on her way to Italy, and she would like a ride to the other coast. He agrees, and in his benign mood tells returning Marianne that he has offered the young girl a ride. As they approach the car, it turns out that two strapping young men are part of the bargain: they are going to Italy with Sara. But Borg seems ready to accommodate them all. In fact, a strange bond exists between him and little Sara, who, now an apparition in his rear-view mirror, adds a dimension of rejuvenation to the day. What is their stage? The three young represent contemporary youth in search of something worthy of their awakening Fidelity; they are working hard at defining their Identity: one of the two boys wants to become a doctor and plays the atheistic rationalist; the other intends to be a minister and defends God's existence. Both, however, when driven to defense or offense, display a certain naive Cynicism, which is the natural contrary to adolescent Fidelity. They both love Sara—or so says Sara, who, appropriately sitting between them, announces to Borg with a charming mixture of cynicism and sincerity that she is playing them out against each other, while remaining a virgin. So now they are hitchhiking to Italy, where young Northerners of that day expected the southern sun to melt away their Identity Confusion.

Before we describe the other surprising appearances, let me point out an implicit scheme in this sequence—a scheme by which Borg meets up, as he now seems almost driven to do, with his past selves and counterplayers. We have "located" his acute crisis in the conflicts natural to old age and Marianne's in those of the center of adulthood; we have also suggested that in his opening dream he had reached back to that somehow unfulfilled center stage in himself. We will find that in each subsequent encounter he faces individuals who personify earlier stages of life (as the young portray the identity crisis) and help him to return to the corresponding stage of his own life through some reverie or dream.

Borg, in watching Sara in the rear-view mirror, seems eminently relaxed, almost meditative. But suddenly, utter fear forces his whole attention forward: he sees a little black car approaching on the wrong side of the road. He swerves his car safely off the road, while the other car overturns into a ditch (one is reminded of the broken-down hearse). What, after a moment of stunned paralysis, they see emerge is a—mysteriously unharmed—middle-aged couple who, it turns out, have been quarreling and immediately continue to do so. The man, the doctor notes, is limping, but he explains that he has been "crippled for years," and (as he says his wife says) not only physically. As they, too, become passengers in the Borgs' car (occupying the folding seats) they continue on with their habitual reciprocal harangue seemingly aggravated by the "death scare" lived through, and yet obviously not the cause of it. The man, who introduces himself as Alman, grants that his wife's scorn may be good psychotherapy for her, while she announces that he is a Catholic who probably perceives the accident to be God's punishment. Thus, the two ministering professions continue as an ideological double theme, full of sarcasm and obscure dread. The husband even accuses his wife, apparently an unsuccessful actress, of playing at having cancer: "She has her hysterics and I have my Catholicism." Suddenly, the wife hits the husband in the face. Marianne, who is now driving, stops the car and quietly orders the couple to get out "for the children's sake" (born and unborn, one senses). And so, Borg records, they "quickly drove away from this strange marriage."

It will have occurred to the viewer that the full car contained a complete representation of the precariousness of adulthood, from the young people in the back seat who are on the way to the land where they hope as yet to find their adult identities as well as each other, to the couple who have just about lost each other and themselves, to the old man and the young woman who are just beginning to find each other in the attempt to prevent a forfeiture of an all too overdefined adulthood. Here, Marianne is the heroine; in her now dominant determination to care, she does not hesitate to break up the antics of the two self-absorbed and hopelessly antagonistic adults as being destructively unethical. For if the simplest moral rule is not to do to another what you would not wish to have done to you, the ethical rule of adulthood is to do to others what will help them, even as it helps you, to grow.

As the car is now relieved of the spectacle of the "strange marriage"—which one suspects seemed so foreign to Borg only because he had not as yet faced the strangeness of that part of his own adult past—he and all the others seem emptied and exhausted, as if they, as well as the car, need refueling. So, first a gas station, then the midday meal.

7. MIDDAY

What grace had saved Borg for those transformations symbolized by that one day's journey? Sara, we now know, had been and still is with him. And in all his self-absorption he apparently had been a good doctor. The gas station happens to be in the very center of southern Sweden where Borg had practiced for fifteen years before he became a researcher and professor in the city. The big, blond gas-station owner immediately recognizes him. After all, the doctor had delivered him and all his brothers. He called his wife ("she beamed like a big strawberry in her red dress") and suggested that they name their coming baby (a boy, of course) Isak. (Will Isak, then, be a godfather to his clientele, yet not a grandfather in his own family?) Payment for the gasoline is refused: "There are some things that can never be paid back." And Isak, with a tragic glance, suddenly thinks aloud: "Perhaps I should have remained here." He should have stayed in touch, then, at least with those to whom he could offer competent and truly needed service—as a member of one of those mediating professions who thereby earn a kind of social and existential exemption. And yet, a pitiless awareness may be telling him then and there how much love one can receive—from patients and students—for what one also does for honor and for money. How many old people, maybe without knowing it, mourn for just that period of their lives?

There follows, again, an idyllic scene: a midday meal on a terrace overlooking Lake Vaettern. Over the table, they now face each other, and with the help of some consciousness-expanding wine, Isak and Marianne become part of a midsummer celebration. Anders, the future pastor, suddenly recites a religious poem. Victor, the scientific rationalist, protests: they had sworn to each other that they would not discuss God. He advocates looking biological death "straight in the eye." Finally, Victor asks the doctor's opinion. But Borg has been musing; and as Marianne lights his cigar for him (he, who had refused to let her smoke her cigarette), Isak, instead of offering an opinion, recites a poem: "Where is the friend I seek everywhere?/ Dawn is the time of loneliness and care . . ./ When twilight comes. . . ." He asks Anders for help, but it is Marianne who continues: "When twilight comes, I am still yearning." And as Sara, moved to tears ("for no reason at all"), says: "You're religious, aren't you, Professor," Isak continues: "I see His trace of glory and power,/ In an ear of grain and the fragrance of a flower," and Marianne concludes, "In every sign and breath of air./ His love is there."

The poem, the setting, the tone seem to confirm the sense in which every human being's Integrity may be said to be religious (whether explicitly or not), namely, in an inner search for, and a wish to communicate with, that mysterious, that Ultimate Other: for there can be no "I" without an "Other," no "We" without a shared "Other." That, in fact, is the first revelation of the life cycle, when the maternal person's eyes shiningly recognize us even as we begin to recognize her. And it is the hope of old age, according to St. Paul's promise.

This poem, no doubt, will accompany Borg to the end of this day. But first, he must encounter life's earliest Other who, so human fate dictates, makes the very origins of Hope a variably discordant matter. After a long silence, Isak arises abruptly and announces that he will visit his old mother, who lives nearby. Marianne wants to come along. She takes his arm, he pats her hand.

From the sunny lakeside, they walk to a house surrounded by a wall "as tall as a man." Inside, his mother, in a black dress with lace cap, looks up sharply from an "incongruous desk." Her estranged living becomes apparent as she, having accepted his embrace, asks with a suspicious glance whether Marianne is his wife and, if so, would she leave the room, for "she has hurt us too much." Introduced, she learns that Marianne has no children and announces that she has had ten; all are dead now, except Isak. None of the twenty grandchildren ever visit her, except Evald. And she has fifteen great-grandchildren whom she has never seen. "I am tiresome, of course . . . and I have another fault. I don't die." They are waiting for her money. . . . She asks to have a large box full of toys brought to her, saying she has "tried to think which of you owned what." She lifts out toys, one after the other, names the owners, chats about them. And then, painfully echoing Isak's opening monologue at his desk, she concludes: "It doesn't pay much to talk. Isn't it cold in here?," and, looking at the darkening sky in the window, "I've always felt chilly . . . mostly in the stomach." She lifts a last item from the box: her father's old gold watch. Drumbeats in the background: the dial is handless! Isak recalls his dream, the hearse, and "my dead self." But his mother concludes with one warming memory: how little Sara always cradled her cousin Sigbritt's infant boy. Now he is going to be fifty years old! She wants to give the watch to him: "It can probably be repaired?" (Again, was the mother once motherly like this Sara?)

When kissing her goodbye, Isak notes that his mother's face is "very cold but unbelievably soft and full of sharp little lines." Marianne, who has watched all this with silent horror, curtsies, and once outside again takes Isak's arm. Isak is now "filled with gratitude toward this quiet, independent girl with her naked, observant eyes." Perhaps he feels that Evald, although his son and his mother's grandson, in marrying Marianne may have reversed the fate that was symbolized by his mother's father's watch, which had mysteriously entered the dream that had started him on this journey. It may have been this hope that gave Isak the courage to confront himself in yet another, more deeply "humiliating" dream.

In the meantime we have learned that old-age Despair and Disgust may be handed on from generation to generation, where conditions (and even quite "comfortable" conditions) have become an inexorable hindrance to renewal.

8. THE LAST EXAMINATION

As Marianne takes the wheel (is she in charge now?) all are resting, the boys in angry sullenness over yet another disputation, little Sara bored with them both. Isak sleeps and dreams profusely. Astonished at his productivity when he writes it all down later, he wonderingly includes a defensive note about his lack of enthusiasm for the psychoanalytic theory of dreams "as the fulfilment of desires in a negative or positive direction." He also wonders whether this new twilight experience of memories and dreams is a sign of senility, or even a "harbinger of approaching death." In abstracting the extraordinary dream sequence here, I can only continue to point to that motivation in old age so miraculously understood by the middle-aged playwright, namely, to experience and, in fact, also to affirm total Despair in order to gain some integrated sense of one's life: for is the life cycle, seen as a whole, perhaps a revelation? (And are dreams not merely "self-revealing?")

Back at the strawberry patch, in a continuation of the morning's reverie, Isak again encounters the original Sara of his youth who, with pitying tears, holds a mirror to his face, forcing him to see himself "old and ugly in the sinking twilight." Is Sara also another Other—his own female Self? For she says that she has been unintentionally cruel by not exposing him to himself. She now announces that she will marry his brother: "It's all a game." He smiles, an unforgettable smile that seems to hurt his whole face. And she says sharply that he, a professor emeritus, ought to know why it hurts, but she is sure he doesn't. She throws the mirror away.

Sigbritt's little boy is crying. She must hurry to him. "Don't leave me," begs Isak. She says she does not understand him, for he stammers. But it doesn't "really matter" anyway.

The day becomes utterly fateful and threatening in a darkening twilight. Blackbirds are screeching like furies. With tears streaming down her face, Sara, up in the arbor, cradles the little boy with lullaby words: "Soon it will be another day." The child calms down, but Isak wants to scream "till my lungs [are] bloody."

The wind dies, the house again looks festive. Sara plays the piano, Sigfrid listens. They sit down to a candlelit dinner, celebrating "some kind of event." Isak watches through the glass door, pressing his hand against the frame, where there is a nail. It pierces his hand, producing a wound like one of the stigmata. As if this identification with Christ the Crucified seemed too self-indulgent a gesture, the scene and the moonlight now turn utterly cold and cruel. Mr. Alman, of all people, appears, stiffly polite, and insists that the professor come into the house, which has turned into some kind of laboratory. Taken into the very lecture room where he used to give his polyclinical examinations, he now must himself take an examination before a silently hostile audience, which includes the young passengers. Asked to inspect a specimen, he can only see his own eye mirrored in the microscope. Asked to read a mysterious formula on the blackboard which tells of a doctor's first duty, he cannot make it out. Alman intones calmly, politely: *"A doctor's first duty is to ask forgiveness."* Yes, of course, he knew that, laughs Isak, reduced to wincing despair. Alman persists: *"You are guilty of guilt."* (Is that sin?) Now the old man, typically, claims infirmity: after all, he has a bad heart! Another judgment: *"There is nothing concerning your heart in my papers."* Finally, Isak is to diagnose a woman patient. She looks like Mrs. Alman (and one is reminded of the implied parallel between the Almans' marriage and his own). His diagnosis: "She is dead." The patient laughs wildly. A third judgment: *He does not know when a woman is alive.* The inquisitor summarizes his guilt as "indifference, selfishness, lack of consideration." He stands so accused by his wife, Borg now learns, and he must confront her. But she has been dead for years? Come, demands the inquisitor.

He leads him out into a primeval forest. The moon is shining "like a dead eye." The ground, covered with decaying leaves, is swampy and porous underfoot, filled with snakes. They now stand by a charred ladder leaning against a burned-out hut. In a clearing, Isak sees Karin, his wife, a strong, sensual woman, being seduced by a disgusting but virile man, and she "received the man between her open knees." The inquisitor states the exact date: "Tuesday, May 1, 1917." May Day. Isak now has seen, but has not heard, the worst. For as the lovers then sit and talk, the woman sadly yet scathingly predicts what Isak will say when she confesses. He will feel sorry for her, like "God himself," and say with a sickening nobility, "You shouldn't ask forgiveness from me. I have nothing to forgive." (But he will not think of asking for forgiveness.)

The inquisitor has the last word, mocking any attempt to gain some superiority from mere self-revelation. "Everything has been dissected. A surgical masterpiece." The Penalty? "Of course, loneliness." "Is there no grace?," asks the dreamer. But the other claims not to know.

Fleetingly, Isak once again tries to appeal to Sara, who once more materializes. "If only you had stayed with me. . . . Wait for me." He wants to cry like a child, but he can't. That escape is also gone.

The message of the dream seems clear: Isak, who has learned how to study, to heal, and to preserve life, has not been alive to a woman's (nor to his own) feelings, and so he has had to watch the women in his life, although they loved him, turn to other men. He has learned, to paraphrase Freud's formula for adulthood, to work but *not* to love. Here, in fact, a psychoanalytic interpretation seems inescapable. For why does he once more turn to Sara, who, again, personifies the young mother: "If you had only stayed with me?" We must assert an infantile trauma behind these scenes of seduction with which, it is clear, he has unconsciously colluded in his adult life. It is what Freud has called the primal scene, the child's observation or imagination of parental lovemaking that makes an Oedipus out of the boy and alienates him from his own Id—the snaky swamp—as well as from the betraying parents. What does the charred ladder mean? Is it an existential or a sexual symbol? Could it not represent the stages of life, rung after rung, here marred by what was burnt out on each?

9. NEW LIFE

As Borg wakes up, he finds that the car is standing still and that he is alone with Marianne. The "children" are in the woods. And he tells her what he thinks his dreams are trying to reveal to him: that he is dead, although he is alive. Her gaze darkens and she, once more perceiving a generational threat, says that Evald had used exactly the same words. "About me?," says Isak, "Yes, I can believe that." But she counters, "No, about himself." A man of thirty-eight! Isak now begs to be told "everything."

So Marianne describes a haunting talk with Evald—the very talk that made her come to see whether Isak might be of help. She had taken Evald for a ride to the sea. Parked there, she had told him that she was pregnant. From her words it is clear that neither Evald nor she had tried much to prevent this. She intended to have the child. Evald had reacted as if trapped. He walked out into the rain, and as she followed him he refused to agree to any development that would force him "to exist another day longer than I want to"—not to speak of being responsible for a new human being. He referred to himself as an unwanted child, conceived in a marriage that was hell—and could he even be sure he was Borg's son? At the end, he cursed her "damned need to live, to exist and create life." Listening silently, Isak can only ask Marianne whether she does not wish to smoke.

She now sums up what we have learned of Isak's mother, of himself, and of his son as "more frightening than death itself." Not even the person she "loves more than anyone else" can take this child from her. Isak suddenly feels "shaken as never before." Perhaps he realizes what his first dream had tried to tell him. "Can I help you?," he asks.

Thus, in seemingly small matters and in small but significant gestures, some measure of Care is restored. But so has the power of Rejectivity been revealed, indeed from generation to generation. For if our generative concerns are held together by a world image which dictates what we consider relevant for the generational succession of our own "kind," it is clear that we are also (more or less consciously) possessed and obsessed by prejudices and convictions which exclude vigorously and even viciously some "other kinds" as weak or bad, foreign or inimical. In fact, such enmity often exists in relation to our closest neighbors—geographic, ideological, conceptual—who may share many of our generative concerns but differ in some minutiae which can suddenly loom devastatingly large; and, of course, it can exist within one's family, or be turned against one's own children, and this especially where conflicting generative concerns make them suddenly appear as outsiders or worse. And while there can be no generativity without rejectivity, human survival demands that rejectivity be counteracted by faith or by insight; for what Freud has called the narcissism of small difference, often expressed in hidden or displaced rejections, can also be projected on an overdefined otherness adhering to the very largest issues and collective antagonisms of mankind, whether these antagonisms are territorial and invite periodical warfare, or credal and deny salvation to the infidels. So we are prepared to see the stage expand from the private and the inner lives of a few individual Swedes to an ancient cathedral rich with symbols and crowded with uniforms.

10. THE CELEBRATION

Now the great Jubilee must be lived through. The "children" come running, bringing him "with friendly, mocking eyes" large bouquets of wildflowers, bowing and chanting that he is so wise and venerable and has, no doubt, learned all prescriptions by heart. A few more hours and they arrive at Evald's house in Lund, greeted by Agda who is breathless from all the preparations while they, she is sure, had a "relaxing and convenient" drive. Evald, very handsome in tails, asks whether Marianne wants to go to a hotel, but she says gaily that she will stay "for another night," and she intends to go to the state dinner with him. Borg, with Agda's help, dresses in his best.

The festivities? In his notes, Borg describes them thus:

> Trumpet fanfares, bells ringing, field-cannon salutes, masses of people, the giant procession from the university to the cathedral, the white-dressed garland girls, royalty, old age, wisdom, beautiful music, stately Latin sentences which echoed off the huge vaults. The students and their girls, women in bright, magnificent dresses. . . .[6]

Truly a crowning ritual for all he was: a doctor, a teacher, a Swede, a Lutheran, a patriot, a venerable old man. But this strange, symbolic rite now seems as "meaningless as a passing dream." Nevertheless, he marches along, upright and obedient, waving to little Sara. The preliminary ceremony in the cathedral (with its Gothic niches, its saints, its crucifix) is endless, and Borg and his two old co-jubilants suffer the specific discomforts of old men in sitting it out. Finally, he stands high up to be topped by the famous Lund doctor's hat. The archetypal comparison with a crown of jewels or of thorns may seem inescapable. But Borg, as he stands there, looks above and beyond the scene and begins "to see a remarkable causality in this chain of unexpected, entangled events." The English caption says something about "an extraordinary logic. . . ." Whatever the words, they seem to bespeak a revelatory sensation of grand simplicity.

In view of the trumpets, the bells, and the cannons in this populous final event, we must pause and change our theoretical tune as well. For Borg is no longer one of a small circle of mutually significant persons containable in an automobile, but one in a row of black-robed men solemnly marching to honor the "immortals" of their own kind. We must recognize in such ceremonies a heritage both of triumph and of deadly danger for human adulthood—the very triumph and the very danger which wisdom here transcends. No doubt, this rather noisy and playful Swedish version of a crowning ceremony is one of the most benign in human history, and one can well see Dag Hammarskjöld in that place—in fact, he is buried in that cathedral. Yet, in its combination of religious, military, national, and academic symbols, it is no doubt meant to remind us that mankind, so far, has been divided into what I have come to call pseudo-species: national, ideological, or religious bodies that consider their own kind the model image of mankind as fully intended in their version of creation and history, for the survival of which they are ready to kill as well as to die. Such shared identity, narrower or broader, in combination with superior accomplishments seems to be necessary for that joint sense of the reality of reality which permits adults in their middle years to be defended against the absolute fact of death—and thus permits the full application, between adolescence and senescence, of matured energies and gifts to what the Hindus call "the maintenance of the world." But this means that adulthood is always also imprisoned in the pseudo-species (we see this, of course, more clearly in foreigners than in ourselves) and thus has remained, to some extent, a pseudo-adulthood, falling short of the potential of an all-human maturity. At the same time, we must acknowledge a universal goal in mankind which has, over the millennia, led to larger and larger units of an ever more inclusive identity. Marx, it seems, believed in a historical trend toward such a maturation by expanding unification. He spoke of history as an *Entstehungsakt*—a word that implies an evolving all-human adulthood. He could not foresee, perhaps, that mankind, when faced with this ultimate possibility, would also invent ultimate weapons for the defense of nations and ideologies and their empires and markets.

Here I should repeat, however, that by "pseudo" I do not mean to emphasize conscious deception but the all-human tendency to create symbols, artifacts and appearances, ideologies and world images in a grandiose effort to make one's own kind a spectacular and unique sight in the universe and in history. It is a prime human dilemma that pseudo-speciation can bring out the truest and the best in loyalty and cooperation, heroism and inventiveness, while committing different human "kinds" to a history of reciprocal enmity and destruction on an increasingly species-wide scale. Therefore, we have every reason to study what this moving picture so strongly reveals, namely, how large-scale adult commitments are prepared in the "politics" of small differences in everyday life and in each successive life stage. And we must learn to differentiate between the way in which such tendencies as Exclusivity and Rejectivity aggravate the *moralistic destructiveness* of public and private morals; and how virtues such as Love and Care, in turn, contribute to a more insightful and universal *ethics*.

As we thus recognize the contraries which arise in every individual as the necessary correlates of human strength, we may well pause to consider the special function which the more inclusive visions of the great religions and ideologies have had in daily life, namely, to counteract the divisive potential arising in every stage of human growth. Such "sinful" tendencies as exclusivity or rejectivity thus were counteracted, say, in the Christian world view by the universal concepts of Agape and Caritas. The subtle sarcasm, however, which pervades the ceremonial scenes of our moving picture serves to point to the ritualisms which in an idolistic and formalistic fashion soon take hold of any innovative world image—ritualisms which for a while may serve some conservational purpose but are apt sooner or later to neglect the vital interplay of historical change and individual life cycles.

In the meantime, we may grant even a certain character type of Swedish doctor and professor, and so obviously an affluent member of the middle class, a moment of integrity which expresses the destiny of the old anywhere, where personal and social conditions favor an integrative revelation offered in the very structure of existence. Where such conditions are wanting, whether for poverty or for affluence, for laissez-faire or autocracy, our critique and our protest must gain purpose and direction from the study of the resulting misery. It is the merit of *Wild Strawberries*, as of any other great drama, that implicit in it is also a social critique: one may consider only the suggestions of possessiveness and feudalism (see the high walls around Mother Borg's lonely house) in Isak's and his son's isolation.

11. THE EVENING

Dr. Borg's moment of revelation is followed by restrained and therefore all the more universal signs that the "remarkable causality" which the old doctor had envisioned at the height of the ceremony is already working in those most closely related to his fate. Borg does not attend the banquet: for him, the day is over. He takes a cab home and finds Agda (who in the cathedral had watched him with possessive pride) making his bed and arranging his things just the way he likes them. In this quiet after the storm he tries to make peace with her. He even apologizes for his behavior that morning, which now seems long ago. She asks him once more whether he is perhaps not quite well. He answers dreamily, in words that must, indeed, alarm her, whether it is really so unusual for him "to ask forgiveness." He even offers her the mutual use of the more familiar *du* (equivalent to addressing one by his first name in English), but she "begs to be excused from all intimacies" and departs, pointedly leaving her door slightly ajar. She is, perhaps, still hoping for *her* ceremony. But all this impresses one as being their normal relationship, with an added touch of friendship.

Then he hears an utterly youthful duet, accompanied by a guitar, in the garden. Lifting the blinds, he sees "the children" serenading him. Sara announces that they have secured a ride all the way to Hamburg (with a deaconess). Finally, little Sara, supported by the garden wall, lifts up her eyes to his inclined face and says with playful feminine intuition: "Goodby, Father Isak. Do you know that it is really you I love, today, tomorrow, and forever?" Then they are gone.

He hears whispering voices in the foyer: Evald and Marianne. Evald comes to say goodnight. Marianne, it appears, has lost a heel, so she *had* to come home before the dance. Isak asks him to sit down. What is going to happen with them?

> *Evald:* I have asked her to remain with me.
> *Isak:* And how will it . . . I mean . . .
> *Evald:* I can't be without her.

Isak: You mean you can't live alone?

Evald: I can't be without *her*. That's what I mean.

Isak: I understand.

Evald: It will be as she wants.[7]

Then Isak finds himself mentioning the loan. Evald protests that he will pay it back. Isak: "I did not mean that." Evald insists. But at least, the "debt" is now a question of money only.

Marianne appears, dressed in rustling white. She asks whether he likes the shoes she is wearing. In some of the longest such shots, they fully face each other, exchanging thanks and saying, "I like you."

The couple leaves. Isak hears his heart bump and his old watch tick. The tower clock strikes eleven. It begins to rain. Preparing for sleep, he wanders back once more to the strawberry patch. It is summer. Everybody is there. Sara runs toward him, calling him "darling" and telling him that there are no strawberries left. The aunt wants him to find his father. Isak says: "I have already searched for him, but I cannot find either Father or Mother." But she takes him by the hand. Down by the beach "on the other side of the dark water," he sees "a gentleman" fishing, and further up the bank, his mother, in bright summer dress, reading. Isak can not make himself heard. But his father waves and his mother nods, both smiling in recognition. A truly primal scene. He tries to shout, but his cries "did not reach their destination." Yet, he felt "rather light-hearted."

Borg has arrived at the beginning: his first childhood. We could now, as usual in our work, reconstruct the stages of life from the first Hope up the whole intact ladder of developmental strengths which old Borg, as any old person, has lived by—or has now learned to mourn. How childlike or how childish his second childhood will be is left open.

II. Notes on a Conception of the Human Life Cycle

I must now amplify and make more systematic the brief formulations of the stages of life that I have so far used only as annotations to Bergman's scenes. I will use these scenes, in turn, as a way of illustrating a conception of the human life cycle to be presented in the form of a checkered chart (see page 25). For if I set down once more the principles that guided me in formulating a succession of life stages, it is in order to reflect on the nature of a total conception. I hope on another occasion to discuss attempts to subdivide such a conception into phenomena that can be measured and tested. Here, let me offer a few notes on the fact that any conception of the whole course, or of any phase, of life, while it may owe its structure and terminology to the sophisticated methods of a given period and field, is apt to inherit some emotional and ideological complications of a very primitive nature.

1. The ceremony just described amply attests to the survival of certain basic qualities common to all adult world views. In my Jefferson Lectures,[8] I have outlined some of the simplest spatial and temporal aspects of the sense of being grown up which are easily circumscribed by the manner in which different languages speak of the condition of adulthood. The family of words related to the designation "adult" attests (to consider only the Latin origins) to a state of having matured (*alescere, adolescere*) both in height and in stature and of having reached the stage of one who now nourishes (*alere*) what he bears and produces. But this means that what has developed in stages must now fit into the structure of an integrated world view which permits the vulnerabilities of human childhood to be turned into generational strengths. To be grown *up*, in any language and vision, has a particular quality of standing tall, so proudly and yet so precariously that there is a universal need to attest and to protest that one knows where one stands and that one has some status in the center of a vision of a new, or, at any rate, forever renewed, human type. One could go through *Wild Strawberries* and describe Dr. Borg's positions and changing points of view from the first dream when, full of dread, he looks at the other self that lies prone in his coffin and attempts to drag him down to the last moment in the cathedral when, his head held high, he is crowned with a special top hat but gazes contemplatively even higher toward a clarifying light. The ceremony further illustrates the collective need of human adults, between the complex process of having been "brought up" and a certain terminal "decline," to affirm ceremonially with whom they have grown up and whose standing in the world they now share—whether they symbolize this by marching in formation, as in the ceremony just witnessed, or, alternately, by sitting in long, receptive rows, watching others march and listening to music and speeches. Under other cultural conditions, of course, the celebrants may link arms and dance vigorously; or, again, they will bow or kneel together or, indeed, prostrate themselves—and all this in order to confirm what they together stand for, or must take a stand against, in the name of high principles personified by those they called "great." And the greatest, more often than not, are those rare persons who have questioned the status quo and have become immortal by creating a new one.

In the pursuit of the basic dimensions of a given world image, one could now proceed from the central fact of the upright existence of the human mind-organism to the periphery of its sensory, muscular, and locomotor reach (vastly augmented as they all are now by tools, instruments, and machinery), where it meets with others in affiliative and cooperative, erotic and antagonistic interplay. As a Navajo medicine man recently put it when asked by a friend for a definition of what is human: indicating the figure of a cross, he said that a person was most human where the (vertical) connection between the ground of creation and the Great Spirit met the (horizontal) one between the individual and all other human beings.

This much about some of the simplest spatial-temporal aspects making up the perspectives of given visions of adulthood, whether they are represented in mythical, ideological, or, indeed, in colloquial terms. These, in turn, are enveloped in world moods such as those associated with any space-time conception of human existence, whether the dominant configuration is that of steps from birth up to maturity and down to decay, maybe serving some historical and technological progress; or of a straight line from birth to death and beyond, whether high up to salvation or way down to damnation; or, indeed, a series of rebirths absorbing the individual and generational cycles in larger cycles of rebirths—and an eventual transcendence. We are thus prepared for the magic power of all-embracing religious and ideological world visions. They, in turn, variously emphasize, between the highest Reason discernible and the "dumb" creatureliness shared with all creation, various core areas of physical existence and efficacy: head, mind, foresight (*sapientissimus* is one of the declamations we hear when Dr. Borg receives his hat), the breath of inspiration and the ritualized intake of food and drink, the passions of the temperaments and the loyalty of the heart, or the potency of the genitals and the generosity of the womb, which serve erotic and procreative union, are sublimated for higher endeavors, or left below to be avoided.

2. Formulated world views also contain, within larger and even eternal temporal perspectives, images of the course of life, or, at any rate, of ideal and evil adulthood, with varying perspectives on the preceding period of growing up toward this middle estate and the final period of decline and dying. The rare emphasis that the gospels place on the relation of a lasting childlikeness to the coming Kingdom must be seen as a prophetic countervoice to the ancient attitude toward the child as one who, if it survives at all, must be fashioned in the adult mold. For all world views must come to terms with the irreversible ambiguities and contradictions arising from the fact that the human species (besides other extreme specializations) must undergo a protracted period in which to grow up and to grow into the specifications of a given group in a given place on earth in a given period of history. Other species "know" where they belong, and their instinctual energies are tuned to their instinctive patterns of living. Human instinctuality employs a drive equipment of loves and hates that must be ready for a great variety of social settings in which to learn the intricacies of technology and the style of customs; wherefore it is characterized by a conflict-ridden dialectic of excessive drive energy and stringent inhibition, of anarchic license and fateful repression and self-restriction. It is, again, the world religions which have striven to provide an all-inclusive world view for the containment of such human extremes as self-seeking vanity and self-abnegating humility, ruthless power-seeking and loving surrender, a search for beliefs worth dying and killing for, and a wish to empathize and understand. As I have put it in my Jefferson Lectures, there seem to be two poles to human endeavor, namely, the felt necessity to "survive and kill" where both the territorial survival and the cultural identity of a human subspecies seem to depend on the defensive or offensive exclusion of (all) others; and the precept "die and become" where, on the contrary, ascetic self-denial to the point of self-sacrifice appears to be the only means to becoming more inclusively human. We know the long and violent history of the attempt on the part of empires and creeds alternately to counterpoint and reconcile or refute and exclude the belief systems that emerge from the truly "dread"-ful human dilemma of having to reconcile a heightened need for generational renewal in a "real" Here and Now with the certainty of individual death.

One must begin with such fundamentals if one wishes to understand the necessity for adults to arrive at some formula of adulthood and to gain some objective perspective on its precursors. Thus, one of the few grand divisions of life into stages, namely, the Hindu *asramas*,[9] clearly acknowledges a broad middle range of "householding" in the service of the "maintenance of the world," preceded by a well defined age of apprenticeship and followed by a transcendence of the individual life cycle and an entry into a cycle of rebirths. This scheme, however, has little to say about the stages of childhood. And in Shakespeare's seven ages there is, between the mewling infant and the sighing lover, only the whining schoolboy. But then we must consider how long it took enlightened humanistic and scientific mankind to acknowledge and to chart the existence of developmental stages—physical and emotional, cognitive and social—in childhood and youth, not to speak of the highly diverse history of the treatment of children through the ages as creatures existing and developing at the whim of fate—and of the adults. No doubt, there has been a deep-seated adult resistance (first discovered and explained by Freud) not only to the remembrance of one's own childhood, but also to the recognition in children of developmental potentials which may upset the adult conviction of occupying in the universe a safe and sanctioned place with a well defined point of view. Only the century of the child has made us study childhood and, indeed, youth, not only as the causal precursors of adulthood as it was and is, but also as a potential promise for what adulthood may yet become. We still face powerful problems arising from the relativity adhering to the adult's task of defining his position as a person and as an observer in ongoing life.

3. As we pursue our specialized conceptions of the cycle of life, matters of overall orientation or mood remain with us, either in the ambiguities and contradictions inherent in the material under observation or in controversies over our choice of formulations. When I, as a psychoanalyst, for example, describe a psychosocial scheme in which I postulate for each stage of life an interplay between certain qualities from which emerges, under favorable conditions, a new "virtue" or vital strength, a number of recurrent questions arise. Do I do this on the basis of clinical interpretation, thus succumbing either to the fatalism of the psychopathologist or to the optimism of the therapeutic utopian? Or am I pursuing a humanistic ideal with unavowed moralistic or esthetic demands impossible to live up to in daily life? Is my view period- and class-bound and does it suggest either conformity to the requirements of a given social milieu or, on the contrary, indulgence in self-actualization? Do the over-privileged abide by such a scheme, and can the underprivileged affort it, should they want it? And, closer to home, are the assumed strivings conscious or unconscious?

Such questions are, of course, legitimate, and we have every reason to pose them to ourselves, whatever our method, for they may open up unduly neglected aspects of the matter. But we must also recognize in them the (often cyclic) recurrence of attempts to resolve in some dogmatic manner the ambiguities and contradictions adhering to adulthood itself. For even quite methodical and well trained persons when faced with the question of adult values are apt to revive the totalistic tendencies of their youth, whether they reassert or disavow the stance once held. For what is at stake here are matters of professional identity and of belief systems couched in theory. Then there are the pervasive trends of the times. For example, in critical and uncritical references to my scheme, the list of "negatives" (Isolation, Stagnation, Despair) are often blithely omitted, wherefore I appear—to some for better and to others for worse—to postulate a series of ideal accomplishments (Love, Care, Wisdom) as desirable "achievements" for which the proper prescriptions should and must be found.

Here, I can do no more than to restate briefly the origin of my formulations in the history of my field. Many of us who have worked not only clinically but also in child guidance and in the development of children have recognized it to be our generation's task to demonstrate the complementarity between the so-called *genetic* point of view in psychoanalysis and a *developmental* one. The genetic approach reconstructs the way major emotional disturbances are rooted in early traumatic events which tend to exert a regressive pull on the present, and it opens the "pre-historic" part of the human life cycle, and thus the unconscious dynamics of human conflict, to systematic inspection. The developmental approach, in turn, is based on the direct observation of children: following the genetic leads, it opens our awareness to the full developmental potentials of all stages of life—that is, both the later stages, when disturbances often become fully manifest, and the earlier ones, to which they are clearly related. Furthermore, in developing or contributing to an inclusive human psychology, psychoanalysis can not shirk the task of accounting not only for the way the individual ego holds the life cycle together, but also for the laws which connect generational cycles with individual ones—and the social process with both. My terms reflect this original task, even as the first formulation of psychosocial stages is grounded in Freud's original discovery of the psychosexual stages in childhood and their fateful relationship to the major psychopathological syndromes at all ages. In my extension of the principle of stages to adulthood and old age, the dystonic aspect of each stage remains related to the potential for a major class of disorders. Although I have abstained from viewing Dr. Borg as a case, Bergman's remarkable clinical intuition would make it quite feasible to describe in his hero some core disturbances that might have made him (given some adverse psychogenic factors) somebody's client—a status which the professor so grimly abhors. If—to speak in diagnostic terms for a moment—his compulsive character in old age borders on the depressive and paranoid, it obviously goes back to some "classical" origins in the analurethral stage of libido development with its retentive-eliminative mode emphases and the resulting over-fastidiousness and strict adherence to mutually exclusive categories in matters of value. Yet, if we let our observations tell us not only what could go wrong in each stage but also what is all set to go right, we can well see what kept such a man together all those years for his crowning day.

But what, some will ask, justifies the introduction into a developmental scheme of such old-fashioned terms as Wisdom or Hope? And what could be their relationship to the unconscious conflicts that Freud has demonstrated to be central to human development? Can hope, for example, be unconscious? The answer is that hope is a prime adaptive ego quality, pervading consciousness and yet immerging in and reemerging from the dynamic interplay of conscious and unconscious forces. Whether somebody judges himself, or is judged by others, to be full of hope and whether or not he is motivated to make the most of it by occasional or persistent display are matters of personality and of social role. Another is the pervasive, though not necessarily always visible, and most contagious rudimentary quality of hopefulness which (as its loss in the deepest regressions indicates) emerges from the earliest experiences of abandonment as well as of closeness and which, throughout life, must rely on the power of unconscious processes as well as on some confirmation by fate—and by faith.

THE INTERPLAY OF SUCCESSIVE LIFE STAGES

	1	2	3	4	5	6	7	8
H. OLD AGE								Integrity vs. Despair, Disgust: WISDOM
G. MATURITY							Generativity vs. Self-Absorption: CARE	
F. YOUNG ADULTHOOD						Intimacy vs. Isolation: LOVE		
E. ADOLESCENCE					Identity vs. Identity Confusion: FIDELITY			
D. SCHOOL AGE				Industry vs. Inferiority: COMPETENCE				
C. PLAY AGE			Initiative vs. Guilt: PURPOSE					
B. EARLY CHILDHOOD		Autonomy vs. Shame, Doubt: WILL						
A. INFANCY	Trust vs. Mistrust: HOPE							

4. If we say that Dr. Borg's initial statement of his old-age conditions seems to describe admirably a state of mind governed by a struggle for Integrity versus a sense of Despair and Disgust, and that out of this conflict a certain Wisdom may emerge under favorable personal and cultural conditions, then we certainly do not postulate the achievement of a total victory of Integrity over Despair and Disgust, but simply a dynamic balance in Integrity's favor. "Versus" is an interesting little word, because it can mean a reciprocal antagonism carried further in "vice versa." Developmentally, it suggests a dialectic dynamics, in that the final strength postulated could not emerge without either of the contending qualities; yet, to assure growth, the syntonic, the one more intent on adaptation, must absorb the dystonic. If Hope is the first and fundamental human strength, emerging from Primal Trust versus Primal Mistrust, it is clear that the human infant must experience a goodly measure of mistrust in order to learn to trust discerningly, and that there would be neither conviction nor efficacy in an overall hopefulness without a (conscious and unconscious) struggle with a persistent temptation to succumb to hopelessness. Dr. Borg's initial condition illustrates how unconvincing a sense of integrity can be if it does not remain answerable to some existential despair and some disgust with the repetitiveness of human pretenses—including, of course, one's own. In speaking here of various "senses of," however, we refer only to their more conscious aspects, while Integrity, like all the other strengths, obviously must have foundations deep in the preconscious and the unconscious as the reservoir of what was distilled in the whole previous course of life, even as Despair and Disgust emerge only as the latest expression of fear, anxiety, and dread that have pervaded previous stages. Despair tells us that time is too short if not altogether too late for alternate roads to Integrity; this is why the elderly try to "doctor" their memories. Rationalized bitterness and disgust can mask that despair, which in severe psychopathology aggravates a senile syndrome of depression, hypochondria, and paranoiac hate. For whatever chance man has to transcend the limitations of his self seems to depend on his full (if often tragic) engagement in the one and only life cycle permitted to him. By the same token, a civilization and its belief systems can be measured by the meaning they give to the full cycle of life, for such meaning (or the lack of it) cannot fail to reach into the beginnings of future generations.

All this was assumed when I came to the formulation that *Wisdom,* in whatever systematic or implicit, eloquent or quiet way it may be expressed, *is the detached and yet active concern with life itself in the face of death itself, and that it maintains and conveys the integrity of experience in spite of the Disdain over human failings and the Dread of ultimate non-being.* It will prove easiest, with the help of our movie, to illustrate the diagrammatic scheme for the cycle of life[10] if we immediately counterpoint this last stage to the very first one. I have postulated that the first and most basic human strength of Hope emerges from the earliest conflict between Primal Trust and Primal Mistrust. Here, the formulation goes: *Hope is the enduring belief in the attainability of primal wishes, in spite of the dark urges and rages which mark the beginnings of existence and leave a lasting residue of threatening Estrangement.* Hope, then, is the ontogenetic basis of what in adulthood becomes faith; it is nourished in childhood by the parental faith which pervades patterns of care. It is almost unnecessary to reiterate that the movie's last scenes, in the face-to-face emphasis on mutual recognition and trust, can be related both to the primal meeting of the eyes of the newborn with those of the maternal person and to St. Paul's dictum about what is beyond the glass darkly.

If I now distribute the stages of life and the life crises in a diagram, Hope "belongs" in the lower left corner and Wisdom in the upper right, while the horizontal and the vertical meet in the upper left. All the earlier conflicts can thus be seen to reach into, and to be renewed on, the level of the last, as they are on each level in between—but always renewed in terms of the conflict which dominates that level. In $A8$, then, Primal Trust and Wisdom meet, and so do Primal Mistrust and Despair. But here another problem of theory enters that easily becomes one of ideology: are we saying thàt the need for a faith is "nothing but" a lifelong fixation on primal trust, childlike in the beginning and illusional at the end? Or that primal trust is "simply" the ontogenetic foundation of a capacity for some faith necessary both for terminal peace and for the renewal of life from generation to generation?

5. The movie, as we saw, links the contemporary cast of individuals who appear in the course of Borg's journey with the important figures of his early years, and it thus gives us a chance to populate the empty boxes on the top line of the chart.

At this point, however, I must spell out the *epigenetic* principle which alone excuses the use of such a chart:

(*a*) Each combination of primal qualities has its stage of ascendance when physical, cognitive, emotional, and social developments permit its coming to a crisis. These stages of ascendance constitute the diagonal.

(*b*) Each such stage has its precursors (below the diagonal) which must now be brought up (vertically) to "their" maturational crisis.

(*c*) Each such crisis (as already stated) must at the advent of succeeding crises (above the diagonal) be brought up to the new level of the then dominant conflict.

✳ In Borg's case it is clear how his own terminal conflicts open up all his earlier ones, as personified by the younger persons who confront him (in fact or in fantasy) on his journey. To enter what we already know on the top line from right to left, his own ruefully unresolved crisis of Generativity versus Stagnation ($H8$) is renewed by his confrontation with Marianne, who herself is undergoing this same crisis in its age-specific form ($H7$) and is forcing her husband Evald to face it on his level. Borg's unresolved Intimacy Crisis ($H6$) we also reencountered, personified in the "accidental" couple, the Almans, and relived in his reveries and dreams.

These are the adult stages proper. They first emerge when a person is ready to commit the strengths, which have matured earlier, to the "maintenance of the world" in historical space and time. They now must combine in the qualities of Love and Care. Love matures through the crisis of Intimacy versus Isolation; it establishes a mutuality with new individuals in wider affiliations, thus transcending the *exclusivity* of earlier dependencies. Care, in turn, is the concrete concern for what has been generated by love, necessity, or accident, thus counteracting the *Rejectivity*, which resists the commitment to such obligation.[10a]

Nobody in this cast, however, nor, indeed, in life is neatly "located" in one stage; rather, all persons can be seen to oscillate between at least two stages and move more definitely into a higher one only when an even higher one begins to determine the interplay: thus, if Borg, in the last stage that can be formulated as developmental, is in a renewed struggle with the two earlier ones, he is so in the face of death or, at any rate, senility; and if Marianne's struggle for generativity is still weighed down by that for intimacy, she is also alarmed at her—and especially her husband's—increasing age and threatening ossification.

Moving further left on the chart and thus to the contemporary representatives of ever earlier stages of life, we encounter the triad of young people. The young men, as we saw, are still in the midst of the struggle for Identity and certainly in the grips of some Identity Confusion which they are trying to resolve by pointing up (and underscoring with blows) each other's inconsistencies. Little Sara, however, will not let them forget the approaching stage when being "in love" must mature into Love and when "intimacies" must amount to a pervasive sense of, and capacity for, Intimacy. What is still awake of Borg's Identity Crisis (*H5*) comes to the fore in the declamations of the midday meal and in a playful, even impulsive, yielding to feelings and notions which might well have become a more important part of his identity had they not been finally subdued by the loss of Sara, who is, as first loves are apt to be, both the female Other and the feminine Self—that is, the Self which such a man considers too feminine to acknowledge. To continue our formulations: *Fidelity is the ability to sustain loyalties freely pledged in spite of the inevitable contradictions and confusions of value systems.* It is the cornerstone of identity, and it receives inspiration from confirming ideologies and affirming companions.

The consideration of the twelve squares in the chart's upper right corner reminds us of another pervasive misunderstanding. For theoretical, as well as clinical, historical, and autobiographic reasons,[11] Identity terms have been emphasized in my writings and have subsequently been widely accepted or rejected on the assumption that in my scheme Identity was the teleological aim and end of growing up. The Identity Crisis is, to say the least, pivotal; but Dr. Borg's case illustrates poignantly what happens when Identity, because of some earlier partial arrests and especially because of a retreat from Intimacy, is overdefined in terms of occupation and civic role and whatever character restriction they may foster. The "achievement" of an over-formulated identity, then, may sacrifice too early a measure of Identity Confusion salutary for some playful variability in later choices.

In this connection, it must be emphasized that all the psychosocial strengths associated with our scheme postulate an active adaptation rather than a passive adjustment—that is, they change the environment even as they make selective use of its opportunities. Thus, the "maintenance of the world" could by no means be effected by mere servitude and compliance; it means rather a continuous reciprocal facilitation of social and psychological development and of larger and smaller institutions and—where such facilitation has become impossible—radical changes in social mores and institutions. It is for this reason that the study of the life cycle leads to that of biography and history and of social and economic conditions. The implication here is that, if individuals do not find in daily ritualizations as well as in the rituals of a society the affirmation and confirmation suggested here, both individual and generational cycles will show symptoms of pathology that point to specific needs for social change. We can, at any rate, recognize in Victor, Anders, and little Sara some readiness for ideological controversies that could, in principle, involve them in a turbulent moratorium or in some ideological movement of varying revolutionary or reactionary potentials. The actual social involvements of our young ideologists seem as yet open, even as they watch with some mixture of awe and mockery how the older generation goes about honoring itself. As for Marianne, I can well see her taking an active hand in communal life, after her encounter with the mixture of professional service and generational isolation presented by her two doctors.

6. To conclude, in speaking of the human life cycle and of the place of adulthood and of old age in it, no conception would be sufficient without reference to the *relativity* of the three cycles:

(*a*) All the emergent strengths are necessary to complete the individual cycle, although, as we saw, no such cycle can escape variable emphases on the inhibiting and isolating qualities of human development which foster fear and anxiety.

(*b*) Any fulfillment of the individual life cycle, far from being simply a matter of finding terminal clarity, can only fulfill what is given in the order of things by remaining responsible and by contributing continuous solutions to the ongoing cycle of generations.

(*c*) The generational cycle in all its intricacies, in turn, is vital to the maintenance of evolving *social structures* which must facilitate the emergence of the life stages or else suffer social and political pathology.[12]

According to the retrospective logic of this presentation, we conclude with a few formulations concerning the stages of childhood. As Dr. Borg, on his journey, crosses the Swedish countryside (and moves further left on our chart), he encounters his erstwhile patients who obviously represent his most satisfying personal involvement in the "maintenance of the world" at a time when his sexual and familial intimacy was slowly going bankrupt. His patients had provided the renewal in his adult life of the strengths he had developed throughout his childhood and youth: the strength of Purposefulness and of Competence which also came to occupy the center of his Fidelity.

Let me add here the corresponding formulations: Rudimentary *Purposefulness is the courage playfully to imagine and energetically to pursue valued goals, uninhibited by the defeat of infantile fantasies, by the guilt they aroused, and by the punishment they elicited.* It invests ideals of action, and it is derived from the example of the child-hood milieu. *Competence, in turn, is the free exercise of dexterity and intelligence in the completion of tasks, unimpaired by infantile inferiority.* It is the basis for coopera-tive participation in technologies, and it relies, in turn, on the logic of tools and skills. But if the first one, namely, Competence, emerges from the infantile struggle of Indus-try versus Inferiority, and Purpose from that of Initiative versus Guilt, these original conflicts are faced in the doctor's reveries and dreams. His examination dream, as we saw, confronts him with the fact that his very competence in professional life has per-mitted him to become insensitive to a deep feeling of inadequacy (here expressed in his failure to recognize when a woman and, by implication, when he himself is "dead" or "alive") and to bypass his deepseated sense of being "guilty of guilt."

The vivid reverie of his early childhood milieu leads back to an even earlier stage in childhood (*B2*) in which the rudiments of a person's Will receive some lasting charac-teristics as it emerges from the conflict between a sense of Autonomy and the sense of Shame—which, like Guilt, is deeply ingrained in the human make-up and is used by all cultures to impose special choices and restrictions on a child's development. *Will is the unbroken determination to exercise free choice as well as self-control, in spite of early experiences of shame and self-doubt caused by uncontrolled willfulness and of rage over being controlled.* As we saw, the great childhood scene illustrates with vital humor how all the children and young people learn to stand up to the demanding and scolding aunt who represents, no doubt, in a reverie all too benign, the potentially cruel, moralistic side of such a milieu. The implication seems to be, quite in accord with psychopathology and characterology, that Isak, more than any of the other chil-dren, submitted to his milieu's moralism to an extent that restricted his spontaneity and playfulness, and that this made him, in fact, the compulsive character that he became.

But as Sara, who had by then assumed the role of the young maternal person, leads Isak to the shore where he and his parents exchange smiles of recognition—if now at the safe distance of terminal resignation—she seems to restore the trust of the first stage, without which Isak could not have become what he is and could not have dreamed as he did.

I hope to have indicated in the first part of this paper that a good story does not need a chart to come alive and, in the second, that a chart, and especially one with so many empty boxes, can use a good story. At any rate, I look forward to seeing this combination used for the demonstration of other conceptions detailing the epigenetic values intrinsic in the human life cycle.*

*This essay was presented in a slightly different version at the symposium on "Human Values and Aging" at Case Western Reserve University in Cleveland on November 10, 1975, as part of a two-year research-design project funded by the National Endowment for the Humanities.

REFERENCES
    [1]Ingmar Bergman, *Four Screenplays* (New York, 1960).
    [2]*Ibid.*, p. 21. Eino Kaila's *Persoonallisuus* appeared in 1934 (Helsinki) and was first published in

Swedish in 1935 (*Personlighetens psykologi* [Helsinfors, 4th edition, 1946]).

[3]As has been done admirably, for example, by Diane M. Bordon and Louis H. Leiter in *Wild Strawberries: A Textbook of Aesthetic Criticism* (California Syllabus, Oakland, 1975).

[4]Erik H. Erikson, *Childhood and Society* (2nd ed., 1963); *Youth and Crisis* (New York, 1968); "The Human Life Cycle" in *International Encyclopedia of the Social Sciences* (New York, 1968).

[5]I will discuss the terms as well as the "versus" later on.

[6]Bergman, *op. cit.*, p. 278.

[7]*Ibid.*, p. 283

[8]Erik H. Erikson, *Dimensions of a New Identity* (Jefferson Lectures, 1973; New York, 1974).

[9]Sudhir Kakar, "The Human Life Cycle: The Traditional Hindu View and the Psychology of Erik H. Erikson," *Philosophy East and West*, XVIII: 3 (1968).

[10]The following formulations are adjusted from the *Encyclopedia of Social Sciences, op. cit.*

[10a]For reasons which I hope are now obvious, I have called these stages *psychosocial*. I should add, however, that Generativity can be shown to have instinctual roots in *psychosexual* development as it continues into adulthood. Psychoanalysis, paradoxically, has tended to separate procreativity from sexuality and even from genital instinctuality, although every genital act climactically involves the procreative organs and their experiential correlates.

Footnote within a footnote: the new *biosocial* point of view makes it plausible that pseudospeciation may also have a more biological root, namely, in instinctive social acts which propagate and defend common genes. The term *generativity* could well include such a meaning, provided it is understood that in man all "instinctive" patterns become enmeshed in instinctual drives. Thus, the "altruistic" sacrifices made for one's genes extend in man to acts of war for one's "kind" and against those deemed inimical to it on the basis of cultural and historical divisions. How, in turn, the world religions have attempted to counteract exclusivity and rejectivity by advocating sacrificial ideologies transcending genealogical vanity and the elitist identities based on it, I have approached in my book *Gandhi's Truth*.

[11]Erik H. Erikson, "Autobiographic Notes on the Identity Crisis," *Daedalus*, Fall, 1970. Revised in *Life History and the Historical Moment* (New York, 1975).

HERANT A. KATCHADOURIAN

Medical Perspectives on Adulthood

Confound not the distinctions of thy life which nature hath divided; that is, youth, adolescence, manhood, and old age: nor in these divided periods, wherein thou art in a manner four, conceive thyself but one. Let every division be happy in its proper virtues, nor one vice run through all. Let each distinction have its salutary transition, and critically deliver thee from the imperfections of the former; so ordering the whole, that prudence and virtue may have the largest section.

Sir Thomas Browne (1605-1682)[1]

CONTEMPORARY PHYSICIANS MAY NOT BE so articulate as their distinguished seventeenth-century colleague, but upon reflection they are likely to share Sir Thomas Browne's life-cycle perspective and to find it essential for the understanding of people and for dealing effectively with their ailments and infirmities. Such a holistic approach is more characteristic of the thoughtful clinician than of the technicians of medicine, for whom the parts of the body sometimes come to wag the whole.[2]

That physicians are aware of the significance of the life cycle is apparent in many aspects of medical practice: for instance, case histories, which constitute the fundamental units of clinical communication, always begin with a statement about the patient's age and sex. These two indices are essential for interpreting the history of an illness, the findings of the physical examination, and any laboratory tests. Because of the overlap between the signs and symptoms of various diseases, the identification of an illness is reached through a process of differential diagnosis whereby the physician makes probabilistic judgments that lead to a definitive decision. As diseases afflict people differently at different ages, the age factor becomes a significant clinical clue in the diagnostic process and an important epidemiological variable. Figures 1-4 illustrate this by showing the discrepant death rates from major illness and external causes at various stages of life.

At an even more fundamental level, a developmental aberration may constitute an illness, that is, the disease may be manifested by the untimely presence or absence of an age-related characteristic. Bed-wetting in an infant or the existence of immature blood cells in his circulation do not carry the pathological connotations that these same phenomena carry in adulthood. Treatment, too, can be age-dependent: choices of procedure and dosage, and even the expected outcome, are significantly linked to age.

33

Despite this pervasive awareness of the life cycle in medical practice, little formal attention has been paid to its various phases generally and to the concept of adulthood in particular. One searches in vain in medical dictionaries for definitions of adulthood. The term "adult" either does not appear at all or, when it does, it is usually defined as "fully grown and mature; a fully grown individual,"[3] or as someone who has ". . . attained full size, strength, and reproductive ability, or the ability to handle personal affairs."[4] The term "adult," like the term "adolescent," derives from the Latin "to grow." Simply put, an adolescent is someone who is growing up and an adult is someone who has grown up. But what does it mean to "grow up"? The answers found in medical texts are not very explicit. Though pediatric texts obviously deal with children, books on adolescence with adolescents, and most other texts with adults, the question of what an adult is is seldom raised.

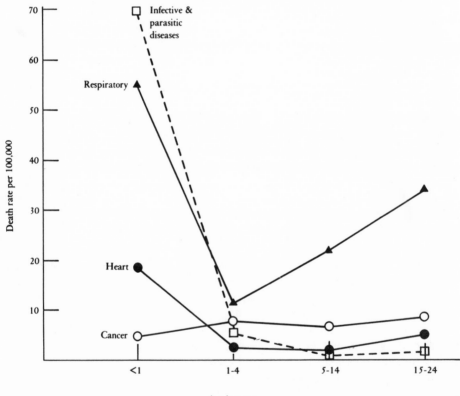

Figure 1. Death rates from major illnesses: birth to young adulthood. The plotted figures for each age group are the average numbers of deaths per year in each 100,000 persons of a given age in the total population. For example, in the four years included under age "1-4," the average number of deaths from respiratory disease was 11.4 per 100,000 children between the years of 1 and 4. The data are from the 1968 Mortality Statistics (Monthly Vital Statistics Report, U.S. Dept. of Health, Education and Welfare, 1971, Vol. 19, No. 12). (Redrawn from W. A. Marshall, Chapter 7, in R. R. Sears and S. S. Feldman, eds., *The Seven Ages of Man* [Los Altos, Calif., 1973]. © 1973 by William Kaufmann, Inc. All rights reserved.)

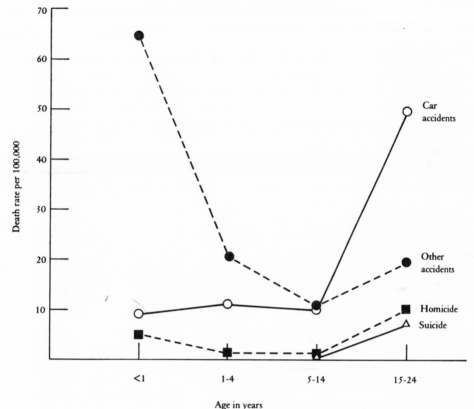

Figure 2. Death rates from major external causes: birth to young adulthood. The plotted figures are comparable to those in the illness chart. (Redrawn from W. A. Marshall, Chapter 7, in R. R. Sears and S. S. Feldman, eds., *The Seven Ages of Man* [Los Altos, Calif., 1973]. © 1973 by William Kaufmann, Inc. All rights reserved.)

The term "adult" does appear as one of the 8,500 subject headings in the *Cumulated Index Medicus*, which is the standard reference to the periodical biomedical literature. But of the 220,000 entries in 1974, it accounts for only two items ("adolescence," "adolescent psychiatry," and "adolescent psychology" fare better with a combined 125 entries).[5] In view of this apparent lack of concern specifically with adulthood, we shall have to consider medical notions about it in more general terms, as they are reflected in medical practice, in the perspectives of human biology, and in psychiatry.

Notions of Adulthood in Medical Practice

Throughout most of the history of medicine (which is almost commensurate with the human record generally), physicians have dealt with their patients in an all-inclusive system of general practice. Specializations based either on the nature of the illness and method of treatment or on the age of the patient are recent phenomena. The first category of specialization includes most present-day medical disciplines. Fields are differentiated by their predominant method of treatment (e.g., the surgical specialties), the part of the body dealt with (e.g., cardiology), attention to a particular class of ailments (e.g., oncology), or even a specific illness (e.g., syphilology). The second category, based on age groupings, is more pertinent to our subject. The one solid offshoot from general medicine in this category is pediatrics. Far less well established are the fields of adolescent medicine and geriatrics (or gerontology).[6]

Pediatrics as a specialty dates back only to the middle of the nineteenth century; prior to that time it was included under internal medicine and, to some extent, obstetrics. But this is not to say that, earlier, physicians did not recognize the special problems of childhood. Even in Egyptian medical documents (such as the Papyrus Ebers of 1550 B.C.), there are sporadic references to diseases of infants and children. They are also found in Babylonian, Indian, and Talmudic texts.

Such references become even more plentiful in Greek and Roman medicine. Hippocrates (ca. 460-377 B.C.) had a good deal to say about childhood illnesses and devoted a whole treatise to dentition. He also noted a late advent of puberty in colder climates. The Roman physician Celsus admonished his colleagues that "children should not be treated as adults," and he pointed out the greater prevalence among youth of acute illnesses, epilepsy, insanity, and consumption.[7] Similar references can be found in the works of Galen (ca. A.D. 130-200), Oribasius (ca. A.D. 325-400), Rhazes (A.D. 850-923), and others. Another early landmark in the history of pediatrics was the publication in 1472 of the *Little Book on Diseases of Children* by Paulo

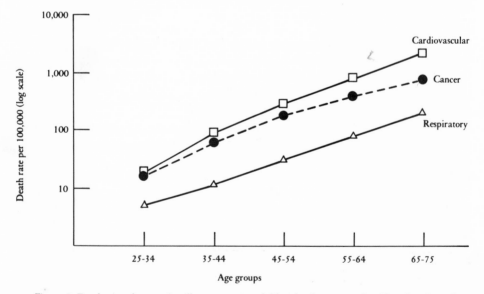

Figure 3. Death rates from major illnesses: young adulthood to later maturity. Note that the scale at left is logarithmic, the actual values would go off the page if they were plotted in conventional form. (Redrawn from W. A. Marshall, Chapter 10, in R. R. Sears and S. S. Feldman, eds., *The Seven Ages of Man* [Los Altos, Calif., 1973]. © 1973 by William Kaufmann, Inc. All rights reserved.)

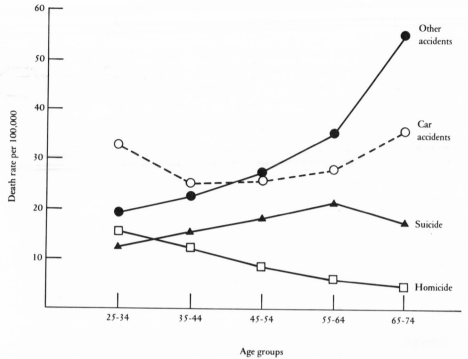

Figure 4. Death rates from major external causes: young adulthood to later maturity. (Redrawn from W. A. Marshall, Chapter 10, in R. R. Sears and S. S. Feldman, eds., *The Seven Ages of Man* [Los Altos, Calif., 1973]. © 1973 by William Kaufmann, Inc. All rights reserved.)

Bagellardus (d. 1472), which was the first printed book entirely devoted to diseases of children.[8] About 1512-13, the *Rosegarten* by Eucharius Röslin (d. ca. 1526) appeared, a work which eventually went through some forty known editions, the last of which was issued in 1730. This was a veritable textbook of pediatrics; all of its thirty chapters are devoted to diseases of children. Starting in the seventeenth century, the treatment of sick children steadily improved in quality, and events of significance in pediatric history become too numerous to mention here. By the mid-nineteenth century pediatrics was being taught in medical schools, and clinics and hospitals had been established for children; by the turn of the century pediatric associations had been founded both in Europe and in the United States.[9]

Adolescent medicine has emerged as a distinct field only during the past several decades, and at this stage of its development it is still being confronted with its own task of identity formation. The absence of a generally accepted label to designate specialists in adolescence is symptomatic. With varying degrees of euphonic abandon, terms like "teenologist," "teeniatrician," "hebiatrician" (Hebe, the goddess of youth), "ephebiatrician" (*ephebeios*, Greek for "youthful") have been put forth, but have so far mercifully failed to find favor.

The problem is real. The transition to adulthood occurs over the second decade: at its inception the individual is a child, at its conclusion, an adult, while in between he occupies biologically and psychologically ambiguous and fluid positions. Which specialist takes care of an adolescent patient often depends on the peculiarities of medical practice in the area, the particular relationship of a family to its family physician, the nature of the adolescent's illness, whether or not he has passed puberty, and other similar considerations. Currently, pediatricians, internists, psychiatrists, dermatologists, orthopedic surgeons, and, in increasing numbers, gynecologists are the specialists most likely to treat teenagers. When the biological process of puberty itself seems disturbed, endocrinologists are often consulted.

The field of geriatrics is also in the process of differentiating itself from general internal medicine. There is increasing recognition that special attention needs to be paid to the biological and psychosocial processes of aging and to the particular illnesses that afflict the elderly. Yet, here again there is some ambiguity as to when in the life cycle geriatrics becomes functional. Aging, after all, is a lifelong process which simply becomes more evident with the progress of adulthood. Nevertheless, just as pediatrics has seceded from internal medicine, so also it appears certain that the decade leading to entry into adulthood and the last decade or two of adulthood itself will also become specialized provinces within medicine. Judging by the number of professional journals and associations of physicians available in these areas, this process is already well advanced. But to what extent the main span of adult life will itself become further subdivided for medical caretaking remains to be seen.

The Concept of Adulthood in Human Biology

Just as medical practice was—and remains—the domain of physicians, investigation of the human body also for a long time belonged exclusively to medicine. More recently, the enormous expansion of knowledge in these fields of research has produced a new type of medical specialist who is not a practicing physician but a research scientist trained in one or another of the basic medical sciences such as physiology or biochemistry.

Another distinction that has become profitably blurred is that between medicine and biology. Traditionally, physicians dealt with people, while biologists studied animals and plants. Today, however, physicians make extensive use of animals in their research, while biologists study human functions as well. It is quite legitimate, therefore, to think of all investigators of the human body as "human biologists" irrespective of their particular disciplinary background: the term is gaining wide currency, and we shall use it here to refer to the work of medical scientists who may or may not be physicians.

One need not be a human biologist to note with wonder the physical transformation of children into adults through the changes of puberty. This is a process crucial for the life of the species, and it is also a momentous event in the life of the individual. In biological terms one can say that adulthood has been achieved when puberty has been successfully completed.

But what is "puberty"? There is as yet no generally accepted definition. The term is often used synonymously with "adolescence" to refer to a vaguely defined transitional period between childhood and adulthood. Since biological and psychosocial developments during this phase of life have fairly distinct characteristics and do not entirely coincide, it would be preferable to use "puberty" for the former and "adolescence" for the latter. Unfortunately long usage has made this distinction difficult to maintain in practice.

The changes that constitute puberty have been classified by Marshall and Tanner as follows:

1) Acceleration and then deceleration of skeletal growth (the adolescent growth spurt).

2) Altered body composition as a result of skeletal and muscular growth together with changes of the quantity and distribution of fat.

3) Development of the circulatory and respiratory systems, leading, particularly in boys, to increased strength and endurance.

4) The development of the gonads, reproductive organs, and secondary sex characters.

5) A combination of factors, not yet fully understood, which modulates the activity of those nervous and endocrine elements which initiate and coordinate all these changes.[10]

There are two major biological consequences to these pubertal changes that have profound psychosocial repercussions. First, the child attains the physique and physiological characteristics of the adult, including reproductive capacity. Second, most of the major adult physical sex differences become established through this process.

The biology of puberty is the subject of an extensive and expanding literature. There is no need for us here to delve into its details, particularly since an account of these matters has been given by a leading authority in a relatively recent issue of this journal.[11] We shall therefore comment only briefly on the five categories of changes listed above.[12]

The pubescent growth spurt is among the more dramatic changes of puberty. Growth in stature is a continous process; by the age of 10, boys have already attained about 78 per cent and girls 84 per cent of their adult height.[13] What makes the growth spurt at puberty noteworthy, therefore, is not so much the amount of growth as its rate.

Among girls, the height spurt typically starts at about 10½ years, reaches peak velocity at 12, and is over by 14.[14] Among boys, the onset is usually at about 12 to 13, the peak at 14, and the end at 16.[15] During the year of peak height velocity a boy grows on an average of three to five inches and a girl somewhat less. In terms of rate of growth, this means an actual doubling in velocity compared to the period preceding puberty and approximates the rapid rate of growth of the two-year-old child.[16] With the culmination of the growth spurt, the rate of growth decelerates rapidly. Most girls at 14 years and most boys at 16 years have reached 98 per cent of their ultimate adult height.[17] Further noticeable growth in stature ceases at about 18 years in women and at 20 years in men.

Concurrent with the growth spurt, there are other changes that shape the adult physique. An important factor in the differences between male and female contours is the amount and distribution of subcutaneous fat. Young children gradually lose their chubbiness, but then, shortly before puberty, they regain some of it. With the growth spurt a negative fat balance is established among boys but not among girls, who usually enter adulthood with more body fat than males, particularly in the region of the pelvis and breasts.

Muscular development is more marked in the mature male. During puberty the muscles increase in size and even more in strength. Prior to puberty, there is no substantial difference in muscular strength between boys and girls, but distinct differences become established at puberty and persist into adulthood.[18] Boys also develop greater speed and coordination in bodily movements, and their reaction to sudden stimuli becomes quicker.

Changes in stature, musculature, and fat distribution constitute the more prominent alterations but by no means the only ones. Essentially, to varying degrees, the whole body becomes transformed. In addition to increased size, the shifts in bodily proportions shape the adult form. Some sex differences in proportion are present at birth: for instance, the forearm is longer relative to height in the male than in the female. But the broader shoulders of the male relative to his hips and his longer legs relative to his trunk are characteristics that emerge at puberty.

Other changes, such as those involving the face, are more subtle. Since the bones of the face grow faster than the cranium, in adulthood the face "emerges from under the skull," as it were. The profile of the adult is straighter, the nose projects further, and the jaw is more prominent. All these features are more marked in the male than in the female. Later in puberty the hairline of the male forehead recedes while that of the female does not change. All these factors, along with the growth of the beard, make the physical transformation of the male face in adolescence more marked than that of the female.

Equally important changes take place internally. The muscles of the heart, for instance, participate in the growth spurt along with the other muscles of the body. Puberty brings on an increase in the number of red blood corpuscles, the blood hemoglobin level, and blood volume. Once again, sex discrepancies are established in favor of males. The same is true for the respiratory system and its functions.

The net effect of these and related changes is to equip the adult with the necessary physiological mechanisms to allow for the effective exertion of his larger and more powerful body. As a result, post-pubescent individuals vastly outperform their pre-pubescent selves in all tasks requiring strength, endurance, and stamina; these changes are also more marked among males than among females.

A word of caution may be in order here. The physical discrepancies that puberty widens between male and female are real. But some extraordinary conclusions have been drawn from them. It is one thing to say that males have generally greater exercise tolerance and another to conclude that women therefore should not drive tractors or play football. While all the physical sex differences that emerge at puberty differentiate male and female populations, they do not equally affect all individuals within them.

There are wide intrasex differences, and there is much overlap between the two groups: in other words, obviously women exist who are taller or stronger than many men. Furthermore, physical strength can be vastly increased by exercise and atrophied through disuse. A great many of the sex discrepancies that occur can be attributed to the selectivity by which males are pushed into physical exertion at work and play.

Much can be made of the male's physical advantages. But an advantage is meaningful only in relation to some specific purpose: to be big as a camel is no advantage if one needs to go through the eye of a needle.) The physical attributes of the male are also generally present in other primates. Our evolutionary forebears differentiated the way they did because of some selective process. Quite plausibly, the male physique was better equipped for tasks such as hunting big game. But what use is this now? And what are the dangers of the male continuing to glory in the prowess of his striking arm and, by extension, in the potency of his weapons? Finally, before too much is made of the male's physical superiority, one should remember that statistically females outlive males, and survival is surely not a trivial test of physical fitness.)

If puberty accomplished only what has been so far described, it would have done the preservation of the human species little good. For, tall and strong as adults may be, to preserve the species they must be able to reproduce. Reproductive capacity is thus the quintessence of biological adulthood, and, as shown by a comparison of various growth patterns (Figure 5), the reproductive system attains its greatest gains at puberty.

The reproductive system, like all other systems of the body, is already present in embryonal life. The genetic sex of the individual is immutably determined at conception: if the sperm that fertilizes the ovum carries an x chromosome, the issue is female; if it carries a y chromosome, the offspring is male. (The genital system makes its appearance during the fifth to sixth week of intrauterine life when the embryo is about one-half to one centimeter long. It is quite undifferentiated at this stage: in both sexes there are a pair of gonads, two sets of ducts, and the rudiments of external genitals. Through an epigenetic process, the reproductive system develops and further differentiates sexually. In the seventh week, it becomes possible to tell if the gonad is going to become a testis or an ovary, and by the fourth month the sex of the fetus is unmistakable even by inspection of the external genitals alone. At birth, with very rare exceptions, a child is unequivocally male or female genetically, anatomically, and hormonally. Although the reproductive systems of male and female are built on the same basic plan, there is thus a progressive divergence throughout development in shape and function between the two. This sexual (dimorphism) is definitively established at puberty. A final installment occurs in women when they experience pregnancy, childbirth, and lactation.[19]

The maturation of the reproductive system in puberty involves the accelerated growth of the internal sex organs and the external genitalia. This is accompanied by the development of the so-called secondary sexual characteristics which include the development of the female breast, the sprouting of pubic and axillary hair, the lowering pitch of the voice, and the appearance of facial hair in the male. In physiological terms, the key events are the activation of ovulation and the menstrual cycle in females and the production of sperm and the ability to ejaculate in males (resulting from the development of the prostate gland which produces most of the seminal fluid).

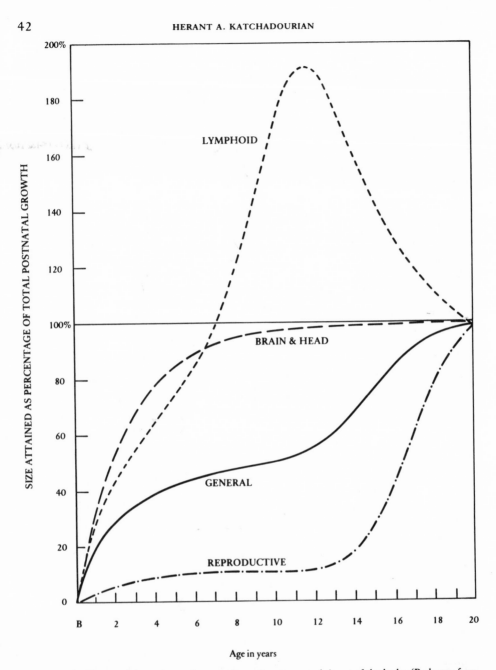

Figure 5. The main types of growth curves for various parts and tissues of the body. (Redrawn from G. A. Harrison, J. S. Weiner, J. M. Tanner, N. A. Barnicot, *Human Biology* [Oxford, 1964], p. 309. © 1964 by the Oxford University Press. All rights reserved.)

It is not possible to assign simple age landmarks for these events, since both the onset and the duration of a given developmental event vary a great deal. For example, breast development, which often is the earliest visible sign of puberty in the female, is regarded as beginning normally at any time between the ages of 8 and 13 and ending normally between the ages of 13 and 18. Pubic hair appears at about age 11 (axillary hair follows a year later), and the adult pattern is established by age 14. Menarche usually occurs about two years after the start of breast enlargement: in the United States, most girls now begin to menstruate at around 12 or 13, but they may also perfectly normally do so as early as 10 years or as late as 16½ years. The early menstrual cycles tend to be irregular and often anovulatory, that is, a young woman does not become reliably fertile until a few years after the initial cycle.

In the male, testicular enlargement is usually the first pubescent change; it starts between 9½ and 13½ years and ends sometime between 13½ and 17 years. Pubic-hair growth occurs between 12 and 16.[20] The growth of the beard is often a later development. The first ejaculation usually occurs at 11 or 12, but mature sperm take a few more years to appear. This relative pubescent sterility in girls and boys, who have otherwise matured sexually, does not, however, amount to reliable contraceptive security, as some teenagers continue to discover to their grief.

In defining adulthood, an important distinction must be emphasized here between sex and reproduction. Whether one accepts Freud's broadly encompassing concept of the libido or Kinsey's far narrower definition of orgasmic "outlets," it can be reasonably asserted that sexuality starts and ends with life. Children are demonstrably capable of sexual arousal and orgasm (although one may question the propriety and wisdom of such demonstration). Sexual functions, like alimentary and eliminative functions, differ somewhat in children and adults, but these differences are not fundamental. The only significant change brought about by puberty is the male capacity to ejaculate during orgasm, and this is primarily of reproductive rather than sexual significance. Pre- and post-pubescent females, pre-pubescent males, and certain post-pubescent males experience orgasm without ejaculation.[21]

A similar statement can be made about sexual behavior. Anthropological and other evidence shows that children are quite capable of engaging in most forms of "adult" sexual activity.[22] That they do not do so overtly and in larger numbers in our culture is at least in part because of social inhibitions. It is not being suggested here that this ought not to be the case, but simply that behavioral differences between children and adults are not entirely biologically determined. Thus, although there are important biological factors that may influence adult sexual behavior, sexuality in itself is not a particularly refined criterion of adulthood. But reproductive capacity is.

A related and crucial developmental phenomenon is gender-identity differentiation. A model for the development of adult gender identity has been proposed by Money and Ehrhardt (Figure 6); it attempts to integrate genetic, hormonal, and social factors as they interact in sequentially defining this major aspect of adulthood.[23]

The trigger that initiates the chain of events involved in puberty is located in the brain. So far as is known, the part of the brain that first stirs is the hypothalamus. The pituitary gland, the testes, ovaries, and the tissues of the body can be stimulated into activity long before the normal time of puberty. But, although potentially responsive, the rest of the body receives its marching orders from the hypothalamus, which issues them in its own good time and possibly under instructions from elsewhere in the brain.

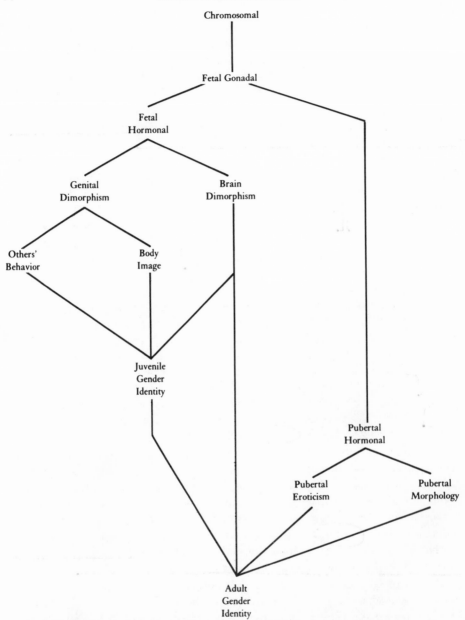

Figure 6. Diagram to illustrate the sequential and interactional components of gender-identity differentiation. (Redrawn from J. Money and A. A. Ehrhardt, *Man and Woman, Boy and Girl* [Baltimore, 1972]. © 1972 by the Johns Hopkins University Press. All rights reserved.)

To initiate puberty, the hypothalamus produces and releases higher concentrations of certain hormones which stimulate the anterior pituitary into increasing the output of two of its own hormones: FSH (follicle-stimulating hormone) and LH (luteinizing hormone). In the female, FSH stimulates the ovarian follicles to mature. These, in turn, produce estrogen which brings about most of the "feminizing" changes of puberty. The function of LH is related to ovulation and to the subsequent formation of the remnants of the ovarian follicle into the "corpus luteum," which produces the second female hormone, progesterone.

In the male, FSH initiates spermatogenesis and LH (which in the male is called interstitial cell-stimulating hormone: ICSH) activates certain cells in the interstices of the seminiferous, or sperm-bearing, tubules to produce the male hormone, testosterone. This, in turn, brings about the "masculinizing" changes of puberty. Although it is customary to refer to these gonadal hormones as "sex hormones" and to assign them gender, such designations must be understood mainly as manners of speech. Testosterone, for example, is as much a growth hormone as it is a sex hormone: it plays a central role in the growth spurt at puberty. Likewise, both classes of hormones are present in each sex; the difference is mainly a matter of relative concentration. (It may be sobering to note that estrogen is found even in the testes of bulls, and that the grand champion of estrogen production is the stallion, which is not the most effeminate creature by most conventional standards.)

Androgens (of which testosterone is only one) are produced in the female by the adrenal cortex and stimulate, for instance, the development of pubic and axillary hair. They also seem to have an erotogenic effect.

The production of these hormones is regulated through an intricate set of feedback mechanisms and follows a cyclical pattern in the female between menarche and menopause. One such feedback mechanism is hypothesized to keep the immature hypothalamus in check prior to puberty. Just as a house thermostat when it is set low does not trigger the furnace although the house is cool, so, prior to puberty, the hypothalamic ('thermostat') is presumably set low and the pre-pubertal levels of circulating pituitary and gonadal hormones are insufficient to activate it (and the bodily tissues do not respond to such low concentrations of estrogen and testosterone). At puberty, the hypothalamus becomes more sensitive, as if its "thermostat" had been turned up. The low levels of circulating anterior pituitary hormones do not inhibit it any longer; thus, higher levels of hypothalamic hormones are produced which stimulate the anterior pituitary and, in turn, the gonads into greater activity, eventually raising the output of the sex hormones to a point where the body responds with the changes of puberty.[24] This negative feedback also controls the menstrual cycle in conjunction with other positive feedback systems that make it possible for increasing levels of a hormone to further stimulate its own production. These feedback loops operate at "short" and "long" ranges, linking the various components of the system. Thus, the neuro-endocrine mechanisms that trigger puberty and maintain the reproductive function of the adult are not so much a hierarchic as a cybernetic system, where the various constituent parts mutually regulate one another.[25]

Other changes in the brain during puberty remain something of a mystery. As was shown in Figure 5, the growth of the brain precedes the growth of other systems. The brain has already attained 25 per cent of its adult weight at birth; 50 per cent at 6 months; 75 per cent at 2½ years; 90 per cent at 5 years; and 95 per cent at 10 years, when the individual is on the threshold of puberty. In contrast, body weight at birth is only 5 per cent and at age 10 only 50 per cent of that of the young adult.

Given the cognitive differences between children and adults and the sequential development in cognition during development (as shown by Piaget, Kohlberg, and others), something other than the meager gain in brain size must account for the neurophysiological changes that underlie and limit the psychological gains. Since most, if not all, nerve cells in the adult are already formed during the first twenty to thirty weeks of intrauterine life, the answer must be sought in increased "connectivity" or communicative linkages between cells. In fact, for the first several years of life and possibly longer, there is a progressive increase in the number and size of dendrites in all layers of the cortex. Studies on myelination show that the brain continues to develop at least until adolescence and possibly into adulthood. Dendrites occupy very little space—even millions of them can be accommodated within the modest brain-weight increases of a few per cent that result in immense gains in the complexity of communicative networks and, hence, cognitive functions.[26] Plausible as this explanation might be, the more precise characteristics of the adult brain remain to be elucidated.

In our discussion so far, we have presented the orderly changes of puberty with only occasional references to its variabilities. Two illustrations will further underscore these variations: each set of three girls and three boys in Figure 7 represents precisely the same chronological age, yet the developmental achievements displayed are obviously wide apart. Figure 8 shows that some boys in their first year of grade school have already reached puberty while others in their last year of high school have not; this is also true for girls.

These are physiologically normal individuals. When one crosses the somewhat arbitrary border into pathologically early puberty, variations become even more extreme. Children, even mere infants, may be found with one or another of the manifestations of precocious puberty. The youngest mother on record, a Peruvian girl, was delivered by caesarian section of a healthy male infant when she was all of 5 years and 7 months of age on May 15, 1939. She had reached puberty at 3 and had become pregnant at 4 years and 10 months. Boys of comparable precocity may have fathered children, but, if so, it would be very much harder to verify. At the other extreme, puberty may be far delayed or its typical changes largely absent, as in the case of eunuchs. Disturbances of puberty result from precocious activity or interference with the function of the hypothalamus, anterior pituitary, or the gonads. They may be due to a wide variety of pathological factors, and sometimes they have no known or demonstrable cause.

The normal process of puberty is subject to a large number of genetic and environmental influences, including familial and possibly racial factors, and the effects of seasons, perhaps of climate, definitely of nutrition, illness, and emotional state.[27] Such factors combine to generate geographic and social class differences in the maturational patterns of puberty. A secular trend of a decline in the age at menarche has been in progress during the last century. In 1840, Norwegian girls on the average reached menarche at about 17 years; now the average is four years younger. Women who reached puberty around 1900 did so one to two years later than teenagers do now.[28] This general trend has progressed at a rate of about four months per decade, but it is beginning to level out in Western countries.[29] A similar pattern of early maturation is assumed to be occurring in boys, although it is more difficult to prove because males lack a comparably distinct event to mark the onset of reproductive maturation.

Another secular trend involves increased height. In successive decades since 1900, adolescents have become taller by 2.5 cm and heavier by 2.5 kg. But since this is a reflection more of earlier maturation than of a more protracted fever of growth, the net gain for adults has been 1 cm per decade: a race of giants is therefore not imminent.[30]

No formal subdivisions of adult life have been distinguished from a human biological perspective. Although aging is studied extensively from the cellular to the organismic level, this work has not as yet been translated into discrete life phases. Using reproductive maturity as the criterion, one could meaningfully divide the life span into three phases separated by puberty and the menopause or climacteric.[31] But the latter event is not so distinct an entity in the male as it is in the female. The landmarks of such a subdivision are also too far apart to provide us with sufficient rungs on the ladder to match the many other important events that characterize adult life. Nevertheless, the climacteric deserves some further comment both as an event of major significance and as a counterpoint to puberty.

A woman is born with several hundred thousand ova which begin to mature cyclically at puberty. Some 300-400 cycles later, ovulation becomes erratic and finally stops as mysteriously as it began. The period of the menopause, which marks this event, usually occurs around the age of 47: about 50 per cent experience it between 45 and 50; 25 per cent before 45; and 25 per cent of women later than 50 years.

The cessation of ovulation results in infertility. Since the maturing ovarian follicle is the source of estrogen and progesterone, the post-menopausal woman also experiences the effects of withdrawal of these hormones. As increased levels of estrogen feminize the pubescent girl, decreased levels of estrogen have the opposite effect: they fail to counter the masculinizing effects of androgens which continue to be produced by the adrenal cortex. As a result, the pitch of the voice is lowered, for example, and the face becomes more hirsute. The other symptoms of the climacteric include "hot flashes," headaches, dizziness, palpitations, and joint pains. Almost all menopausal women experience these effects, but only about one in ten is significantly perturbed by them. Equally important are mood changes which occasionally culminate in the severe depressions of involutional melancholia. Although the reproductive system undergoes atrophic changes, the climacteric need not lead to sexual apathy or malfunction. Some women in fact experience an enhancement of erotic responsiveness, possibly due to the effect of androgen as well as to psychological factors such as freedom from the fear of pregnancy.

The male climacteric is a far more dubious entity. Gonadal function in the male does not generally cease as abruptly as it does in the female. Only rarely does a true male climacteric occur that includes symptoms such as hot flashes and similar signs of hormone withdrawal. More typically, there is a gradual decline in testicular function, with concomitant loss of fertility and potency, beginning in middle age. Nevertheless, males, too, can remain sexually active (and some even fertile) into old age.

In both sexes the hormonal decline in middle age is at the gonadal level. The pituitary hormones continue to be produced, but the testes and the ovary do not respond as before. Since estrogen can be readily administered, the biological changes of the climacteric can be significantly retarded and modified in women. Such hormonal replacement is of dubious value in males.

Psychiatric Viewpoints on Adulthood

Since its nineteenth-century emergence as a distinct medical specialty, psychiatry has been concerned with mental illness rather than with normative human development. Psychiatrists have traditionally labored in mental institutions, which for the most part have functioned as warehouses for the storage and custody of lost and unclaimed human beings. The great advances in the early history of psychiatry were thus in the more humanitarian treatment of the insane[32] and in the classification of mental illness.[33] It was Freud who brought psychiatry out of the madhouse.

Freud treated adults primarily, although his famous stages of psychosexual development were restricted to childhood. Even adolescence as a stage of life did not come into focus until the next generation of psychoanalysts, notably Anna Freud, August Aichhorn, Peter Blos, and, of course, Erik Erikson. Among the early psychoanalysts,

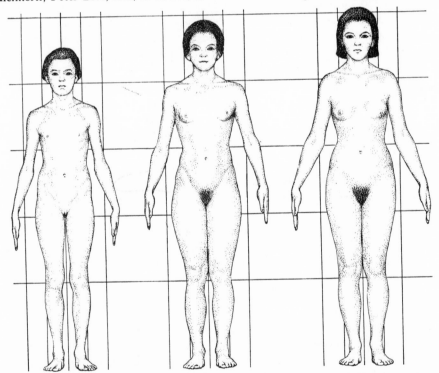

Figure 7. These three girls, all with the chronological age of 12.75 years, and the three boys depicted on the opposite page at 14.75 years show dramatic differences in development depending on whether they have not yet reached puberty (left), are partway through it (middle), or have completed their development (right). (From Tanner, "Growing Up," *Scientific American,* September, 1973. © 1973 by Scientific American, Inc. All rights reserved.)

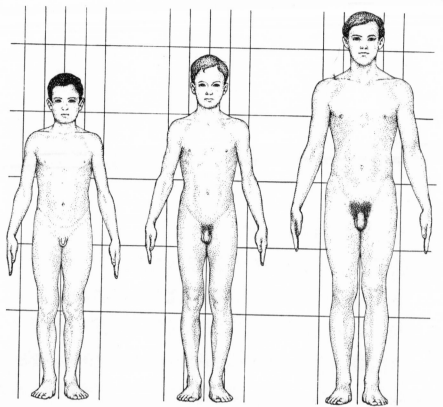

Jung was one who addressed himself to life stages beyond adolescence;[34] in fact, he started with the stage of "youth" that he defined as spanning the period between post-pubescence and adulthood. Jung visualized this phase as one of disengagement from childhood aspirations, confrontation with the issues of sexuality and self-esteem, and a general broadening of life perspective. Between the ages of 35 and 40, according to Jung, personality changes slowly begin to occur: some childhood traits may reemerge, and a reshuffling of motivations and interests takes place. These changes gradually become stabilized, and attitudes and convictions begin to harden, so that by age 50 a tendency toward rigidity and intolerance is established.

Jung dwells at length on old age, which he sees as characterized by further deep-seated psychic reorganization. There may be a tendency to change in the direction of the opposite sex, such as when older men become more "feminine" and women more "masculine." Eventually, the main task becomes the confrontation of death. Rather than compete with the young or cling to the past, the individual must discover in death a meaningful goal to strive for rather than a peril to shrink from: ". . . an old man who cannot bid farewell to life appears as feeble and sickly as a young man who is unable to embrace it."[35]

The major effort so far to examine the entire life cycle has come from Erik Erikson. Given the fame of his work, the difficulty of summarizing his thoughts without greatly

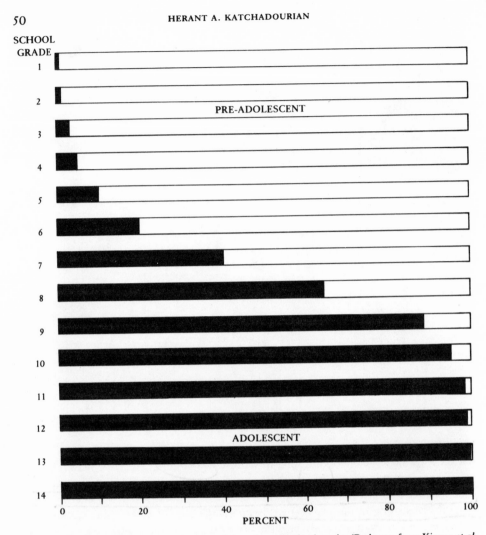

SCHOOL
GRADE

Figure 8. Per cent of adolescent (pubescent) boys in each school grade. (Redrawn from Kinsey *et al,*
Sexual Behavior in the Human Male [Philadelphia, 1948], p. 187).

diminishing them, and his own contribution to this volume, it would be otiose of me to
discuss his theories here in any detail, but we also cannot possibly omit all reference to
them even in this brief account.[36]

Erikson's theory of psychosocial development postulates a sequence of eight phases
or "ages of man." These phases derive in part from Freud's stages of psychosexual and
libidinal development, but they also go beyond them and encompass the entire life
span. Each stage is defined by a phase-specific task and follows a general chronology
without being linked to specific, arbitrary age limits. The first four phases pertain to
childhood, the fifth to adolescence, and the last three to adulthood.

These assignments hold true only in the sense that the phase-specific tasks reach
their critical point of resolution during their respective phases. Otherwise, their solu-

tions are prepared in previous stages and elaborated in subsequent ones. At each phase, components from each of the eight major tasks are present simultaneously as "precursors," "derivates," and as the decisive "crisis" itself. Consequently, it is not possible to discuss any phase of development in isolation. Thus, childhood does not end nor adulthood begin with adolescence. Rather, the adult is anticipated in the child and the child persists in the adult. This is the thread that gives continuity to Erikson's developmental scheme.

The model for this scheme is epigenetic and based on a fundamental principle of embryonal development whereby the differentiation of each part progresses from the simple to the more complex, each part having its time of ascendance while all parts grow simultaneously. This process is also firmly rooted in a social context and relies on a coordination between the developing person and an average expectable environment. Through a "cog-wheeling" of life cycles, phase-specific needs of children are interlocked to those of caretaking adults as representatives of society. Added to the internal strands that hold an individual life cycle together are the external ties which link various life cycles in an expanding circle of interpersonal bonds.

The psychosocial transition to adulthood is accomplished during adolescence (Erikson's Stage V) through the achievement of a sense of ego Identity. This, in turn, permits the establishment of a sense of Intimacy by the resolution of the first phase-specific task of adulthood proper (Stage VI). Such intimacy involves relations with the other sex but also with others of the same sex, and one's own self as well.

The counterpart to intimacy is Isolation as manifested in the ability and willingness to repudiate, isolate, or even destroy forces and people inimical to oneself. Erikson defines these phase-specific tasks in terms of the polar opposites of successful outcome or failure. In this sense, isolation constitutes the failure of intimacy. But, in another sense, the negative outcome has its own desirable features: given the state of the world, a person with no ability or will to protect himself would soon be overwhelmed. The outcome of a given stage is thus never either one or the other alternative because such "pure forms" cannot exist and would be maladaptive if they did.[37]

The next phase of adulthood (Stage VII) confronts the issue of Generativity versus Stagnation. Continuing with the heterosexual paradigm, Erikson sees the central task here as the establishment, "by way of genitality and genes," of the next generation through the production and care of offspring. This same purpose may also be achieved by some who forgo parenthood and express their generativity through other altruistic and creative acts. Likewise the mere fact of biological parenthood or the desire for children does not in itself amount to true generativity. The failure to advance to this stage results in a stagnation that may take the form of obsessive pseudo-intimacy or a narcissistic self-indulgence whereby the person treats himself as if he were his "own one and only child."

The final phase of adult life must resolve the task of Integrity versus Despair and Disgust. Integrity is the "fruit of the seven stages" and the outcome of having taken care of things and people, adapted to triumphs and disappointments, originated others and generated things and ideas. It is the "acceptance of one's own and only life cycle and of the people who have become significant to it as something that had to be and that, by necessity, permitted no substitution."[38] If this "one and only life cycle is not accepted as the ultimate of life," the result is despair, since there is no time for fresh starts. Such despair leads to contempt of oneself and disgust with the world.

Adulthood in a more specific sense has so far received less attention in Erikson's work than adolescence. None of its phase-specific tasks would elicit the same recognition that the concept of Identity produces. Only those precursors of adult crises that appear in connection with adolescence (and none of the derivatives of the adult crises) have been spelled out. In his earlier presentation, Erikson designated the adolescent precursors of the three phase-specific adult tasks as Sexual Identity versus Bisexual Diffusion; Leadership-Polarization versus Authority Diffusion; Ideological Polarization versus Diffusion of Ideals.[39] In later versions of his table, these terms appear as Sexual Polarization versus Bisexual Confusion; Leader-and-Followership versus Authority Confusion; Ideological Commitment versus Confusion of Values.[40]

In concluding his Jefferson Lectures, Erikson noted that we have had a century of the child and something like a century of youth, and he wondered when the century of the adult would begin.[41] This remark presages, perhaps, a shift in his own focus of interest.

In contemporary psychiatry a few other efforts dealing with normal adulthood in a developmental scheme deserve mention. Engel[42] and Lidz[43] have written thoughtful accounts bringing together insights from medicine, psychoanalysis, and the social sciences, but they are long on childhood and short on adulthood.[44] Grinker has studied normal young males whom he calls "homoclites."[45] Though the psychiatric literature on adulthood remains sparse, there is some evidence that increased attention is being directed to this phase of life: one encounters an occasional report of new research,[46] and middle age is now discussed in considerable detail as a distinct topic in standard texts of psychiatry.[47] There is also a substantial literature on the psychiatric aspects of old age.[48]

Since psychiatry draws heavily on research in the behavioral sciences, a full account of the psychiatric perspective on adulthood would also have to take account of this literature, which is a task we cannot take on here. By way of illustration, we might mention the monumental volumes of G. Stanley Hall on adolescence[49] and old age[50] which were published at the turn of the century. Currently, the work of Neugarten is particularly noteworthy,[51] and there are other contributors.[52]

Toward a Definition of Adulthood

Prerequisite to a clearer delineation of adulthood as a phase of life is a better understanding of what constitutes a "phase of life" in the first place. The presence of such stages can neither be taken for granted nor dismissed out of hand by the argument that "life is too complex to be pidgeonholed." Other things have been profitably classified that are not simple either; besides, "complexity" is as much a function of the level of analysis as it is inherent in the subject of study itself.

Taxonomy is the "law of arrangement" whereby, on the basis of certain characteristics, a group of objects, ideas, or phenomena is placed in a pattern for a particular purpose. Since there are many ways of classifying something, a single item can be part of any number of classifications: books, for instance, can be sorted out not only by author and subject, but also by size, shape, color, or weight. All such arrangements are artificial, but any one can be legitimate for some specific purpose. Still, they are not all equally relevant so far as the fundamental purpose of the objects being described is concerned.

In its attempts to look for order in the world, science assumes that, in addition to artificial categorizing of varying usefulness, there are also natural orders which, when elucidated, constitute natural laws. When Dmitri Mendeleyev (1834-1907) discovered that chemical elements show a periodic recurrence of properties when arranged in the order of increasing atomic weight, he laid one of the cornerstones of modern chemistry. This Periodic Table permitted him to detect errors in previously accepted atomic weights of elements based on their position, and the "gaps" that existed in the series permitted him correctly to predict the existence and properties of the elements gallium, scandium, and germanium fifteen years before their actual discovery. Similarly, after the discovery of helium and argon, the periodic law led to the prediction of the existence of neon, krypton, xenon, and radon. Classifications are thus not only convenient summaries; they can also be powerful research tools. Their "empty boxes" are part of their function and are not merely a reflection of incompleteness.

For a classification to be useful, it need not necessarily elucidate a fundamental natural law. Carl von Linne (1701-1778), for instance, relied on the number and arrangement of stamens and pistils in a flower for his placement of plants in various categories. Though an artificial system, it has proven enormously useful. But unlike his systematization of the animal and plant kingdoms, Linne's attempts at classifying minerals and diseases (he was trained as a physician) have not proved particularly useful.

The task of defining adulthood and its stages is basically a taxonomical venture. But it needs to be clarified if one is to "discover" divisions of the life cycle in the manner of "natural laws." Does one pick and choose certain aspects of adult life to fit into a schematic pattern or "invent" a pattern, as it were, for a purpose? The former presupposes the existence of life stages and subdivisions in an almost immutable sense. The latter model is far more modest and consistent with the notion that adulthood and its phases may be perceived differently at different times and places, depending on the aspects of adult biology and behavior that are chosen as the bases for assignment.

Since we are unlikely to find a single basic dimension, comparable to the atomic weight of elements, for defining life phases, the stages to be constructed must have various delineating limits. The nodal points must constitute significant landmarks that are appropriately spaced. If the rungs of the ladder are too far apart, the connectivity is lost and the system is not sufficiently differentiated. Likewise, if there is a profusion of stages, the scheme will be too fragmented. There are lessons to be learned in this regard from biology. For instance, one taxonomic pitfall is the fallacy of describing variant individuals as separate species by failing to account for intraspecies variability. There is likewise a danger in discovering "pseudostages" of the life cycle that are merely variants. Finally, for classification schemes to be useful, they must allow for continued correction or expansion, while leaving the essential character of the system intact. (For instance, to date, 330,000 plant and 1,000,000 animal species have already been

named, 15,000 to 20,000 new species are discovered each year, and the Linnaean system still continues to assimilate them. Although the number of life stages is far fewer,
the principle is the same.)

Any comprehensive definition of adulthood will have to be based on an understanding of our biological substrate and our psychosocial characteristics and be reflective of the mind and the spirit that lend meaning to life. Given the complexities of
human nature and the pluralistic and rapidly changing nature of the world, to agree on
such definitions is a difficult task. We are surely not going to arrive at a definition to
end all definitions for all time. But we hope that approximations can be found that will
be widely accepted, at least temporarily, within certain cultural confines and that will
in turn perhaps reveal some universals.

Medicine has important bearings on several aspects of this problem. First, it contributes the indispensable dimension of normative biological development into and during adulthood. Second, it focuses on illness and debility which come progressively to
preoccupy adult life. Third, it significantly alters the life span itself.

Biological maturity in the sense of the completion of growth and reproductive
capacity is essential to any definition of adulthood. Yet this dimension may seem to be
as much a source of difficulty as it is of help. At the ages when these biological gains are
achieved, most persons in contemporary Western society are still hopelessly dependent,
their identities nebulous, and their stations in life undetermined. Furthermore, like all
biological phenomena, these changes follow a variable timetable which simply does not
lend itself to the fixed and arbitrary schedules that society uses to certify people as
adults. The result is the well known disparity between the biological and social imper-
atives of adulthood. To bridge this gap there is little point in espousing a return to a
"natural" world where biological functions are allowed to be what they may. We may
be primates, but we have also come down from the trees, and it would be difficult for us
to climb back up again.

Yet it is also naive to expect that we can keep biological adults "on ice" until the
social structure allows their full-fledged integration into the adult world and legitimiza-
tion of the expression of their biological maturity. One solution to this dilemma may be
a more differentiated response from society regarding which or what aspect of maturing functions are to be kept in check and which ones allowed reasonable expression.

A case in point is adolescent sexuality. In past times, because association between
sex and reproduction was unpredictable, social inhibitions had to be imposed on sexual
behavior, since no society could trifle with the welfare of its young and hope to survive
for very long. Sex and reproduction are now reliably and safely separable; however,
societal response remains ambivalent. Increasing numbers of young people are taking
the matter in their own hands, but they frequently mismanage it and the relativistic
morality which guides them in principle sometimes comes within whispering distance
of amorality in practice.

There is no ready solution to this dilemma, but greater awareness of biological
variation may temper the rigidity with which social schedules are set up in defining
adulthood. It is a curious fact that we claim to put so much stock in the natural world,
yet we either remain ignorant of it or disregard its true nature. From that bulwark of

Catholic theology, Thomas Aquinas, to countless lesser figures, "rules of nature" and Natural Law have been invoked as guides to human behavior, yet there is often no discernible association between what we think exists and what actually does exist in nature, in terms both of our biological selves and of the living world at large.

The logistical problems involved in substituting a developmental for a chronological timetable in defining adulthood are enormous. It would certainly disrupt the pace of bureaucratic gymnastics and cause much administrative grief. Yet the current alternatives seem equally cumbersome: we assume young people to be what is convenient to adults for them to be and we then get upset when they are not. Neither does the answer lie in self-determination, however: for every youth truly more mature than his years, there are ten who are queue-jumping.

Serious questions can be raised as to whether our socially determined tempo of adult life is sufficiently linked to the concurrent progress of physiological processes. Our work schedules do allow us times to eat and rest, but, beyond such obvious accommodation, there is probably a great deal more that could be done to bring social schedules into step with biological rhythms. We are all aware of the alternation of sleep and wakefulness, but few realize that as many as a hundred other functions also follow daily cycles. These include the rates at which cells divide and metabolic processes fluctuate. For instance, body temperature drops at night, urinary output increases during the day, and other functions change rhythmically. As a result, the body's response to drugs, for example, is not uniform but depends, at least in some cases, on the time of administration (e.g., diabetics are far more sensitive to insulin at night). Likewise, experimental evidence shows that the time of exposure to a noxious agent may in part determine whether or not the organism will succumb to it. Such rhythmicity is characteristic of all living systems, including unicellular organisms. As Colin Pittendrigh has put it, "Gertrude Stein to the contrary notwithstanding, a rose is not necessarily and unqualifiedly a rose; that is to say, it is a very different biochemical system at noon and at midnight."[53]

The biological clocks ticking away in each of us are not restricted to the silent regulation of psychological processes. Such rhythms are also involved in behavioral regulation varying from fluctuations in the speed of problem-solving to shifts in mood. Much of the research in this field has involved circadian rhythms,[54] but biological rhythms, such as the monthly menstrual cycle, can also have shorter or longer "periods."[55] The longer the period of the rhythm, the harder it is to detect and study; the considerable variation of the same rhythm in different people further complicates its study. Such rhythms are not restricted to normal functions, but are also manifested in various medical and psychiatric conditions such as manic-depressive psychosis.

The study of metabolic rhythms and biological clocks is a fascinating field still in its infancy, but one with great potential to enhance our understanding of the biology of behavior—a subject with wide social ramifications.[56] One possible though partial explanation for the current plague of psychosomatic ailments and stressful lives is that the culturally set pace of life in industrialized societies is frequently out of phase with its basic metabolic rhythms. The entire evolution of man took place while he was a hunter. The agricultural way of life accounts for less than one per cent of human history, and no biological changes seem to have occurred during that time.[57] Thus, our bodies and the rhythms by which they oscillate are more or less the same as those of our remotest ancestors. But our societies and cultural determinants of behavior are quite obviously far from the same: hence the dysrhythmia.

Even prehistoric man must have been aware of the effects that significant disruptions had in his daily round of life: soldiers of all time have had to experience sleepless nights and forced marches. But these have been sporadic events, not ways of life. Today, such disruptions seem to have become routine. A case in point is long-distance east-west jet travel. The resultant symptoms of "jet lag" are well known; they constitute a physiological burden that has been widely imposed on people only during the past decade or two, but that we seem already to have accepted as if it were a preordained part of human destiny. The point is not to denigrate the tremendous advantages of jet travel but to indicate the uncritical willingness with which we expose our bodies to stresses whose long-term effects have yet to become fully manifest. When one moves from earthbound flights to travel in deep space, the dislocations entailed are difficult even to envisage.

All this perhaps has little bearing on adulthood except that adults set up the social schedules to which they then expose the rest of the populace as well, and that it is those adults in the most "adult" roles of leadership who are the most subjected to the effects of biological dysrhythmia. In fact, a willingness and seeming ability to defy the innate rhythms of the body for social or personal ends has become one of the hallmarks of adulthood in the Western world.

For medicine to contribute more significantly to this problem, considerable sifting and sorting of existing information as well as the acquisition of further data will be necessary. The stresses that result from the incongruous social demands on the body are serious, but we do not have to pay attention to them if we are willing to write off the toll in distress and casualties as part of the cost of modern life or of being adult.

Both personally and professionally we often harbor a rather curious attitude toward illness. Even though we know perfectly well that a great deal of life, especially adult life, will be afflicted by it, when we fall ill, we nevertheless have a tendency to feel slighted and aggrieved, or to be nagged by thoughts of failure and a sense of guilt. The "normal" state of being is assumed to be one of robust health, and death is a calamity whenever it comes.[58] If medicine could convey the notion that illness and death are part of life rather than aberrations imposed upon it, the conceptual and practical gains in understanding the life cycle would be considerable.

The impact of health measures on prolonging life hardly needs to be belabored. People in the West now have a life expectancy of 70 years and, by the end of the century, this figure will probably have reached 80 years. In contrast, life expectancy in classical Greece was 18 and in Rome 22 years. Much of this disparity is a reflection of the decline in infant mortality rates, but it is also true that more people are living longer today than ever before.

The impact of such changes on our concept of the life cycle is enormous. Napoleon was an army captain at 16, emperor at 32. Mozart died at the age of 35 years and 10 months.[59] Were Napoleon and Mozart "young adults" as we now understand the term when in their early thirties? These and countless other examples suggest that there is nothing fixed or immutable about life phases. They simply cannot be dealt with out of historical and cultural contexts. This is also why a purely biological definition of adulthood would be futile, quite aside from the fact that biology itself is subject to change.

Looking further into the future, there may even come a time when it will be possible to tamper with the biological clocks that regulate the very processes of growth and aging (or "ripening and rotting," as Hayflick puts it).[60] If and when that time comes, decisions may have to be made about what part of the life cycle to prolong. Within a life span of, say, one hundred years, would we want to foreshorten childhood or prolong it? If adulthood is to be stretched out, can it occur during our "prime" or will it simply prolong the period of decrepitude? And in relation to what function will "prime time" be determined? As we live longer, will we accomplish more and have fuller lives? Or will we simply stretch out what we do to fill up the time allotted according to some Parkinsonian principle?

Such problems and prospects have a way of suddenly catching up with us while we are preoccupied with one or another seemingly important matter. There are also plenty of life-cycle-related problems that are already urgent. Despite the rapid expansion of, and marked changes in, the older population, our notions of old age as a phase of life have undergone little revision. We go on marveling at the number of active, alert, "youthful" people in their seventies without recognizing that the same chronological age span now perhaps represents a different state than it did in the past (or may in the future). And if we keep piling "old people" upon "old people" as dependents on society, our welfare and supporting institutions will soon be pushed further toward the breaking point. But if we can reappraise who these people are, what their needs and capabilities are, and how this life phase should now be perceived, then matters can be quite different.

To deal with such issues, we need to confront them, perhaps, not so much with a grim determination to "solve" life's problems, but first with an attempt to understand them better. As Dostoevsky declared in his diary, his purpose as a writer was to "find the man in man." It is equally our task to try to find the adult in the adult in this day and age.

REFERENCES

[1]Sir Thomas Browne, *Religio Medici, Letter to a Friend, Christian Morals, Urn-Burial, and Other Papers*, Part III, Sect. 8 of *Christian Morals* (Boston, 1878).

[2]William Osler (1849-1919), the great clinician of our time, was so ardent an admirer of Sir Thomas Browne that a copy of the *Religio Medici* was placed in his coffin. Cited by J. H. Talbot, *A Biographical History of Medicine* (New York, 1970).

[3]Thomas Lathrop Stedman, *Medical Dictionary* (Baltimore, 1961).

[4]Blakiston's *New Gould Medical Dictionary* (Philadelphia, 1949).

[5]*Cumulated Index Medicus* (Chicago, 1974).

[6]Neither of these two fields yet constitutes a formal specialty in the United States as reflected by the existence of Specialty Boards. The credentials given by these Boards establish a physician as a specialist,

but a certification for the practice of medicine is at the discretion of state licensing bodies. In principle, at least, any licensed physician is allowed to treat any and all illnesses.

[7]H. F. Garrison, "History of Pediatrics," *Abt-Garrison History of Pediatrics* (Philadelphia, 1965), p. 43.

[8]L. Clendening, *Source Book of Medical History* (New York, 1942), p. 261.

[9]The growth of modern pediatrics during the nineteenth century has been described by Abraham Jacobi (1830-1919), who himself contributed greatly to its development and is regarded as the "Father of American Pediatrics." Jacobi's collected works are in *Collectanea Jacobi*, W. J. Robinson, ed. (8 volumes; 1909). For Jacobi's biography, see Talbot, *op. cit.*, pp. 1119-21.

[10]W. A. Marshall and J. M. Tanner, "Puberty," *Scientific Foundations of Paediatrics*, J. A. Davis and J. Dobbing, eds. (London, 1974), p. 124.

[11]J. M. Tanner, "Sequence, Tempo, and Individual Variation in the Growth and Development of Boys and Girls Aged Twelve to Sixteen," *Daedalus* (Fall, 1971), pp. 907-30.

[12]For further details, see the references to Tanner. Also, F. P. Heald and W. Hung, eds., *Adolescent Endocrinology* (New York, 1970); B. T. Donovan and J. J. Van den Werff Ten Bosch, *Physiology of Puberty* (Baltimore, 1965); A. W. Root, "Endocrinology of Puberty," *The Journal of Pediatrics*, 83 (1973), pp. 1-19.

[13]D. Sinclair, *Human Growth After Birth* (London, 1973), p. 26.

[14]W. A. Marshall and J. M. Tanner, "Variations in the Pattern of Pubertal Changes in Girls," *Archives of Disease in Childhood*, 44 (1969), p. 291.

[15]W. A. Marshall and J. M. Tanner, "Variations in the Pattern of Pubertal Changes in Boys," *ibid.*, 45 (1970), p. 13.

[16]J. M. Tanner, "Physical Growth," *Carmichael's Manual of Child Psychology*, P. Mussen, ed. (3rd ed., New York, 1970), I, p. 94.

[17]Sinclair, *op. cit.*, p. 26.

[18]H. E. Jones, *Motor Performance and Growth. A Developmental Study of Static Dynamometric Strength* (Berkeley, 1949).

[19]See F. A. Beach,"Human Sexuality and Evolution," *Reproductive Behavior*, W. Montagna and W. A. Sadler, eds. (New York, 1974).

[20]Despite the chronological variability in onset, the progressive changes in breast, genital, and pubic-hair growth are consistent enough to be grouped into stages that act as developmental landmarks. For a discussion of these stages, see J. M. Tanner, *Growth at Adolescence* (2nd ed., Oxford, 1962).

[21]In the last category are males whose prostate gland has been removed (but without damaging the relevant nerves in the region). One could also include practitioners of the Indian technique of "Karezza" or "coitus reservatus" (not to be confused with "coitus interruptus"), although strictly speaking this may involve retrograde ejaculation into the urinary bladder rather than orgasm without ejaculation. This practice was commonly used as a means of birth control in the nineteenth-century communal Oneida colony in upstate New York. See N. Bishop, "The Great Oneida Love-in," *American Heritage*, 20 (1969), pp. 14-17, 86-92.

[22]For a cross-cultural review of childhood sexual behavior, see C. S. Ford and F. A. Beach, *Patterns of Sexual Behavior* (New York, 1951), and the relevant sections in A. C. Kinsey et al., *Sexual Behavior in the Human Male* and *Sexual Behavior in the Human Female* (Philadelphia, 1948 and 1953).

[23]J. Money and A. A. Ehrhardt, *Man and Woman, Boy and Girl* (Baltimore, 1972).

[24]For an extensive consideration of the mechanism of the onset of puberty, see M. M. Grumbach, G. D. Grave, F. E. Mayer, *The Control of the Onset of Puberty* (New York, 1974).

[25]One is reminded of the Roman general who claimed that his young son was the most influential person in the world because Rome controlled the world, the Emperor controlled Rome, the general himself controlled the Emperor, the general's wife controlled him and was in turn controlled by their little boy!

[26]J. M. Tanner, "Growth and Development of the Brain," *Carmichael's Manuel, op. cit.*

[27]For instance, randomly chosen and unrelated girls reach menarche at an average of 19 months apart. This difference is 13 months in sisters who are not twins, 10 months between nonidentical twins, and only 2.8 months between identical twins living together under average West European economic conditions.

[28]For a list of ages at the onset of menarche in various countries, see Table 7 compiled by Marshall and Tanner in Dobbing, *op. cit.*, p. 144.

[29]This phenomenon is ascribed in part to environmental factors, such as improved nutrition, but other factors may also be operative. Even increased exposure to light due to the widespread use of artificial lighting has been suggested as a cause (based on experimental work with animals), although the fact that blind girls reach menarche earlier than others would seem to contradict this. See N. A. Jafarey, "Effect of Artificial Lighting on the Age of Menarche," *Lancet*, 1 (1971), p. 707.

[30]F. Falkner, "Physical Growth," *Pediatrics*, H. L. Barnett and A. H. Einhorn, eds. (15th ed., New York, 1972), p. 239.

[31]"Menopause" refers to the permanent cessation of menstruation due to aging. "Climacteric" is a broader term that includes the various related changes experienced at this point. Strictly speaking, the latter term, but not the former, is applicable to males, although in current usage the two terms have tended to become synonymous.

[32]Pioneered by Philippe Pinel (1745-1826) in France, William Tuke (1732-1822) in England.

[33]The foundations of psychiatric nosology were laid down by Emil Kraepelin (1856-1926); Eugene Bleuler's (1851-1939) redefinition of schizophrenia was another major landmark.

[34]C. G. Jung, "The Stages of Life," in *The Collected Works of C. G. Jung*, Vol. 8 (New York, 1960).
[35]*Ibid.*

[36]The first detailed presentation of Erikson's concept of the life cycle is in "Identity and the Life Cycle," *Psychological Issues*, 1 (1959), pp. 50-100. Adulthood is dealt with in pages 95-99. See also *Identity, Youth and Crisis* (1968), and *Childhood and Society* (2nd ed., New York, 1963).

[37]This argument also holds well for Mistrust which is the opposite of Basic Trust, the phase-specific task of Stage I. But it is more difficult to see much virtue in the negative outcomes of some of the other stages such as Inferiority (II), Identity Confusion (V), Stagnation (VII), and Despair (VIII).

[38]Erikson, "Identity and the Life Cycle," *op. cit.*, p. 98.
[39]*Ibid.*, p. 120.
[40]Erikson, *Identity, Youth and Crisis, op. cit.*, p. 94.
[41]Erik Erikson, *Dimensions of a New Identity* (New York, 1974).
[42]G. Engel, *Psychological Development in Health and Disease* (Philadelphia, 1962).
[43]Theodore Lidz, *The Person* (New York, 1968).
[44]See Bernice L. Neugarten's review of T. Lidz's book in *Contemporary Psychology*, 14 (1969), pp. 409-11. See also John Romano in the *Journal of the American Medical Association*, 207 (1969), p. 244.
[45]R. R. Grinker, Sr., R. R. Grinker, Jr., and J. A. Timberlake, "A Study of the 'Mentally Healthy' Young Males (Homoclites)," *Archives of General Psychiatry*, 6 (1962), pp. 27-74.
[46]R. L. Gould, "The Phases of Adult Life: A Study in Developmental Psychology," *The American Journal of Psychiatry*, 129 (1972), pp. 33-J31. A project still in progress at the Psychophysiology Laboratory of the Institute of Living Hospital, Hartford, Conn., under the direction of C. F. Stroebel and B. Glueck, Jr., is also attempting to obtain daily records of life events, moods, and bodily changes from both patients and normal subjects.
[47]R. N. Butler, "Psychiatry and Psychology of the Middle-Aged," in A. M. Freedman, H. I. Kaplan, and B. J. Sadock, eds., *Comprehensive Textbook of Psychiatry*, 2 (2nd ed., Baltimore, 1975), pp. 2390-2404; B. L. Neugarten and N. Datan, "The Middle Years," in S. Arieti, ed., *American Handbook of Psychiatry*, Vol. 1 (2nd ed., New York, 1974).
[48]For an overview, see J. Weinberg, "Geriatric Psychiatry," in A. M. Freedman *et al., op. cit*, 2405-20.
[49]G. Stanley Hall, *Adolescence* (New York and London, 1904).
[50]*Idem, Old Age* (New York, 1922).
[51]B. L. Neugarten, *Personality in Middle and Later Life* (New York, 1964); "Personality and Aging," in J. E. Birren and K. Warner Schaic, eds., *Handbook of the Psychology of Aging* (in press).
[52]See, for instance, C. Buhler, "The Course of Human Life as a Psychological Problem," *Human Development*, 2 (1968), pp. 184-200; D. J. Levinson *et al.*, "The Psychosocial Development of Men in Early Adulthood and the Mid-Life Transition," in D. F. Ricks *et al.*, eds., *Life History Research in Psy-*

chopathology, Vol. 3 (Minneapolis, 1974); much of this research is discussed by D. C. Kimmel in *Adult-hood and Aging* (New York, 1974).

[53]Quoted by R. R. Ward in *The Living Clocks* (New York, 1971), p. 278.

[54]The term "circadian" is derived from the Latin for "about" (*circa*) and "day" (*diem*). It is preferred to "daily" because these oscillations do not precisely coincide with the earth's daily rotation. "Diurnal" is also confusing since it is sometimes used in contradistinction to "nocturnal" and at other times in the sense of "daily." Pittendrigh in R. R. Ward, *op. cit.*, p. 276.

[55]For a review of psychological changes related to the menstrual cycle, see J. F. O'Connor, E. M. Shelley, and L. C. Stern, "Behavioral Rhythms Related to the Menstrual Cycle," *Biorhythms and Human Reproduction*, M. Perin *et al*, eds. (New York, 1974), pp. 309-24.

[56]For surveys in this field written for the general reader, see G. G. Luce, *Body Time* (New York, 1971); R. R. Ward, *op. cit*. The former has extensive bibliographical references.

[57]Sherwood L. Washburn and C. S. Lancaster, "The Evolution of Hunting," *Perspectives on Human Evolution*, S. L. Washburn and P. C. Jay, eds., Vol. 1, (New York, 1968), pp. 213-29.

[58]For reflections on this issue, see L. Thomas, "Biological Aspects of Death," *The Pharos of Alpha Omega Alpha*, 37 (1974), pp. 83-89.

[59]R. Tomlinson, *Demographic Problems: Controversy Over Population Control* (Belmont, California, 1967).

[60]L. Hayflick, "Why Grow Old?," *The Stanford Magazine*, 3 (1975), pp. 36-43.

ROBERT N. BELLAH

To Kill and Survive or To Die and Become:
The Active Life and the Contemplative Life as Ways of Being Adult

> Every third thought shall be my grave.
> —Prospero in *The Tempest*

THE RHYTHM OF ACTIVITY AND REST is one of the basic characteristics of all life, certainly of human life. The terrestrial rhythm of day and night echoed in the biological rhythm of waking and sleeping has been enormously elaborated in the psychological, social, and cultural life of man. In many cultures the wisdom of the night in the form of dreams provides a refreshing counterpoint to the trials of the day. The contrasts of action and passivity, work and enjoyment, initiative and receptivity have been woven into patterns of personal and social organization. A spatial correlate of this basically temporal rhythm is to be found in the common distinction of inner and outer, which may be elaborated in terms of private and public, the inner life versus life in the world. The focus of this paper is on the highest cultural expression of this fundamental rhythm: the contrast between sacred and profane, between the religious and the secular.

It is important to stress from the beginning that we are not dealing with irreconcilable opposites, with watertight, exclusive categories. The contrasts I have in mind are the two ends of a polarity, each implying the other. That is why the temporal metaphor of rhythm is perhaps to be preferred to a spatial image, though the rhythm of sacred and profane time is certainly echoed in the rhythm, if I may so speak, of sacred and profane space. In any case one of the most basic patterns of life in primitive societies is the annual alternation of work and ritual that Durkheim described with classical precision in *The Elementary Forms of the Religious Life* and that Victor Turner has recently elucidated in his admirable book *The Ritual Process*. Not infrequently, the annual cycle among primitive peoples reflects still another terrestrial and biological cycle—that between summer and winter, growth and quiescence. The great rituals are often performed during periods when the earth is relatively unfruitful and does not yield to human labor. That the rituals themselves are often thought to contribute to earthly fruitfulness is another reminder that we are dealing with dialectical poles, not logical opposites.

But the series of contrasts going from activity and rest to profane and sacred would not be so germane to our subject of adulthood if they remained merely rhythmic alternations of all human life. They have, however, been taken as reference points for the elaboration of roles in almost all societies. Legitimately or not, they have been used to help define sex roles, stages of the life cycle, and the differentiated pattern of adult occupations. In most human cultures, though this is being questioned today, the "inner" and the "receptive" have been identified with the feminine and the "outer" and the "active" with the masculine. It is interesting that it is much rarer, though to some degree characteristic of our own society, to identify the feminine with the religious, or at least to identify religion with women. But some psychoanalytically oriented observers believe that the male claim to religious preeminence, so common in most primitive and advanced cultures, is a claim to "feminine" capacities at a higher level. Jealous of female superiority in the realm of biological creativity, the argument runs, the men lay claim to a "higher" spiritual creativity. It is beyond the limits of this essay to pursue this question, but we may note that certainly the saint has often been in some sense less "masculine" than the warrior, even when the saint has been the highest ideal of male personality.

It is with the double problem of the use of the religious/secular contrast for the differentiation of adult roles and for categorizing stages of the life cycle that this essay will be concerned. Erik Erikson has contributed significantly to our understanding of both of these uses. His most helpful statement of the role-differentiation problem is to be found in his recent book on Jefferson, *Dimensions of a New Identity:*

> . . . human communities, whether they consist of a tribe set in a segment of nature, or of a national empire spanning the territory and the loyalties of a variety of peoples, must attempt to reinforce that sense of identity which promises a meaning for the cycle of life within a world view more real than the certainty of death. Paradoxically speaking, however, to share such a transient sense of being indestructible, all participants must accept a ritual code of mortality and immortality which . . . includes the privilege and the duty, if need be, to die a heroic, or at any rate a shared death, while also being willing and eager to kill or help kill those on "the other side" who share (and live and kill and die for) another world view. The motto of this immortality, whether in combat or competition, can be said to be "kill and survive."
>
> The men who inspire and accomplish such a world view we call great and we bestow a form of immortality on them: While they must die, as we must, their image, cast in metal, seems to survive indestructibly in the monuments of our town squares or in the very rock of Mount Rushmore.
>
> But there is the other, the transcendent, effort at insuring salvation through a conscious acceptance of finiteness. It emphasizes nothingness instead of somebodyness. It is "not of this world," and instead of a competition for the world's goods (including those securing the earthly identity) it seeks human brotherhood in self-denial. It courts death or, at any rate, self-denial as a step toward a more real and everlasting life. It prefers self-sacrifice to killing. And it visualizes the men and women who can make this aspect of existence convincing, not as great and immortal, but as saintly and as partaking of an eternal life. This way of identity is personified by the great religious leaders who in their own words represent the naked grandeur of the I that transcends all earthly identity in the name of Him who *is* I Am. The motto of this world view could be said to be "die and become."[1]

That Erikson has here given expression so eloquently to the classic Western contrast between the *vita activa* and the *vita contemplativa* has provided both the theme and the title of this essay. I should point out at once that the contrast that seems so absolute in the above quotation (and often seems so absolute in the Western understanding of the active and contemplative lives) is not meant as absolute by Erikson, for in context he means to say that Jefferson participated in *both* ideals, however much we would have to place him primarily as an exemplar (and one of the greatest) of the first one.

But in Erikson's work we should not be surprised to find that what at first seems to be a contrast of adult role types (even if a contrast only of emphasis) also turns out to be related to life-cycle stages. This becomes quite clear in *Gandhi's Truth* where there is a discussion of the Hindu theory of the life cycle with its clear distinction between the early adult householder stage (*Grhastha*) concerned with procreativity but also with "family relations, . . . communal power, . . . and productivity,"[2] and the final two stages of life that are defined as "*Vanaprastha*, or the inner separation from all ties of selfhood, body-boundness, and communality and their replacement by a striving which will eventually lead to *Moksha*: renunciation, disappearance."[3] But in the Hindu pattern there was also a way of bypassing the cycle of stages and choosing early a life of renunciation, which could still imitate the householder stage as Erikson suggests:

> We have seen how deeply Gandhi at times minded having to become a householder, for without his becoming committed to a normal course of life by child marriage, he might well have been a monastic saint instead of what he became: politician and reformer with an honorary sainthood. For the true saints are those who transfer the state of householdership to the house of God, becoming father and mother, brother and sister, son and daughter, to all creation rather than to their own issue.[4]

Erikson avoids any simple equation of his life-cycle pattern with that of the Hindus. He would perhaps resist relating it to the classical distinction between active and contemplative lives. Yet I think there is a clear relation between his last two stages and the active and contemplative lives. This comes out best, perhaps, in the discussion of the virtues (what a service Erikson has rendered us in helping to make this ancient word available to us once again) connected with the stages.[5] For Erikson finds that the virtue associated with the stage of generativity, characteristic of the middle years of adulthood, is *care*, and care defined as he defines it ("the widening concern for what has been generated by love, necessity or accident . . .")[6] is not only etymologically related to the characteristic feature of the active life as defined by Augustine: *caritas* (New Testament: *agape*) or charity. And Erikson associates the virtue of *wisdom* with the final human stage of integrity, characteristic of old age. The contemplative life has most frequently been characterized by the same word, which translates *sapientia* or *sophia*. Nor could Erikson's definition, "detached concern with life itself, in the face of death itself,"[7] be much improved on, especially if we add that concern for eternity that Erikson ascribed to the saint in the Jefferson book.

It would be interesting to pursue in detail the many relationships between Erikson's scheme and the traditional Christian one. The eight virtues that he attributes to the eight stages of the life cycle are surprisingly similar, though not identical, to the moral and theological virtues of traditional Christianity. It is particularly interesting that all three theological virtues (faith, hope, and charity) are there. And these relations in turn would reveal that Erikson brings a religious dimension into his life cycle far earlier than the final stage. At least as important would be the first stage of trust, characterized by the virtue of hope, and the adolescent stage of identity, characterized by the virtue of fidelity. Indeed, it is the essence of Erikson's scheme that only if basic trust has been established early and a sense of faithfulness established in adolescence will it be possible to hope for wisdom in old age. But with this suggestive stimulus from Erikson I would like to turn now to some historical reflections on the vicissitudes of action and contemplation as adult ideals in the West, with a few side glances at East Asia for comparative purposes.

While the contrast between sacred and profane can be found in all cultures the idea of the *vita activa* and the *vita contemplativa* is historically specific. It originates first in the text of Plato (though perhaps in the life of Socrates).[8] Since it is grounded in a strikingly non-primitive conception of religion it differs markedly from comparable contrasts among primitive and archaic peoples and in this respect it is paralleled by developments in Israel, India, and China.[9] But in this essay I will be mainly concerned with the particularities of the Western development, and only in connection with the Chinese comparison will a few more general considerations emerge.

What is new in the Platonic text is the claim for a radical superiority of contemplation (*theoria*) or philosophy (love of wisdom) over other modes of life. The actual phrase "contemplative life" (*bios theoretikos*) is found first in Aristotle[10] where it is contrasted with the political life (*bios politikos*) and the life of pleasure. Plato contrasts love of wisdom with love of victory and love of gain.[11] Only later would the political, the military, the economic, and the pleasure-seeking be aggregated as the active life (*bios praktikos*) in contrast to the contemplative.

What is really striking in the Platonic corpus is not so much the terminology, although that, even if requiring later systematization, remains decisive for the later tradition, as the personification of the contrast. The new claim is embodied in a person, Socrates, and that which is being rejected as the highest ideal is also embodied, though in a poetic person, Achilles.

Achilles was the greatest hero of Homer, and the spirit of Homer, the "educator" of the Greeks, was still vibrant in the Athens of Pericles in Socrates' youth. Perhaps no one has linked Homer and Periclean Athens more vividly than Hannah Arendt and thus disclosed to us what Socrates rejected when he offered himself in Achilles' stead:

> The *polis*, as it grew out of and remained rooted in the Greek pre-*polis* experience and estimate of what makes it worthwhile for men to live together (*syzēn*), namely, the "sharing of words and deeds," had a twofold function. First, it was intended to enable men to do permanently, albeit under certain restrictions, what otherwise had been possible only as an extraordinary and infrequent enterprise for which they had to leave their households. The *polis* was supposed to multiply the occasions to win "immortal fame," that is, to multiply the chances for everybody to distinguish himself, to show in deed and word who he was in his unique distinctness. . . . The second function of the *polis*, again closely connected with the hazards of action as experienced before its coming into being,

was to offer a remedy for the futility of action and speech; for the chances that a deed deserving fame would not be forgotten, that it actually would become "immortal," were not very good. Homer was a shining example of the poet's political function, and therefore the "educator of all Hellas"; the very fact that so great an enterprise as the Trojan War could have been forgotten without a poet to immortalize it several hundred years later offered only too good an example of what could happen to human greatness if it had nothing but poets to rely on for its permanence . . . .

The *polis*—if we trust the famous words of Pericles in the Funeral Oration—gives a guaranty that those who forced every sea and land to become the scene of their daring will not remain without witness and will neither need Homer nor anyone else who knows how to turn words to praise them; without assistance from others, those who acted will be able to establish together the everlasting remembrance of their good and bad deeds, to inspire admiration in the present and in future ages . . . .[12]

Not historically, of course, but speaking metaphorically and theoretically, it is as though the men who returned from the Trojan War had wished to make permanent the space of action which had arisen from their deeds and sufferings, to prevent its perishing with their dispersal and return to their isolated homesteads . . . .[13]

What is outstandingly clear in Pericles' formulations—and, incidentally no less transparent in Homer's poems—is that the innermost meaning of the acted deed and the spoken word is independent of victory and defeat and must remain untouched by any eventual outcome, by their consequences for better or worse. . . . Thucydides, or Pericles, knew full well that he had broken with the normal standards of everyday behavior when he found the glory of Athens in having left behind "everywhere everlasting remembrance [*mnēmeia aidia*] of their good and evil deeds."[14]

Surely Socrates' criticism of Achilles,[15] as well as his criticism of Pericles,[16] can be understood in this context. The amoral pursuit of shining glory and immortal fame, the narcissistic obsession with "everlasting remembrance," could not be the basis of a good life or a good *polis*.

In contrast to Achilles (and Pericles) is Socrates, the contemplative man, forbidden by his *daimonion* to engage in politics,[17] who was described by Alcibiades as on one occasion standing from sunrise to sunrise rapt in thought.[18] But, though his life differed so markedly from the Homeric heroes, Socrates, too, was a hero. Indeed Alcibiades prefaces his account of the incident with the ironic words: "And now I must tell you about another thing 'our valiant hero dared and did,' "[19] quoting a tag line from the *Odyssey*. And in the *Apology* Socrates compares himself to Achilles, calling to mind his own steadfastness in battle and asking how he could be any less steadfast in adhering to his divinely imposed duty to lead the philosophic life.[20] With the courage of Achilles he will give a most un-Homeric model of what human life can be. It is in the *Republic* that Plato most insistently substitutes Socrates for Achilles. In his commentary to Book III, Allan Bloom writes:

> Socrates brings Achilles to the foreground in order to analyze his character and ultimately to do away with him as *the* model for the young. The figure of Achilles, more than any teaching or law, compels the souls of Greeks and all men who pursue glory. He is the hero of heroes, admired and imitated by all. And this is what Socrates wishes to combat; he teaches that if Achilles is the model, men will not pursue philosophy, that

what he stands for is inimical to the founding of the best city and the practice of the best way of life. Socrates is engaging in a contest with Homer for the title of teacher of the Greeks—or of mankind. One of his principal goals is to put himself in the place of Achilles as the authentic representation of the best human type.[21]

Later, in Book VI of the *Republic*, we begin to perceive more positively the outline of the new mode of life and of what makes it new:

> And there is this further point to be considered in distinguishing the philosophical from the unphilosophical nature.
> What point?
> You must not overlook any touch of illiberality. For nothing can be more contrary than such pettiness to the quality of a soul that is ever to seek integrity and wholeness in all things human and divine.
> Most true, he said.
> Do you think that a mind habituated to thoughts of grandeur[22] and the contemplation of all time and all existence can deem this life of man a thing of great concern?
> Impossible, said he.
> Hence such a man will not suppose death to be terrible?
> Least of all.[23]

Finally, toward the end of Book VI, we learn that the object of contemplation is the Good, about which Socrates is unable to say anything directly. He speaks instead of the sun, which is to the visible world as the Good is to the intelligible world. But the Good is not merely intellectual, it is the end for which man yearns, the final object of *eros*. At the beginning of Book VII, the parable of the cave completes the teaching about the Good. But it also gives the new Platonic teaching about action. For the true contemplative man, who has left the cave to gaze on all things in the direct light of the sun, elects to return and to assist the dwellers in the cave, even unto death. Guided by the vision of the heavenly city,[24] which exists in the mode of eternity, the contemplative man can act for the welfare of the earthly city without being blinded by illusions of shining glory and immortal fame.

The new understanding of contemplation and action, though adumbrated in pre-Socratic times by Parmenides and Heraclitus, Aeschylus and Sophocles, is brought to its fruition in Plato. It is a powerful reaction against the corruption and disintegration of archaic Greek culture. The older balance between ritual and deed was already depicted as problematic in Homer, where the heroes are not balanced by priests of comparable stature. By the time of Pericles, the Sophists, Euripides, and other skeptics have riddled the Homeric theology and the city religion. The city founder and the lawgiver have been replaced by the ambitious politician, the imperialist tyrant, and the glory-seeking general, all uninhibited in their ever expanding egoism. The fruit of that unrestrained egoism was the disaster of the Peloponnesian War. But, in the midst of the shambles, in the mind of the philosopher emerges a new conception of contemplation (*theoria*) in correlation with a new conception of the divine, and from this new experience comes a new set of standards for worldly action, standards which replace "glory" with "care" as the key to the active life. On the basis of a comparable, if less poetically expressed, experience of the divine presence in the mind (*nous*) of the philosopher, Aristotle worked out those standards in the *Ethics* and the *Politics* in ways that have remained to some degree normative for the Western tradition ever since.

At no great distance in time from Plato and Aristotle, Confucius and Mencius were engaged in a comparable task in China. Appalled by the political and social conditions in the late Chou Period, in which ambitious feudal retainers overthrew their lords and embarked on policies of sheer self-aggrandizement, Confucius attempted to revive the normative order of the early Chou Period. Instead of the continuity between Achilles and Pericles, Confucius discerned a great disparity between the Duke of Chou and the princes of his own day. His attitude toward tradition is thus profoundly different from that of Socrates. Instead of rejecting and replacing the Duke of Chou, Confucius identified with him and contributed to the deepening of his meaning for subsequent Chinese culture. Yet surely this is not merely because of Confucius' "traditionalism" as against Socrates' "iconoclasm." For in the Chinese tradition the Duke of Chou did not exemplify obsessive narcissism and the quest for "shining glory." He was a modest and retiring man, forgoing the throne in favor of regency for his nephew and preaching a political doctrine based on virtue and benevolence.

For all his "traditionalism" and love of the ancient rituals, Confucius breaks with archaic religion as decisively as does Socrates. For Confucius, too, it is in the mind (*hsin*, cf. Greek *nous*) of the sage that transcendence is recognized. There is a recognition of Heaven (*ten*) as of God (*theos*) in Plato. But Confucius is as reticent to speak of the highest things[25] as Plato is.[26] Even in connection with the highest virtue (*jen*, which Tu Wei-ming translates "humanity," but Waley[27] translates "Goodness," perhaps remembering Plato's *Agathon*), Confucius is no more able than Plato to give a definition of the Good. The new experience of transcendence in the mind of the sage is related to a mode of life that is comparable to, though not identical with, the *bios theoretikos*. Perhaps the key Chinese terms are "learning" (*hsüeh*) and, in Mencius, the process known as "exhausting the mind and knowing the nature" (*chin hsin chih hsing*). Perhaps it would be well to give the whole passage from which the latter phrase comes, for it makes an interesting comparison with the passage from Book VI of the *Republic* quoted above.

> Mencius said, "It is the man who has stretched his mind to the full [*chin ch'i hsin*] who fully understands man's true nature. And understanding his true nature, he understands Heaven. To guard one's mind and to nourish one's true nature is to serve Heaven. Do not be in two minds about premature death or a ripe old age. Cultivate yourself [*hsiu shen*] and await the outcome. In this way you will attain to your allotted span [*ming*].[28]

All this is not to find "world rejection" in Confucius and Mencius. But neither is it really legitimate to find world rejection in Plato and Aristotle. All four were profound political philosophers. All four gave new definition and direction to political and practical life as well as to the life of the mind. But all were frustrated in their attempts to actualize their political teachings. All of them recognized a dimension of transcendence beyond the political even though they believed it had to be actualized in the political. To put it in Western terms, the new recognition of transcendence did not lead to an exclusive emphasis on the contemplative life but to a new conception of the balance between contemplation and action and a new understanding of the meaning of action as well as of contemplation.

Nevertheless, deepening pessimism about the "world" did lead to genuine movements of world rejection not many centuries later both in the West and in East Asia. And subsequently world rejection was the dominant mode in East and West, an experience that has indelibly colored all of our thinking about the contemplative life in relation to action. In the West, the note of world rejection was carried predominantly by Christianity; in the East, by Buddhism. It is to the impact of these great religions on the balance between contemplation and action that we must now turn.

In this brief essay we must bracket discussion of the break with archaic religion that occurred in ancient Israel.[29] Suffice it to say that there, too, a new balance between the divine and the human was worked out, a new understanding of the implication of the divine demand for political existence. As in Greece and China a powerful experience of the divine—in Israel in the specific mode of prophetic revelation—did not entail world rejection but a renewed effort to realize ethical action in the world. With the emergence of Christianity, however, we find quite a different situation. The radical eschatological note, the imminent expectation of the end of the world, led to the nearly complete rejection of the larger political world in the (relatively brief) time of waiting that remained. To the extent that ethical problems did consciously emerge they had to do with the personal lives of the converts, or at most with the problems of coherent community in the new churches. Nothing like a Christian political philosophy can be discerned at least until the time of Augustine. Yet very early the *bios theoretikos* and the *bios praktikos* became foci of Christian reflection. What the terms meant in the new context we must now consider.

It is actually in Philo (ca. 25 B.C.–ca. A.D. 40) that we can first discern the new interpretation that will later be taken up by the church fathers.[30] In Philo the concern for the complexities and modulations in the variety of "practical lives" that we found in Plato and Aristotle has largely dropped out. In a sense the *bios praktikos* has now been absorbed into the *bios theoretikos* as a preparatory stage of ascetic discipline. The new articulation of the two lives as successive stages will be of great consequence in later Christian thought, but it is not without preparation in Plato. The contrast between phases of life is a not infrequent theme in Plato—indeed among the many contrasts between Achilles and Socrates not the least important is the hot-blooded death of the former in the bloom of youth and the philosophic death of the latter at the age of seventy. Particularly in the *Laws*, Plato worked out an ingenious pattern of change over the life cycle (even though the element of play and dance remained central at every age) culminating in the philosophic life of the elders who are the guardians of the laws. But Plato's Magnesia is a total community in which a full political life is possible, whereas in Philo and the early church fathers the carapace of the empire is taken for granted and the concern of the religious community is largely with its own internal life. Origen (ca. 185–ca. 255) builds on Philo when he says, "Contemplatives are in the house of God, while those who lead an active life are only in the vestibule."[31] But, however much the active life was downgraded relative to the contemplative—a tendency more common in the Eastern than in the Western church—even in Origen it is cer-

tainly not rejected. In commenting on the New Testament incident of the Transfigura-
tion, Origen wrote:

> Peter was eager that they should continue in the vision he was privileged to see, but
> that was not to be. By leaving the vision and going down to serve His brethren once
> more, Our Lord demonstrated to him that the active life must always continue with the
> contemplative, that the *bios theoretikos* and the *bios praktikos* are inseparable.[32]

That this passage echoes Book VII of the *Republic* as well as the New Testament will
also be true of Augustine.

As in so many other respects so with the reflection about the active and contemplative lives, Augustine marks a turning point in Christian history. He takes up
and completes the striving for personal holiness so evident in the early fathers but he
puts this striving in a far broader social context. For him there is no question as to the
superiority of the contemplative life. Both active and contemplative lives are lived in
the space between the divine and the human and both partake of the tension of that
space. But the contemplative life is already a foretaste of the goal.

Augustine picks up from Origen the reference to Martha and Mary in Luke
10:38–42 as types of the two lives:

> Martha's part is holy and great: yet Mary hath chosen the better, in that while her
> sister was solicitous and working and caring for many things, she was at leisure and sat
> still and listened. Mary's part will not be taken away from her, Martha's will—for the
> ministering to the saints will pass away; to whom will food be given, where none hun-
> gers? Mary's part does not pass away, for her delight was in justice and truth, and in this
> same will be her delight in eternity. What Mary chooses waxes greater; for the delight of
> the human heart—of a faithful and holy human heart—in the light of truth and the
> affluence of wisdom, if it be sweet now, will then be sweeter far.[33]

But though the hierarchical ordering is clear, no one has seen better than Augustine
that true Christian existence requires both lives and that the active life is not merely
another name for the ascetic disciplines preparatory to contemplation but involves full
participation in the ethical and political life of the world. Perhaps the key passage is in
the *City of God*, xix, 19:

> As for the three kinds of life, the life of leisure, the life of action, and the combination of
> the two, anyone, to be sure, might spend his life in any of these ways without detriment to
> his faith, and might thus attain to the everlasting rewards. What does matter is the
> answers to those questions: What does a man possess as a result of his love of truth? And
> what does he pay out in response to the obligations of Christian love? For no one ought to
> be so leisured as to take no thought in that leisure for the interest of his neighbour, nor so
> active as to feel no need for the contemplation of God. The attraction of a life of leisure
> ought not to be the prospect of lazy inactivity, but the chance for the investigation and dis-
> covery of truth, on the understanding that each person makes some progress in this, and
> does not grudgingly withhold his discoveries from another.
>   In the life of action, on the other hand, what is to be treasured is not a place of honour
> or power in this life, since "everything under the sun is vanity" but the task itself that is

achieved by means of that place of honour and that power—if that achievement is right
and helpful, that is, if it serves to promote the well-being of the common people, for as we
have already argued, this well-being is according to God's intention. . . . So then, no one
is debarred from devoting himself to the pursuit of truth, for that involves a praiseworthy
kind of leisure. But high position, although without it a people cannot be ruled, is not in
itself a respectable object of ambition, even if that position be held and exercised in a
manner worthy of respect. We see then that it is love of truth that looks for sanctified leisure, while it is the compulsion of love that undertakes righteous engagement in affairs.[34]

Not for glory and not for power but for the welfare of the people under the compulsion
of love the political functions of the active life have value and meaning.

The early church, alternately persecuted and protected by the Roman Empire,
largely abstained from participation in political life and remained particularly aloof
from military life. But, after Christianity became the official religion of the empire, a
more positive conception of political life (and an abandonment of Christian pacifism)
developed. The return of classical political philosophy in Christian guise in the writings
of Augustine greatly facilitated this process, which would be resumed in the High
Middle Ages especially by Thomas Aquinas. But at the same time the spread of
monasticism, which was just beginning in Augustine's time, had new implications for
the understanding of the active and contemplative lives. For the early church as well as
for Augustine there was no suggestion that the contemplative life was only for clergy or
the active for laity. Both clergy and laity ought, of necessity, to participate in both lives.
But in the Middle Ages the contemplative life tended to be confused with the monastic
life, or even with the life of particular orders (friars were committed to the "active
life"), even though this identification never became complete. On the other hand, the
increasing recognition of the validity of secular life and the concomitant recovery of
pre-Christian classical culture contributed to the crisis over the articulation of the contemplative and active lives that occurred in the sixteenth century.

We may now glance briefly at the history of Confucianism in China and its relation to the rise of otherworldly religion after the third century of the Christian era. Pre-
Han Confucianism was by no means the predominant school of Chinese thought, and
even in its first great period of prosperity under the Han Dynasty (roughly 200 B.C. to
A.D. 200) it had to contend with other schools. With respect to our central concern the
two major alternative ancient schools contrasted neatly with Confucianism. Legalism
was the ideology of pragmatic manipulators interested primarily in the extension of
state power. They represented a hypostatization of the active life, having no concern
with the dimension of the transcendent. Taoism, on the other hand, was certainly primarily contemplative and even otherworldly if we mean by that term rejecting the
public and political realm. Confucianism, as we have seen, maintained a balance
between active and contemplative modes and indeed throughout history Confucianism
seems to have had the potentiality to shade off toward Legalism, on the one hand, or
Taoism, on the other. While the functioning bureaucrat was often a theoretical Confucianist but a practical Legalist, there is also much truth to the adage: "A Confucianist
in office; a Taoist out of office." Thus while Confucianism has never totally dominated
Chinese culture it has through most of history provided the central integration of it.
The period of the Han Dynasty was by and large one of such successful integration.

With the collapse of the Han Dynasty and the subsequent loss of political unity, Confucianism no longer seemed wholly adequate even as a political ideology. The increasing existential anxiety accompanying a period of political turmoil seemed to require some more radically religious response than Confucianism could offer. Consequently we see in the centuries that followed the greatest challenge to the dominance of Confucianism as the organizing philosophy of Chinese culture in the entire history of imperial China. The challenge came first from religious Taoism, but, from the fourth century on, Taoism was overshadowed by Buddhism, which had arrived in China from India during the later Han Dynasty as the major challenge to Confucianism. Far more otherworldly than Christianity, Buddhism was an essentially contemplative religion with little to say about worldly action. While never replacing Confucianism, Buddhism remained the dominant cultural force in China for some six centuries (fourth to tenth), a fact that both Chinese and Western scholars seem to prefer to forget.[35]

This is not the place for even a cursory discussion of Buddhism. Suffice it to say that it is a tradition based on a profound experience of religious transcendence that has given rise to extraordinary systems of metaphysical speculation and subtle practices of meditation and devotion. Buddhism was in part shaped by the Chinese environment, so that by the seventh century it had become Chinese Buddhism, but by the same token neither Taoism nor Confucianism was ever the same after their prolonged exposure to Buddhism. When in the tenth and eleventh centuries a resurgent Confucianism (generally called "Neo-Confucianism" in the West) displaced Buddhism as the dominant force in Chinese culture it did so only after having imbibed much from its opponent. Though it strongly rejected monasticism, the revived Confucianism was deeply contemplative. Under the Buddhist stimulus it greatly elaborated the incipient metaphysics of the ancient texts and developed every hint of meditational techniques. The failure of radical Confucian reforms in the Sung Period gave an overtone of political pessimism to Neo-Confucianism that may not have approached Augustine's somberness but was, and remained for centuries, far from optimistic about the possibility of action in the world even though it never abandoned the ideal of responsible political leadership. Curiously enough it was in the sixteenth century that there arose, with no direct influence from the West, the first gentle hint of a major shift away from the contemplative mode and toward the active.

In the West the shift was not gentle and it was far more than a hint. In the extraordinary figure of Niccolò Machiavelli, who stands at the head of modern Western philosophy, we encounter a radical criticism of Christianity, a tacit rejection of classical philosophy, and a dramatic reversal of the hierarchical relation between the contemplative life and the active life—or rather, the abandonment of the contemplative life altogether. We seem suddenly to be back in the world of Pericles, if not that of Achilles, though Machiavelli's heroes are more often Romans than Greeks. But the amoral aggrandizement of one's city and often the amoral aggrandizement of oneself (the pursuit of "shining glory," whether by good or evil deeds) have replaced the rule of the moral and theological virtues. Indeed the very word *virtus* has become ambiguous in its Italian guise of *virtù*, which now has as much to do with natural capacity or strength as it does with morality.[36] Machiavelli glories in action, and he is one of the greatest of all analysts of it. But with contemplation he wants no part. He criticizes

Christianity as a weak and uncivic religion, preferring the "bloody" pagan religion of ancient Rome.[37] Nothing draws his contempt so much as the unarmed prophet—Savonarola is his most common example, though Jesus of Nazareth, whom he studiously avoids mentioning, is probably another. Moses he admires because he was an armed prophet, and he mentions him together with others whom he admires, such as Cyrus, Theseus, and Romulus.[38] Throughout the texts of *The Prince* and the *Discourses* he mentions Plato and Aristotle only once. Neither the transcendence of revelation nor the transcendence discerned in the soul of the philosopher is of any interest to him. For those who view "secularization" as a gradual process Machiavelli must always come as a shock. It would be hard to imagine what it would mean to be more secular than Machiavelli.

Machiavelli, of course, was not without precursors. Hans Baron has shown how Florentines such as Salutati and Bruni in the late fourteenth and early fifteenth centuries resuscitated the honor of the active life on the basis of a "civic humanism" which learned much from the ancient world.[39] But these early civic humanists did not reject the contemplative life, even in its most cloistered monastic form. They simply argued that it was not necessarily best for all people under all circumstances and that under certain conditions the active life could be of equal or even superior dignity. As Salutati wrote, "To devote oneself honestly to honest activities may be holy, and holier than laziness in solitude. For holiness in a [quiet] country life is useful only to itself, as St. Jerome says. But holiness in a busy life raises the lives of many."[40] Nor did the early civic humanists (and many later ones) reject ancient philosophy. Plato and Cicero were particular favorites. Thus the teaching of the civic humanists was not a reversion to pre-Socratic politics as in the case of Machiavelli, but only an adjustment within the context of the Classical-Christian tradition in favor of a greater dignity of the active life. In view of the late medieval tendency to link the contemplative life to clerical life and the active life to secular life one might with reason consider the rise of civic humanism a "secularizing" trend. But even that is far from the whole story. Part of what was happening, as is evident in the Salutati passage, is that a *religious* dignity is being claimed for the active life. With Savonarola the Florentine tradition of civic humanism was fused with an eschatological interpretation of the mission of Florence which had the ironic consequence of linking civic humanism, with its sense of the dignity of the active life, to a more intense religiosity than that displayed by the Roman church of which it was critical.[41] An ideologist of Venetian republicanism like Paolo Paruta was in his defense of the active life far closer to this early strand of civic humanism than he was to his contemporary, Machiavelli.[42]

Indeed there is much in common between the Florentine and Venetian civic humanists and the Protestant reformers in their revival of the religious dignity of the active life. The tendency to denigrate contemplation as the exclusive preserve of lazy, selfish, and conceited clerics did not at all mean an abandonment of many elements of the classic definition of the *vita contemplativa*, such as faith, prayer, and worship. Luther, perhaps, put it most bluntly when he wrote:

> If the monks really wanted to escape from people, they should honorably and honestly flee, not leave a stench behind them; that is, they should not by their fleeing give other

vocations and offices a stench as though these were utterly damned and their own self-chosen monasticism were pure balsam. When a person flees from human society and becomes a monk it sounds as though he were saying, "Shame on you! How these people stink! How accursed is their vocation. I want to be saved and let them go to the devil!" If Christ had fled like this too and become such a holy monk, who would have died for our sin or atoned for us poor sinners? Do you suppose it would have been the monks with their unsociable and austere mode of life?[43]

Perhaps behind those words we can see the reemergence of all that complexity of activities and occupations in the world to which Plato and Aristotle gave so much attention. Not just "the active life," but the political, military, mercantile, manufacturing lives were beginning to require ethical and religious recognition. The Lutheran and Calvinist doctrines of "calling" were precisely designed to give those occupations religious meaning and value. Yet again this was no simple "secularization." The contemplative life, even though no longer called that, continued to permeate the active life, which was, as the Protestants insisted, to be pursued "in, but not of, this world." Perhaps the most compressed way of summing up the position that spans both civic humanists and reformers is the phrase that one of Ignatius Loyola's devoted disciples, the Jesuit Father Jerome Nadal, applied to that great Counter Reformation leader: *contemplativus in actione.*[44]

But if one aspect of the early-modern West involves a reordering of the place of action and contemplation within the continuing Classical-Christian tradition, we must not forget that other aspect, which we already observed in Machiavelli, the utter abandonment of the tradition. From this point of view, Thomas Hobbes is the first-born son of Machiavelli and outdoes his master, not in the radicalness of his views, but in the thoroughness of his theoretical support for them. For Machiavelli, theorist of political action though he was, seldom reflected on the first principles of the human condition. Hobbes we might call the first theoretical social scientist, just as Machiavelli was the first empirical one. For Hobbes meets the philosophical tradition on its own ground of first principles. He abandons entirely the fundamental Platonic-Aristotelian understanding of man as motivated primarily by *eros* toward the Good, just as he abandons the Christian understanding of man as in need of, and utterly dependent on, divine grace. Hobbes builds his understanding of man almost exclusively on one motive—the biological need for self-preservation. If he adds anything to this primary need it is the urge to dominate and excel others (which may be only an extrapolation of the primary need). In constructing a whole theory of social order on this principle, Hobbes creates a pre-Socratic political philosophy that far outdoes the meager attempts of the Sophists to do the same. Naturally in this theory there is no room for contemplation, for there is no room for transcendence. Like his predecessor, Hobbes is interested in religion, but primarily as a device for political control of the masses. About its inherent value and meaning Hobbes remains silent.

There is one important difference between Machiavelli and Hobbes that has caused their influence to be somewhat divergent in subsequent history. However radically individualist Machiavelli can sometimes be, his starting point is never the isolated individual but the city. Because of his constant preoccupation with the city and its needs, there is a link to the tradition of civic humanism that was never broken. Machiavelli's defense of republican liberty has been instructive to those who find in that liberty an ethical and religious meaning utterly lacking in Machiavelli. Another way of putting it is to say that Machiavelli was always profoundly political and that politics can be understood in an Aristotelian as well as a pre-Socratic way. But Hobbes is not finally political at all, for his radically individualist understanding of man is more economic than political. It is but a step from Hobbes to Locke's basic understanding of man in terms of labor. If we may adopt Hannah Arendt's useful subclassification of the *vita activa*,[45] we may say that the *homo politicus* of Machiavelli is beginning to be replaced by the *homo faber* and the *animal laborans* of Hobbes and Locke. In Arendt's terms this means that first work and then labor become more important than action. But whatever the tensions between the various radical champions of the active life, they all abandon contemplation. This had the ironic consequence that not only was religion undermined, but philosophy itself became a far more insignificant handmaiden than it had ever been in the Middle Ages.[46]

At this point we must allude to another crucial development that plays into our problem in important ways: the rise of modern science. Early-modern science involved a dramatic break with classical philosophy, particularly Aristotle, but it did not necessarily involve a break with religion. One of the early great ideologists of science, Francis Bacon, saw it as part of the same divine providence that brought about the Reformation:

> . . . we see before our eyes, that in the age of ourselves and our fathers, when it pleased God to call the Church of Rome to account for their degenerate manners and ceremonies, and sundry doctrines obnoxious and framed to uphold the same abuses; at one and the same time it was ordained by the Divine Providence that there should attend withal a renovation and new spring of all other knowledges.[47]

Yet the new science, even when understood in religious terms, came down heavily on the side of action rather than contemplation, as is explained admirably by Eugene Klaaren:

> For the venerable Augustinian tradition knowing consisted of *participation* in the known, an activity reinforced by the primacy of *sapientia* (wisdom). . . . This ontological orientation of knowledge was reinforced by the high value of contemplative knowledge, which genuinely symbolized the theology of Being in all things. The presupposition that the order of knowing followed that of being was basic.
>
> When Boyle and Bacon, like Descartes, reversed this traditional order, a venture of knowing itself emerged. As practical and experimental knowledge gained primacy in use and value over contemplative knowledge, the very activity of knowing acquired an integrity of its own. Henceforth, this activity closely approximated making or reconstruction rather than participation or abstraction. In this epochally new order the directing if not spontaneous significance of will, which presupposed the often distant yet all-powerful will of God, disregarded the old maxim that the will moves according to the last dictate of understanding. Sharp distinctions between Creator and creation and man and world were also manifest between knower and known. A new field for individual will emerged.[48]

But where God must be known indirectly through his works and not directly through participation the very experience of transcendence itself is endangered. As Klaaren himself points out, the belief in an "often distant" God in the seventeenth century gave way to Deism in the eighteenth and atheism in the nineteenth, at least among those who seriously pursued the relation of science and theology.

We have already indicated that in early-modern China (and Japan, too, as we shall see in a moment) the reversal in primacy of contemplation and action was also taking place, even if pianissimo, so to speak, compared to the West. With the seventeenth century the great age of metaphysical speculation is just about over, to be replaced by the development of "scientific" philology and a turn toward "practical studies." The practice of meditation (quiet sitting) was not immediately abandoned, but its prestige, particularly among the most influential and innovative scholars, declined. De Bary in a magisterial review of the "enlightenment" tendencies in seventeenth- and eighteenth-century Chinese Confucianism speaks of its "pragmatic and positivist spirit,"[49] its liberation from the "ascetic and transcendental influences of Buddhism"[50] that had infiltrated Sung Neo-Confucianism, and its emphasis on "the reality of the actual, physical natures of man and things."[51] Few Chinese Confucianists openly rejected the ancient Confucian notion, expressed classically in Mencius, that the mind (hsin) is the sensorium for transcendence (through nature, hsing, to heaven, t'ien). And yet if De Bary is right that by the seventeenth century "sagehood as a goal of spiritual attainment had become almost as rare as had sainthood in the twentieth-century West,"[52] then we can ask whether early-modern Chinese Confucianism was not reverting to a "pre-Confucian" philosophy, just as the West was reverting to a "pre-Socratic" one.

While controversy over the meaning of the texts is still going on, it does seem to me that at least one influential eighteenth-century Japanese thinker, Ogyū Sorai, did make that reversion. Openly rejecting Mencius and tacitly rejecting Confucius, Sorai exalted the "ancient kings" whom he alleged had received the original modes and orders of human society from a rather distant Heaven. There is a strong naturalism in Sorai. He takes seriously the basic desires, talents, and abilities of men and considers society as the context for men to fulfill these desires and abilities. But what holds society together are the objective normative orders administered by the ruler, who acts in later ages in the place of the ancient kings. For Sorai there is no longer any direct link to heaven through the mind. He ridiculed contemporary followers of Mencius by saying: "To use one's own mind to control one's own mind is like a lunatic controlling himself by means of his own lunacy."[53] The rejection of contemplation and the emphasis on the dynamism of political society made Sorai an important forerunner of the Meiji state. Indeed, we are beginning to be aware that modern China and Japan were far from unprepared for the modern period. Radical ideas from the West would never have been absorbed so quickly and effectively if there had not been a preparation from within. Nevertheless, in neither country was the traditional pattern of thought wholly destroyed either by the indigenous early-modern thinkers or by the incursion of modern Western thought.

Our final task is to bring what has become a sweeping excursion into intellectual history back to our original concern with patterns of individual adulthood. If comparative ethnography indicates that most human cultures have shown an alternating rhythm of concern with the sacred and the profane and if Erik Erikson has found that the mature personality expresses itself in both action and contemplation, then we might ask whether a culture that exclusively emphasizes action (or contemplation either, for that matter) can be a very healthy environment for human growth. The relation of history and life-history is problematic at best, and the relation between intellectual history and life-history is even more problematic. What the reigning intellectuals believe is not necessarily what everyone believes. Even the cultural resources available to intellectuals may not exhaust the cultural resources available to others. It is common knowledge, for example, that the religious life of Americans could hardly be gauged from the religious life of American university professors. Nevertheless the prolonged dominance of an intellectual tendency cannot but affect the larger culture. The loss of respect for the *vita contemplativa* by Western (and Eastern) intellectuals for several centuries has certainly put it on the defensive, even where it survives. The most viable survival technique under these circumstances, as we have seen in the West (there are comparable examples in East Asia), is to combine the two ways of life in some sort of synthesis. But to be in but not of the world or to be *contemplativus in actione* is enormously difficult, as Calvinists and Jesuits have learned. The "in" tends to become "of" just as action tends to obliterate contemplation. The Catholic turn toward the world in the twentieth century, in an effort to make the Jesuit model the model for the church as a whole, has further endangered the contemplative life by weakening one of the last lines of its defense.

And yet, however unfavorable the cultural environment, an individual can still put together for himself (and for others) a coherent pattern of personal identity. Even in America, which was born in action, so to speak, and where contemplation has always had a foreign ring, it has been possible to find wisdom and to express it to others. I want to mention in this regard two quite extraordinary but exemplary Americans: Jefferson and Lincoln.

The reference to Jefferson comes naturally from the Erikson discussion mentioned at the beginning of this paper.[54] Almost everything in Jefferson's intellectual equipment would seem to militate for an exclusive concern with the active life. His intellectual heroes were Bacon and Newton and Locke. His study of eighteenth-century French thought brought him to a basically materialist and sensationalist conception of man, which was more radical than that of his English teachers. In his preoccupation with useful invention and his scorn for useless speculation he was typical of the best minds of his age. Yet even in his early life, when he was in the thick of action, there is a grandeur of vision, a concern for universal truth that prevented him from being only a pragmatic politician. Without that larger vision it would not have been possible for the Declaration of Independence to have been the revolutionary document that it was, for America and for the world.

But it is in his late years that the contemplative side of Jefferson comes out best. There is something almost classical about his enjoyment of a leisured life in the country, not for lazy self-indulgence, but for the intellectual exploration of the world. In that exploration the Latin classics were a great comfort to him (he also studied the Greek texts but could make no sense of Plato). Erikson is quite right to point out that this contemplative mode reached a kind of culmination in his careful study of the Bible and his construction of a purified text of the teachings of Jesus. For Jefferson, Jesus was the highest model of humanity because of his deep concern for others. Even if what Jefferson left out is as instructive as what he kept in his "revised version," this enterprise shows beyond doubt that Jefferson transcended the utilitarian and pragmatic mode. And the fruit of these years of retirement, the enormous correspondence—particularly that with John Adams—is not the least of what he has left to his country.

Lincoln's is a deeper and more obscure example.[55] There were no late years of retirement in which wisdom could culminate. There is the probable rationalism of his early years and the certain fact that he never joined a church. Yet if there was ever a contemplative in action it was Lincoln. The enormous consistency of his vision from the late eighteen-thirties to the end of his life and the care and concern that went into his most casual writings give evidence of an extraordinary concentration. Aware as perhaps no other American of the moral price that every day of the existence of slavery exacted from all Americans, he nevertheless always controlled his actions, limiting them to what was politically possible, what was just beyond the national consciousness but not so far beyond as to be rejected. Lacking Jefferson's education he was yet more deeply educated. His three greatest teachers were the two texts that shaped the consciousness of Americans in those days, the Bible and Shakespeare, and Jefferson himself.

As with all great contemplatives, there are many things we will never know about Lincoln. But out of the darkness of the war years, out of the concern and the care that he could never lay aside came two great documents that, like the Declaration of Independence, transcend the particularities of their origin and speak to mankind. The message they speak is not only that of inalienable rights, but also of charity, reconciliation, and rebirth.

In 1940 Jacques Maritain wrote:

> As I have said . . . contemplation is particularly important to this continent. Is it not a universally repeated commonplace that America is the land par excellence of pragmatism and of the great undertakings of human activity? There is truth in this, as in most commonplaces. Whitman celebrates the pioneers in a manner which is certainly characteristic of the American soul. But, in my opinion, there are in America great reserves and possibilities for contemplation. The activism which is manifested here assumes in many cases the aspect of a remedy against despair. I think that this activism itself masks a certain hidden aspiration to contemplation. . . . On the other hand, the tendency, natural in this country, to undertake great things, to have confidence, to be moved by large idealistic feelings, may be considered, without great risk of error, as disguising that desire and aspiration of which I spoke.
>
> To wish paradise on earth is stark naïveté. But it is surely better than not to wish any paradise at all. To aspire to paradise is man's grandeur; and how should I aspire to paradise except by beginning to realize paradise here below? The question is to know what paradise is. Paradise consists, as St. Augustine says, in the joy of the Truth. Contemplation is paradise on earth, a crucified paradise.[56]

Perhaps Maritain was too optimistic. Perhaps America is too deeply committed to the active life in its pathological hypostatization to find again the healing balance of contemplation. Even Maritain himself went on to speak of "contemplation overflowing in action," which may be too easy a compromise with the reigning ethos. But at a moment when many Americans find the pragmatic world meaningless, perhaps Maritain's hopes for this continent were not utterly misguided.

REFERENCES
    [1]Erik H. Erikson, *Dimensions of a New Identity* (New York, 1974), pp. 42–43.
    [2]*Idem, Gandhi's Truth* (New York, 1969), p. 37.
    [3]*Ibid.*, p. 38.
    [4]*Ibid.*, p. 399. Erikson seems fascinated by men who were torn between the active and contemplative life, for Luther as well as Gandhi was such, and Erikson even discerns a touch of the same tension in Jefferson.
    [5]See Erik H. Erikson, *Insight and Responsibility* (New York, 1964), especially Chapter 4, "Human Strength and the Cycle of Generations."
    [6]*Ibid.*, p. 131.
    [7]*Ibid.*, p. 133.
    [8]Two important books bearing on the subject of this essay came to my attention too late to be taken into account in the body of the text. One is Joseph Pieper's *Leisure the Basis of Culture* (revised edition, New York, 1964). The other is Nicholas Lobkowicz's *Theory and Practice: History of a Concept from Aristotle to Marx* (Notre Dame, Indiana, 1967). Lobkowicz cites a rather late tradition deriving from Cicero and Iamblichus to the effect that the distinction between the kinds of life and the special respect for contemplation should be traced back to Pythagoras (pp. 5ff).
    [9]For a discussion of the characteristic differences between primitive, archaic, and historic (Greece, Israel, India, China) religions, see "Religious Evolution" in Robert N. Bellah, *Beyond Belief* (New York, 1970).
    [10]*Nichomachean Ethics*, 1095*b*.
    [11]*Republic*, 581*c*.
    [12]Hannah Arendt, *The Human Condition* (Chicago, 1958), pp. 196–97.
    [13]*Ibid.*, p. 198.
    [14]*Ibid.*, pp. 205–6.
    [15]*Republic*, 390*e*–391*e*.
    [16]*Gorgias*, 515.
    [17]*Apology*. 31*c*–32*a*.
    [18]*Symposium*, 220*c*.
    [19]*Ibid.* Michael Joyce's translation in Edith Hamilton and Huntington Cairns, eds., *The Collected Dialogues of Plato* (New York, 1961), p. 571.
    [20]*Apology*, 28*b*–29*b*.
    [21]Allan Bloom, *The Republic of Plato* (New York, 1968), p. 354.
    [22]"The Greek word is *megaloprepeia* and means literally 'that which is fitting or seemly for a great man.' " *Ibid.*, p. 461, n. 2.
    [23]*Republic*, 468aff. Paul Shorey translation in Hamilton and Cairns, *op. cit.*, p. 722.
    [24]*Republic*, 592*b*.
    [25]*Analects*, 17:19, etc.
    [26]*Seventh Letter*, 341*c*.
    [27]Arthur Waley, *The Analects of Confucius* (London, 1938).
    [28]Mencius, VII, 1:1. W. A. C. H. Dobson, *Mencius* (Toronto, 1963), p. 143.
    [29]See Eric Voegelin, *Order and History*, Vol. I, *Israel and Revelation* (Baton Rouge, La. 1959).
    [30]Lobkowicz (*op. cit.*, Chapter 4) traces this shift to the Neoplatonists, but takes as his representative figure Plotinus. While Plotinus is clearly not the crucial figure for the early Christian tradition there is another respect in which Plotinus made a decisive contribution. It was he who distinguished decisively between *logos* in the sense of conceptual thought and *theoria* in the sense of unitive vision. Allowing for

shifts in linguistic usage we may equate this contrast to the contemporary one in which theory means abstract conceptualization and contemplation means religious insight. While the connection between the ideas of theory and contemplation has never been wholly lost, to trace fully the development of the deepening split between them in the West is beyond the scope of this paper. Lobkowicz is concerned primarily with the contrast theory/practice in the modern meanings of those terms. I am concerned with the contrast contemplation/practice.

[31]In *Psalm* cxxxiii, cited by Sister Mary Elizabeth Mason, O.S.B., *Active Life and Contemplative Life* (Milwaukee, 1961), p. 19.

[32]In *The Song of Songs; Commentary and Homilies*, cited in Mason, *op. cit.*, p. 25.

[33]*Sermo* cixix, 17, cited by Mason, *op. cit.*, p. 36.

[34]Henry Bettenson translation of St. Augustine, *Concerning the City of God Against the Pagans* (Penguin, 1972), pp. 880–81.

[35]This lapse has been pointed out in a recent doctoral dissertation, Wai-lun Lai, "The Awakening of Faith in Mahayana (*Ta-ch'eng ch'i-hsin lun*); A Study of the Unfolding of Sinitic Mahayana Motifs," Harvard University, 1975.

[36]J.G.A. Pocock has some interesting reflections on *virtus*: "A term which was originally, and largely remained, part of the ethos of a political and military class, *virtus* became assimilated to the Greek *aretē* and shared its conceptual development. From the meaning of "civic excellence"—some quality respected by other citizens and productive of leadership and authority over them—*aretē* had been refined, by Socrates and Plato, to mean that moral goodness which alone qualified a man for civic capacity, which could even exist without it and render it unnecessary, and which, at the highest levels of Platonic thinking, rendered existence and the universe intelligible and satisfactory. *Aretē* and *virtus* alike came to mean, first, the power by which an individual or group acted effectively in a civic context; next, the essential property which made a personality or element what it was; third, the moral goodness which made a man, in city or cosmos, what he ought to be." *The Machiavellian Moment* (Princeton, 1975), p. 37. Needless to say the Christian use of the term was a development of the Platonic usage, whereas Machiavelli's *virtù* is a reversion to the most primitive stage of the concept.

[37]*Discourses*, I, 11–15.

[38]*Prince*, 6.

[39]Hans Baron, *The Crisis of the Early Italian Renaissance* (Princeton, 1966).

[40]*Ibid.*, p. 111.

[41]See Donald Weinstein, *Savonarola and Florence: Prophecy and Patriotism in the Renaissance* (Princeton, 1970).

[42]William J. Bouwsma, *Venice and the Defense of Republican Liberty*, (Berkeley, 1968), pp. 202ff. Sarpi would seem, in the crucial respects, to be closer to Paruta than to Machiavelli.

[43]From "On the Councils and the Church," in *Luther's Works*, Vol. 41 (Fortress Press, 1966), p. 39. But Saint Gregory the Great, who had such an enormous influence on medieval monasticism, was long before aware of Luther's problem. In taking Christ as his example, he wrote: "He set forth in himself patterns of both lives, that is, the active and the contemplative, united together. For the contemplative differs very much from the active. But our redeemer by becoming Incarnate, while he gave a pattern of both, united both in Himself. For when he wrought miracles in the city, yet continued all night in prayer on the mountain, He gave his faithful ones an example not to neglect, through love of contemplation, the care of their neighbours; nor again to abandon contemplative pursuits through being too immoderately engaged in the care of their neighbours; but so to keep together their mind, in applying it to the two cases, that the love of their neighbour might not interfere with the love of God, nor again the love of God, cast out, because it transcends, the love of their neighbour." *Morals on the Book of Job*, xxviii, 33, cited in Mason, *op. cit.*, p. 66.

[44]Mason, *op. cit.*, p. xi.

[45]Arendt, *op. cit.*

[46]Cf. *ibid.*, p. 294.

[47]From *The Advancement of Learning*, cited by Eugene M. Klaaren, "Belief in Creation and the Rise of Modern Natural Science," Ph.D. Dissertation, Harvard University, 1975, p. 106. Lobkowicz (*op. cit.*,

Chapter 7) has a very valuable discussion of Bacon as the inheritor of the medieval artisan tradition. Out of this tradition comes the special stress on "making" as a central part of action, Arendt's *homo faber*.

[48]Klaaren, *op. cit.*, p. 144.

[49]W. Theodore de Bary, ed., *The Unfolding of Neo-Confucianism* (New York, 1974), p. 144. This and the following quotations are from De Bary's own article, "Neo-Confucian Cultivation and the Seventeenth-Century 'Enlightenment,' " pp. 141–216.

[50]*Ibid.*, p. 194.

[51]*Ibid.*, p. 201.

[52]*Ibid.*, p. 204.

[53]*Bendō*, in Yoshikawa Kojiro *et alia*, eds., *Ogyū Sorai, Nihon Shisō Taikei*, 36 (Tokyo, 1973), p. 28.

[54]See note 1 above.

[55]My understanding of Lincoln has been greatly enhanced by Harry V. Jaffa's extraordinary book, *Crisis of the House Divided* (New York, 1959), as well as by some of the essays in the same author's *Equality and Liberty* (Oxford, 1965).

[56]From an essay entitled "Action and Contemplation," in Jacques Maritain, *Scholasticism and Politics* (New York, 1940), pp. 192–93.

WILLIAM J. BOUWSMA

Christian Adulthood

THE ELASTICITY OF CHRISTIANITY, as it has accommodated itself to two thousand years of cultural change, is well known; and it poses special problems for the identification of a peculiarly "Christian" conception of what it means to be an adult. It is also likely to make any attempt at such definition seem arbitrary. I shall nevertheless try to show in this essay that Christianity does contain a characteristic conception of healthy human maturity, but to do so it will be necessary to distinguish between what I shall call *historical* and *normative* Christianity. Historical Christianity reflects the composite of those cultural impulses that make up what is commonly thought of as Christian civilization; much of it is not specifically Christian, although it constitutes a large part of what has been believed by Christians. Its conception of "adulthood" is often an eclectic mixture of somewhat contrary impulses, and it is likely to be unstable. But normative Christianity is an ideal type. It is normative in the sense that it builds on and is consistent with those biblical norms about human nature and human destiny that give to Christianity whatever precise identity it may possess. It is also, therefore, heavily indebted to Judaism. It is not ahistorical, but it can rarely be found in a pure form. Its conception of adulthood can be stated with some coherence.

The conception of maturity in historical Christianity can be further described as a mixture of two quite different notions, which I shall call the idea of *manhood* and the idea of *adulthood*. The significance of this second distinction may be suggested by the differing etymologies of the two terms. The Germanic *man* is considered by most linguists to be derived from an Indo-European verb meaning "to think" (cf. the Latin *mens*); it thus refers to a supposedly qualitative difference between human beings and other animals, and "manhood" would thus imply entrance into a fully rational existence. But *adult* comes from the Latin *adolescere*, "to grow up." It is (or can be) neutral about the nature of growth; it implies a process rather than the possession of a particular status or specific faculty. The two terms, which are often confused in our culture, can also be taken to represent the two major but contrasting impulses in the Western tradition. *Adulthood*, as I will use it here, is related to the anthropology of the Bible; and its suggestion of process hints at the distinctively dynamic qualities of the Hebrew language.[1] But *manhood* is a creation of classical antiquity, and it reflects the need of classical culture to organize all experience in terms of absolute, static, and qualitative categories.

81

The idea of manhood is elaborated in the classical formulations of *paideia* or *humanitas*, which pointed, for the Greek and Latin educational traditions, to the peculiar excellence of the human species. Unlike adulthood, manhood tends, with rare exceptions, to be sexually specific, and thus it is one source of the tendency to deny full maturity to women.[2] It also differs from adulthood in its rejection of individuality, and it is oriented to the goal rather than the processes of human development. We can see this in the relative indifference of classical humanism to the psychology of the child and its significance for the formation of the man.[3] Childhood, in this conception, was conceived not as the positive foundation of maturity but as formlessness or chaos, and manhood was the result of the imposition on this refractory matter, by education, of an ideal form. With the achievement of manhood, childhood was decisively and happily left behind.

Embedded in this conception were both the metaphysical distinction between form and substance, with its hints of anthropological dualism, and a characteristic distinction, within man, among the several elements of the human personality: soul and body, or reason, will, and passion. These were seen not merely as analytical devices but as real, qualitative distinctions corresponding to distinctions in the structure of all reality. Similarly, childhood and manhood had to be qualitatively distinct; they could not coincide, for insofar as a human being was still a child he could not be a man. Here we may discern the characteristic resistance of ancient rationalism to ambiguity and paradox.

In this view, some of man's faculties were also ontologically superior and sovereign, others inferior, dangerous except in subordination, and thus demanding suppression. Manhood was specifically associated with the rule of reason, which was at once the spark of divinity in man, his access to the higher rationality of the divinely animated cosmos, and the controlling principle of human behavior; the function of reason was to order the personality into conformity with the larger order of the universe as it was apprehended by the mind. The principles of reason thus come from "above," and the ideal man is therefore a fully rational being who pits his reason against the chaotic forces both within himself and in the world.

The assimilation of this conception into historical Christianity has been responsible for its tendencies to an idealism in which the religious quest is understood as a commitment to higher things, with a corresponding contempt for lower. Anthropologically, this has often pitted the soul (more or less associated with reason) against the passions and the body; it has also been responsible for the doubtful association of Christianity with the notion of the immortality of a disembodied soul. And certain conclusions have followed for the ideal of human maturity often encountered in historical Christianity. This conception is the source of a Christian ethics of repression, directed (like the pagan ethics of the Hellenistic world) chiefly against sexuality as the most imperious of the bodily passions; of Christian distrust of spontaneity, a quality especially associated with childhood; and of the notion of the mature Christian—this might be called the Christian ideal of manhood—as a person who has so successfully cultivated his own bad conscience, his guilt for his persistent attraction to lower things, that he can only come to terms with his existence by a deliberate and rigorous program of self-discipline and self-denial in the interest of saving his soul. The Christian man, in this conception, has consciously separated himself as far as possible from his childhood, in obedience to a higher wisdom that is readily distinguishable from folly.[4]

We can encounter this conception of Christianity in many places, notably among its modern critics. Nietzsche's morbid caricature of Christianity owed a good deal to the conception,[5] though Nietzsche also understood the significance of biblical Christianity better than many of his Christian contemporaries.[6] And of course this kind of Christianity is now peculiarly vulnerable to attack. A case in point is a recent work by a British psychologist, whose position will both help to bring out the human implications of the classical strand in historical Christianity and throw into relief what I will present as normative Christianity. This writer addressed herself especially to the historical impact of Christianity on human development. Noting Jesus' association of childhood with the kingdom of heaven, she remarked:

> Socrates encouraged his young followers to develop towards maturity; Jesus tried to reduce his to the level of children. The Gospels contain numerous statements in which the attitudes of children are compared favorably with those of adults. . . . These statements are so often quoted with approval that probably few pause to consider whether it is really a good thing for adults to think and behave like children. What attracted Jesus towards "little children," obviously, was their unquestioning trust in adults, and his ideal was to be surrounded by adults who had a similar trust in him.

This writer's somewhat uncritical commitment to the classical ideal of a manhood that leaves childhood behind seems reasonably clear, though her sense of the implications of that ideal and of the historical roots of the kind of Christianity she indicts is somewhat confused. But her attitude is not uncommon, and her depiction of one prominent strand in historical Christianity is not unfounded. She discerns in Christianity an authoritarian impulse that, rejecting true adulthood, aims to reduce adults to a childish malleability, and so proves also destructive of the positive qualities of childhood. Christianity, in her view, is a "harsh, joyless, guilt-obsessed religion that makes happiness suspect and virtue unattractive." It is, in essence, an "ascetic, other-worldly religion which for centuries has served to stifle the free intelligence and to limit disastrously the range of human sympathies." It is dominated by "a self-centred preoccupation with one's own virtue and one's own salvation," and accordingly the Christian has a "negative, passive, masochistic character and [an] obsession with suffering and sacrifice."[7]

But this indictment neglects to notice that similar charges against historical Christianity have been periodically made from within the Christian community, a fact which suggests that we may find in Christianity itself a very different understanding of the Christian position. Thus it has not escaped the attention of Christians that the authority claimed for Christian belief has at times tended to degenerate into an authoritarianism that contradicts the central meaning of Christianity. It is undeniable, for example, and certainly by Christians, that the Christian clergy have in some periods claimed, as Christ's successors, to be "fathers" with a more than legitimate paternal authority over the laity, their "children." In 1301, for example, Boniface VIII brought a long tradition of such paternalism to a climax in a stern letter to the king of France. "Hearken, dearest son," he wrote, "to the precepts of thy father and bend the ear of thy heart to the teaching of the master who, here on earth, stands in place of Him who alone is master and lord."[8] But the practical authoritarianism in Christian history is easily exaggerated; the claims of ecclesiastical authority have rarely gone unchallenged. Those of Pope Boniface, indeed, resulted in a major disaster for the papacy at the hands of men who also considered themselves Christians. Some Christians have also rejected in principle the attitudes he represented. Calvin, for example, placed a highly unfavorable construction on clerical paternalism. "Hence it appears," he declared, "what kind of Christianity there is under the Papacy, when the pastors labor to the utmost of their power to keep the people in absolute infancy."[9] Indeed, the papacy itself has shown recent indications of sympathy for Calvin's position. The *aggiornamento* of John XXIII has been widely interpreted as an admission of the coming-of-age of the laity, and Pope John himself suggested a new understanding of adulthood in his transparent inability to take seriously his own status and dignity as an adult. Paradoxically, this was somehow interpreted by many of those who observed him as the most persuasive evidence of his maturity.

The paradox of Pope John takes us to the heart of the conception of adulthood in normative Christianity, which I shall now approach directly through a text in the Pauline letter to the Ephesians:[10]

> So shall we all at last attain to the unity inherent in our faith and our knowledge of the Son of God—to mature manhood, measured by nothing less than the full stature of Christ. We are no longer to be children, tossed by the waves and whirled about by every fresh gust of teaching. . . . No, let us speak the truth in love; so shall we fully grow up in Christ. He is the head, and on him the whole body depends. Bonded and knit together by every constituent joint, the whole frame grows through the due activity of each part, and builds itself up in love.

Here we are immediately introduced to several important themes. One is the strictly metaphorical meaning of "childhood," whose characteristics may be encountered in men of all ages; another is the association of maturity with personal stability. Still another is the identification of full adulthood with the loving solidarity of mankind, and this will concern us later. But it is of particular importance for our immediate purposes that the measure of true adulthood is finally "the full stature of Christ," for this is an absolute standard, in relation to which no man, whatever his age, can claim to be fully an adult. This peculiarity of Christian adulthood especially struck Calvin, who emphasized it in commenting on the text:[11]

> As [the apostle] had spoken of that full-grown age toward which we proceed throughout the whole course of our life, so now he tells us that, during such a progress, we ought not to be like children. He thus sets an intervening period between childhood and maturity. Those are children who have not yet taken a step in the way of the Lord, but still hesitate, who have not yet determined what road they ought to choose, but move sometimes in one direction, and sometimes in another, always doubtful, always wavering. But those are

thoroughly founded in the doctrine of Christ, who, although not yet perfect, have so much wisdom and vigor as to choose what is best, and proceed steadily in the right course. Thus the life of believers, longing constantly for their appointed status, is like adolescence. So when I said that in this life we are never men, this ought not to be pressed to the other extreme, as they say, as if there were no progress beyond childhood. After being born in Christ, we ought to grow, so as not to be children in understanding . . . although we have not arrived at man's estate, we are at any rate older boys.

Here the paradox is fully stated: that the Christian, however ripe in years, cannot think of himself as a completed man. Christianity has, then, a conception of full adulthood; the goal of human development is total conformity to the manhood of Christ. But since this is a transcendent goal, the practical emphasis in Christian adulthood is on the process rather than its end. Since it is impossible to achieve perfect maturity in this life, the duty of the Christian is simply to develop constantly toward it. The essential element in the Christian idea of adulthood is, accordingly, the capacity for growth, which is assumed to be a potentiality of any age of life. It is in this sense that the Christian life is like adolescence, that stage in which the adult seems, however ambiguously, trembling to be born.

But adolescence also suggests the coexistence, within the personality, of the child and whatever it is that he promises to become, and this points to another peculiarity of the Christian view: its insistence on the continuity, rather than the absolute qualitative difference, between the child and the man. The developing adult is assumed to incorporate positively the individual and (in fact) irrepressible character of the child. Adulthood assumes that the child cannot be left behind, but is the basis of the more mature personality. Thus the child lives on in the man, so that child and man are somehow identical, a conclusion, from the standpoint of classical manhood, that is paradoxical and absurd. It is evident also that the idea of adulthood is related to various other Christian paradoxes: that the last shall be first, that foolishness is wisdom, and that God, who is himself "highest," should lower himself to become a corporeal man—and indeed, as though this metaphysical confusion were not sufficiently degrading, that he should come not as a hero or a king but as a humble figure who is put to death for others. The paradox of adulthood points to the folly of the cross.

Similarly adulthood does not recognize real qualitative and hierarchical distinctions *within* the personality; it sees man, whether child or adult, as a living whole. It may sometimes use such terms as "spirit," "soul," "mind," or "flesh"; but this vocabulary (which also reflects the difficulties of translating the thought of one culture into the language of another) is intended to describe various modes of activity of what is, in itself, an undifferentiated unity. The anthropology of normative Christianity can only be pictured, not as a hierarchy of discrete faculties, but as a circle organized around a vital center, the core of human being (cf. Latin *cor*, "heart"), whose qualities, for good or evil, permeate the whole.[12] Thus, where classical anthropology sought to understand man by identifying the several faculties of the personality and ranking them according to their objective value, normative Christianity has been inclined to accept and even to celebrate the mysteries of the total personality.[13]

This conception of Christian adulthood is, of course, not only normative; it has also found concrete historical expression, though I think it has rarely been dominant in the history of Christianity.[14] Nevertheless, the availability to Christians in all subsequent ages of the canonical Scriptures and the constant effort to penetrate to their meaning have meant that, however obscured by misunderstandings arising out of the cultural limitations of their readers, a biblical conception of adulthood has always played at least a counterpoint to the classical conception of manhood. It has never altogether disappeared from later Western culture, however muted it may have become; it has regularly helped to block radical intrusions of the classical idea of manhood into Christianity (I suspect that both Arianism and Pelagianism are linked to that conception); and occasionally, though usually only briefly, it has swelled out unmistakably as a major theme. It is prominent in the mature Augustine, in the more Pauline manifestations of the Catholic and Protestant Reformations, and in twentieth-century neo-orthodoxy and biblical theology, with their heightened cultural relativism and their enhanced sensitivity to history.

This conception of adulthood is in fact so inextricably linked to normative Christianity as a whole that we can trace it through a series of basic and specifically Jewish and Christian doctrines and, in this way, explore its implications more deeply. Its foundations can be discerned in the biblical account of the creation, which incorporates a number of insights basic to Christian thought. This is not, as in the creation myths of surrounding peoples, the culmination of a primordial struggle between a creator and the forces of chaos, coeternal with, perhaps even anterior to, him; it is a true beginning. This has various implications. God created the universe; and, as this was eventually understood, he created it out of nothing,[15] a doctrine that establishes both the absolute transcendence of God and his full sovereignty over every aspect of creation.[16] And since the creation specifically included the heavens as well as the earth, the story subverts the classical distinctions between high things and low.[17] If hierarchies of any kind are admissible in the biblical universe, they cannot, at any rate, have any sacred basis. They possess only relative value; all created things are, in the only relationship of absolute significance, on the same level, as creatures.[18] For man this means not only that he must recognize his creatureliness but that he must see it in every aspect of his being. No part of him is divine, and therefore none can claim to rule by divine right over the others.[19] Among its other implications, this precludes the possibility of repression as a way of ordering the personality. Because man was created as a whole, indeed in God's own image, every aspect of man is good and worthy of development, for "God saw all that he had made, and it was very good" (Gen. 1:31).[20]

In addition, this good creation is depicted as a work of time, and, as the sequel reveals, God has built into it the dimension of process and change. Time and change, so dimly regarded in the classical world of thought, are therefore also necessarily good; the biblical God underlined their positive significance by presenting himself, after the fall, as the Lord of history who encounters and reveals himself to man in temporal experience.[21] The Old Testament is fundamentally historical, and the New is based on a further series of historical events in which God uniquely enters and sanctifies time.[22] In this conception the past acquires peculiar significance. It is that aspect of time which man can know through memory, which indeed he must ponder deeply because it gives meaning to the present and promise to the future.[23] The past demonstrates God's care and will for man and therefore it cannot be ignored or repudiated. This explains why the Scriptures so frequently summon man to *remember* the past, for in an important sense it is contemporaneous with all subsequent time.

The significance of the past also points to the indelible importance of all human experience. It gives meaning to the particular temporal experiences that have shaped each individual during the whole course of his life, so that the biblical idea of time is the foundation for the conception of the worth of the individual personality.[24] But it also gives meaning to the collective experiences of mankind into which all individual experience is ultimately submerged, a conception basic to the discovery of the great historical forces that transcend individual experience.[25] Fundamental to the Christian view of man is, therefore, an insistence on a process of growth in which the past is not left behind but survives, shapes, and is absorbed into the present.[26] The unalterable past provides a stable base for the identity alike of each individual and of every society. St. Augustine's *Confessions*, with its vivid delineation of a personality changing yet continuous with its past, is a product of this conception.[27] The absence of genuine biography in the classical world has often been remarked.[28] By the same token, the great classical histories sought to reveal the changeless principles governing all change, while the biblical histories were concerned with change itself as God's work and with its shaping impact on men.

The Christian life, then, is conceived as indefinite growth, itself the product of a full engagement with temporal experience involving the whole personality. The Christian is not to evade the challenges, the struggles, the difficulties and dangers of life, but to accept, make his way through, and grow in them. He must be willing to disregard his vulnerability and to venture out, even at the risk of making mistakes, for the sake of growth.[29] This understanding of life finds expression in the figure of the Christian as wayfarer (*viator*) or pilgrim; Christian conversion is thus not, as in the mystery religions, an immediate entrance into a safe harbor but rather, though its direction has been established, the beginning of a voyage into the unknown.[30] As movement in a direction, it also implies progress, but a progress that remains incomplete in this life.[31] The "other-worldliness" of Christianity is significant, in this context, as the basis of the open-endedness of both personal and social development.

From this standpoint, just as the essential condition of Christian adulthood is the capacity for growth, the worst state of man is not so much his sinfulness (for sins can be forgiven) as the cessation of growth, arrested development, remaining fixed at any point in life. In these terms, just as adulthood requires growth, its opposite—what might be called the Christian conception of immaturity—is the refusal to grow, the inability to cope with an open and indeterminate future (that is, the future itself), in effect the rejection of life as a process.

There is, however, a close connection between the rejection of growth and the problem of sin; the refusal to grow is, in an important sense, the source of all particular sins. The story of the fall reveals the connection, and may also be taken as the biblical analysis of the causes and the consequence of human immaturity. It contrasts essential man, as God created him, with actual man, man as he appears in history, who is fearful of the future and afraid of growth. The story explains this as a result of man's faith-lessness. For the fall is caused not by a breach of the moral law but by man's violation of the relationship fundamental to his existence; it belongs to religious rather than to ethical experience. Primordial man, whose goodness stems from his dependence on God, is depicted as rejecting the creatureliness basic to his perfection and claiming independent value and even divinity for himself. He seeks to become "like gods," and implicit in this pretension is the rejection of his own further development. By com-placently making himself *as he is* the divine center of his universe, he rejects the possi-bility of change and learns to fear all experience. Thus he loses his openness to the future and his capacity for growth; in short he repudiates his capacity for adulthood.[32] The claim to divinity, therefore, paradoxically results in a pervasive anxiety. And out of this anxiety man commits a whole range of particular ethical sins, the end products of his faithlessness. Thus, too, he begins to suffer particular sensations of guilt.[33]

A further symptom of his immaturity may be seen in man's perennial tendency, implicit in his claim to divinity, to absolutize his understanding of the universe in a frantic effort to hold his anxiety in check. This, I take it, would be the Christian explanation for the relatively small influence of a biblical understanding of the human situation in Christendom itself. Man solemnly invests his culture, which is in fact always contingent on his own limited and self-centered vision and need, with ultimate meaning, thereby imprisoning himself within a man-made, rigidly bounded, and internally defined universe that further destroys the possibility for growth. He philoso-phizes, claims access to the real truth of things, to being-in-itself. This is the significance normative Christianity would assign to the absolute qualitative distinctions of classical culture, a man-made substitute for biblical faith. Harvey Cox has described such con-structions as a "play-pen," a nice image in its implications for human development.[34] Their power to inhibit human sympathy, with its special value for personal growth, is suggested by the need of the Greek (in an impulse with which we are all quite familiar) to see the man who differed from himself as a barbarian. Without faith—what Tillich has called the courage to be, which is also the courage to become—the only escape from man's intolerable fear of chaos is the idolatry of cultural absolutism. So, without faith, man tends to bigotry, for any grasp of the universe other than his own is too dangerous for him to contemplate. It is in this light that we can understand the full implications of the pagan charge that the early Christians were enemies of culture. In a sense this was true then, and it remains true; for normative Christianity all culture is a human arti-fact, and no absolute validity can be attached to its insights. Such a position is always likely to be disturbing, as every social scientist has discovered.

Yet normative Christianity does not deny the practical values of culture. It simply insists that, just as man is a creature of God, so culture is a creature of man, not his master. Secularized in this way, culture can serve many useful human purposes, and it can even become a vehicle of Christian purposes when men fully recognize their dependence on God.[35] But culture can never be ultimately serious. Indeed, there are tensions in the Scriptures that suggest that some dimensions of biblical religion itself may be understood as products of culture, or at any rate set in a larger context within which, like culture, they can be seen to possess only relative authority. Job discovered this in his confrontation with an inscrutable but infinitely holy God, and we can also sense something of this in the tension in the Old Testament between prophetic religion and the law. The law is like culture in the sense that it defines and particularizes sins, and the prophets do not deny the validity of such definition. But prophetic religion also insists, not simply that there is more to be said about man's situation before God than this, but, in addition, that definition is significant only in relation to the indefinite and open.[36]

If the Christian analysis of the evils in historical existence can be understood as a diagnosis of immaturity, the Christian conception of salvation can be similarly construed as a description of the only way to recover that capacity for growth in which true adulthood consists. The basic problem here is to replace anxiety with faith, so that man can enter an open future with confidence and grow through his experience. But here he encounters a problem he cannot solve. Faith is a function of man's dependence on God, but it is precisely this relationship that man in historical existence has repudiated. In effect he has destroyed the "true self" God made, and he must therefore be remade. And as Augustine asked, "If you could not make yourself, how could you remake yourself?"[37] Described psychologically, the predicament in which man finds himself is one of entrapment and bondage—in short, of total helplessness.[38] Furthermore, because man was created a living whole and repudiated his creatureliness as a whole, there is no area of his personality left untouched by his alienation from God and thus from his true self. This is the precise meaning of the often misunderstood doctrine of total depravity: it signifies that man has no resources by which he can save himself.

Yet exactly here, in the recognition that this is the case, lies the first step toward the resumption of growth. Once man sees himself as he is, acknowledges his limits, perceives the contingency of all his own constructions, and admits that they have their sources only in himself, he is well on the way to accepting his creaturehood and open to the possibility of faith. Faith begins, then, not in illusion but in an absolute and terrifying realism; its first impulse is paradoxically the pereeption that faith itself is beyond man's own control, that there is no help in him, that his only resource is the grace of a loving God. The Christian, as Barth remarked, is "moved by a grim horror of illusion." "What is pleasing to God comes into being when all human righteousness is gone, irretrievably gone, when men are uncertain and lost, when they have abandoned all ethical and religious illusions, and when they have renounced every hope in this world and in this heaven. . . . Religion is the possibility of the removal of every ground of confidence except confidence in God alone. Piety is the possibility of the removal of the last traces of a firm foundation upon which we can erect a system of thought."[39] Salvation thus begins with confession, the admission of sin and ultimately of faithlessness, which is therapeutic in the sense that it demands total honesty and is directed to the removal of every false basis for human development. Augustine's *Confessions* might be described as the Christian form of psychoanalysis, the retracing, in God's presence and with his help, of the whole course of a life, which aims to recover the health of faith.[40]

By confession and repentance, themselves a response to faith, man recognizes his helplessness and thus becomes open to help. This help is revealed and made available by God himself through the saving work of Christ, in which God again demonstrates his infinite concern with history. The response to Christ in faith expresses man's full acceptance of that creatureliness which is the essential condition of his authentic existence and growth; the answer to sin is not virtue but faith. By faith man is dramatically relieved of his false maturity, his claims to a self-defined "manhood," and enabled to begin again to grow. This is why conversion can be described as a "rebirth," which resembles birth also in that it is not subject to the control of him who is reborn; baptism, the ritual of rebirth, is an initiation into true existence. Freed from the anxieties of self-sufficiency by faith, man can grow, both individually and collectively. Indeed, only now has he the strength to face directly the contingency, the inadequacy, the slavery and sinfulness of all merely human culture. He can risk seeing it clearly because, with faith, he has also received the gift of hope. From this standpoint the Gospel is the good news because it frees man for adulthood.

But this is an adulthood that involves, always, the whole man; thus its goal is symbolized not by the immortality of the soul but by the resurrection of the body as representing the total self that must be made whole. As Augustine exclaimed in old age, "I want to be healed completely, for I am a complete whole."[41] Christian maturity is manifested, therefore, not only in the understanding but more profoundly in the affective life and in the loving actions that are rooted in the feelings. Christ is above all the model of absolute love. Conformity to this loving Christ is the goal of human development; in Augustine's words, "he is our native country." But he is also the key to Christian adulthood, for "he made himself also the way to that country."[42] The Christian grows both in Christ and to Christ.

Again we encounter a set of paradoxes, the first of which is that man's full acceptance of his creatureliness, the admission of his absolute dependence on God in Christ, proves to be the essential condition of human freedom. For the only alternative to the life of faith is bondage to the self, to the anxieties and the false absolutisms embedded in human culture, by which man is otherwise imprisoned. Faith, in these terms, is the necessary condition of true autonomy, of freedom not from the constraints of experience—the Stoic ideal—but freedom to grow in and through them that is essential to adulthood. The Pauline injunction to work out one's own salvation in fear and trembling suggests this freedom, and suggests also the strains attendant on growth, but it would be impossible to fulfill without the faith that "it is God which worketh in you both to will and to do of his pleasure" (Phil. 2:13). This kind of freedom supplies the strength to challenge authority maturely, without the rebelliousness, arrogance, and destructiveness symptomatic of insecurity, or to criticize the definition of one's own life and to examine the dubious sources of one's own actions.[43]

At the same time, obedience to God paradoxically proves a far lighter burden than obedience to human ordinances or the requirements of culture, even though—another paradox—it is, in any final sense, impossible. For Christian righteousness consists not in a moral quality that must be maintained at all costs but in a relationship of favor and peace with God that is the source (rather than the consequence) of moral effort. If the Christian is in some sense virtuous, his virtue arises from love rather than duty, and if he fails, he can count on forgiveness. Thus, though he must recognize and confess his guilt as part of his more general realism, he is not to nourish or cling to it, for this would amount to the rejection of God's love. Repentance means allowing our guilt to be God's concern, and all guilt, otherwise so paralyzing for the moral life, must be swallowed up in love and gratitude. Christian adulthood is a growth away from, not toward, guilt.

By the same token it cannot be repressive, not only because no power in the human personality is entitled to excise or even to control any other (this is the happy implication of total depravity), but above all because such an effort, since it cannot touch the quality of the heart, would be superficial and in the end futile. Christian thinkers have sometimes displayed great insight into the nature of self-imposed control. Calvin's description of the process implies some acquaintance with its physiological consequences, as well as realism about the social necessity for restraint in a world in which those, too, who are growing in Christ must recognize that they are not fully and dependably adult: "the more [men] restrain themselves, the more violently they are inflamed within; they ferment, they boil, ready to break out into external acts, if they were not prevented by this dread of the law. . . . But yet this constrained and extorted righteousness is necessary to the community. . . ."[44] But the ideal of Christian adulthood is not control but spontaneity; it is, in Augustine's words, to "love and do what you will."[45]

The spontaneity in the Christian ideal of adulthood points to still another paradox: its deliberate cultivation of, and delight in, the qualities of the child, now understood less metaphorically.[46] Childhood, after all, assumes growth, and it is in this respect fundamentally different from childishness, which rejects it; in this sense childhood is a model for adulthood. Indeed, childhood welcomes the years, unaware that they bring decay and death, and the deep and fearless interest of the child in his experience permits him to ask simple but profound questions that, later, may seem wearisome or too dangerous to be entertained. The child is not afraid to express wonder and astonishment.[47] Thus the confident trust in life of a healthy child, so different from the wariness that develops with age, has often been taken in Christian thought as a natural prototype of faith; in this sense, the adult Christian life is something like a return to childhood. As Kierkegaard remarked, it seems to reverse the natural order: "Therefore one does not begin by being a child and then becoming progressively more intimate [with God] as he grows older; no, one becomes more and more a child."[48] But there is, in this reversal, realism about the actual results of maturation, which ordinarily destroys the openness and wonder of childhood and replaces it with disguises and suspicion, with sophistication and a "knowingness" that chiefly serve to exclude a profounder knowledge. For the man, a return to the values of childhood is only possible when the inadequacies of his pretended manhood have been recognized in repentance and confession and he can take the way of faith. Then the growth of the man can again be like that of the child.[49]

This suggests a further peculiarity in the Christian view of adulthood: its lack of interest in chronological disparity. All Christians, insofar as they are growing in Christ, are equally becoming adults—or equally children.[50] Baptism is no respecter of age. An important consequence of this is to limit the authority and influence of parents, for where parent and child are both growing up in Christ,[51] the parent cannot be the only, or even the primary, pattern of maturity.[52] The Christian parent has failed unless his child achieves sufficient autonomy to establish his own direct relation to Christ. Nor is there sexual differentiation in the Christian conception: girls and boys, women and men are equally growing up in Christ.

But there is still another respect in which Christian adulthood merges with childhood: in its appreciation for play. This may be related to Paul's contrast between the wisdom of this world and the divine foolishness by which its hollowness is revealed.[53] The recurrent figure of the Christian fool, both child and saint, has sought to embody this conception. But it also has lighter, if equally serious, implications. The security of dependence on a loving God makes it unnecessary to confront life with a Stoic solemnity; the Christian can relax, even (again paradoxically) when he is most profoundly and actively confronting the sinfulness of the world. He can enjoy playfully (which also means to delight in, for itself, not to exploit instrumentally, for himself) the goodness of the creation. His culture can be an unbounded playground for free and joyous activity. He can risk the little adventures on which play depends. The loving human relationships of the Christian life can find expression in mutual play, through which we give pleasure to one another. Play is a natural expression of the joy of faith, which makes it possible to engage in life, even the hard work of life, as a game that has its own seriousness (for without their special kind of seriousness games could scarcely interest us), and that yet can be enjoyed precisely because the ultimate seriousness of existence lies elsewhere, with God.[54] But play is also related to that seriousness. Bushnell saw play as "the symbol and interpreter" of Christian liberty and pointed to its place in the eschatological vision of Zechariah 8:5: "And the streets of the city shall be full of boys and girls, playing in the streets."[55]

I have treated these various elements in the Christian conception of adulthood as aspects of an ideal for individual development, but to leave the matter at this would be to neglect an essential dimension of the Christian position. Like Judaism, Christianity has usually seen the individual in close and organic community with others. The Pauline description of growing up in Christ, though it has obvious implications for the individual, is primarily concerned with the growth of the Christian community; it is finally the church as one body, and perhaps ultimately all mankind, that must reach "mature manhood." The primary experiences through which the Christian grows are social experiences. One encounters Christ and the opportunity to serve him in others; the maturity of the individual is realized only in loving unity with others.[56] The power of growth is thus finally a function of community, and, at the same time, maturity finds expression in identification with other men; Christ, the model of human adulthood, was supremely "the man for others."[57] Through this identification of the individual with the body of Christ, the Christian conception of adulthood merges finally into history and eschatology. —)In times

REFERENCES

[1]Cf. Thorlief Boman, *Hebrew Thought Compared with Greek*, tr. Jules L. Moreau (New York, 1970), esp. pp. 28-33, 45-69.

[2]An exception can be found in Seneca's letter to his mother, known as the *Consolation to Helvia*, in which he recommends a standard program of literary and philosophical studies to console her for his exile.

[3]Cf. H. I. Marrou, *A History of Education in Antiquity*, tr. George Lamb (New York, 1964), pp. 297-98.

[4]A good example of this ideal is John Chrysostom's address to Christian parents on the upbringing of children, translated by M. L. W. Laistner in his *Christianity and Pagan Culture in the Later Roman Empire* (Ithaca, 1951), pp. 85-122. "Thou art raising up a philosopher and athlete and citizen of heaven," Chrysostom declared; for this he recognized "wisdom" as "the master principle which keeps everything under control," the height of which is "refusal to be excited at childish things." The purpose of education for him is to make the Christian boy "sagacious and to banish all folly": that is, to make him a precocious little Stoic sage. He is to "know the meaning of human desires, wealth, reputation, power" that he "may disdain these and strive after the highest." And the fruit of his maturity consists in the ability to control his passions: if he can only learn "to refrain from anger, he has displayed already all the marks of a philosophic mind."

[5]Cf. *The Antichrist*, no. 51, tr. Walter Kaufmann: "We others who have the *courage* to be healthy and also to despise—how we may despise a religion which taught men to misunderstand the body! which does not want to get rid of superstitious belief in souls! which turns insufficient nourishment into something 'meritorious'! which fights health as a kind of enemy, devil, temptation! which fancies that one can carry around a 'perfect soul' in a cadaver of a body, and which therefore found it necessary to concoct a new conception of 'perfection'—a pale, sickly, idiotic-enthusiastic character, so-called 'holiness.' Holiness—merely a series of symptoms of an impoverished, unnerved, incurably corrupted body." From the standpoint of normative Christianity, this seems fair enough as a characterization of much that has professed to represent Christianity. Wagner's *Parsifal* is a familiar and particularly morbid expression of this conception.

[6]For a perceptive essay on Nietzsche's relation to Christianity, see Karl Barth, *Church Dogmatics*, III:2 (Edinburgh, 1960), pp. 231-42.

[7]Margaret Knight, *Honest to Man* (London, 1974), pp. 41-42, 193, viii, 21, 196. The popular character of this work by no means reduces its value for our purposes.

[8]Quoted by John Mundy, *Europe in the High Middle Ages* (London, 1973), p. 323.

[9]*Calvin's New Testament Commentaries*, XI, tr. T. H. L. Parker (Grand Rapids, 1972), p. 183 (on Ephesians 4:14).

[10]Ephesians 4:13-16. I use the translation in *The New English Bible*. The precise authorship of this epistle is a matter of dispute, but there seems to be little doubt about its Pauline inspiration.

[11]*New Testament Commentaries*, XI, pp. 182-84. On Paul's metaphorical use of childhood, see Paul Ricoeur, *The Symbolism of Evil*, tr. Emerson Buchanan (Boston, 1969), p. 149.

[12]For biblical anthropology in general, see Hans Walter Wolff, *Anthropology of the Old Testament*, tr. Margaret Kohl (Philadelphia, 1974), esp. pp. 7-9. On Paul's anthropological terminology, so often misunderstood in historical Christianity, cf. Günther Bornkamm, *Paul*, tr. D. M. G. Stalker (London, 1971), p. 131.

[13]Cf. Augustine, *Confessions*, tr. R. S. Pine-Coffin (London, 1961), p. 224: "What, then, am I, my God? What is my nature? A life that is ever varying, full of change, and of immense power. . . . This is the great force of life in living man, mortal though he is." There is much of this attitude also in Pascal's *Pensées*, for example, no. 434: "What a chimera then is man! What a novelty! What a monster, what a chaos, what a contradiction, what a prodigy! Judge of all things, imbecile worm of the earth; depositary of truth, a sink of uncertainty and error; the pride and refuse of the universe!" Barth, *Church Dogmatics*, III:2, pp. 110-11, has this: "[Man's] existence is he himself, who in his very subjectivity, in his very indefinability, is seeking after the mystery of himself. . . ."

[14]The common notion of the "infinite elasticity of Christianity" (in Hegel's phrase) is somewhat misleading; this quality might, with approximately equal justice, be called the infinite elasticity of Hellenism.

[15]There is a useful survey of this idea in the early church in Barth, *Church Dogmatics*, III:2, pp. 152-53. I do not mean to suggest that creation *ex nihilo* is clear in the Genesis account; cf. E. A. Speiser, *Genesis* [The Anchor Bible] (Garden City, 1964), pp. 13-14. But Job 26:7 suggests it, and it is clearly spelled out in 2 Macc. 7:28.

[16]Cf. Reinhold Niebuhr, *The Nature and Destiny of Man* (New York, 1941), I, pp. 133-34.

[17]Cf. Barth, *Church Dogmatics*, III:2, pp. 350-51.

[18]Wolff, *Anthropology*, p. 162.

[19]Augustine appears to be struggling toward this conception in *De natura et gratia*, ch. 38: "I am of the opinion that the creature will never become equal with God, even when so perfect a holiness is accomplished within us as that it shall be quite incapable of receiving an addition. No, all who maintain that our progress is to be so complete that we shall be changed into the substance of God, and that we shall thus become what He is should look well to it how they build up their opinion; upon myself I must confess that it produces no conviction." But there is a tentativeness here that suggests the difficulty of the idea of man's creatureliness for the Hellenistic Christian.

[20]Niebuhr, I, p. 167, suggests that "sometimes the authority of this simple dictum . . . was all that prevented Christian faith from succumbing to dualistic and acosmic doctrines which pressed in upon the Christian church."

[21]Augustine's *Confessions* is, of course, a kind of extended essay on this theme; cf. his *On Christian Doctrine*, tr. D. W. Robertson, Jr. (Indianapolis, 1958), p. 64: ". . . the order of time, whose creator and administrator is God. . . ."

[22]Cf. Emil Brunner, "The Problem of Time," in *Creation: The Impact of an Idea*, ed. Daniel O'Connor and Francis Oakley (New York, 1969), p. 124.

[23]Cf. Augustine, *Confessions*, 222-23: "Who is to carry the research beyond this point? Who can understand the truth of the matter? O Lord, I am working hard in this field, and the field of my labors is my own self. I have become a problem to myself, like land which a farmer works only with difficulty and at the cost of much sweat. For I am not now investigating the tracts of the heavens, or measuring the distance of the stars, or trying to discover how the earth hangs in space. I am investigating myself, my memory, my mind." See also Rudolf Bultmann, *Primitive Christianity in its Contemporary Setting*, tr. R. H. Fuller (Cleveland, 1956), pp. 144-45.

[24]On this point, cf. Charles Norris Cochrane, *Christianity and Classical Culture* (New York, 1957), p. 456; Niebuhr, I, p. 69; Bultmann, p. 180; and Kierkegaard, *The Concept of Dread*, tr. Walter Lowrie (Princeton, 1957), p. 26: ". . . the essential characteristic of human existence, that man is an individual and as such is at once himself and the whole race, in such wise that the whole race has part in the individual, and the individual has part in the whole race."

[25]Eric Auerbach, *Mimesis*, tr. Willard Trask (Garden City, 1957), chs. 1-3, is especially perceptive on this characteristic of biblical, as opposed to classical, literature.

[26]Kierkegaard's conception of the stages on life's way may perhaps be taken as a reflection of this tendency in Christian thought; Kierkegaard's three stages do not simply replace each other, but the later stages absorb the earlier.

[27]Cochrane, pp. 386ff.; Peter Brown, *Augustine of Hippo: A Biography* (Berkeley, 1967), p. 173.

[28]As in Bultmann, p. 130.

[29]This seems to be implied in the *Divine Comedy*, in which the way to Paradise begins with the full moral experience of the Inferno.

[30]Cf. Brown, p. 177, on Augustine's understanding of conversion as a beginning. As Augustine remarks in *Christian Doctrine*, p. 13, the Christian life is "a journey or voyage home." The notion of life as movement was also important for Luther: "For it is not sufficient to have done something, and now to rest . . . this present life is a kind of movement and passage, or transition . . . a pilgrimage from this world into the world to come, which is eternal rest" (quoted by Gerhard Ebeling, *Luther: An Introduction to His Thought*, tr. R. A. Wilson [Philadelphia, 1970], pp. 161-62). Calvin devoted particular attention to this theme (*Institutes*, III, vi, p. 5): "But no one . . . has sufficient strength to press on with due eagerness, and weakness so weighs down the greater number that, with wavering and limping and even creeping along the ground, they move at a feeble rate. Let each one of us, then, proceed according to the measure of his puny capacity and set out upon the journey we have begun. No one shall set out so inauspiciously as not daily to make some headway, though it be slight. Therefore, let us not cease so to act that we may make some unceasing progress in the way of the Lord. And let us not despair at the slightness of our success; for even though attainment may not correspond to desire, when today outstrips yesterday the effort is

not lost. Only let us look toward our mark with sincere simplicity and aspire to our goal; not fondly flattering ourselves, nor excusing our own evil deeds, but with continuous effort striving toward this end: that we may surpass ourselves in goodness until we attain to goodness itself. It is this, indeed, which through the whole course of life we seek and follow. But we shall attain it only when we have cast off the weakness of the body, and are received into full fellowship with him" (Battles tr.). Bunyan's *Pilgrim's Progress* vividly dramatizes the conception.

[31]Ricoeur, pp. 272-74, is instructive on the conception of progress implicit in Paul's understanding of the transition from the law to the grace of Christ: "the fall is turned into growth and progress; the curse of paradise lost becomes a test and a medicine." Augustine interpreted his own life as a progression in understanding: "I am the sort of man who writes because he has made progress, and who makes progress—by writing" (quoted by Brown, 353). For Thomas à Kempis, the Christian life is marked by a concern "to conquer self, and by daily growing stronger than self, to advance in holiness" (*Imitation of Christ*, tr. Leo Sherley-Price [London, 1952], p. 31). For Luther, progress was a condition of all existence, for "progress is nothing other than constantly beginning. And to begin without progress is extinction. This is clearly the case with every movement and every act of every creature." Thus one must "constantly progress, and anyone who supposes he has already apprehended does not realize that he is only beginning. For we are always travelling, and must leave behind us what we know and possess, and seek for that which we do not yet know and possess" (quoted by Ebeling, pp. 161-62).

[32]Bultmann, esp. p. 184.

[33]This interpretation of the fall owes a good deal to Ricoeur. For the transition from anxiety to sin, see Niebuhr, I, pp. 168, 182-86.

[34]*The Secular City* (New York, 1965), p. 119.

[35]For a survey of Christian attitudes to culture, see H. Richard Niebuhr, *Christ and Culture* (New York, 1951).

[36]Ricoeur, pp. 58-59, 144-45, 321.

[37]Quoted by Gerhart B. Ladner, *The Idea of Reform: Its Impact on Christian Thought and Action in the Age of the Fathers* (Cambridge, Mass., 1959), p. 406.

[38]Ricoeur, p. 93.

[39]*The Epistle to the Romans*, tr. Edwyn C. Hoskyns (London, 1933), pp. 68, 87-88.

[40]Cf. Brown, p. 175.

[41]Quoted by Brown, p. 366.

[42]*Christian Doctrine*, p. 13.

[43]Cf. Paul Tillich, *The Eternal Now* (New York, 1956), p. 158.

[44]*Institutes*, II, vii, p. 10. Melanchthon was particularly subtle about human behavior that does not correspond to the impulses of the "heart"; the result is not, in fact, rationality, but, to follow Lionel Trilling's distinction, *both* insincerity *and* inauthenticity: "Therefore it can well happen that something is chosen which is entirely contrary to all affections. When this happens, insincerity takes over, as when, for example, someone treats graciously, amicably, and politely a person whom he hates and wishes ill to from the bottom of his heart, and he does this perhaps with no definite reason" (*Loci communes theologici*, tr. Lowell J. Satre, in *Melanchthon and Bucer*, ed. Wilhelm Pauck [London, 1969], p. 28).

[45]Quoted by Anders Nygren, *Agape and Eros*, tr. Philip S. Watson (New York, 1969), p. 454.

[46]On the virtues of a childlike spontaneity, cf. Horace Bushnell, *Christian Nurture* (New Haven, 1916; first ed., 1888), p. 5: "A child acts out his present feelings, the feelings of the moment, without qualification or disguise."

[47]Cf. Niebuhr, *Beyond Tragedy* (New York, 1937), pp. 143-48.

[48]*Journals and Papers*, tr. Howard V. and Edna H. Hong (Bloomington, 1967), I, p. 122, no. 272.

[49]Niebuhr, *Beyond Tragedy*, pp. 148-52. At the same time Augustine's portrayal of infancy in the *Confessions* should warn us, in its realism, that Christianity is not merely sentimental about childhood, in which it can also detect the flaws of maturity. But this is again to suggest their identity.

[50]Bushnell noted, p. 136, that the apostolic church included children and observed, pp. 139-40, that "just so children are all men and women; and, if there is any law of futurition in them to justify it, may be fitly classed as believing men and women."

[51]Cf. Bushnell, 10: ". . . since it is the distinction of Christian parents that they are themselves in the nurture of the Lord, since Christ and the Divine Love, communicated through him, are become the food of their life, what will they so naturally seek as to have their children partakers with them, heirs together with them, in the grace of life?"

[52]Barth emphasizes this, *Church Dogmatics*, III:4, p. 248. It is a significant feature of the Christian conception, indeed in a patriarchal society a revolutionary feature, that the Son, rather than the Father, is the model of adulthood. Lest this peculiarity seem to invite too simple an interpretation, however, the paradoxical unity of Father and Son in the Trinity must also be kept in mind.

[53]Cf. Tillich, *Eternal Now*, pp. 155-57.

[54]For Christianity and play, I have been stimulated by Lewis B. Smedes, "Theology and the Playful Life," in *God and the Good: Essays in Honor of Henry Stob*, ed. Clifton Orlebeke and Lewis B. Smedes (Grand Rapids, 1975), pp. 46-62. In view of common misunderstandings about the normative Christian attitude to sexuality, it is worth quoting Smedes—who certainly represents the normative position—on the playfulness of sex, p. 59: "The sexual component of our nature testifies that man was meant to find the most meaningful human communion in a playful relationship. In mutual trust and loving commitment, sexual activity is to be a playful festivity. It attests that human being is closest to fulfilling itself in a game. To be in God's image, then, includes being sexual, and sexuality is a profound call to play." Smedes also has useful comments on recent theologies of play.

[55]Bushnell, pp. 290-92.

[56]Cf. Augustine, *City of God*, XIX, v: "For how could the city of God . . . either take a beginning or be developed, or attain its proper destiny, if the life of the saints were not a social life?" Luther was emphatic: "We ought not to isolate ourselves but enter into companionship with our neighbor. Likewise it . . . is contrary to the life of Christ, who didn't choose solitude. Christ's life was very turbulent, for people were always moving about him. He was never alone, except when he prayed. Away with those who say, 'Be glad to be alone and your heart will be pure' " ("Table Talk," no. 1329).

[57]Cf. Barth, *Church Dogmatics*, III:2, pp. 222ff.

IRA M. LAPIDUS

Adulthood in Islam:
Religious Maturity in the Islamic Tradition

Introduction

ISLAM HAS A CONCEPTION OF ADULTHOOD. Though Muslim tradition is not self-consciously occupied with it, especially as opposed to childhood or youth, it does provide a
notion of what the fully matured person should be. A Muslim legal concept that is close
to our own sense of adulthood defines the *mukallaf*—the legally and morally responsible person—as one who has reached physical maturity, is of sound mind, may enter
into contracts, dispose of property, and be subject to criminal law. Above all, he is
responsible for the religious commands and obligations of Islam, for bearing the burden
(*taklif*) laid upon him by God.[1]

Islam, of course, is very diverse. What I have in mind when speaking of Islam is
the Sunni religious tradition, embodied in Muslim scripture—Koran, *hadith* (the
sayings of the Prophet), and law—and in Muslim commentary on scripture, theology,
and mysticism. I leave aside Shi'ite, gnostic, and philosophic versions of Islam, and I
also leave aside the common ideas of common people as they vary the world over. In
choosing this approach I have had to sacrifice consideration of diverse Islamic doctrines
and of particular Islamic beliefs and practices as the anthropologist might see them.
The scriptural tradition, however, especially the Sunni tradition, represents the fundamental beliefs of most Muslim peoples and has a profound influence on Muslim lives.

Moreover, this tradition in Islam seems closest to our own ideas of adulthood, for
Sunnis look for religious fulfillment in the same world of everyday reality which we
regard as the terrain of adulthood. Along with its teachings about God and the world to
come, Islam lays heavy stress on matters of this world and on the moral, ethical, and
psychological nature of man. In Islam a religious life is generally an active life, con-
sisting of everyday occupations in politics and business, of marriage and family, inter-
mixed with the practice of ritual and other religious obligations. To be a good Muslim
means to live properly within the religious and moral law and in accord with the traditions of Muslim societies. Islam also teaches that the fulfillment of social, moral, and
ritual obligations of the Muslim requires a certain quality of soul. An active worldly
Muslim life has to be based on certain inner qualities, particularly belief in, or commitment to, God and the Muslim tradition, and other ethical virtues and psychological
strengths. The integration of outward deeds and inner states defines Muslim religious

97

maturity, though it is not a recipe for maturity. Islamic religious culture recognizes a great variety of life qualities and accomplishments as expressions of the Islamic ideal. It also recognizes the incompleteness of every human being.

The Scripture and Guidance

The best place to begin our account of Muslim conceptions of religious maturity is with the scripture itself, which is God's revelation of the "guidance" for Muslims. The Koran opens with a prayer for guidance:

> In the Name of God, the Compassionate, the Merciful
> PRAISE be to God, Lord of the worlds!
> The compassionate, the merciful!
> King on the day of reckoning!
> Thee only do we worship, and to Thee do we cry for help.
> Guide Thou us on the straight path,
> The path of those to whom Thou hast been gracious:—with
> whom thou art not angry, and who go not astray.[2]

The scripture teaches what men should believe about God, nature, and sacred history; it gives precise rules in great detail about what men should do and not do in religious ritual and in relation to their fellow men. It also presents images of moral qualities and images of the spirit which should infuse ritual, social, and legal obligations.

The ritual and legal rules of the Koran law and *hadith* are often very specific, but the crucial aspect of the guidance does not lie in the specific injunctions. Beyond precise specification is the moral spirit in which a man lives. The Koran leaves each man to judge what constitutes proper fulfillment of God's command. For example, the Koran's law about night vigils is not a rule but a permission—a permission to adapt the injunction to pray to individual circumstances.

> Thy Lord knoweth that thou prayest almost two-thirds, or half, or a third of the night, as do a part of the followers. But God measureth the night and the day:—He knoweth that ye cannot count its hours aright, and therefore, turneth to you mercifully. Recite then so much of the Koran as may be easy to you. He knoweth that there will be some among you sick, while others travel through the earth in quest of the bounties of God; and others do battle in his cause. Recite therefore so much of it as may be easy . . . .[3]

Another example is more important to us. The law of marriage and the scriptural idea of women illustrate how Muslim religious doctrines are tied to those everyday human concerns that are central to the Muslim, to our own, and, perhaps, to any, conception of adulthood. First, the Koran defines the legal boundaries for valid marriages:

> Forbidden to you are your mothers, and your daughters, and your sisters, and your aunts, both on the father and mother's side, and your nieces on the brother and sister's side, and your foster-mothers, and your foster-sisters, and the mothers of your wives, and your step-daughters who are your wards. Forbidden to you also are married women except those who are in your hands as slaves: This is the law of God for you.

Then the Koran adds a moral concern which extends beyond the rules:

> And it is allowed you, besides this, to seek wives by means of your wealth, with modest conduct, but without fornication . . . .

And then, the open-ended permission; within the cadre of the law there is the actual living of the marriage, built on agreement between husband and wife:

> This is the law. But it shall be no crime in you to make agreements over and above the law. Verily, God is Knowing, Wise![4]

The *hadiths*, the sayings of the Prophet Muhammad, go beyond the Koran and give emotional attitudes as well as legal rules. *Hadiths* accept sexuality as natural and desirable, are opposed to celibacy, and favor marriage. *Hadiths* do not renounce the animal side of man but rather integrate it into a religious life. Marriage not only channels sexuality; marriage is held to have exceptional religious and spiritual value:

> When a man marries he has fulfilled half of the religion; so let him fear God regarding the remaining half.

The prophet says further: "You have seen nothing like a marriage for increasing the love of two people."

This is a moving phrase, but it may not mean the same thing to Muslims as it means to us. In the *hadiths* a husband's love is protective and indulgent.

> Ayisha said: "I swear by God that I have seen the Prophet standing at the door of my room when the Abyssinians were playing with spears in the mosque and God's messenger was covering me with his cloak in order that I might look over his shoulder at their sport. He would then stand for my sake till I was the one who departed; so estimate the time a young girl eager for amusement would wait."

A wife's love is obedient. The best wife is the

> . . . one who pleases [her husband] when he looks at her, obeys him when he gives a command, and does not go against his wishes regarding her person or property by doing anything of which he disapproves.

The marriage depicted in these quotations is unequal. It assumes a benevolent superiority of the husband over a dependent, childlike, and submissive wife. As we might guess, a relationship of this kind is filled with ambiguity. Indeed, the attitude toward women presented in the *hadiths* is hostile as well as adoring. The Prophet says: "The whole world is to be enjoyed, but the best thing in the world is a good woman." But the Prophet also says: "I have not left behind me a trial more injurious to men than women." And further:

> I had a look into paradise and I saw the poor made up most of its inhabitants, and I had a look into hell and saw that most of its inhabitants were women.[5]

The apparent contradictions in the emotional attitudes expressed in the *hadiths* are not accidental, for the scripture means not only to give legal rules and moral standards, but also to foster inner growth through emotional awareness. The contradictions hold a mirror to reality—a mirror of the confusion which is naturally found in the hearts of believers. Useful guidance does not consist in upholding a static ideal, but in provoking awareness of the contradictory truths of the heart, an awareness which may engender emotional or religious growth and may help develop the emotional capacities which underlie ritually and ethically correct behavior. Thus, to fulfill the scriptures implies living within legal norms, in accord with moral standards, and dealing with the truths of the heart which underlie legally, ritually, and morally correct behavior. The Muslim reads scripture not just for the final word, for the once-given revelation, but as a living dialogue with himself which gives birth to ever renewed self-awareness.

> When a man reads the Koran again and again, even such a short Surah as the "Surah of the Opening," new meanings occur to him during this process, which have never occurred to his mind before. And this new awareness often causes the man to feel as though the Surah were being revealed for the first time at that very moment. He believes in these [new] meanings, and both his "knowledge" and "work" increase. Those who read the Koran carelessly do not experience this, but anyone who reads it with any attentiveness has experiences of this kind.[6]

The tension in the Muslim scriptures between specific injunctions and open inspiration is high. However, where specific rules do not apply the Koran gives further guidance in the form of images of the kind of person who makes a good Muslim. The good Muslim is a *halim*—a man who preserves self-control and patience in the face of the passions which arise within him.

> Prosperous are the believers
> who in their prayers are humble
> and from idle talk turn away
> and at almsgiving are active
> and guard their private parts save
> from their wives . . .
> and who preserve their trusts and their convenant
> and who observe their prayers. Those are the inheritors
> who shall inherit Paradise
> therein dwelling forever.[7]

He subordinates passion and impulse to reasonable and ethical self-restraint. He faces life's trials with patient endurance and fortitude (*sabr*). Patience and restraint are grounded in self-knowledge, especially in wisdom about the limits of man's powers and his humble place in the world. They are also grounded in faith and awe of God whose power the Muslim knows and to whom he is grateful for the gift of life. Insight into the reality of God and man is the basis of ethical dispositions and appropriate worldly behavior.

By contrast, the *jahil*—the unbeliever—is self-assertive, arrogant, and rash. He shows a touchy pride in himself and contempt for others. Lacking inner controls, he is swayed by passion and anger. The *jahil* is driven by the need to prove his power, his self-sufficiency, and his worthiness because he cannot bear to recognize his true weakness and helplessness before God. For lack of insight into God's being and his own, the *jahil* lacks an inner sense of direction and is impulsive and unreliable in his daily life.[8]

The *halim*, then, is the person at peace with himself and his limitations, dedicated to God's command, who has the capacity to act in a purposive but humble way with sensitivity and ethical restraint. The scriptural image of the *halim* is central to the whole of the Muslim tradition. The *halim* is the wise man whose wisdom governs the living of everyday life. He is the ideal Muslim—the Muslim who possesses a wholeness of being in which knowledge, virtue, and action have been wholly integrated.

Later Muslim tradition defines this integrity in terms of faith. The concept of faith expresses the harmony of inner faculties and outer actions, which is the ideal of Islam. Faith turns a man from ignorance to knowledge of the truth, from passion to virtue, and from evil to good deeds. Thus, Muslim faith, called *iman*, is different from faith in our sense of the word. *Iman* means knowing the truth and believing in it, but then it expands in meaning until it issues as something for which we have no single word in English—the very whole and the wholeness of a man's existence grounded in belief in God.

In the Muslim view, faith begins in the intellect, knowing that God exists, knowing of His attributes, His prophets, His will—and accepting this knowledge as the truth (*tasdiq*). Faith is not just a matter of knowing, the way we know that Muslims believe in God and Muhammad, but knowing this to be reality, the way we know each other's presence. *Tasdiq* is an attitude of believing, of accepting, a conviction about what has been preached, recorded, and told, an experience of what is known in a way that binds the heart and becomes the basis of a commitment to live one's life in accord with that reality.

Muslim authors stress that *iman* is an emotion in the heart as well as a thought in the mind. It is a state of devotion; it entails trust in and submission to God, fear and love of God, and above all love of what God wants men to do and hatred for what he has forbidden.

> The word *iman* originally means in Arabic *tasdiq*. But God in his revelation has used it in such a way that it means the whole of the acts of obedience and the avoidance of the acts of disobedience.

True faith blends into true *Islam*; total inner assent merges into total submission in all that a man feels and says and does. The believer surrenders his own willfulness and his point of view and accepts God's revelation and commands; he abandons the obstinate resistance in himself—that pride, haughtiness, confidence in himself alone which is the basis of deeds not of God's choosing—to submit the heart and the will and the actions of the limbs completely to God's commands and God's wishes. The heart tamed, other values excluded, *iman* issues in devoted worship, in every deed of everyday life carried out as an expression of God's will. Here, the feeling in the heart becomes a living confirmation of the theological doctrine of man's passivity in the world that God has created. By faith the believer recreates the reality of the universe in his own heart. He becomes the person who lives in accord with the most fundamental truths. He has become an epiphany of the text and the teachings.

Muslim faith is not a static quality, but something which grows. In every faith there is a measure of doubt; every *iman* is tainted by hypocrisy (*nifaq*), by a whisper of Satan, until the white spot of faith eventually excludes the shadow of doubt. Muslim thinkers define the several stages by which faith grows from knowledge of the truth to that absolute certainty and firmness of conviction, to that ever present knowledge of what God has commanded, which marks the highest degree of faith.

For some the process is a dialectical one. On the one hand, faith is the passive opening of the heart to the truth of God's will. To be a Muslim at all, one must believe. Belief may rise spontaneously in the heart. *Iman*, says al-Ghazali,

> . . . is a kind of illuminating "light" [*nûr*] which God Himself throws into the hearts of his servants as a free and gracious gift. Sometimes it comes in the form of a firm and irresistible conviction welling up from the innermost soul, which is completely ineffable.[9]

On the other hand, also according to al-Ghazali, it is a quality which grows in the heart as a result of worship and of good deeds. Passive self-surrender and submission of will can only be reached by acts of obedience and by the disciplined practice of Islam. Just as the active fulfillment of Islamic teachings is rooted in passive surrender of the self to God's will, the inner faith is built up by a lifetime's devotion to the practice of Islam. Worship and the exercise of good deeds increase the confidence of the believer and his subjective conviction in the reality of Islam. Faith grows by the interaction between passive surrender and active mastery of the self.

Faith, then, and the process by which it grows, is a metaphor of the development of the whole of man's life. It is more than belief, it is a man's personality, his knowledge of reality blossomed into insight, suffusing his emotional existence, and expressed in every word and gesture. Muslim lives turn about the quest for this integrity; Muslim writers ponder its implications.

Two Lives

Al-Ghazali: The teachings and example of Abu Hamid Muhammad al-Ghazali, born in 1058, died in 1111, scholar and saint, are accepted by Sunni Muslims as a revitalization of the true faith. Al-Ghazali studied law and theology in Tus and Nishapur. At the age of thirty-three he was appointed professor in the Nizamiyya school of Baghdad, one of the most prestigious positions of the time. He wrote treatises on law and theology, mastered philosophy and esoteric subjects, gave authoritative legal decisions, and lectured to hundreds of students. He was widely regarded as living an exemplary Muslim life. Yet he was beset by doubts. ". . . as I drew near the age of adolescence the bonds of mere authority (*taqlid*) ceased to hold me and inherited beliefs lost their grip upon me." At the time of his greatest success, his doubts flowed into a deep sense of unworthiness.

> I considered the circumstances of my life, and realized that I was caught in a veritable thicket of attachments. I also considered my activities, of which the best was my teaching and lecturing, and realized that in them I was dealing with sciences that were unimportant and contributed nothing to the attainment of eternal life.
>
> After that I examined my motive in my work of teaching, and realized that it was not a pure desire for the things of God, but that the impulse moving me was the desire for an influential position and public recognition.

Al-Ghazali yearned to give up this false life, to sever the attachment to worldly things, leaving "wealth and position and fleeing from all-consuming entanglements." But he could not do it. The conflict absorbed his energies.

> One day I would form the resolution to quit Baghdad and get rid of these adverse circumstances; the next day I would abandon my resolution. I put one foot forward and drew the other back. If in the morning I had a genuine longing to seek eternal life, by the evening the attack of a whole host of desires had reduced it to impotence.

One voice cried, "To the road! To the road!" The other, "This is a passing mood . . . do not yield to it, for it will quickly disappear." It did not.

> For nearly six months beginning with Rajab 488 A.H. [= July, A.D. 1095], I was continuously tossed about between the attraction of worldly desires and the impulses towards eternal life. In that month the matter ceased to be one of choice and became one of compulsion. God caused my tongue to dry up so that I was prevented from lecturing. One particular day I would make an effort to lecture in order to gratify the hearts of my following, but my tongue would not utter a single word nor could I accomplish anything at all.
>
> This impediment in my speech produced grief in my heart, and at the same time my power to digest and assimilate food and drink was impaired; I could hardly swallow or digest a single mouthful of food.

Al-Ghazali had come to an emotional crisis. His doctors said wisely but helplessly:

> This trouble arises from the heart and from there it has spread through the constitution; the only method of treatment is that the anxiety which has come over the heart should be allayed.

His decision was made. Al-Ghazali took up the life of a wandering Sufi. In the years that followed he was initiated into the mysteries of Sufism; he composed his masterpiece, *The Revival of the Religious Sciences*, and he taught privately. In the end, however, Al-Ghazali returned to a public position, a professorship at Nishapur. He had resolved the doubt in his heart; he had come to certain knowledge of the truth of God's existence and of the nature of his obligations to Him. He saw his return as a return to his old work in a new way.

> In myself I know that, even if I went back to the work of disseminating knowledge, yet I did not go back. To go back is to return to the previous state of things. Previously, however, I had been disseminating the knowledge by which worldly success is attained; by word and deed I had called men to it; and that had been my aim and intention. But now I am calling men to the knowledge whereby worldly success is given up and its low position in the scale of real worth is recognized.

Al-Ghazali did not renounce the world; what he did was abandon false goals in worldly activity.

Sufism brought al-Ghazali to certain knowledge of God and certain knowledge brought him back to Muslim beliefs, prayer, and teaching, to the Given Way of scripture and tradition. For a Muslim, maturity entailed a return to, and a fulfillment of, the fundamentals of the religion. His master of theology, al-Juwayni, had already said:

> I had read thousands of books; then I left the people of Islam with their religion and their manifest sciences in these books, and I embarked on the open sea, plunging into the literature the people of Islam rejected. All this was in quest of the truth. At an early age, I fled from the acceptance of other's opinions [taqlid]. But now I have returned from everything to the word of truth.
> "Hold to the religion of the old women."[10]

Ibn Khaldun: A politician and scholar, born in 1332, died in 1406, Ibn Khaldun is known primarily for the *Muqaddima*, the Introduction to his universal history. This is a learned, almost encyclopedic, commentary on Muslim history, society, and culture, contained in a framework that attempts to account for the origins and evolution of human culture in general. The author, a native of Tunis, of a distinguished family of politicians and scholars, was schooled to follow in the path of his ancestors in Muslim religious studies and in philosophic literatures. His education, however, was relatively unusual in that it stressed philosophic knowledge rather than minor literary accomplishments, and in that it contained more than the usual smattering of lessons in preparation for a scribal career. Ibn Khaldun was one of those rare scribes who was a genuinely accomplished scholar. In this respect his education was only too ideal, for implicit in it were conflicts between religious and secular learning, between the scholar's vocation and the scribe's functions. Ibn Khaldun's career unfolded in inner conflict and outward uncertainty about his ambitions and the proper course of his life.

His early career was spent as a client, scholar, scribe, and administrator at the courts of various North African and Spanish princes. He made his way from humble apprenticeships to the post of *hajib* or head of government at Bougie. At the same time he kept alive his scholarly interests, wrote treatises on logic, philosophy, and jurisprudence, and studied and taught religious law. When he was thirty-five years old, circumstances shattered his career. A new phase of his life began in which he reacted strongly against public life and yearned to devote himself to research and teaching. But for another decade he oscillated between political ambitions, obligations, and involvements and devotion to research, teaching, and worship. Finally in 1375, pressed by exhaustion of his political prospects, by insecurity, by ennui with the world of affairs, by yearning for devotional and scholarly fulfillment, he retired from public life and took up a four-year-long retreat, during which he conceived his theories of history and politics and culture, and wrote the *Muqaddima* and a history of the Berbers.

The issues involved in the oscillations between politics and religion in Ibn Khaldun's early career and the significance of his retirement into scholarship are rooted in the tradition in which he was raised. From early Islamic times the scribe was conceived to be the servant of a ruler, helping the ruler make good decisions, guiding him to right actions, and executing his will. To fulfill these duties, the scribe had to have a sound secular education which was the basis of his knowledge of worldly affairs, of men and politics, and he had to have a sound religious education, because to cope gracefully with the realities of public life required deep moral and religious virtues such as loyalty, generosity, self-control, and cooperativeness. Religion nourished the virtues that led to success in worldly affairs. To fulfill his role as courtier and administrator, the Muslim scribe had to be a person in whom religion, morality, education, and politics, in whom knowledge, virtue, and the right use of power were conjoined. As in the religious tradition generally, the ideal was to integrate worldly activity with inner virtue. Ibn Khaldun's career illustrates how elusive this integration could be, for the ideal of the scribe required a blend of elements which were in constant tension. Religious devotion, moral character, scholarly erudition, and political efficiency are not easily cultivated in the same person.

In turning from the activities of the scribe to reflections about history, Ibn Khaldun kept alive the tensions implicit in his education and early career. Muslims thought of history as a didactic subject comprising a record of persons and events that were of political or religious concern. In his Introduction, however, Ibn Khaldun attempted to devise a philosophic foundation for the study of history which merged discrete instances into a general framework of understanding. History remained didactic, but now the experience as a whole, rather than the anecdotal example, was to be instructive. His theories turned on the rise and fall of empires, but his essential concern was how changes in the conditions of life affected the possibilities for individual moral and religious fulfillment. Ibn Khaldun's theory of history was a theory of the relationships between secular and religious life at the level of historical experience; it also served as a didactic, orienting experience at a juncture in his personal development.

After four years of retirement and absorption in historical studies, Ibn Khaldun returned to public life and, in 1382, left North Africa for Egypt to begin a new career as a professor of law and *qadi*—a judge who administers the religious law for the members of the Muslim community. The choice of a new career and a new homeland marked both a significant break with the past and a profound continuity. In the Muslim tradition, the judge or *qadi* was the very embodiment of the Muslim religious law. A student of law, the judge applied religious law to daily life and upheld Muslim religious norms. At the same time, the post of chief judge, which Ibn Khaldun occupied in

Egypt, was a political position. Appointed by the Sultan, often a client of the ruler or of other powerful officials, a judge was expected to be loyal to the government in political matters. Thus, the position of the *qadi*, though in principle a religious post, embodied the characteristic Islamic tension between this-worldly and other-worldly purposes. In the deepest traditions of Islamic religious thought, in cultural values and role definitions, in personal experience, in mundane daily activity, religious and personal fulfillment turned on the reconciliation of the secular and the religious, or worldliness and pious retirement, on the harmony of inner spirit and outer deed.

The lives of al-Ghazali and Ibn Khaldun are obviously very different, but they both illustrate some of the parameters in which Muslim lives develop. For all their differences both are active worldly lives in which piety and learning are at the service of society. Al-Ghazali was a teacher, a lawyer, and a religious adviser to princes; Ibn Khaldun was a politician, administrator, and judge as well as a scholar. Both men accepted the given world; they did not attempt to transcend or to revolutionize the society in which they lived. Their basic assumption was that personal fulfillment lay within their tradition.

To find that implicit fulfillment, each man had to go through a profound crisis, a kind of conversion: not a turning to a new life, as it would be in a Christian context, but a struggle fully to realize the values implicit in the old life. In the Muslim context the crisis of conversion was part of the process of personal maturation in relation to a society and cultural values which were accepted as beyond question.

In this world, the task of living was to bring together the ways of the world and the values of the heart. Al-Ghazali at the acme of success discovered that he was a hypocrite. He doubted the truth of his teaching, and he pursued his career for the sake of fame and prestige rather than for the love of God and the love of learning. To fulfill his life he had in some way to bring into harmony what he knew, what he felt, and what he did. His quest for God was the quest for that kind of knowledge which would bring his inner and outer existence into harmony with the truth, and with each other. Ibn Khaldun similarly had to integrate his inner and his outer experience and reconcile piety and learning with a public life. He struggled, in each phase of his life, for some resolution to the nagging polarity in his experience, and he reached out for that elusive wholeness of being which comes from harmony within the self and harmony with the world.

Confidence and Humility

While men struggle with these problems, Muslim religious writings discuss the spiritual and psychological issues involved in the development of an integrated adult personality. There is no systematic discussion of the problems of religious maturation, but several themes are held to be important to personal and religious development.

One crucial theme is the balance between confidence and humility. Muslims know how heavy God's burden is, how difficult to follow properly the ritual and social life enjoined in the scriptures, how difficult to develop a genuine personal commitment to these obligations, and how persistent the doubt in the midst of faith. Our brief biographies illustrate how complex and sensitive men may bend or even break over the intricacies of cultural values and real situations. Muslims ponder: Can this be done? How much can a man expect to achieve? What are his strengths and his limitations? How much is in his own control and how much is he dependent upon God's mercy and grace? Is he responsible for his successes and failures?

The theologians who debate these issues hold two basic positions about man's ability to fulfill the burden of adulthood. On the one hand, they hold man to be essentially helpless. This is at once a theological position, a perception of reality, and a feeling of despair. As a theological position, a deep strain in Muslim religious feeling exalts God absolutely, conceives no qualifications on his Majesty, and holds that God by His power, His will, His foreknowledge and His other attributes determines all matters, great and small. No man has any true autonomy or capacity for choice and action of his own. This is a predestinarian doctrine. A *hadith* says: "The pens have been lifted and the pages are dry." As a realistic perception, Muslims are sensitive to the fact that man does not control his destiny. They have in mind that fortunes change, the rich may become poor, the healthy, sick; all men die. As a mood, the sense of helplessness is expressed in fatalism and resignation.

On the other hand, the theologians also hold to a measure of human strength and responsibility. Some hold that God is the ultimate author of man's existence, the creator of all his thoughts and acts, but in some sense man "acquires" these acts; they become his. Man does not create the fundamental energy or reality of his life, but he is a passive participant in his own existence. He has become responsible.

Other theologians assume a different balance between fate and freedom or rather between an attitude of passive acceptance of fate and an attitude of active relatedness and responsibility. For example, al-Shahrastani recognized freedom of will within the individual, but the power of executing the will, he held, derives from God. Every man, al-Shahrastani argued, is aware of his need for God's help and knows that nothing is created or brought into existence without Him. God has given man the capacity to choose alternatives, but not the resources to be fully independent or self-determining. Al-Nasifi, however, was not so pessimistic about man's powers in the external world. He held that believers may be confident that their own serious endeavor induces God's help. God allies himself with man's purposes for either good or evil, complementing man's limited power with His unbounded might. Without asserting a brash confidence in man's powers to govern the world, al-Nasifi had implicit confidence that man could shape reality by his choices—with God's collaboration and assistance. Man could realize his inner freedom and see the outside reality as responding and relating to his choices. With all man's actual limitations he is fully responsible.[11]

Finally, there are the theologians who have complete confidence in man's free will, his ability to choose belief as against unbelief, to choose good as opposed to evil, and who believe in his capacity to carry out his choices in daily life. These theologians have implicitly ignored God's omnipotence; they accord man a complete freedom and responsibility in his realm.

Muslim theologians have never resolved these differences nor defined a Muslim orthodoxy. Islam is a religion without an authoritative church hierarchy, and Muslims accept a wide range of opinions as valid expressions of Islam. The debate does not lead to a logical resolution, to a formula which defines man and his nature; it leads rather to a collective understanding of what are the central issues in man's spirituality and to a confrontation of several possible positions. This debate deepens the Muslim's awareness of two truths which do not displace each other. A Muslim knows that he is helpless before his own overwhelming and baffling inner life and helpless to remake the world which is beyond him. But he also knows that he is endowed with resolute capacities to shape, in some degree, both his inner life and the outer world. Neither position displaces the other; rather they must be pitted against each other. Each individual must weigh them against each other to form a point of view about the boundaries of his own abilities and strengths, the measure of his confidence in his own potentialities, the degree of his responsibilities, and the extent of his courage to sustain his convictions and commitments. An inner balance between confidence and humility, an acceptance of responsibility, and a recognition of fundamental human limitations generate the poise and restraint needed to forge and to sustain a coherent "adult" way of living in consonance with, and in creative relation to, the values and the customs of Muslim culture and society. In this view, a man must balance the tides of helplessness, worthlessness, and inadequacy with his experience of confidence and capacity to form and realize religious and moral purposes and to measure his true responsibilities so that he may without false enthusiasms or false despair proceed with the life that scripture, society, and his own convictions require of a Muslim adult.

Activity and Passivity

Following the emphasis on human capacities and responsibility, Muslim religious writers give strong emphasis to the importance of self-discipline and striving to do the good. To perfect the performance of religious rituals, to behave in an ethically correct way, to live as a good Muslim require endless attention and discipline. Al-Ghazali admonishes:

> You will never arrive at fulfilling the commands of God, my dear student, unless you watch over your heart and your members every single movement from morning to night. God most high is aware of your secret being; He observes your inner and your outer man. . . .
> Let your endeavour be that your master may not see you where he forbade you to be and may not miss you where he commanded you to be. You will not manage to do this, however, unless you plan out your time and order your activities from morning to evening. From the moment you wake from sleep until the time when you return to your bed be diligent in performing the commands God most high lays upon you.[12]

Only by lifelong training and perseverance can a soul be tutored, directed, and organized to live in a correct way.

Ethical writers give similarly stern suggestions. Children should be held to praiseworthy deeds, by force if necessary, for the acts themselves impose on the soul and set the pattern of later behavior. One should always seek good companions, for they set the example. A true friend and mentor who will not hesitate to expose one's shortcomings can be helpful. But most important is self-discipline. Each man is responsible for overcoming the defects of nature and his childhood. "He must strive by degrees to wean his soul of bad customs and unpraiseworthy habits, not despairing of the difficulty of the way. . . ." The soul must be held strictly to account; any departure from right ways must be punished lest it recur; not a single infringement or oversight is allowable. A man

> . . . must keep before him a minute regard to all manners of motions and rests, words and actions, regulations and dispositions, in order that nothing contrary to the intelligent will may proceed from him. . . .
>
> . . . At the conclusion of each day, he should carry out an examination of every action performed during that day, thoroughly and without overlooking any single one. . . .[13]

Muslim writers are equally aware that, however rigorous, striving for self-control does not fully avail. They also know man's limitations and dependence upon God's help for his success. Following this point of view, they stress a passive way to religious fulfillment—the way of renunciation of worldly values, submission of one's own will to God's will, faith, and trust in God. As an illustration of this passive way, I shall take al-Ghazali's discussion of *tawakkul*—abandonment of self or trust in God.

In the *Revivification of the Religious Sciences*, al-Ghazali explains that trust in God means to leave everything to God and to have no will, initiative, or activity of one's own. There are three levels of this extraordinary state. One is akin to the trust of a man in the attorney who represents his interests. The man turns over his affairs to the management of another in whose honesty, energy, and ability he has confidence. This delegation, however, is limited to a particular case, and the subject does not surrender his awareness of what is going on, his judgment, or his ultimate right to make choices. This modest degree of trust may continue indefinitely.

The second degree of trust is akin to the dependence and confidence of a very small child in his mother. The infant cannot take care of himself; he knows only his mother, seeks refuge with her, and depends on her support. The infant has no capacity for initiative of his own, but he can cry, call for his mother, run after her, and tug her dress. At any distress, his first thought is of his mother; he has complete confidence that she will meet his needs. This is like the man who trusts entirely to God and has complete confidence that he will be nourished by the Almighty to whom he addresses his prayers and petitions. This state of passivity may last a day or two, like a fever, before it passes and the mystic is returned to an everyday condition.

The third state is to be in the hands of God as a corpse in the hands of the washer. The mystic sees himself as dead, moved by God, certain that he does not move, or will, or know, save by God's decree. In this state, the mystic trusts completely that he will be sustained. He does not call out like a child nor pray like an adult. This third state, al-Ghazali says, lasts no longer than the pallor produced by fear.[14]

These images convey the state of being that al-Ghazali has in mind. The trust of the child in his mother is a man's trust in his basic security, his confidence that his being will be sustained. The trust of the corpse in the washer, that passivity that can only be communicated by images of death, whose interval is the moment of fear, lies beyond the infant's trust. To know it, one passes through the helplessness of infancy, through the fear of death, through the terror of nonexistence. This trust is known by the abandonment of one's own efforts and resources, by the testing of one's capacity to endure a total surrender of one's own life to the very ground of all life. To know this trust is to know that one's existence is assured without striving, effort, or will of one's own. It is assured as such.

Renunciation of the will, of the self, abandonment to God, and trust in God do not represent detachment in a physical sense from the ongoing life of the world, but moments that come to pass and return as part of the flow of man's psychic reality. These moments of passive grounding in trust become the basis of an active Muslim life and of the active virtues that pervade the scriptural and traditional imagery.

The Muslim who trusts in God has the full measure of his own capacities and limitations; he knows the boundaries of his autonomy and his abiding dependence. Knowing this he is able to accept God's will. He no longer clings to worldly things as if he could not live without them. He no longer has need for the defenses, the false strivings, and the false values that men pursue and that the Koran denounces as the pagan quality of the *jahil*. He who makes this test of his fundamental security has no need to control the world or to manipulate men to meet his presumed wants. Rather, refreshed by inner peace, he is able to devote himself to his religious purposes. Trust in God becomes the basis of active striving to fulfill His command. The passive way and the active way are understood to be equally important to a Muslim adulthood.

Conclusion

Human potentialities are endlessly diverse. Muslim culture has its own vision of a fulfilled human life, stressing some possibilities and neglecting others. In the Muslim view religious maturity is the integration of the individual with the norms of his religion and culture. It is a personal reconciliation to the reality of the world and of man's place in it as God has willed it to be. It is inner peace expressed and achieved through living in the world in accord with the revealed reality.

In other world cultures, the balance between the individual and society is differently conceived. In the Confucian tradition, as in Islam, personal cultivation requires responsible social relationships and the fulfillment of the ritual norms of Confucian culture. Professor Tu, however, stresses—as Muslim authors would not—the importance of the individual's inner sense of direction and the uniqueness of each manifestation of adulthood. Muslim authors were not so much concerned with the ineffable qualities of individual experience as with ethical and ritual obligations, the essential modes of individual self-expression. Moreover, while Muslim writers would agree with the Japanese view that concentration upon a particular way of living is essential to self-cultivation, they would take the whole of a man's living, in the family, in society, and in his profession, the whole of his daily existence, rather than his specific occupation or profession, to be the terrain of religious realization. With these variations, in Islam as in Chinese and Japanese societies, adulthood is realized in terms of a concrete, culturally defined, worldly way of living.

In Christianity spiritual maturation transcends any given social situation or set of cultural values. Adulthood is realized by an individual in relation to God. Christianity has refused to be committed to any particular culture; conversion to Christianity implies a turning away from specific social and cultural commitments as ultimate values in order to follow Christ. Muslims would agree that only God is absolute and that nothing in this world may be held equal to Him, but Muslim society is nonetheless the temple of Muslim religious life.

In different world cultures the nature of the life process itself is differently conceived. Islamic adulthood is presented in scripture and in the traditional religious literatures in terms of an ideal inner harmony and harmony between the individual and the world. This goal, however, is not a static ideal, rigidly applied, nor is it exclusive of valid human possibilities in Islam. Muslims are well aware that the struggle to approximate the ideal makes up the course of spiritual development. The ideal may never be attained, but it defines the direction in which a Muslim life proceeds.

In this respect Islam seems to differ markedly from the other world religions. It differs from Confucianism in that it pays little attention to the rhythms and the sequence of development or to the characteristic difficulties of each stage of life. Though Muslim mystics analyze the successive psychological and spiritual phases of their ascent, there is little emphasis on the stages of a temporal life cycle. Also in Confucianism and normative Christianity, the way, the wayfarer, being "on the way" are more important than the end to be realized. Muslim adulthood, bound to a specific cultural universe, must hold in mind both the open road and the final resting.

Yet for all these differences, there are common realizations about man's humanity, religious fulfillment, and becoming an adult. One is this: In Islam and Christianity spiritual self-realization is engaged through faith. By faith, as Professor Bouwsma explains, man is relieved of false maturity and of the anxiety of self-sufficiency to face the inadequacy of all that is merely human. So, too, in Islam trust in God and humility open the way to the inward healing and outward responsibility which is "on the way" to adulthood.

REFERENCES

[1]R Brunschviq, "Théorie générale de la capacité chez les Hanafites médiévaux," *Revue Internationale des Droits de l'Antiquité*, I (1949), 157-72. Joseph Schacht, *Introduction to Islamic Law* (Oxford, 1964), *passim*.

[2]Koran, Sura 1.

[3]Koran, Sura 73/20.

[4]Koran, Sura 4/27-28.

[5]J. Robson, tr., *Mishkat al-Masabih* (Lahore, 1963), II, 658, 660, 689, 694, and A. Jeffrey, *Reader on Islam* (The Hague, 1962), p. 83.

[6]Ibn Taymiyya, quoted in T. Izutsu, *The Concept of Belief in Islamic Theology* (Tokyo, 1965), p. 189.

[7]Koran, Sura 23/1-11.

[8]T. Izutsu, *God and Man in the Koran* (Tokyo, 1964), pp. 198-211, and *Ethico-Religious Concepts in the Koran* (Montreal, 1966). I. Goldziher, *Muslim Studies*, S. M. Stern, ed. (London, 1967), I, 201-08.

[9]Izutsu, *The Concept of Belief, passim*; quotes pp. 69, 136.

[10]W. M. Watt, *The Faith and Practice of al-Ghazali* (London, 1953), pp. 21-22, 54-58, 74-77, 91, 151-52, and *A Muslim Intellectual: A Study of al-Ghazali* (Edinburgh, 1963), pp. 23-24.

[11]A. Guillaume, *The Summa Philosophiae of al-Shahrastani* (Oxford, 1934), pp. 30-38, and al-Nasifi, "Bahr al-Kalam," in A. Jeffrey, *Reader on Islam*, pp. 375ff.

[12]Watt, *The Faith and Practice of al-Ghazali*, p. 91.

[13]Nasir ad-Din Tusi, *The Nasirean Ethics*, tr. G. M. Wickens (London, 1964), pp. 111, 119, 121-22.

[14]G. Anawati and L. Gardet, *Mystique Musulmane* (Paris, 1964), pp. 154-59.

TU WEI-MING

The Confucian Perception of Adulthood

ACCORDING TO THE CONFUCIAN *Book of Rites*, the "capping ceremony" (*kuan-li*) is performed on a man's twentieth birthday and declares that he has come of age. But only after he has married and become a father in his thirties is he considered a fully participating member of society. His career as a scholar-official normally begins at forty. He is then considered mature and responsible. If all goes well, he reaches the apex of his public service at fifty, and he does not retire from it until he is well over seventy. The "capping ceremony" is also preceded by an equally elaborate process of maturation: education at home begins at six, sex differentiation in education at seven, etiquette at eight, arithmetic at nine, formal schooling at ten, and by thirteen the student will have studied music, poetry, dance, ritual, archery, and horsemanship.[1] Thus from childhood to old age the learning to be human never ceases.

Adulthood conceived in this way is not so much a state of attainment as a process of becoming. The initiation rite as a gateway to manhood does not feature prominently in Confucian symbolism. And the idea that one's life on earth can and should be differentiated into discrete modes of existence and is, in essence, a preparation for an afterlife does not seem to have occurred in the Confucian tradition either. The emphasis instead is on the process of living itself. The maturation of a human being is viewed as an unfolding of humanity in the world. For without self-cultivation as a continuous effort to realize one's humanity biological growth becomes meaningless. Adulthood, then, is "to become a person." The present paper is intended as an exploration of the underlying structure of this claim.

Metaphor

Tseng Tzu, one of Confucius' most respected disciples, envisioned the task of becoming a man as one of embarking on an endless journey with a heavy burden on one's shoulders.

> The true Knight of the Way [*shih*] must perforce be both broad-shouldered and stout of heart; his burden is heavy and he has far to go. For Humanity [*jen*] is the burden he has taken upon himself; and must we not grant that it is a heavy one to bear? Only with death does this journey end; then must we not grant that he has far to go?[2]

The image of being "on the way" is also present in Confucius' comment on his best disciple, Yen Hui, whose premature death deeply agonized him: "Alas, I saw his constant advance. I never saw him stop in his progress."[3] Similarly, as the *Analects* records, once standing by a stream the Master was moved to remark, "Could one but go on and on like this, never ceasing day or night!"[4] As many commentators have pointed out, the continuous flow of the water here symbolizes a ceaseless process of self-realization and is therefore an apt description of the Confucian understanding of the authentic way of being human.

Yet the Way, which is inseparable from the person who pursues it, is never perceived as an external path. Instead, it is assumed to be inherent in human nature and thus, as the *Doctrine of the Mean* clearly notes, cannot even for a moment be detached from it.[5] To follow the Way, so conceived, is neither a rejection of, nor a departure from, one's humanity. It is rather a fulfillment of it. Therefore, in a strict sense, a man does not follow the Way as a means to an end. Nor does he imitate the Way so that he can realize a specifiable destiny. The idea of achievement is not at all applicable to this mode of thinking. In fact, Confucius himself insisted that "the Way cannot make man great" and that "it is man who can make the Way great."[6] Understandably, in Confucian literature the imagery of *seeing* the Way is hardly used. The Way can be heard (presumably as an inner voice), obtained, and embodied, but it can never be found by casting our gaze outward.

The internality of the Way as an experienced presence is what accounts for much of the moral striving in Confucian self-cultivation. Since the Way is not shown as a norm that establishes a fixed pattern of behavior, a person cannot measure the success or failure of his conduct in terms of the degree of approximation to an external ideal. The Way is always near at hand, and the journey must be constantly renewed here and now. An often quoted dictum in the *Great Learning* simply reads: "If you can renovate yourself one day, then you can do so every day, and keep doing so day after day." The instruction is not only to do what one ought to do but to "try at all times to do the utmost one can."[7] And furthermore, if one encounters difficulties, "do not complain against Heaven above or blame men below."[8] It is like the art of archery: "When the archer misses the center of the target, he turns around and seeks for the cause of failure within himself."[9] The Way, then, does not provide an ideal norm or a set of directives to be complied with. It functions as a governing perspective and a point of orientation.

The Confucians believe that ideally only those who steer the middle course can completely realize themselves and hence manifest the Way in its all-embracing fullness. But they are also aware that, although the course of the Mean is perfect, few people have been able to follow it consistently, "if just for a round month." The seemingly common and direct path of self-cultivation is in practice extremely difficult to maintain. It was probably not merely for dramatic effect that Confucius is alleged to have said, "The empire, the states, and the families can be put to order. Ranks and emolument can be declined. A bare, naked weapon can be tramped upon. But the Mean cannot [easily] be attained."[10] Thus the pursuit of the middle course is much more demanding and significant than even the most outstanding demonstration of power, honor, or *what is "the way"?*

valor. This may give one the impression that only those who can always pursue the due medium are the "true Knights of the Way." But, having come to the realization that the quality of the Mean rarely exists, Confucius was particularly concerned about finding the "ardent" (*k'uang*) and the "aloof" (*chüan*). For "the ardent will advance and lay hold of the Way; the aloof will keep themselves from pursuing the wrong ways."[11]

The Way is, then, particularly open to those who have the inner strength to "get hold of it, grasp it firmly as if wearing it on his breast and never lose it"[12] and to those who are able to wait for the right moment to follow it. But it is more or less manifested in the lives and conduct of ordinary people as well. Even men and women of simple intelligence are in a sense witnesses of the Way.[13] Only the so-called "hyperhonest villager" (*hsiang-yüan*) has little chance of manifesting it. Confucius' distaste for this sort of person is shown in his characterization of him as "the enemy (or thief) of virtue."[14] The reason why Confucius was particularly disapproving of the hyperhonest villager is elaborated by Mencius as follows:

> If you want to censure him, you cannot find anything; if you want to find fault with him, you cannot find anything either. He shares with others the practices of the day and is in harmony with the sordid world. He pursues such a policy and appears to be conscientious and faithful, and to show integrity in his conduct. He is liked by the multitude and is self-righteous. It is impossible to embark on the way of Yao and Shun [the Confucian Way] with such a man. Hence the name "enemy of virtue."[15]

At first glance Confucius does seem unusually stringent toward the hyperhonest villager. One wonders what harm he has done merely because he believes that "[b]eing in this world, one must behave in a manner pleasing to this world."[16] After all, one of the primary Confucian concerns, also, is to bring peace and harmony to this world. Again, Mencius elaborates on how Confucius might have responded to our puzzlement:

> I dislike what is specious. I dislike weeds for fear they might be confused with rice plant; I dislike flattery for fear it might be confused with what is right; I dislike glibness for fear it might be confused with the truthful; . . . I dislike the hyperhonest villager for fear he might be confused with the virtuous.[17]

The real problem with the hyperhonest villager is his total lack of a commitment to the Way. Despite his apparent compatibility with the established social norms, he is absolutely devoid of any "ambition" for self-improvement. His complacency, as a result, is no more than a reflection of a hollow and unreal personality.

The Knight of the Way, however, never ceases to "set his heart on the Way." Nor does he relax his "firm grasp on virtue." Indeed, he always endeavors to "rely on humanity and find recreation in the arts"[18] so that he can broaden himself with "culture" (*wen*) and refine himself with "ritual" (*li*).[19] His "ambition" is to become a "man of humanity" who, "wishing to establish his own character, also establishes the character of others, and wishing to be prominent himself, also helps others to be prominent."[20] His learning is "for the sake of himself" (*wei-chi*),[21] and he does not regard himself as an "instrument" (ch'i), for his mode of existence is to be an end rather than a tool for any external purpose.[22] To be sure, this by no means implies that he some-how exemplifies the amateur ideal of "doing his own thing" for love alone. As we shall see, he is as much motivated by a duty-consciousness[23] as by an aesthetic need for self-perfection.

In fact, no matter how hard he works and how much distance he covers, a true man is, as it were, all the time "on the Way." The aforementioned Tseng Tzu was gravely serious when he said that "only with death does this journey end." Even the sigh of relief he uttered with his dying words—"I feel now that whatever may betide I have got through safely"—was preceded by a verse from the Book of Odes:

> In fear and trembling,
> With caution and care,
> As though on the brink of a chasm,
> As though treading thin ice.[24]

Approach

The Way as a root metaphor or basic analogy is vitally important for understand-ing the Confucian concept of man, an understanding necessary for an appreciation of the Confucian idea of adulthood. Since the process of maturation is conceived as a con-tinuous effort toward self-realization, the creative development of a person depends as much upon a sense of inner direction as upon a prior knowledge of the established social norms. For a person to manifest his humanity, it is not enough simply to model himself on the proper ways of life and conduct approved by society. He must learn to control his own course through experience and furnish it with contents shaped by his concrete action. And as the Way cannot be fully mapped out in advance, he must, with a sense of discovery, undergo a dynamic process of self-transformation in order to com-port with it.[25] The Way, then, is always a way of "becoming" (ch'eng).

Understandably, the Confucian term for adulthood is ch'eng-jen, which literally means one who has become a person. Since the word ch'eng, like many other Chinese characters, is both a noun and a verb, the former signifying a state of completion and the latter a process of development, it is not far-fetched to understand the ch'eng-jen basically as one who has gone far toward a fully developed humanity. The notion of ch'eng-jen thus denotes not merely a stage of life but a many-sided manifestation of man's creative adaptation to the inevitable process of aging, a proven ability to mature further, as well as an obvious sign of maturity itself. The assumption is that the person who "has the Way" (yu-tao) has not only experiential knowledge of the Way but the wisdom and strength to lead the Way.

Strictly speaking, if adulthood means the process of becoming a person and an adult means not only a mature person but also a person capable of further maturing, it is difficult to imagine in such a context how "adulthood" could merely signify a culmi-nating point of "adolescence." The idea of adolescence as a state of growing up, pre-sumably from puberty to maturity, is alien to the Confucian view of life. For one thing, maturity can never be achieved in the sense of suddenly enveloping a hitherto incomprehensible mode of existence. Since the process of aging begins with birth, it does not make much sense to characterize a particular stage of human life as "growing up." It is one thing to underscore a distinctive pattern of physical maturation in youth and quite another to define the process of becoming human in terms of a period of nine to eleven years of alleged transition.

However, this should by no means suggest that the distinction between youth and manhood is absent in Confucian thought. It is only that attention is not so sharply focused on a "between" period, alleged to be characterized by mental and emotional instability as well as by other ingratiating attributes associated with this early stage of life. Since, in Confucianism, maturation is perceived mainly in terms of self-cultivation, human growth as a holistic process of realizing that which is thought to be the authentic human nature begins in early childhood and does not end even with old age. Despite the critical quality of adolescence in both the "nature" and "art" of maturing, it is by and large equal in importance to other vital periods of life history. By implication, although old age must be recognized as a delicate situation and at times even confronted as a difficult problem, it is intrinsically valuable as a concluding chapter in man's self-realization.

Against this background, the tripartite division of "youth" (shao), "manhood" (chuang), and "old age" (lao) in the Analects must be taken as denoting three equally significant periods of human life and thus three integral aspects of adulthood (which, to reiterate an early point, means the state of being well on the way to becoming a fully realized person). The three things against which a Knight of the Way must, as Confucius recommended, be on his guard can therefore be seen as an integrated teaching on adulthood:

> In his youth, before his blood and vital humors have settled down, he is on his guard against lust. Having reached his prime, when the blood and vital humors have finally hardened, he is on his guard against strife. Having reached old age, when the blood and vital humors are already decaying, he is on his guard against avarice.[26]

The young adult should be on his guard against excessive indulgence in sex not so much because of an aversion toward sexual activity itself as because of the detrimental effect it is thought to have on one's mental as well as physical health. The physiological theories underlying this consideration, which are still prevalent in China, hold that a careful preservation of one's "blood and vital humors" at this juncture of maturation is a prerequisite for a wholesome growth. The development of a personality, like the planting of crops, must not be hurried. The story of the farmer of Sung in Mencius whose over-zealousness led him to help his crops grow by artificially pulling up seedlings is a vivid description of how harmful imposition can frustrate the natural process of aging.[27] Just as unnecessary assistance withers the crops, "lust's effect," far from comforting to the body and mind, "is tempest after sun."

Similarly, strife is threatening to true manhood because the energy available for personal development and public service is misdirected. To be sure, Confucius encouraged moral striving. And the reason why he was particularly pleased to teach the "ardent" is precisely because the latter have a strong will to forge ahead.[28] But competitiveness, which is what "strife" means in this connection, is a clear demonstration that the way of being human is here pursued not for the sake of self-realization but "for the sake of the others" (*wei-jen*).[29] So long as one's self-image is mainly dependent upon the external responses of others, one's inner direction will be lost. As a result, the ability to "endure adversity" or "enjoy prosperity" for long will also be weakened.[30] Despite the fact that physically one's "blood and vital humors have finally hardened," one is not necessarily strong in the sense of being truly "steadfast" (*kang*). In fact, steadfastness in the Confucian sense means the ability to remain unaffected by external influences in determining how one is to pursue and manifest the Way.[31]

If strife, reflecting a profound inner uncertainty, becomes a kind of impulsive aggressiveness, "avarice" in old age seems to indicate a defensive attachment to what one has already gained. The Chinese character *te* in this particular context also suggests "possessiveness." The remark in the *Analects* may have been the source of a widely cir-culated proverb which characterizes the small-minded person as one who is "distressed in mind trying to get more, and then troubled lest he lose it." A possessive old man may not present any serious threat to society. But from the viewpoint of self-realiza-tion, if one is overpowered by possessiveness in old age, the possibility for a safe and sound passage in the last phase of one's "lifelong" journey will be slim. Otherwise, old age may truly be the fruition of one's earnest endeavor to learn to be human through self-effort. Thus, like lust in youth and strife in manhood, the real danger of avarice lies in its detrimental effect on what ought to be a ceaseless process of realizing full human-ity. In a deeper sense, since one of the most persistent attachments is to life itself, the art of dying is undoubtedly the principal challenge in old age. Unless one can peacefully accept the termination of one's life as a matter of fact, one still somehow falls short of a successful completion. This may have been the reason why a great many biographies of Confucian scholar-officials contain detailed descriptions of the last moments of their lives.

The common belief that, under the influence of Confucian thought, Chinese cul-ture has developed a special respect for old age needs some explanation. Notwithstand-ing gerontocratic tendencies in Chinese history, old age in itself commands little admiration. Respect for the old is actually based on the assumption that, in the long and unavoidable journey of self-improvement, an old man ought to have forged way ahead in furnishing his life with inspiring contents. Ideally, therefore, being advanced in age is a sign of wisdom and resourcefulness as well as of experience and per-severance. But this hardly implies that in practice seniority of age automatically becomes an undisputable value. Simply "being old and not dying" does not get one very far. The manner in which Confucius approached an old man in the *Analects* may appear shockingly un-Confucian on the surface, but it is consistent with his overarching concerns:

> Yüan Jang [an unmannerly old man of Confucius' acquaintance] sat waiting for the Master in a sprawling position. The Master said to him, "In youth, not humble as befits a junior; in manhood, doing nothing worthy of being handed down. And merely to live on, getting older and older, is to be a useless pest." With this he hit him on the shank with his staff.[32]

Confucius' candid attitude toward Yüan Jang, by which many a commentator including Arthur Waley has been deeply perplexed,[33] is not at all inconceivable in light of the Confucian belief that old age, as a more matured manifestation of adulthood, is itself still "on the way." It is perhaps also in this sense that the Master instructed his followers to respect the young: "How do you know that they will not one day be all that you are now?" And since the emphasis is on actual performance as well as on promise of moral growth, Confucius continued, "[Only] if a man has reached forty or fifty and nothing has been heard of him, then I grant there is no need to respect him."[34] It would be misleading to suppose, however, that one's moral growth can significantly surpass one's physical maturation. An attempt to get on quickly without proper cultivation merely assumes the form rather than the content of maturity. A youth whom Confucius employed to carry messages is a case in point. When a friend commented that he seemed to have made great progress, the Master said, "I observe that he is fond of occupying the seat of *a full-grown man*; I observe that he walks shoulder to shoulder with his elders. He is not one who is seeking to make progress *in learning*. He wishes quickly to become a man."[35]

It should be noted in this connection that learning (*hsüeh*) in the tradition of Confucian education is broadly defined to include not only intellectual and ethical growth but the development of the body as well. Actually the involvement of the body is such an integral part of the Confucian ideal of learning that the Confucian Way itself has been characterized by the Neo-Confucians as "the learning of the body and mind" (*shen-hsin chih chiao*). Indeed, each of the "six arts" (*liu-i*) that constitute the core of Confucian teaching involves the total participation of the body. Although only archery and charioteering are intended to be physical exercises, ritual and music both require the harmonization of bodily movements. Even in calligraphy and arithmetic, the importance of practice in the sense of acquiring an experiential understanding of the basic skills is always emphasized. One might even say that it is precisely in this sense that the Neo-Confucian masters often instruct their students to "embody" the Way. Therefore, the one who seeks to make progress in learning must have the courage and patience to wait for the "ripening of humanity" (*jen-shu*). After all, "only when the year grows cold do we see that the pine and cypress are the last to fade";[36] likewise, human self-realization depends much upon what may be called one's staying power.

The idea that youth, manhood, and old age are three inseparable dimensions of adulthood is compatible with the Confucian belief that a fully developed person should first be incited by "poetry," then established by "ritual," and finally perfected by "music."[37] It may not be far-fetched to suggest that adulthood, as a process of becoming, can be understood as a continuous "ritualization" from "poetry" to "music."

The poetic state, so to speak, symbolizes the eagerness and excitement of the young adult who has already developed an inner sense of direction. The technical term used to designate this kind of commitment is *li-chih*, which literally means "to establish one's will." The absolute necessity of an existential decision, not only as a commencement but also as an affirmation to be continuously reenacted, is taken for granted in Confucian literature. Thus, the Master insisted, "Only one who bursts with eagerness do I instruct; only one who bubbles with excitement, do I enlighten."[38] In a strict sense, unless the young adult is personally motivated to embark on the Way, no teacher can force him to pursue it. Having been fully aware that, especially for the young, "the desire to build up [one's] moral power is never as strong as sexual desire,"[39] Confucius recommended the study of poetry as a guide for harmonizing basic emotions. He felt that the odes of the classical tradition can, among other things, "serve to stimulate the mind," "be used for purposes of self-contemplation," "teach the art of sociality," and "show how to regulate feelings of resentment." Through a careful reading of them, he further maintained, not only "the more immediate duty of serving one's father and the remoter one of serving one's prince" can be learned, even knowledge about natural phenomena can also be acquired.[40] On the other hand, he who does not have any acquaintance with the odes is "as though he stood with his face pressed against a wall!"[41] In such a situation, he can hardly advance a step toward self-realization. Poetry then marks an initial but critical step on the Way.

Similarly, ritual, symbolizing the state of manhood, is both a structure and a movement whereby one's character as a mature person is established. Like the tradition of the *Odes*, it involves a set of highly integrated rules of propriety which the young adult must learn in order to become a full participating member of society. Also, like poetry, it harmonizes as well as directs human emotions toward a socially recognizable mode of expression. Since a person in the Confucian sense is always a center of relationships rather than an *individual* complete in himself and separable from others, the structure and movement by which he expresses himself in the context of human-relatedness becomes a defining characteristic of his humanity. Ritualization so conceived, far from being depersonalizing, is a necessary way of learning to be human. However, the order of priority as specified by Confucius clearly indicates that ritual itself must also be based on human feelings: "If a man is not humane [*jen*], what can he have to do with ritual?"[42] Ideally ritualization should be in perfect accord with humanization. And ritual is not thought to be a social imposition upon nature but a refinement of nature according to well articulated cultural values. It is perhaps in this sense that Confucius maintained that only through ritual can those human feelings that exhibit basic virtues be properly manifested:

> Respectfulness without ritual becomes laborious bustle; carefulness without ritual becomes timidity; boldness without ritual becomes turbulence; straightforwardness without ritual becomes rudeness.[43]

It is also in this sense that the Master felt he could finally talk about the real meanings of the odes with Tzu-hsia, because this disciple had come to the realization that just as the art of laying on the colors follows the preparation of the plain ground, so is ritual subsequent to poetry.[44]

Example

The perception of adulthood as a continuous development from poetry to music is an idealized way of conceptualizing the process of growing up in accordance with the middle path. A close approximation to this pattern of maturation is certainly the case of Confucius himself. Yet, although the *Analects* does provide a good example of this, it has never been taken as a norm in the Confucian tradition. For the process of self-realization is so dependent upon one's particular circumstances that it is pointless to set up one concrete experience as the single most important archetype. The Confucian Way, in a strict sense, is not one and the same as the way of Confucius. Strictly speaking, even the word "Confucianist" is a misnomer because the follower of the Confucian Way does not accept the Master's life and conduct as revealed truth; nor does he believe that Confucius actually attained the highest possible level of human perfection. His ultimate concern, then, is not to become a Confucianist but to become a genuine human being, a sage. To be sure, Confucius the symbol has been honored as the complete sage for more than two thousand years. But this by no means suggests that Confucius the person has ever been celebrated as the only true interpreter of the Human Way (jen-tao). In fact, Confucius never claimed that he had himself attained sagehood. The way of Confucius therefore should be taken mainly as a standard of inspiration:

> At fifteen I set my heart upon learning.
> At thirty I established myself [in accordance with ritual].
> At forty I no longer had perplexities.
> At fifty I knew the Mandate of Heaven.
> At sixty I was at ease with whatever I heard.
> At seventy I could follow my heart's desire without
> transgressing the boundaries of right.[45]

"Learning" (hsüeh) was to Confucius much more than the acquisition of empirical knowledge; nor was it simply a method of internalizing the proper manner of behavior in society. It was the thing he did as a conscious human being. Through learning, which means through an ever deepening personal knowledge about how to be human, he transformed his life into a meaningful existence. Learning in this particular association was so much a cherished idea that Confucius almost refused to grant anyone else the characterization of being "given to learning": "In a hamlet of ten houses you may be sure of finding someone quite as loyal and true to his word as I. But I doubt if you would find anyone with such a love of learning."[46] And he admitted that, after the death of his best disciple, no students of his were really "given to learning."[47] Confucius was absolutely serious about his self-image as a devoted learner; once after a disciple reported that he had been at a loss to describe his Master to a questioner, Confucius said, "Why didn't you say that I am a person who forgets his food when engaged in vigorous pursuit [of learning], is so happy as to forget his worries, and is not aware that old age is coming on?"[48]

If the setting of his heart upon learning at fifteen signifies the opening of a new and continuous process of intellectual and moral growth, the establishment of his character in accordance with ritual at thirty further suggests a more refined expression of maturity. As ritual involves a network of human relations, self-establishment in this connection specifically points to the responsibility one assumes in reference to a variety of primordial ties. Concerning the major dyadic relationships, Confucius is alleged to have said that he had not been able to accomplish any of them:

> To serve my father as I would expect my son to serve me: that I have not been able to do.
> To serve my ruler as I would expect my ministers to serve me: that I have not been able

to do. To serve my elder brothers as I would expect my younger brothers to serve me: that I have not been able to do. To be the first to treat friends as I would expect them to treat me: that I have not been able to do.[49]

Confucius' self-criticism, far from being simply a heuristic device, indicates that in assuming ordinary responsibilities there is bound to be room for improvement. Loyalty, filiality, brotherhood, and friendship are common virtues, but the processes of ritualization through which they can be fully realized are long and subtle. Maturity in this sense means both the ability to manifest virtues like these properly and the awareness that one must never cease to make further effort to establish oneself in ritual. The mature person is therefore "earnest and genuine."[50] For he knows that the burden is heavy and the journey is long for the realization of true humanity.

This duty-consciousness is predicated on the Confucian golden rule: "Do not do to others what you would not want others to do to you."[51] The golden rule is always negatively stated because the emphasis is on self-cultivation. Given the centrality of one's own quest for personal knowledge, perhaps it is neither necessary nor desirable to impose upon others what one believes to be right for oneself. Underlying the golden rule, then, is the premise that "conscientiousness [chung] and altruism [shu] are not far from the Way."[52] The inner demand for being truthful to one's humane self is inseparable from the social need to care for others; and the learning for self-realization is also the learning for harmonizing human relations. The real threat to a genuine manifestation of the humane self is not society but one's own selfish desires. Altruism is thus not a consequence of conscientiousness but its inalienable complement. The positive character of this Confucian doctrine is implicit in the assertion that the Way is pursued not by insisting upon its abstract universality but by assuring that which is best for one's humane self, the self that forms a community with others.

As the transformation from a commitment to learning in the poetic state to an assumption of social responsibilities in the ritual state symbolizes Confucius' maturation as a young adult, "no longer having perplexities" symbolizes Confucius' disposition in the middle years. "No perplexities" first suggests an independence of mind. His will had by then become so firmly set on the Way that wealth and honor were to him like "floating clouds"[53] with no danger of casting any shadow on his mind. This ability to remain disinterested, however, was hardly a recoil from social involvement. It was a form of self-possession, suggesting inner strength and repose: "I have listened in silence and noted what was said. I have never grown tired of learning nor wearied of teaching others what I have learned—these are just natural with me."[54] The unperturbed mind, to borrow from Mencius, is the resultant effect of "righteous deeds."[55] It is a wisdom which, despite active participation in society, perceives the total situation clearly. Thus, only "the wise have no perplexities."[56]

Yet the unperplexed adult is not only intellectually alert but emotionally stable and strong. His independence of mind is as much an indication of moral courage as a sign of wisdom. When Tzu-lu asked what constituted "a complete man" (a truly mature person), Confucius said:

If anyone had the wisdom of Tsang Wu-chung, the uncovetousness of Meng Kung-ch'o, the valor of P'ien Chuang-tzu, and the artistic talents of Jan Ch'iu, and graced these virtues by the cultivation of ritual and music, then indeed I think we might call him "a complete man."

However, realizing that what he had described was too much an ideal for his disciple to emulate, he continued with Tzu-lu, who was noted for his moral courage, particularly in mind:

> But perhaps today we need not ask all this of the complete man. The man, who in the view of gain thinks of righteousness; who in the view of danger is prepared to give up his life; and who does not forget an old agreement however far back it extends—such a man may be considered "a complete man."[57]

If "beyond perplexities" signifies the wisdom and courage of manhood, "knowing the Mandate of Heaven" points to an even more sophisticated frame of mind in which the coming of old age is confronted squarely both as an inevitable process of maturation and as a great promise of reconciliation. Indeed, the meaning of the Mandate of Heaven is twofold. It connotes the limitation of one's own fate as well as the fulfillment of a "transcendent" command. At fifty Confucius had experienced many hardships in life, among which the deaths of several of his best disciples and the repeated failures of his hope to set the world in order must have been especially agonizing. By then Confucius had become acutely aware of the inescapable limitation of human efforts to exert lasting influence on the brute realities of life. His personal encounters with dehumanizing forces in social conflicts and in fiercely contested political arenas had totally frustrated his "dream" of returning to the great peace of the Chou dynasty. As his advice and protests time and again fell upon heedless ears, he felt that his alienation from the world was complete: "Only Heaven knows me!"[58] Nevertheless, as a confirmed humanist, he refused to forsake the world and herd with birds and beasts: "If I am not to be a man among other men, then what am I to be? If the Way prevailed under Heaven, I should not be trying to alter things."[59] As he was approaching old age he felt more strongly the tension between a profound sense of the finitude in man and an equally profound belief in the perfectibility of human nature. Yet, his own choice of action was clear: recognizing that what he could do to set the world in order was extremely limited, still he could not but do it.

"Knowing the Mandate of Heaven" can therefore be conceived as an expression of Confucius' spiritual crisis. A distinctive character of it is a deeply felt sense of mission. Despite the bitterness of his lot, his concern for the human world became even greater. To be sure, once he conveyed to Tzu-kung his wish not to say anything. When the disciple wondered how the Way could be revealed if the Master chose to remain silent, Confucius responded, "Heaven does not speak; yet the four seasons run their course thereby, the hundred creatures, each after its kind, are born thereby. Heaven does no speaking!"[60] Yet Confucius' tacit understanding of the Mandate of Heaven is not a sign of passivity but of total commitment, a positive effort to carry out a lifelong task. In fact, he made it clear that the Mandate of Heaven is not an object of speculation but a thing to be feared and respected.[61] To know the Mandate of Heaven is therefore more than an attainment of comprehension. When Confucius' life was seriously threatened by a military officer in the state of Sung, when he had reached the age of fifty-nine, he is recorded to have said, "Heaven produced the virtue that is in me; what can Huan T'ui do to me?"[62] This sense of being chosen to fulfill a transcendent command is further evidenced by another incident which had happened three years previously:

> When Confucius was in personal danger in K'uang, he said, "Since the death of King Wen, is not the course of culture [wen] in my keeping? If it had been the will of Heaven to destroy this culture, it would not have been given to a mortal [like me]. But if it is the will of Heaven that this culture should not perish, what can the people of K'uang do to me?"[63]

Against this background, Confucius' self-definition as a transmitter rather than a maker[64] assumes a shape of meaning seldom understood and appreciated by students of Chinese thought. A transmitter is tradition-bound only in the sense that for the sake of self-knowledge he never ceases to learn from the past. To him, the value of history is judged not only by its usefulness and relevance to the present but also by its uninterrupted affirmation of the authentic possibility of humanness in the world. He does not assume the role of a maker, not because he fails to recognize the power of creativity but because by a conscious choice he refuses to cut himself off from the humanizing processes that have significantly contributed to his own maturation. In fact, as a transmitter, he continuously renews himself by delving deeply into the sources of his chosen heritage. His respect for the ancients does not lead him to a glorification of the past. Rather, his intention is to make sure that the humanity of the former sages always remains a felt presence in the world. His mission, then, is to assure cultural continuity through personal knowledge. In a deeper sense, Confucius' unqualified dedication to the transmission of what has for centuries been called the Sagely Way is not at all in conflict with his acute awareness of the finitude in man. Thus, independence of mind, suggesting both wisdom and courage, is now further refined. To know one's limitation, instead of inhibiting one's determination to forge ahead, actually enhances one's commitment to action. And one's sense of mission, far from suggesting hubris, is based upon a realistic appraisal of one's circumscription as well as one's inner strength. The encroachment of old age seems to have given another dimension to Confucius' adulthood.

"I was at ease with whatever I heard" suggests receptivity. The art of listening, especially as contrasted with that of seeing, is neither aggressive nor possessive. It is an affirmation of the world in a spirit of detachment. For it manifests maternal virtues of caring, forgiving, and accepting without at the same time exhibiting an unexamined attachment to a love object. It seems that by then Confucius' inner demand to change the world had been transformed into a silent appreciation of it. In the words of a twelfth-century commentator, "when sound enters, the mind opens up without rejection or resistance; as the art of knowing has reached its ultimate perfection, the mind can have it without reflection."[65] This penetrating responsiveness of the mind was surely the result of a long and strenuous self-examination. Understandably, Confucius, as depicted by his students, had succeeded in freeing himself from four defects of the mind: opinionatedness, dogmatism, obstinacy, and egoism.[66] It is vitally important to note, however, that the spiritual "carefreeness" of Confucius at sixty implies neither eremitism nor asceticism. Rather, it symbolizes self-realization through the experience of unconflicted continuity with the world in all its aspects. The Master did say, "In the morning, hear the Way; in the evening, die content!"[67] But the Way can never be heard by leaving the world. Indeed, the true peace of mind is not attained by deliverance from, but by participating in, the world. And only those who are really in the world are on the Way and thus have a chance of hearing the Way.

"I could follow my heart's desire without transgressing the boundaries of right" implies harmony. This last phase of Confucius' adulthood seems to symbolize the final fruition of a long process of maturation. The commitment to learning at fifteen, the establishment of the self in ritual at thirty, the attainment of an unperturbed mind at forty, the knowledge of the will of Heaven at fifty, and the receptive appreciation of the world at sixty all converged, as it were, into a new state of realization. As Mencius suggested that "the great man does not lose his childlike heart,"[68] the joy of unrestrained freedom in the septuagenary Confucius seems to have been an artistically cultivated spontaneity, a second childhood in old age. "Poetry" and "ritual" are no longer fitting descriptions; the degree of integration characterized by a harmonization of what one is and what one ought to be can now be better understood in the symbolism of music as performed in Lu, Confucius' native state: "[I]t began with a strict unison. Soon the musicians were given more liberty; but the tone remained harmonious, brilliant, consistent, right on till the close."[69] The closing with "jade tubes" which produce a deep, euphonic sound is, in Mencius' words, "the concern of a sage."[70] Only then can we say that the Way is heard and even death is welcome

However, as already mentioned, the example of Confucius' adulthood does not serve as an absolute norm but as a standard of inspiration in the Confucian tradition. Actually the Master never instructed his students to follow him in order to find the Way. Instead, he inspired them to pursue the Way by realizing humanity—or adulthood, if you will—in themselves. His real strength as an exemplary teacher then came from a persuasive power which, in the words of his admirers, was as gentle and refreshing as the spring breezes. Yen Hui, who died in his early thirties, never attained the level of adulthood his Master was confident he could have reached, but his description of the Confucian Way is worth quoting:

> The more I strain my gaze upward toward it, the higher it soars. The deeper I bore down into it, the harder it becomes. I see it in front; but suddenly it is behind. Step by step the Master lures me on. He has broadened me with culture, restrained me with ritual. Even if I wanted to stop, I could not. Just when I feel that I have exhausted every resource, something seems to rise up, standing sharp and clear. Yet though I long to pursue it, I can find no way of getting to it at all.[71]

Even among Confucius' closest disciples, the paths of self-realization are varied. Between Yen Hui's premature death and Tseng Tzu's longevity, there are numerous manifestations of adulthood. The case of Confucius is but one of them. It is therefore conceivable that a person in his eighties or nineties may be able to advance further on the Way than Confucius had in his seventies. It is also conceivable that people under new circumstances may choose to pursue the Way in a mode which differs significantly from what traditionally has been sanctioned as authentically Confucian. After all, from the Confucian perspective, the approaches to sagehood are as many as there are sages. And by implication, although adulthood can be recognized, it can never be defined.

REFERENCES

[1]See the *"Nei-che"* chapter in *Li-chi* (1815 edition), 28:20a-21b.

[2]*Analects*, 8:7. See Arthur Waley, trans., *The Analects of Confucius* (London, 1938), p. 134. Also cf. Wing-tsit Chan, trans., *A Source Book in Chinese Philosophy* (Princeton, 1969), p. 33, and James Legge, trans., *Confucian Analects* in *The Chinese Classics* (7 vols.; Hong Kong, 1966; reprint), I, 210-11. For an inspiring discussion on the imagery of the Way in the *Analects*, see Herbert Fingarette, *Confucius—The Secular as Sacred* (New York, 1972), pp. 18-36.

[3]*Analects*, 9:20.

[4]*Analects*, 9:16. See Waley, p. 142. As Waley points out, the extensive discussion on the metaphor of the water in *Mencius* (IVB:18) also addresses itself to the same idea.

[5]*Chung-yung*, I:1.

[6]*Analects*, 15:28. See Chan, p. 15.

[7]*Ta-hsüeh*, II. See Chan, p. 87.

[8]*Analects*, 14:37. The same passage is also found in *Chung-yung*, XIB:3. See Chan, p. 101.

[9]*Chung-yung*, XIV:5. See Chan, p. 102.

[10]*Chung-yung*, IX. See Chan, p. 99.

[11]*Analects*, 13:21.

[12]*Chung-yung*, XIII. See Chan, p. 99.

[13]*Chung-yung*, XII:1-2.

[14]*Analects*, 17:13.

[15]*Mencius*, VIIB:37. See D. C. Lau, trans., *Mencius* (Penguin Classics, 1970), p. 203.

[16]Lau, p. 203.

[17]*Ibid.* The term *hsiang-yuan* is rendered by Lau as "village honest man."

[18]*Analects*, 7:6.

[19]*Analects*, 9:10.

[20]*Analects*, 6:28. See Chan, p. 31.

[21]*Analects*, 14:25.

[22]*Analects*, 2:12.

[23]"Duty-consciousness" is here contrasted with "rights-consciousness." While the latter emphasizes one's legitimate claims, the former is concerned about the moral imperative, a sense of commitment, completely independent of outside influence.

[24]*Analects*, 8:3. See Waley, p. 133. A different version of the poem is found in James Legge, trans., *She-king (Book of Poetry)*, in *Chinese Classics*, IV, pt. 2, 335.

[25]For a methodological discussion on this, see A. S. Cua, "Confucian Vision and Experience of the World," *Philosophy East and West*, XXV, no. 3 (July, 1975), 327-28.

[26]*Analects*, 16:7. See Waley, pp. 205-06.

[27]*Mencius*, IIA:2, sec. 16.

[28]*Analects*, 13:21.

[29]*Analects*, 14:25.

[30]*Analects*, 4:2. See Waley, p. 102.

[31]*Analects*, 5:10.

[32]*Analects*, 14:46. See Waley, p. 192.

[33]Waley did not believe that Confucius could have been so rude to an old man; and so he arbitrarily decided that Yüan Jang was in fact a young boy, although he was fully aware that his view contradicted virtually all traditional commentaries. See Waley, p. 192, n. 3. Legge did accept that Yüan Jang was an old man, but he also felt that Confucius' candid remarks were quite unusual. For his apologetic comments, see Legge, trans., *Confucian Analects*, pp. 292-93, n. 46.

[34]*Analects*, 9:22. See Waley, p. 143.

[35]*Analects*, 14:47. See Legge, p. 293.

[36]*Analects*, 9:27. See Waley, p. 144. I am indebted to Joan Erikson for calling my attention to this important dimension of Confucian education.

[37]*Analects*, 8:8.

[38]*Analects*, 7:8. See Waley, p. 124.

[39]*Analects*, 9:17. See Waley, p. 142.

[40]*Analects*, 17:9. See Legge, p. 323.

[41]*Analects*, 17:10. See Waley, p. 212.

[42]*Analects*, 3:3.

[43]*Analects*, 8:2. See Legge, p. 208. *Li* is rendered by Legge as "rules of propriety."

[44]*Analects*, 3:8.

[45]*Analects*, 2:4.

[46]*Analects*, 5:27. See Waley, p. 114.

[47]*Analects*, 6:2; 11:6.

[48]*Analects*, 7:18. See Chan, p. 32. It seems clear that the "something" "in vigorous pursuit of something" refers to "learning."

[49]*Chung-yung*, XIII:4. See Chan, p. 101. This statement seems incompatible with Confucius' remark, "I can claim that at Court I have duly served the Duke and his office; at home, my father and elder brother. As regards matters of mourning, I am conscious of no neglect, nor have I ever been overcome with wine. Concerning these things at any rate my mind is quite at rest." (*Analects*, 9:15; Waley, p. 144.) But the apparent contradiction between the two views can easily be resolved, if the whole matter is understood as involving different levels of self-cultivation. Surely, Confucius did not consider himself a failure in carrying out the basic requirements of loyalty and filiality. However, neither was he satisfied with what he was able to accomplish. Although his mind was quite at rest, his effort to improve himself remained persistent.

[50]*Chung-yung*, XIII:3.

[51]*Analects*, 15:23. Also see *Chung-yung*, XIII:3.

[52]*Chung-yung*, XIII:3.

[53]*Analects*, 7:15. The entire statement reads: "He who seeks only coarse food to eat, water to drink, and bent arm for pillow will without looking for it find happiness to boot. Any thought of accepting wealth and rank by means that I know to be wrong is as remote from me as the clouds that float above." See Waley, p. 126.

[54]*Analects*, 7:2. See Waley, p. 123, with minor modifications.

[55]*Mencius*, IIA:2, sec. 15.

[56]*Analects*, 9:28; 14:30.

[57]*Analects*, 14:13. See Waley, p. 183, for the first part and Legge, pp. 279-80, for the second part. It should be noted that the term *ch'eng-jen*, rendered by Waley as "a perfect man," is also the term for "adult" or "adulthood."

[58]*Analects*, 14:37.

[59]*Analects*, 18:6. See Waley, p. 220.

[60]*Analects*, 17:19. See Waley, p. 214.

[61]*Analects*, 16:8.

[62]*Analects*, 7:22. See Chan, p. 32.

[63]*Analects*, 9:5. See Chan, p. 35.

[64]*Analects*, 7:1.

[65]See Chu Hsi's commentary on the *Analects*, in *Ssu-shu chi-chu* (Taipei, 1952; reprint), p. 7.

[66]*Analects*, 9:4.

[67]*Analects*, 4:8. See Waley, p. 103.

[68]*Mencius*, IVB:12.

[69]*Analects*, 3:23.

[70]*Mencius*, VB:1. See Lau, p. 150.

[71]*Analects*, 9:10. See Waley, p. 140.

THOMAS P. ROHLEN

The Promise of Adulthood in Japanese Spiritualism

A TIME-TESTED ELEMENT in the Western folklore about Japan states that age is respected there, that the old are well cared for, and that aging is viewed in a positive light. The inquiring visitor today will certainly find great quantities of evidence to the contrary, and Ruth Benedict's observation about the characteristic shape of the Japanese life cycle—a "U" with the high points representing the much greater ease, gratification, and freedom of childhood and old age—seems to be losing its empirical base in urban, industrial Japan. But, for all the change, there is still something to our first naive impression that the Japanese view the progress of individual lives differently than we do, and many aspects of the contemporary scene still confirm this.

Japanese leaders, for example, whether politician, businessman, or scholar, are generally much older than their Western counterparts. Age at all social levels is a central principle in the ordering of social rank, and this holds for the most modern as well as the more traditional kinds of organizations. Age also remains positively correlated with Japanese ideas of creativity, wisdom, and authority. While it is true that most older Japanese today slip into obscurity (and some into destitution), it is surprising how many older people remain publicly active, influential, and respected long after Americans of similar ability and accomplishment would have picked up their marbles and moved to Florida. Japan has legions of local-level Averell Harrimans, that is, and this holds for just about every form of career and institution in the country. The ideals and understandings of a past age are still influential, and, more importantly, they have a good deal to teach the modern, Westernized world about alternative views of adulthood. In fact it was precisely the instructive value of the contrast between the two cultural views of age and aging that inspired the folklore in the first place.

Old age is not adulthood, of course, but its culmination. A consideration of what people take to be life's high and low times, however, is a first step toward grasping the shape the life cycle is understood to have. The traditional Japanese view has adulthood arranged as leading to a very satisfactory old age. This obviously could not be said of the contemporary American view despite the attractions retirement comes to hold for some. Clearly we hope to recapture something of youth ("sixty years young," "you're only as old as you think") upon setting aside the burdens of job and career. Our view, even at its most optimistic, is patently not a glorification of age or aging, but a belief that even in old physical age we can recapture something of the carefree, mobile, active

129

state typical of youth. As has often been said, it is youth that epitomizes the American sense of well-being, and we pay homage to its gods time and again throughout an adulthood that inevitably leads us away from many of its prerequisites.

What characterizes the attractions of old age for Japanese? Certainly the ease, gratification, and respect given the aged as part of the traditional family pattern is part of the story. We can grasp this attraction immediately because it speaks to a universal set of wishes, but there is a much more profound and challenging side to the traditional Japanese view of aging—one that has nothing to do with the traditional family, the pleasure principle, or the automatic rewards of time. It centers on personal growth, demands considerable effort and application, looks to a release from "the self" rather than to its satisfaction, and stands as a most important yardstick of personal achievement and the life well led.

I. The Traditional Outlook

A. TIME AND CHANGE

The Japanese have an acute awareness of aging viewed as a subtle change in one's relationship with the world.[1] They live in a society ordered around differences in age. They speak a language that to be spoken properly requires a precise knowledge of the relative ages of the parties concerned. Women especially dress according to a rather minutely worked out aesthetic that relates patterns and color to fine gradations in age. And the Japanese inhabit a cultural world profoundly concerned with the turn of seasons, of years, and of whole lives. Time is a flow of change that is essentially universal in its pattern. To resist or ignore it is the height of folly. Just as each season has its character and its particular beauty, so each part of a life should be accepted and appreciated for what it brings. As we shall see, acceptance and appreciation of this kind of nature-given reality, a form of truth that not only surrounds human existence but *is* human existence, involves a submission of the "self." Much of human culture and particularly its product, the self-consciousness of individuals, has been built on other man-made assumptions of reality that we tenaciously cling to for security and power. Giving up self-centered awareness is far from an easy task. Life, however, is a stern and implacable teacher, and part of the fascination of the Japanese view of biographical time is that it is at once fatalistic (nature has its way) and yet, contrary to our understanding of that fatalism, simultaneously preoccupied with the challenge and potential for human perfection contained in the submission of "self" to a greater reality. Acceptance of the process of aging, for example, brings the person into closer contact with all natural change. This to Japanese is a form of religious fulfillment.

The process of learning acceptance (of becoming part of) begins with early socialization. William Caudill and Helen Weinstein in their very detailed comparative study of Japanese and American infant care observed that:

> In Japan, the infant is seen more as a separate biological organism who from the beginning, in order to develop, needs to be drawn into increasingly interdependent relations with others. In America, the infant is seen more as a dependent biological organism who, in order to develop, needs to be made increasingly independent of others.[2]

The process of becoming more and more *psychologically* a part of society continues long past childhood and graduation from school. Japanese adulthood witnesses many kinds of socialization, some voluntary and some not. Companies give their new employees rather stiff introductory courses, for example, and vast numbers of Japanese enroll in courses of training that contribute to their further development as members of society. In all this, personal growth in spiritual terms is part of a greater acceptance of, and integration with, society as a nature-given reality. Society weighs heavily in the life of Japanese, and learning to accept the burdens and limitations involved is a major first step on the road to maturity.

Caudill's observation is echoed in the example given by a Japanese friend in explanation of the important phrase *ningen ga dekita*, which translates something like "for him, the process of becoming human is complete," a highly complimentary expression made of mature individuals. How one becomes a human being is crucial to grasp if the Japanese ideal of personal growth is to be understood. My friend explained:

> Take a person who as a student was a radical—an extremist. After graduating he takes a job, begins to work with people, and gradually comes to see other people's points of view. He slowly learns the sensibleness of moderation in his own conduct. At this point, people would observe that he appears to be on the way to achieving humanity [*ningen ga dekiso*]. A person described as completing this process is one who does not push his ideas or feelings on others, but, on the contrary, is deeply receptive to the thought of others. His empathy and openness allow him to make others part of himself [*jibun no naka ni aite o ireru*—literally "putting others inside himself"].

Obviously, the "humanity" stressed here establishes as ideal a very particular form of social interaction, and out of it a very particular sense of society is likely to develop. We will return to this issue in the last section of this essay. The point most immediately at hand is that this "becoming human" tells us much about intentional effort at personal cultivation. The process involved is not an automatic one or one limited to a set period or stage of life. People can and should work all their lives at becoming more human. The compliment *ningen ga dekita* is not given lightly. In my experience, it is typically made about those in their forties or older. And it is common to assume that people given posts of leadership and those of considerable achievement in the arts will possess a character deserving of this praise. Their successful performance, people will tell you, depends on the insight, self-control, and developed skill that only those having reached this stage are likely to possess. This expectation calibrates (as an ideal at least) the rather tight Japanese relationship between age, rank, and moral attainment.

Biographical time is also divided into numerous, vaguely defined age periods and states of being based on the convergence of age and social-role transitions. Women, for example, are said to experience the transformation from premarital "flowering" to "womanhood" to a stage marked by declining concern with appearance and so on. Men experience stages focused around their mastery of work, and most especially on their growing capacity to devote themselves wholeheartedly to it (a quality that closely reflects character development and is termed the "flowering of manhood"). Old age (by contrast) is a time when sex differences diminish, social roles in family and work

are less central, and, in a sense, each individual is released from the grip of social definition—free to venture down more private paths. Here, too, we find a rich vocabulary
describing achievements and qualities particular to or possible at this point in life.
There is a term, for example, for those who greatly enjoy going around helping others.
Most expressions, however, refer to matters of spiritual cultivation and maturity.

The crucial point is the simple one that the Japanese are not at all inclined to the
idea or unconscious presumption that being an adult is to dwell in one long, rather static stage of life. That our term "adulthood" finds no easy equivalent in Japanese is quite
revealing. The continuing aspects of an individual's position as a responsible member
of society and the apparent plateau qualities of physical maturity are neither ignored
nor underestimated in Japan, but they only form the background for change. Adulthood is a time of becoming, not being. This becoming is typically part of a *life-long*
socialization process (not, as in America, a search for the "real self" that characteristically requires individual independence and, of late, visualizes society as the villain
obstructing this goal). Time, rather than hindering or limiting this process of growth, is
seen as contributing to it through the tempering agencies of experience and aging.

B. HUMAN NATURE AND HUMAN PERFECTION

Time means inevitable change, but valued, meaningful change depends most heavily on individual effort. Such terms as personal cultivation, maturation, spiritual
strengthening, and so on, are all labels applied to a dynamic process of growth and
character development that underlies the Japanese understanding of the "spiritual."

The Japanese, it is often remarked, have a way of acknowledging many established
religions and yet giving little devotion to any of them. When it comes to the matter of
continuing personal growth and perfection, however, we find the Japanese deeply
interested in and inspired by examples of spiritual accomplishment regardless of their
cultural, theological, or other settings. It is my opinion that in fact the Japanese quest
for character improvement is close to being a national religion, and it is from this angle
that we will next consider Japanese adulthood. The quest begins simply enough with
various disciplines and routines, most of which are part of the mundane social work-a-
day world, but the ultimate aims of the training and effort are states of understanding
and being for which the labels "enlightenment" and "salvation" are as close as we can
get in English. The framework of meaning that serves as the road map for efforts at
personal cultivation has been conceived on the basis of deeply spiritual and profound
forms of insight.

It is difficult to imagine a culture that does not contain promises that invest adulthood with direction, a sense of dynamic growth, and the satisfaction of meaningful
effort. Obviously, the pursuit of status, wealth, fame, power, freedom, and so forth, are
formed, governed, rewarded, and made sacred by cultural and social circumstances. It
is no different for other kinds of ambitions, Japanese spiritualism being one and American self-fulfillment being another. In these latter instances, at least, the most crucial
first item of business in the comparative study of such ambitions is to understand the
implicit assumptions about human nature that are involved and from there to trace out

the relationships of time, conduct, and society that center on each particular (cultural) conceptualization. Accordingly, it is to the Japanese idiom of the person, the everyday statements of human nature, that we next turn.

When speaking about people, and thus by implication about human nature, the Japanese are likely to structure a rich, coherent, and dynamic world of expression around a very small set of nouns that represent the elemental "substances" and geography of an inner, "spiritual" (seishin) world. This is a world that can be visualized through spoken expressions and seen in the physical manifestations of body-states—such things as posture and the nuance of conduct. The unobservable and highly subjective realities of body-state, character, and the spirit are thus expressed in the more tangible imagery of speech and action. This same language, reversing the direction, is crucial to much of the effort to cope with and perfect subjective reality. The two-way traffic is so frequent that only at a great remove is their separation apparent.

The two crucial "substances" are ki and kokoro, nouns as ubiquitous in spoken Japanese as the verbs "to feel" and "to think" are in English. They are central to what would be, in our terms, an immense variety of personal characteristics—including will, insight, sensibility, self-control, and emotion. There is little justification for labeling ki and kokoro as concepts, since that would imply a narrowness of definition and a precision of logic that is not to be found.[3] Rather, these nouns are so common that they are at once simple and yet impenetrable. Words of this sort have an extraordinary density of association and are not to be grasped as part of lexical sets.

An understanding of the "spiritual" view of adulthood requires that we develop a deep empathy for the implications about human perfectibility inherent in the usage that surrounds ki and kokoro. We must recognize at the outset that daily life is so saturated with their mention that both the unconscious minutiae and the deeply considered ambitions of life are anchored in these words, and their significance largely derives from this fact. Rather than dry axioms at the base of a philosophical system, we find in ki and kokoro an extraordinary world condensed. Simply to say kokoro is to evoke a profound value.

Both terms, furthermore, have a long and rich history as crucial elements in traditional Chinese[4] and Japanese thought.[5] The Confucian Analects, the writings of early Taoism, the aesthetic language of Japanese literature, and the explanations of Japanese Buddhism all utilize them. They represent human nature and human potential, and yet they have not been defined (in the Western philosophical sense), but rather their meaning has been assumed, implied in the usage, and often left intentionally vague for greater suggestive power.

Words require the sustenance of tangible form. One finds a concern with ki and kokoro threaded through different kinds of training, through some psychological therapies and prophylactic practices, through work, through the stages of life, through aesthetic matters, and so on. Largely because of the common insight and vocabulary they provide, these activities all come to have an affiliation that is particularly Japanese. Adulthood is not a concept or a subject but a time dimension in a more complex whole centering on human nature and its fulfillment.

The characters for both *kokoro* and *ki* have Chinese origins, and scholars trace their initial meaning to very ancient Chinese. *Kokoro* appears to have first meant "heart," in the corporal sense, and over time it came to stand also for "core," "essential," and "basic nature." In contemporary Japanese the term occupies a pivotal position in a broad field of expressions related to human psychology. Because written characters are remarkably conservative in terms of preserving early meanings, the original Chinese meaning of corporal heart has not been totally lost, and *kokoro* retains a natural, of-this-world quality. Certainly, the supernatural aspect of "spirit" in English is foreign to it. Also of considerable importance is the fact that the location of *kokoro* is the chest area, and the processes of perceiving, distinguishing, and knowing are not, thereby, solely or even primarily products of simple cognition.

Ki, too, has a natural quality to it. In the early Chinese, the character apparently stood for vapor (particularly of cooked rice). It came to mean breath, wind, air, and weather. *Ki* thus partakes in a general pan-cultural pattern in associating breath with vitality and spirit in contrast to the lifeless body lacking these animating qualities. The Hebrew *ruach*, the Greek *pneuma*, and the Sanskrit *prana* are other examples. Like *kokoro*, *ki* is also the center of an extensive set of expressions having to do with human psychology.

What happens to *ki* and *kokoro*, what they do, and what qualities obtain for them when taken in total constitute their inherent dynamic, and this becomes a picture of human nature. It is through the typical transformations of *ki* and *kokoro* that the assumed inner world of character participates in the world of outward, observable action and form. Knowing what inner changes are possible and likely, therefore, puts us on the road to understanding the significance of many outward concerns and activities focused on the perfection of character.

Ki enjoys a remarkable range of qualities and conditions which bridge our rather more separate worlds of feelings (easily changed, universal) and personality (more inherent, individual, specific). Consider the following list: (1) *ki* is heavy—i.e., the person is dull, sluggish; (2) *ki* is fast—excitable; (3) *ki* is long/short—patient/impatient; (4) *ki* is large/small—generous/timid; (5) *ki* is strong—strong-willed, persistent; (6) *ki* sinks—disappointed; (7) *ki* is easily changed—unsettled, fickle. Even from this short list we can appreciate the problems of translation, for the very same *ki* in closely similar phrases is analogous to mind, will, person, and temperament in English. An integrated view of personal character is retained, and nothing illustrates this better than the expression for madness—"*ki* is different," implying that the person's *ki* has changed in some fundamental way, has gone outside the normal range of flux.

While rational calculation is readily discussed by other vocabularies, willingness, inclination, attention, and energy are at issue in the case of *ki*, and actions may be considered in terms of calculation, but are more often seen as products of the state of *ki* at a given time. The essential changes a person experiences, according to the *ki* framework, are the ups and downs of energy, activity, and mood. These are impermanent conditions that collectively constitute an image of flux and often fragility. Basic to these conditions is the orienting, attending capacity of *ki* as illustrated in: (1) to use *ki*—to care about, to attend to, to worry about; (2) *ki* points toward—the person is inclined to do;

(3) *ki* is numerous—the person is of many minds, has fragmented attention; (4) *ki* is attached to—the person is careful of, attends to, focuses on; (5) *ki* is turned around—the person imagines too much; (6) *ki* fades away—the person feels faint; (7) *ki* is taken—the person is absorbed in; (8) *ki* is drunk up—the person is overawed; (9) *ki* is loose—the person is off guard; (10) *ki* is entered by—the person has something weighing on his mind, is troubled.

In most of this our initial reference to the person's "inner world" seems misleading since *ki* operates in a perceptual field (including memory) that surrounds the person. Just as breath enters and leaves the body, so *ki* orients to, and is affected by, what occurs in the world around the person. The *ki* of two people "meet," and knowing how another holds *ki* is to be sensitive to his or her feelings and intentions.

The fact that *ki* is vulnerable is of special interest in this regard, for "the way one holds *ki*" is crucial in the effective focus of attention (not fickle or scattered, but steady and concentrated), in the enhancement of perception, in the concentration of energy, and even in the defense against illness and depression. The phrase "illness comes from *ki*" is usually interpreted as meaning illness enters when one is off guard, when *ki* is improperly held. The onset of depression (i.e., when *ki* loses animation or will not move forward) is often taken as the product of what we might term the mismanagement of *ki*. Alertness and readiness, matters of focus, are expressed as having a firm hold on *ki* and are crucial to a wide variety of desirable outcomes. Good health (*genki*) is literally "basic" or "original" *ki*, and this is best interpreted as having a steady, adequate flow of energy (*kiryoku* or *ki* "power"). "Good health" also means "not tired."

All this is readily distinguished in the daily conduct and presence of people. The alert, energetic person, poised and ready, stands in sharp contrast to one who is lethargic, distracted, or confused, and the difference is explained in terms of *ki*. Learning to hold *ki* well is thus quite important to practical affairs, and it is a foundation for spiritual growth.

With *kokoro* we directly enter the idiom of cultivation, and thus we begin to consider the potential that "adulthood" can have for Japanese. *Kokoro*, often translated as "mind" or "spirit," can be improved, whereas the essential nature of *ki* is unchanging and only the individual's ability to manage and utilize it is subject to improvement.[6] One may cultivate, put in order, strengthen, foster, forge, temper, and purify *kokoro*. Since it lies behind *ki*, its perfectibility establishes a basic link between the phenomenal world related to *ki* and the efforts directed at education and perfection. For this reason, *kokoro* is the term used in discussions of growth and aging, of morality and aesthetics, and of human nature in the more considered realms of religion and philosophy. Spiritual enlightenment is spoken of in terms of *kokoro*; yet, however altered a state that might be, its characteristics are ones that begin to appear as one holds *ki* properly.

The general location of both *kokoro* and *ki* is the torso.[7] Ideas "float" into the chest (and *kokoro*), and the terms for chest and stomach are commonly interchangeable with those of *ki* and *kokoro* when excitement, tranquillity, anger, and so on, are discussed. Physiological change and the close relationship of *ki* and *kokoro* to it (in contrast, say, to the head or to supernatural spirits) underlie the elaborate Japanese concern with this central zone of the body. Given this perspective, one can feel the physiological impediments to concentration and energy flow, just as we have learned to "feel" guilt. Once again, Japanese spiritualism is anchored in the tangible, experiential, and immediate. It has a naturalistic, commonsensical quality.

To attain an inner calm and stability is the ultimate object of various forms of Japanese traditional training, all conceived as forms of yoga.[8] This state is desirable because it greatly enhances receptivity to outward reality, because it is the basis for energy flow, and because it is essential to readiness for action. These arts, from flower arranging to judo, really constitute one complex. In all of them repetitive practice gradually leads to physical stability, increased concentration, deeper insight, and greater emotional tranquillity.

Posture is a primary initial concern here. Whether seated or standing, a relaxed but alert posture that opens the central area and provides stability is often taught as the first step in managing *ki*. The early practice of *Zazen* is a matter of learning to sit correctly, and posture is crucial to learning virtually all the traditional arts. There is no more powerful symbol of the perfected inner life than that of outward composure.

An orderly, well-kept daily existence is another clear indication of the proper maintenance of *ki* and, in turn, such behavior is understood to be an important foundation for the process of growth and cultivation itself. The alertness, energy, and self-discipline required for efficiency in even the most mundane affairs invest just about any routine with great potential significance in terms of the spiritual perspective.

One cannot but sense throughout Japanese social life a tautness and precision of conduct akin to the military mode of existence. The morality behind the social order is here again deeply enmeshed in the judgmental frameworks and ambitions concerning personal cultivation. To be neat, proper, and orderly—whether in housekeeping, factory routines, personal relations, or daily ceremonies—is to possess the necessary will, energy, and attention. Japanese social order is buttressed by the idea that orderliness is an expression of something far more important—the character of those being orderly. Coercive order, however, has no long-term value in this scheme; ideally, compliance and efficiency are to come from each person.

The goals of concentration and concentrated experience mean that pursuing a variety of things at once, or switching from one pursuit to another, is viewed as debilitating and as an indication of character weakness or malady. The esteemed life is one of persistence and singularity of focus in work, in social relations, and in long-term goals. Time works for those who concentrate attention on a particular ambition or corner of the world but not for those switching careers, relationships, or points of view. It is almost unthinkable for someone to attempt to do several sports seriously, for example, and Japanese scholars tend to devote their entire careers to a particular (often, by our standards, narrow and soon outdated) theory or research topic. An artist in his sixties tells me he needs twenty years more of study. The man who cannot learn to stay still, to be patient, or to be loyal is thus judged as lacking character. The image of such a person contrasts, of course, with one of personal stability and calm. One ultimate rationale for this valuation of single-mindedness is the "spiritual" insight that such concentrated effort and attention foster.

The very important *michi* (or *do*), meaning "way" or "path," which is suffixed to the names of virtually all traditional pursuits (thus, the "way" of tea, the "way" of fencing, etc.), expresses this notion. In Japan, to cultivate a particular "way" means essentially to spend a very long time practicing an "art," thus deepening one's intuitive grasp of its inherent nature. The conceptual framework of "way" has roots in ancient Chinese and Japanese thought, but the crucial point here is that the cultivation of the human spirit (*kokoro*) is deeply involved with the overall, long-term form of personal careers. Unswerving endeavor in work or in a "way" or in a family role carries a very high value, and this holds for all levels of society. The policeman and the housewife doing their duty faithfully over a lifetime are as involved in the pursuit of spiritual insight as are the artist and the Zen priest who self-consciously seek such a goal. All roles and duties in daily life are thus potentially sacred, and I have on several occasions heard serious discussions of the need to articulate the "way" of the modern businessman. This emphasis on spiritual development within daily affairs obviously contributes to the great dynamic of an ostensibly secular Japanese society.

The virtue in sticking to a narrow career path is coupled to the idea that as the ability to concentrate develops (with all that it implies about heightened perception and deeper understanding) it naturally extends to all of life, and that the "spiritual" goals of any career or study, any human life in fact, are essentially the same. All paths lead in the same direction, one defined by the universality of external truth and comprehended by the developing *kokoro*. Insight is a product of character-strengthening and vice versa—the two can hardly be separated. Discipline, persistence, and all else that represents self-control thus set the stage for a maturity of understanding that focuses on the unchanging reality that lies behind the mercurial shifts of human ambition and language-bound thought. Time and practice teach profound insight to those willing and able to learn to listen, and almost any career or "way" offers this possibility if undertaken seriously for many years. While the discipline of work and other social duties is a crucial framework for early development, teaching a kind of mastery which in turn teaches acceptance and humility, the final stages of life should ideally witness a transcendance of social forms and cultural formulations.[9] The individual now becomes more directly responsive to intrinsic reality. It is often said by Zen priests that the movement of personal growth comes full circle with this final stage, for those who see clearly achieve the spontaneity and directness of childhood.

The general interest in such things as artistic creations, autobiography, and biography is also revealing. Famous careers tell the story of spiritual growth; an artist's work deepens as he grows older, and the artistic products of cultivated men reveal to the sensitive observer great spiritual insight. Samples of the calligraphy, painting, and other works of exceptional people become treasured for the inspiration they contain. Anecdotes revealing the character of great men, similar to our Lincoln stories, are remarkably popular and commonly used as part of "spiritual" instruction. The great life, not a supreme being or a set of normative pronouncements, lies at the center of Japanese spiritualism. We should also note, however, that spiritual greatness is thought to be revealed in a remarkable (but seldom miraculous) act, one that illustrates

Maslow ... of needs.

the spiritual accomplishment of a long period. There is a serious problem here, for acts and action can become the dominant focus. Instead of being no more than illustration, action can become an end in itself, in which case the nature of Japanese spiritualism is radically altered. Japanese history and literature are filled with heroic (typically sacrificial) acts that reveal character. In some historical times and places, the Japanese have been taught to emulate such acts rather than pursue individual cultivation in its biographical fullness. We will shortly turn to consider the consequences of just such a shift in prewar Japan.

Returning to aesthetic matters, to appreciate the *kokoro*, or the "essence," of a poem, a novel, or a picture is to appreciate the *kokoro* of its creator, and the very ability for such appreciation is understood to be in direct proportion to the development of the beholder's *kokoro*. The word *kokoro* can thus become a shorthand for the near oneness of things—creator, created, and the eternal truth which binds them. The product of one spiritual pursuit has meaning and affinity for those whose lives have been devoted to separate careers, because the spiritual underpinning of all effort is essentially the same. Here human nature is no longer a separate reality. A rich and seemingly paradoxical world that we might label "mystical" is thus fashioned without recourse to the supernatural. All things come to be understood as essentially allied, but this alliance is *perceived*, not created by individual thought.[10] Remember, the *kokoro* is not a cognitive system, but the center of the whole being, a center that has memory, learns, is physiologically sensitive, scans interior and exterior worlds, and synthesizes all this and much more in the conduct of a personal life. The power to perceive deeply, to know, comes from long, devoted training, patience, and concentration focused on some "way."[11]

Naturally, older Japanese have a special awareness of, and preoccupation with, life in these terms. The concentration of energy and alertness is important for all ages, but the maturing stages of *kokoro*—the time when the description "a cultivated *kokoro*" becomes appropriate—comes rather late. While time has brought the decline of many faculties, "retirement" is supposed to bring a rich harvest in spiritual terms. The pursuit of traditional arts, aesthetic wanderings, and other personal quests increases, especially among the educated and well-to-do. Older men and women may find their followers venerating them as living testimonies of a certain "way." Whether they are comfortable in the role or not, they seldom have much choice; for this is the shape the ideal life should take, and every denial of spiritual certitude or personal virtue only confirms the expectations of those following in the "way" that old age brings great humility, eccentricity, and ironical insight. The stark image of an ancient, gnarled tree, standing open and revealed to the elements and thus past the time of active generativity and the deceptions of luxuriant growth, epitomizes the promise of tranquillity and the approach to unity with all life. This is not, of course, a promise open to empirical scrutiny.[12]

The understanding of human nature implicit in the daily usage and patterns of behavior surrounding the terms *ki* and *kokoro* thus establishes a broad field of relationship between the minutiae of daily conduct and most aspects of Japan's formal religious and philosophical heritage. What is central is not some division between sacred and profane, but the matter of personal cultivation itself. Human perfectibility is the connecting link between everyday routine and the eternal truth that lies hidden within it. In between, in terms of time, we find many recognized levels of growth, change, and accomplishment, and these are closely associated with life-cycle changes and advancement in the social hierarchy; but the whole framework of understanding would lose much of its ultimate influence were it not for the fact that its upper reaches connect quite easily into the long heritage of Japanese interest in mystical insight and thirst for oneness with the world. So far as the general tradition of human perfectibility goes, the duty-filled world of the Confucian scholar laboring at self-discipline and personal cultivation merges naturally with the independent, iconoclastic world of the laughing Zen priest. As images and symbols of a life well led and of spiritual accomplishment, both greatly enhance the sense of adulthood outlined here. I might add that these images also stand for the advancement of freedom, a freedom, that is, based on the atrophy of the self, not on an escape from the pressures and demands of the world.[13]

II. The Vicissitudes of Spiritualism in Modern Japan

So far, the spiritual meaning of Japanese adulthood has been presented as essentially a product of the intersection of a particular sense of time and a particular sense of human nature. Out of necessity these ideas have been considered initially as if they existed in some pristine state requiring a social, political, and historical vacuum, an approach we must now abandon in order to explore the equally "factual" matters of modern change, confusion, and tragedy. There is much to be learned in the fate history has dealt this attractive and rather benign view of human nature.

Inevitably, what is of value and meaning to individual spheres of life—matters of ethics and personal growth—becomes entangled with the machinery of great political and social ambitions. Large-scale efforts recognize and attempt to create a specific kind of ideal person suited to the requirements of large-scale mobilization. The loyal soldier ready to die for country, the assertive Red Guard ready to criticize a superior, or the critically independent citizen ready to make democracy work are all of a common type. The ideologies that arise on a national political scene, to reverse the direction of influence, almost of necessity are phrased partly in the readily appreciated language and metaphor belonging to the personal ethical sphere. Characteristically the millennium provides the opportunity to realize the highest ideals of personhood and personal relations. Appeals to any political banner, that is, are made in terms that are originally meaningful at a very different level of existence. In their combinations and permutations the original or pristine character of each is by definition transformed. Furthermore, formulations of value that ostensibly hold only for one level actually gain dynamic form through the contrasts involved. Personal morality is all the more important because of a philistine political world. And so, too, is political activism readily justified as a means of eliminating evils of popular character. The lines of relationship between the two quite different levels or realms of meaning and action are thus historically complex.[14] Here we can do no more than briefly outline this story for Japan over the last century, and yet without this outline our sense of the matter would be far from complete.

That enormous upheaval, the Meiji Restoration of 1868, brought a newly constructed nation-state into a rapidly industrializing, essentially Western world. The spiritual outlook, while never the exclusive possession of any class in feudal times, was central to the way of life of one group in particular—the samurai. The instrumental values of samurai spiritualism, namely highly polished military skills, effective organization, and fearless action, were never clearly separated from matters of quiet self-cultivation and religious transcendence. Zen Buddhism, for example, was primarily of interest to warriors. For early-modern Japan the spiritual legacy came largely from samurai. Particularly important were those who generated much of the commotion and voiced the unfulfilled nationalist ambitions during the period immediately prior to 1868. They set the stage for the Meiji Restoration and were thereafter deified as heroes. Much of the myth-making focused on their strength of character. These young samurai became symbols of the political and especially revolutionary applicability of Japanese spiritualism. Violent impatience with the world's problems in this version was justified in terms of personal sacrifice. The goals of quietude and wisdom were subordinated to action, and youthful impetuousness was equated with purity of motive.

The new government, led by many of the samurai of the restoration movement, faced the enormous task of achieving international security and independence for Japan through economic and military development. In this undertaking, which proved to be so remarkably swift, a disciplined and dedicated populace was of crucial importance. Here, personal character became entangled with issues of the efficiency of the modern state. As the country's leaders, men who were once young revolutionaries, grew older and more politically entrenched, they shifted their outlook on what in the spiritualist tradition was most important. A pattern of state-sponsored moral education and military training gradually emerged that aimed primarily at efficient mass action. The requirements of large-scale mobilization thus provided another reason to set aside the ideal of gradual and highly individual progress. As in the case of the restoration activists just mentioned, the focus turned toward youth, but unlike the activists' example, the emphasis in state-supported spiritualism was on loyalty rather than dissent. Thus, as the spiritual outlook became more deeply entangled in the modernizing ambitions of the late nineteenth century, its individual-level qualities became publicly distorted.

This distortion took place most visibly in the worlds of public institutions and political schemes, but it left many areas of social and personal life untouched. There the less instrumental view of personal growth remained in force. In fact, it was to the private sphere that many Japanese turned to escape the hustle, the growing jingoism, and ultimately the authoritarianism of the pre-World War II era. In that private sphere, the spiritual outlook I have described remained, and while it was nativistic and opposed to the utilitarian character of Western civilization, it was also generally opposed to authoritarianism and dubious about the ultimate worth of modern society.

There are other facets to the history of late-nineteenth-century Japanese modernization involving traditional values and the personal level of relevance. Japanese work hard and with great discipline, a matter crucial to the prosecution of industrialization. Such habits were not created by the modern state, nor by traditional, self-conscious spiritualism. Once the outlook of Western utilitarianism entered the nineteenth-century Japanese framework of conscious concern with virtue and motivation in work, however, the good work habits of Japanese came to be viewed as consistent with, and bolstered by, tradition. Foreign individualism and materialism were seen as threatening these valuable qualities.

Another Japanese quality that contributed greatly to national success is the willingness of her citizens to adapt to and adopt from powerful foreign civilizations. The understanding at the personal level that truth lies outside the self (that it is natural and thus universal) is crucial, I believe, to understanding the Japanese capacity for accepting and mastering Western industrialism. The special epistemology at work in Japanese tradition makes borrowing, copying, adapting, and imitating perfectly reasonable, and, furthermore, the pejorative implications about the person (namely, lack of independence and creativity) that we almost invariably see in acts of copying are not encouraged by the Japanese view of the person. In fact, imitation is central to all forms of self-cultivation. Once the Pandora's box of foreign ideas and customs was opened, however, many Japanese came to see their most treasured virtues and cultural insights threatened by the wave of Westernization. Before the inherent antipathies of two fundamentally different civilizations had become clear to the Japanese, they had entered enthusiastically on a course of borrowing in every possible area of knowledge. Slogans distinguishing spiritual from technological matters, in the hope of preserving the Japaneseness of the former while allowing continued Western influence in the latter, were constantly reiterated. It is clear that such a separation was quite impossible for Japan, however, and, furthermore, political or economic policy could hardly be made exclusively subject to only a spiritual or technical perspective.

The confusion generated by change—technical, social, but, above all, cultural— became a major element in the frustration and instability that underlay the politics of Japan in the nineteen-thirties, as the government, increasingly dominated by the military, attempted to raise the spiritual tradition into a national ideology and thus exorcise Japan of the bewitching power of foreign influence. As before, the tradition was greatly distorted. Political authority was inserted where personal experience (and perhaps a personal teacher) had been appropriate. What was to be learned from life was replaced by codified rules and principals. Action of service to the state was made the central concern.

Let us turn back for a moment. With Westernization and modernization to provide new temporal and cultural contrasts after 1868, the assumptions, ideals, and commonplace values of a previous age came to be gathered into the less vital but more discernible category of "tradition." A new cultural consciousness was produced by the emerging dialectical framework built on the contrasts East/West and modern/traditional. The deepening awareness and reflective concern with past fundamentals (previously taken so much for granted as to be in one sense unknown) that arose did not immediately threaten the variability, flexibility, and potential profundity that characterizes the spiritual outlook at the personal level. Kenneth Pyle, for example, has shown that a major problem among intellectual nativists in the period before the Russo-Japanese war was their inability to articulate or agree upon a definition of Japanese tradition. This is no surprise, since "traditional" had come to mean all that was not foreign. It is of great significance, then, that these thinkers abandoned their scholarly dilemmas at the time of the war in a rush to be part of the action.[15] Perhaps it is too simplistic an assertion, but it does appear that the appeal of nationalistic action was greatly enhanced, then and later, by the confusion about personal and political meaning in a Japan rapidly becoming culturally more and more complicated.

This confusion encouraged greater and greater government intervention into the realm of morality and values. As the clouds of war gathered in the thirties and military men achieved a greater voice in government, this intervention reached its zenith in an effort to make a truly Japanese national ethic. The official view of Japanese spiritualism gave emphasis to the qualities of patriotism, diligence, duty, endurance, and sacrifice. The sense of biographical growth was subordinated to that of instant moral achievement. The official view emerged first in the military and in the schools and was strongly supported by the police and numerous government-sponsored mass organizations.[16] The brand of spiritualism that emerged echoed strongly the previous samurai reformer version, with its emphases on instrumental action, youth, and the State. What, in its benign form, constituted many paths to personal fulfillment now became limited to those officially acceptable. Thus, the authority of the state was used to effect a uniform national identity and moral strictness based upon a kind of traditionalism that ironically was new to Japanese history, consciously fabricated as it was by a modern state for nationalistic purposes. Thus, political oppression and ultimately war were carried on in the name of a spiritual outlook only part of which they actually represented. Careers in the military, death on the battlefield, and the rearing of good future soldiers, goals that did indeed represent forms of spiritual strength, superseded the more profound, personal, and quietistic goals of the tradition. What was lost was the sense of personal cultivation for its own sake. One is tempted to say that in attempting to solve the national disease of immoderate and disjointed modernization, an impatient and disorganized government turned to Japan's strongest tradition for some remedy—just as individual Japanese in hard times have always been encouraged to rely on their spiritual strength—and yet for all of its resources this tradition proved itself inappropriate as the social philosophy of a modern nation.

Many Japanese understood this in the thirties, it appears, but they remained generally silent, preferring to keep personal opinion and national policy separate. The failure of democratic institutions in that era is in part to be understood as the result of a paradoxical situation in which most citizens remained loyally patient (many who held critical opinions kept silent) while extremists in the name of patriotism subverted political institutions by radical action. The only popular opposition came from the left, where activism was also the dominant philosophy. Both the silent and the forceful contributed to the collapse of political order, and each in its own way illustrated why the Japanese spiritual tradition is regarded by some as incompatible with democratic government.

The Japanese have never ceased experiencing spiritualism in this paradoxical sense—at one and the same time it is a critical source of national strength, a dangerous avenue to national excess, a profound source of understanding of the human condition and of personal progress and, yet, because it contrasts with imported Western ideas, a source of contradiction, doubt, and confusion. It can encourage action, but it is more typically understood as supporting patient endurance and the separation of private opinion from public duty. Finally, the problem of social order has become a question in modern times of the propriety of governmental initiative and authority in the realm of private morality. None of these matters has declined in importance since 1945.

Since the war, however, their arrangement in actual social life has changed radically. Now one finds a general preoccupation with publicly avoiding all expressions reminiscent of prewar militarism. This has meant that the vocabulary of spiritualism is taboo for the government, the political parties, and most other prominent national entities. In the media the image of self-sacrifice is often a laughing matter. The government's required courses in morals for the public schools are good illustrations of the almost total reversal of affairs from prewar days. Today, high-school morals textbooks devote considerably more pages to Western religions and ethical systems than to native Japanese conceptions, and the course is an anemic failure. Furthermore, the occupation left to Japan a democratic government and the ideals of American citizenship, neither of which fit all that comfortably with traditional values and understanding. Japanese leftists, discontent with the occupation's capitalist legacy, go even further, for their ideal is of the person who persistently refuses to accept external (corrupt) reality, holding out instead for the ultimate realization of some utopian scheme defined in social, not spiritual, terms. A powerful leftist teachers' union now opposes every effort to make the schools sources of a revived nationalism. For most of the intelligentsia spiritualism is anachronistic and still dangerous. But, with no truly appealing alternative at the personal level (democracy is hardly interesting as an ideal for the conduct of personal lives), Japan remains culturally leaderless and the occupation comes to appear more and more like a cultural decapitation.

Companies and other intermediate-level institutions, however, continue to recognize the instrumental value of the traditional outlook, and an increasing number are conducting spiritual training programs in order that they can at least benefit from effective, dedicated, and satisfied workers.[17] Many individuals, furthermore, dismayed by the direction of industrial change and increasingly skeptical of the value of foreign (particularly American) cultural solutions, are attempting to consider more deeply the possibilities within the Japanese spiritual heritage. The tradition is being considered once again, but this time with an eye to pinpointing what is of value outside the samurai legacy. Bookstores are filled once more with semipopular attempts to define the essence of Japaneseness, and the traditional arts are enjoying a boom.

To conclude this brief historical review, then, the contemporary scene is characterized by a separation of national-level and personal-level matters, spiritualism is once more rather benign, but there is also widespread confusion and discontent over the lack of ethical clarity, and many harbor private desires that the government once more step in as spiritual educator and cultural arbitrator. I firmly doubt history is going to repeat itself, but the issues of value and meaning that make the question of cultural definitions of adulthood so fascinating have taken a particular shape in modern Japanese history, one that is thoroughly entangled with shifting national approaches to social order and cultural identity.

The last century has witnessed another more unilinear kind of change in Japanese social institutions, a change that seems to be permanently altering the traditional view of biographical time. Rapid economic advancement has changed the shape of many working careers. Modern patterns of living and employment are also reshaping the domestic cycle of the Japanese family. Despite the predictions of wholesale conversion to American ways coming from some specialists, the relatively intense Japanese commitment to work (and mothering) roles has not changed much since the end of the war, but the social context and institutional meaning of such responsibilities have been changing significantly.

Most Japanese men today are salaried employees of companies or the government, and for most of them it is a bureaucratic kind of career path they follow. Education is a basic distinguishing mark, personal ability has some influence, but seniority is the crucial principle upon which rank, responsibility, status, and monetary reward are ordered over time. Experience is more valued than in America. Men move up slowly, and there are age limits for promotion. As a result, the hierarchy of bureaucratic authority in factories as well as offices is age graded. A man is judged relative to his age-mates, all working their way up in competition with one another. The obvious failures prove to be those who are not promoted at various crucial age-determined stages. The bureaucratic framework, in sum, creates an ideal career arc that progresses slowly from subordination to supervisory position, from dependence and inexperience to a capacity to lead and assist others, from the necessity of humility to the necessity of self-confidence.

The conceptual ideal behind this bureaucratic ladder largely echoes the outlook and the values of the traditional family enterprise.[18] The young son worked hard learning from his father. Gradually, as the son gained in experience, he is allowed greater initiative. The father, as he aged, became less important to the daily rounds of work but remained crucial for the wisdom he provided. Midway through this, the son himself became a father and assumed responsibility for the education of the next generation. Even in retirement, the old father remained a valued advisor. Obviously, this ideal model gave no recognition to oedipal tensions or to any need for generational autonomy. The idea of growth through independence found no place in this scheme. The family ideal placed the full life cycle firmly in a social nexus. It tied authority to both seniority and to experience, and it visualized personal growth as the product of discipline and experience.

The same ideal is generally true of modern Japanese organizations.[19] The rub comes in the fact that the great majority of today's employees cannot be promoted to bureaucratic positions analogous to fathers in the traditional family. Moreover, men are generally retired from their firms or government bureaus in their mid-fifties, and, following this, economic necessity requires that they work in subordinate roles in other companies. The company ideal is that of "one big family," and yet at retirement the company "family member" is sent away. Only a tiny group of men, those who achieve executive rank in their late forties or early fifties, are permitted by the nature of modern organizations to assume the satisfying role of respected seniors. The scale of contemporary organizational structures, in other words, has created far greater distance between the ideal and reality than existed in the past. For many young Japanese men, work is not the time-honored pivot of their existence and growth that it had been. Many are hedging their bets with more private pursuits, and in this development lies the possibility of some, perhaps many, new conceptions of life's progress. The conception of male adulthood as "flowering" in the toil of work will undoubtedly remain the major theme, but new and different species of human fulfillment are appearing in reaction to the organizational environment.

The woman's life cycle in the now nuclear and rather isolated family of the salaried worker revolves not around an organizational framework, but around marriage, child-raising, and the increasingly long period that follows the departure of her children from home. Her "flowering" may come with physical beauty, but her life's central time comes with child-bearing, which to the Japanese represents a woman's highest achievement in terms of social responsibility, sacrifice, and the expenditure of creative energy. Unlike the case of many men, who today are never given the organizational opportunity to "flower" or reach a pinnacle of socially recognized productive maturity, motherhood remains an almost universal possibility. On the other hand, the arrival of the two-generation family as the national type symbolizes the fact that a serious discontinuity now exists in the lives of most women after their children's departure. Americans take this for granted, but Japanese are just learning to adjust to it. Greater longevity (now exceeding United States rates) has exacerbated these social-role and structural-place problems for men and women alike, especially since the traditional place for the aged—living with their own children in a known community—is steadily declining as a possibility. It is a fact that past Japanese society provided a firmer foundation for a role-centered ideal of self-cultivation than exists today.[20]

In conclusion, however, I would like to emphasize that what is significant in Japanese spiritualism is the promise itself, for it clearly lends meaning, integrity, and joy to many lives, especially as the nature of adult existence unfolds. It fits the physical process of aging. It recognizes the inherent value of experience. It gives strong witness to the importance of a lifelong effort to retain and develop personal integrity. It reinforces the notion that social structure is justifiably gerontocratic. And for all its emphasis on social responsibility, discipline, and perseverance in the middle years, it encourages these as means to a final state of spiritual freedom, ease, and universal belonging. It would seem that here we have a philosophy of life that emphasizes what the experiences of adult life are likely to teach and a vision of the social order more likely to suit the changing perspectives of age. Time is not eroding life's prospects, nor can the superficial changes of technology or verbal fashion alienate an aging generation from its approach to the deeper, more essential truths of life. Here is a philosophy seemingly made for adulthood—giving it stature, movement, and optimism.

There are, of course, may problems: As we have seen, it is also a philosophy most certainly at odds with much of value we would call modern; it has been used as an apology for many forms of political folly, cruelty, and injustice; in one sense, it gives youth little weight or significance, in another far too much; it makes people slaves (in our terms) to duty and social role, and typically (but not at all necessarily), it is a powerful force supporting the status quo. None of this should ever be denied.

But since we are primarily interested at this time in definitions of adulthood, we might reverse the coin and ask whether the progressive efforts of the last century to further modern institutions and rationality, self-conscious individuality, and freedom from social constraint (all coupled, of course, with the profound effects of technological change) have not taken much of the value and dynamic out of our understanding of adulthood. Social progress and progressivism seem to be alienating us from a sense of biographical progress. Old age has come to mean obsolescence, retirement, senescence, loneliness, and the shame of unavoidable dependency. Work and virtue seem to grow further apart year by year. Have we not, in the words of Laurens vander Post, "abolished superstitions of the heart only to install a superstition of the intellect in its place?"[21]

The Japanese spiritualism I have attempted to outline here is an ideal, one among many in today's Japan, and it cannot be said to correspond neatly to a discrete set of objective facts. I have also made it far simpler and more coherent than it actually is to Japanese. It is a vision, one that grows rather naturally from the everyday Japanese idiom of human nature, and as a vision it has the power greatly to influence the course of individual lives and, at times, the course of the nation's destiny. I strongly doubt we could (or would want to) attempt to create a similar vision, but the comparison is striking, and in this Japanese vision there is much truth, especially regarding aspects of the experience of adulthood about which our modern world has become increasingly silent.

REFERENCES

[1]For a few details generated by a cross-national survey approach, see D. W. Plath and K. Ikeda, "After Coming of Age: Adult Awareness of Age Norms" in *Psychological Anthropology* (The Hague, 1975).

[2]W. Caudill and H. Weinstein, "Maternal Care and Infant Behavior in Japan and America," *Psychiatry*, 32 (1969), pp. 12-43.

[3]Nothing better illustrates the pitfalls of over-conceptualization than the recent efforts of two outstanding Japanese psychiatrists to define the layman's term *ki* into a place in psychiatric theory. See T. Doi, *Amae no Kōzō* (Tokyo, 1971) and B. Kimura, *Hito to Hito No Aida* (Tokyo, 1972).

[4]Cf. D. J. Munro, *The Concept of Man in Early China* (Stanford, 1969).

[5]Cf. Y. Akatsuka, *Ki no Kōzō* (Tokyo, 1974).

[6]In this regard, compare the discussion of *ki* in K. Tohei, *Aikido in Daily Life* (Tokyo, 1966) with that of *kokoro* in P. Kapleau, *Three Pillars of Zen* (Tokyo, 1965).

[7]Cf. K. Dürckheim, *Hara: The Vital Center of Man* (London, 1962).

[8]Cf. *idem, The Japanese Cult of Tranquility* (London, 1960).

[9]The transcendence of culture is here represented by the replacement of dialectical categorization by silent awareness of unity. In Japanese religion, the dialectic is the disease.

[10]Consider the simple teaching of Dōgen Zenji, a Zen priest: "To study Buddhism is to study oneself; to study oneself is to forget oneself, to forget oneself is to be enlightened by all things." *Zen Center of Los Angeles Journal*, Winter/Spring, 1975.

[11]H. Herrigal's *Zen in the Art of Archery* (New York, 1953) is one good account of the difficulties of training in a "way" and the results as experienced by a sensitive Westerner.

[12]Although some elderly Japanese have expressed doubt and disappointment at the end of lives lived in accord with such a promise, there is no form that disproof or general denial can take because personal experience is crucial, and, within the realm of experience and change, nothing is automatic.

[13]Although it cannot be explored adequately here, it is true that the Japanese language of selfhood is more fragmented than ours. There is a variety of different and distinct terms that translate as "self." To kill the "self" is a positive act, for example, but a particular kind of "self" is involved.

[14]For an account of this relationship in modern Germany, see W. H. Bruford, *The German Tradition of Self-Cultivation: "Bildung" from Humbolt to Thomas Mann* (London, 1975).

[15]*The New Generation in Meiji Japan: Problems of Cultural Identity 1885-1895* (Palo Alto, 1969).

[16]Cf. K. Tsurumi *Social Change and the Individual: Japan Before and After Defeat in World War II* (Princeton, 1970).

[17]Cf. T. Rohlen, *For Harmony and Strength: Japanese White Collar Organization in Anthropological Perspective* (Berkeley, 1974).

[18]Cf. H. Hazama *Nihonteki keiei no keifu* (Tokyo).

[19]Cf. *For Harmony and Strength, op. cit.*

[20]Plath has explored in greater depth the question of the life cycle in the context of modern Japanese society. See D. W. Plath, "The After Years" in D. Cowgill and L. Holmes, eds., *Aging and Modernization* (New York, 1972), pp. 133–50; and D. W. Plath, "The Last Confucian Sandwich: Becoming Middle Aged," *Journal of Asian and African Studies*, X: 1-2 (1975), pp. 51-63.

[21]*The Heart of the Hunter* (New York, 1961), p. 137.

SUSANNE HOEBER RUDOLPH AND LLOYD I. RUDOLPH

Rajput Adulthood: Reflections on the Amar Singh Diary

OUR INTERPRETATION OF ADULTHOOD IN INDIA is based on a personal document, the diary of a North Indian Rajput nobleman, Amar Singh,[1] and particularly on his account, in the first seven of its eighty-seven volumes, of his late adolescence and early married years (1898-1905).[2] In these years he completed his education, became a professional soldier, and entered his extended family as husband, father, and heir to the title and estate of Kanota, in the princely state of Jaipur. We approach adulthood from the perspective of the family, not the family in an evolutionary universal history, or the family abstractly, as an ideal type or heuristic construct, or the family as it ought to be in the light of a given set of values. Rather, we approach it contextually, in a particular time and place, Rajputana, in northwestern India, at the end of the nineteenth century, a society of princely states under British "paramountcy," feudal and patrimonial, in which agriculture, commerce, and state service provided livelihoods and resources.

We approach adulthood via the family in part because we have extensive and rare evidence, an actor's detailed account of reasons and motives, rules and roles, strategies and outcomes, in part because the extended family in the "big house" of a hundred souls related to several other big houses is a complex social unit that occupies much more social and psychic space than does the conjugal family. It organizes, supports, and directs a wide range of distinct activities and roles. In twentieth-century Europe and America many of these activities and roles are, on evolutionary and normative grounds, expected to be structurally and functionally "differentiated" in "secondary" associations such as production or service enterprises, schools, occupational groups, voluntary associations, and media publics. The distinction between primary and secondary, difficult enough to establish and maintain in analyses of contemporary industrial societies, will not occupy a central place in our analysis. Instead, we take the differentiated, complex, and corporate extended family as our unit of analysis for the study of adulthood.

We do not claim to speak about "Indian" adulthood. We are interested in adulthood understood in terms of what is appropriate to an extended family[3] of the ruling stratum in Rajputana, India, circa 1900. Indeed we are skeptical of accounts of adulthood that do not take account of regional, class, and social differences. Comparison, generalization, and judgment follow contextual analysis. The society that nurtured Amar Singh is passing away, but the upper-class extended family survives. Hence, some of the generalizations we formulate may have significance well beyond the aristocratic Rajput circle in which they arise, in other upper-class extended families in India and elsewhere, including East-Coast family summer compounds in America. In any case, they suggest an alternative form of psychic and social organization and its consequences for limiting and fulfilling life.

Adulthood—or maturity—is often defined in terms of independence, understood in part as the opposite of dependence, and individualism (which we would distinguish from individuality), understood in part as the ability to articulate, defend, and pursue self-definition and self-interest against the collective. For Amar Singh, being a mature adult meant creating and maintaining individuality and initiative in an interdependent, corporate setting. Being individualistic in the extended family and the big house was disruptive and costly, but articulating and expressing a distinct self was not.

I

We start with the fact that Amar Singh was a Rajput, not a Brahman, Vaish, or Kayastha, the social orders traditionally associated with literate vocations. These social orders involve rather different adulthoods. He shared the norms of the Kshatriya social order whose traditional calling was to rule as warriors, not those of the non-martial twice-born, of whom the Brahman is often taken as the leading exemplar. Brahman norms feature asceticism, self-control, non-violence, and correct religious ritual in the service of purity and the avoidance of pollution. To transcend passion and desire, to conserve the limited supply of that precious bodily fluid, semen—source of power and creativity—entailed limiting or eliminating the appetites, maintaining the inviolability of living creatures, avoiding contaminating substances and persons as well as "hot" foods and meat, and practicing rituals of purification. Brahmans aspired to be *brahmacharyas*, celibates with respect not only to sexual expression but also with respect to anger, appetite, and all the other passions that enslave men, destroy their tranquillity and serenity, and enhance rather than diminish their egoistic selves. Those who celebrate as well as those who denigrate Indian spiritualism have reference, in one form or another, to Brahmanic culture, taking it for Indian.

Rajput culture is very different.[4] In the great sweep of Indian history, across its centuries and regions, *Kshatriya* culture probably had a more central place than Brahman among dominant elites and provided the norm that most conquering or socially mobile groups emulated. Rajputs were expressive, not ascetic, valuing and practicing activities that released the passions. They were preeminently warriors and rulers, guardians of society's security and welfare. Feudal play, of which the highest expression was combat but which also included blood sports (pig-sticking, goat-cutting, hunting big and small game) and latterly polo, was a central occupation and preoccupation; its disciplines and austerities hardened the Rajput and prepared him for battle. Rajputs ate meat, took alcohol and opium (not as an underground or challenging counter-cultural practice, but to prepare for or to celebrate wars and weddings and as a support for ordinary social intercourse), kept concubines and enjoyed dancing girls. Their core value was not purity and the avoidance or eradication of pollution, but honor and the avoidance or eradication of dishonor. Courage, valor, and prowess animated the Rajput sensibility.

Political, not religious, ritual expressed and regulated the allocation of honor: to wear the gold anklet of the *tazimi sardar* at court ceremonials entitled the bearer to be greeted by the maharaja standing, folding his hands, and bowing twice. Wars were fought and kings unseated over who should occupy the first seat below the throne. The heroes of Rajput history are those who fought and died valiantly in battle or, among Rajput women, those who sacrificed themselves to encourage their men to do so and who performed *johur*, ritual self-immolation, to avoid the dishonor of capture after defeat.

There is no evident legacy or reason in the Kshatriya dimension of Rajput culture for Amar Singh to have become a writer or a diarist; if anything, its worldly activism and respect for physical prowess should have inhibited, even precluded, that result. But, like all complex high cultures, the Rajput style and world view included a variety of orientations, some more conducive to the writer's craft than others. Critical for Amar Singh, the potential writer, was the Charan component of Rajput culture, particularly as it was mediated by the Charan Barath Ram Nath jee Ratnu.

Being taught by Barath Ram Nath jee distinguished Amar Singh's education from that of other young princes and nobles taught by Charans. After an early-morning gallop or hunt and after exercising Jodhpur Lancer horses, Amar Singh repaired at eleven to the prince regent's bungalow to meet with his teacher. Although formally the tutor of Amar Singh's contemporary, the young Maharaja Sardar Singh, and other young men at the Jodhpur court, Ram Nath jee took a special interest in Amar Singh who proved to be a uniquely apt and rewarding student.

Keepers and cultivators of Rajput history and traditions, the Charans defined Rajput codes of conduct and ideals. At their best, they criticized without malice, praised without flattery. Genealogists, historians, and teachers, sometimes leading state servants, they collected and wrote *dohas*, a couplet literary form whose recitation was at once entertaining, informative, and moral. Their place in Rajput society was filled in other parts of Hindu society by a certain kind of Brahman.[5]

Whether as history or aphorism, the *doha* is meant to instruct as well as to entertain. As moral instruction it has something in common with another important influence in Amar Singh's education, the Victorian texts Ram Nath jee put in his way. He found, for example, the hortatory tone of Samuel Smile's *Duty* not unfamiliar and its moral and practical guidance attractive and useful in Rajput as well as English society. Encouraged by Ram Nath jee to read books that would broaden his knowledge of the world and quicken his imagination as well as instruct him, Amar Singh read widely in the early years of the diary, from Alexander Dumas and Victor Hugo to H. Rider Haggard and Marie Corelli, from biographies of George Washington and Napoleon Bonaparte and their generals to historical and cultural accounts of the nations of Europe and Asia.

Perhaps the most important text for the diary, if not for the diarist in his early years, was Plutarch's *Lives*. Amar Singh began reading it soon after he converted his memorandum book to "the diary," and continued doing so for almost a year. He was obviously much taken with it, although its power over him had its limits: "I was trying to read Plutarch's *Lives* when my eyes closed in slumber." Citations from Plutarch rival *dohas* at the beginning of diary entries, and it was Plutarch's example that led him to modify the diary form by recording, after the daily entry, the character and times of important persons he knew. This change in turn led to the extended essays on a variety of subjects written over several days and weeks.

Amar Singh was influenced, too, by the great literature of Indian civilization, the *Mahabharata* and the *Ramayana*. He read them not only because Ram Nath jee set them as texts and out of conventional respect but also because he wanted to know whether they measured up generally and in relation to English texts. Neither Ram Nath jee, the teacher, nor Amar Singh, the student, was *parti pris* about Western and Eastern literature; without pretense, indeed, without articulating their concern, they pursued quality and meaning, defining each with reference to the other. In the context and circumstances in which they found themselves, they were free from the cultural aggressiveness sometimes associated with Indian nationalism and the cultural alien- ation and self-hatred that many Indian intellectuals expressed in their affirmation and rejection of things English and Indian.

Being taught by a Charan was conventional; being taught by Ram Nath jee was not. Amar Singh learned from him to respect and value the best in Rajput culture and to avoid and criticize persons and practices that corrupt or degrade it. He learned, too, to understand and judge it from the outside, from the perspective of English and West- ern values and practices. In part from reading, in part from experience, he found those rules best that were appropriate to the context. Indian food tasted best, he found, when eaten from *thalis* with the hand, English food, when eaten off plates with knives and forks.[6] To transpose the rules was to spoil the food. His education had taught him that, in English society as in Indian, part of being adult was knowing what was appropriate, to know from specific contexts and circumstances what one was to do and how to do it well.

Being an adult for Amar Singh meant, in the first instance, being a good Rajput in a *fin de siècle* princely India influenced by British India. These environments were the necessary but not the sufficient conditions for adulthood. The extended family, depicted in intimate detail in the diary, provided the sufficient conditions. Its densely populated, expansive, multifarious world contrasts sharply with the sparsely populated, bounded, and narrow world of the nuclear family. Living well in the world of the extended fam- ily requires rather different skills, strategies, and character from those required to live well in a nuclear family. We have learned a great deal from the diary about the com- plex corporate structure of an extended family, about its sense of dynastic history, about the influence of physical space—how forts and *havelis*, men's and women's quarters, rooms off courtyards, back stairs, and front gates shape movements and manners— about generational and male/female relationships under conditions of gerontocratic authority and male dominance; about peer solidarity and conflict; about the expectation that sons, particularly first sons, will be as good as and similar to, not better than and different from, their fathers;[7] about the need for and balance between initia- tive and subordination, innovation and compliance. The diary enables us to observe these features of the extended family and to discern the reasons, rules, and strategies of the actors involved.

The contrast between the Rajput extended family and models and descriptions of nuclear families in Europe and America takes various forms. Affect in the extended family is more diffuse and, for the most part, more dilute than is likely to be the case in a nuclear family. One important consequence is that key affective relationships are less intense. Because there are more players who matter, rivalry among participants in the extended family involves lower psychic risks and costs than does rivalry in the sur- charged, high-stake monopolistic competition characteristic of the nuclear family. Con- flict and cooperation are more often carried on collaboratively among factions and allies than dyadically between single players. Authority and affection are less likely to be located or concentrated in the same person. The relationship between some biological and social life stages is patterned very differently: young married adults "join"—rather than leave—the family and older adults gain—rather than lose—authority (if not power). More generally, adulthood in the extended family involves the capacity to achieve individuality while living interdependently in a collective universe of significant others, not the capacity to achieve independence from the private universe of one con- jugal family and then to live in another.

II

The achievement of adulthood in the Freudian paradigm features the unravelment of the individual personality from the parents. Freudian ontogeny depicts the realiza- tion of autonomy in terms of primary and secondary differentiations as they are expressed in the struggle over organ modes:

> From the time of puberty onward the individual must devote himself to the great task of freeing himself from the parents; and only after this detachment is accomplished can he cease to be a child and so become a member of the social community. . . . In neurotics, however, this detachment from the parents is not accomplished at all; the son remains all his life in subjection to his father. . . .[8]

This formulation of individual ontogeny is closely related to Western man's view of his phylogeny. The oedipal struggle is the personal and familial counterpart of the much larger struggle against all forms of embeddedness in the corporate structures and collectivities of an older society. The psychological concepts that inform modern West- ern man about the meaning of adulthood also reflect the ideological and social transfor- mation that made such an adulthood possible and desirable.

In their projections of mature men in mature societies, psychology and sociology reflect the triumph of individualism in nineteenth-century European thought. In their scientific imagery, individuals trapped in corporate units are social and psychological victims of the *ancien régime*, to be liberated by the inexorable processes of modern- ization or the political act of revolution. Just as psychological ontogeny required unraveling the individual from the family to achieve adulthood, so the phylogeny of the race required unraveling it from social embeddedness to achieve specie adulthood. The legacies of this ideological struggle abound in contemporary social-science concepts and explanations and influence its normative and empirical vision. Extended families obstruct entrepreneurship and economic development; political freedom depends on individualism; the decline or destruction of traditional collectivism is a requisite of prosperity, happiness, and freedom.

The Freudian paradigm's interpretation of adulthood can be read as a description or ideological justification of, or as a metaphor for, individualistic liberalism's vision of man's destiny. It supports the view that other civilizations are destined to be phylogenetic failures unless they can make appropriate adjustments in their psychological ontogenies.

This "function" of Freudian thought is captured in the work of O. Mannoni, a French colonial official of unrevised Freudian persuasion. His observations in *Prospero and Caliban* of the colonial and the colonized capture the core of the argument.[9] Mannoni believed that the colonial situation arose out of an uncanny fit between the neuroses of the colonized and the neuroses of the colonial. The colonial suffered from the inferiority complex created by his excessive individualism, his only too successful unravelment from supportive corporate structures; at the extreme, he embodied the misanthropic neurosis that drove Robinson Crusoe to the island. The colonized, in turn, suffered from a dependency complex that arose out of his reliance on ancestors, as expressed in an ancestor cult, and his subjection to the powers of dead family members. Mannoni was confident that Malagasies specifically, and "orientals" more generally, because of their embeddedness in the social situation of the lineage group and the age-graded society, had no opportunity to develop an ego: "The ego is wanting in strength . . . the individual is held together by his collective shell, his social mask, much more than by his moral skeleton."[10] Unlike civilized men, Malagasies accepted without doubt their cultural and social environment: "We do not find in him that disharmony, amounting almost to conflict, between the social being and the inner personality which is so frequently met with among the civilized."[11] By contrast: "The personality of the occidental was long ago transformed by breaking with the ancestral customs and the removal to heaven of a universalized paternal authority."[12]

There are many problems in Mannoni's formulation, not the least of them the fact that it failed to account for the fifty years in which the dependency-ridden Malagasies physically resisted the imposition of French rule: it ultimately came by dint of military force, not psychological fit. But he represents a more general tendency of some psycho-analytically inspired sociological and anthropological literature to view the personality structure created by collectively organized societies as incomplete, undeveloped, and immature.

Mannoni has much company. William J. Goode's comprehensive comparative work on the family rests on the presumption that all the world is moving toward the conjugal West—to its improvement. The nuclear family "asserts the worth of the individual as against the inherited elements of wealth or ethnic group . . . a strong theme of 'democracy' runs through [its] ideology." "It has had an independent effect on industrialization."[13] David Guttman, a psychoanalytically oriented social scientist, sums up a good bit of social-science writing when he concludes: "The extended family is valued in cultures which resist change, which value stability over innovation, and by those who give priority to conformity over expressiveness."[14]

Erik Erikson, who analyzed the problem associated with growing up in the tight communal organization of American Indian tribes and transferring from it to "America," is also heir to the uneasy feeling that embeddedness must diminish self and obstruct maturity. Noting the Hindu philosophical and religious emphasis on "immersion in different orders of self-abandonment," he finds in it clues to the basic quality of family life:

> The deep nostalgia for fusion is reborn, it seems, from generation to generation out of the diffusion of the mother in the joint family, in which she must respond to each and, at the same time, to all, and thus can belong to the individual child only in fleeting moments.[15]

For Erikson, the combined effects of diffused mother and closed embeddedness within a network of relatives often produce patterns of guilt, dependency, and passivity:

> Thus many live always dependent, expectant, demanding, sulking, despairing, and yet always seeking the fusion which affirms, confirms, fulfills. Such an expectance of reunification by fate *can*, in turn, lead to an utterly passive sense of non-responsibility as an individual, and to a waiting for salvation by some form of re-immersion.[16]

To the concern of other observers that tradition and corporate families produce dependency, Erikson adds diffuse female cultural feeling as a factor that generates not only dependency but also a non-instrumental orientation:

> Every Indian, be he ever so well educated and pragmatic, lives also in a feminine space time that is deep inside a HERE and in the very centre of a NOW, not so much an observer of means and ends but a participant in a flux marked by the intensity of confluence.[17]

These statements are good Vedantic philosophy, reflecting the dissolution of the self in the eternal oceanic from which it has come. But one senses here the too ready propensity of Judeo-Christian writers to assimilate the philosophically and spiritually oceanic to the amniotic oceanic and to suggest the appropriately regressive conclusion. But, because the Rajput families depicted in the diary engage in instrumental socialization and often produce, out of a complex balance between collective living and individual initiative, a viable interdependence, we are inclined to emphasize other themes.

Philippe Ariès is perhaps the most powerful exponent of a wholly different valuation of the transformation of Western society from corporatism to individualism and from the extended to the nuclear family. Although unromantic about medieval life, he attends to the losses post-eighteenth-century life suffered as a result of nuclearity. He calls our attention to an intensification over time of the concept of the family and a strengthening of its moral hold. In the earlier society, which made few distinctions between children after weaning and adults, children

> ... went straight into the great community of men. ... The movement of collective life carried along in a single torrent all ages and classes, leaving nobody any time for solitude and privacy. In these crowded, collective, existences there was no room for a private sec-

tor. The family fulfilled a function; it ensured the transmission of life, property and names; but did not penetrate very far into human sensibility.[18]

By contrast, beginning in the seventeenth century, he sees family and schooling together removing the child from adult society.

> The school shut up a childhood which had been free within an increasingly severe disciplinary system. . . . But this severity was the expression of a very different feeling from the old indifference, an obsessive love, which was to dominate society from the eighteenth century on.[19]

> . . . The modern family satisfied a desire for privacy and also a craving for identity: the members of the family were united by feeling, habit and their way of life. They shrank from the promiscuity imposed by the old sociability.[20]

To Ariès, the new society is infinitely more restrictive than the old. It is less varied, pluralistic, open. "The new society provided each way of life with a confined space . . . and . . . each person had to resemble a conventional model, an ideal type, and never depart from it under pain of excommunication."[21]

The theme of adult dependency never surfaces as a significant element in Aries' characterization of medieval psyches. He sees men moving in the interstices between and within a pluralism of structures to make their fate, if anything, more freely than nineteenth-century men. Contrary to Goode and other American social scientists of Parsonian persuasion, who associate the rise of the family with the open society, achievement, and mobility, Ariès associates it with an intensification of social distances and a closing off of intercourse among races and ethnic and social groups. These insights appear to issue from a Rousseauistic frame of mind, normatively attuned to more generalized communities. He speaks of a "withdrawal" into the conjugal family, a narrowing of the bounds of sociability and sentiment, and a transfer to the private sector of affect which had been public. "The concept of family feeling took the place of the other concepts of loyalty and service and became predominant, even exclusive."[22]

We do not need to follow all of Ariès' arguments. But in an essay concerned with issues of dependence and initiative in relation to adulthood, we note that he reverses the terms of analysis suggested by the accounts cited above. In his eyes, the son of Oedipus is less free in consequence of the intense combat in which he engaged.

III

If the oedipal struggle is understood as an ideological construct that helped to establish and legitimize an individualistic society, does the formula cited before—"only after this [great task of freeing himself from the parents] is accomplished can he cease to be a child and so become a member of the social community"—cease to be a guide for adulthood in settings other than the European and American? Must we accept the notion that in extended families and corporate societies that do not feature the oedipal struggle adulthood is problematic or unrealizable? Or do we need a wholly different interpretation of adulthood based on different assumptions and conditions? To anticipate, our argument will be that Freud's view has a certain universal applicability because the tasks of unravelment are everywhere requisites for adulthood. But we do not find that the extended family induces dependency, at least no more so than the nuclear family. The belief that it does arises from taking cultural norms that call for compliant behavior as descriptive of, or identical with, intentions, motives, and inner states. Inner states are more appropriate evidence for revealing psychic conditions than cultural norms and social roles. While behavior governed by cultural norms and social roles, on the one hand, and meaning arising from intentions, motives, and inner states, on the other, are interdependent, they are not identical. Roles and rules are subject to choice, interpretation, and strategic manipulation. The evidence from the diary makes it clear that if Rajput males, instead of unraveling themselves from the family, are obliged to knit themselves into it, they do not thereby lose the psychic capacity to free themselves from their parents in ways that enable them to cease to be children and to become adults.

Amar Singh's sense of corporate identity arose in the first instance from a dynastic sense of his family's historical continuity. He was also conscious that he was a Champawat Rathore. The Rathores were the ruling clan of Jodhpur; the Champawats, the descendants of Champa, brother of Jodha, founder of Jodhpur. The exploits of Champawat heroes appear in the diary along with reports of Amar Singh's own feats in battle. While in China he speared three Boxers; the event acquired historical meaning as Amar Singh assimilated it to the Champawat legacy and knew himself enhanced by doing so. The feat was his, but not his alone. He achieved, as it were, by ascription.

His corporate identity arises, too, out of the constant demonstration of architectural and geographic space associated with the extended family. It lives in the *haveli* ("big house") in the city of Jaipur; it spreads out to the garden house in the suburbs and still further to the fort in the country, located in the midst of the estate's revenue-paying villages. All these things are Kanota. But the feeling of corporate space is even wider; it includes two related lineages and their estates, Naila and Gondher, descendants of the granduncles who came to Jaipur with Amar Singh's grandfather and made their careers at the same time he did. Their *havelis*, gardens, and forts are integrated into Amar Singh's sense of family space and corporate identity.

Historical consciousness and physical representation do not exhaust the embodiments of corporate identity. They are continually renewed by time spent with members of it. Amar Singh calls upon his mother and his two aunts, upon his grandfather, upon his two granduncles and their several wives, and upon his numerous cousins and their wives. Calling on them affirmed the solidarity of the group; not to do so was unfriendly, even suspicious. There was, too, the special world of the men's society, not only in the *mardana* ("men's quarters") but most especially on the polo ground, at the hunt, dining and carousing, and long intimate conversations with favorite cousins. Ariès notes a similar quality in the French corporate survivals of the seventeenth century: ". . . groups called for a whole network of daily contacts, involving an unimaginable number of calls, conversations, meetings and exchanges. . . ."[23]

It has often been pointed out that in Asia extended families are much more frequent among the wealthy than among the poor.[24] That finding is related to the necessary condition of having the resources to maintain a large establishment. The diary makes clear, too, that the extended family, like other complex organizations, requires ample time for rituals of respect and communication.

Relevant persons in the big house are not, of course, limited to family members. In some families, though not the diarist's, the line between family member and servant was blurred by the presence of natural sons of the master, sometimes the children of kept women who had a regularized role in the women's quarters, sometimes the children of servants. In any case, servants were part of the political and sentimental society of the household. In the Kanota *haveli* there were the fifteen "orderlies" of grandfather; fifteen servants for the horses and cattle; seven clerks who helped manage the estate; fifteen servants of mother; ten servants of father's brother; three servants of father's brother's wife; three servants of father's deceased brother's wife; fifteen servants of Amar Singh's wife; Amar Singh's three servants; as well as grandfather, mother, two aunts, one uncle, three male and three female cousins, six brothers, one sister, and Amar Singh (the father lived away, in the service of the Maharaja of Alwar). There were some one hundred souls in the Kanota city household alone, another hundred in the country fort, and many more, of course, in the households of the related lines at Naila and Gondher. Together the population of the extended corporate "family" reached at least five hundred, the equivalent to the population of a small village.

Such units enhance life chances in important ways that explain why they hold together even where feuds and personal incompatibility lead to conflict. The three Champawat houses together controlled a substantial portion of the senior administrative posts in Jaipur, including the prime ministership, the police, and the management of relations with feudal-estate holders. When some fell out of favor at court, others held on and could help. The family network facilitated marital negotiations, a basic coin of status. And, when the elders were imaginative, the family could educate and send into varied and new occupations younger sons who, under the prevailing system of primogeniture, would not inherit. It was more in the family's economic and political interest to move sons into new occupations and adapt to the changing times than it was merely to pass on customary occupations, much less to sit back and consume or diminish landed income or capital. Four of the five Kanota house sons who had active careers were sent to new-style English schools, Mayo College, the "Eton" of India, and military and agricultural colleges. They began service outside the Jaipur state, three at the courts of other princely states, one, Amar Singh, in the Indian army; the fifth became the family's estate manager.

The larger lineage unit was composed of three extended families, Kanota, Naila, and Gondher, and was a corporate entity also, less clearly bounded, organized, and directed than each of the extended families taken separately, but, on occasion or for certain purposes, a formidable force. Within Kanota house, authority was hierarchical, concentrated in the oldest male, Amar Singh's grandfather, Zorawar Singh. Among the three houses, the pattern of authority was more horizontal in that each could influence or constrain the other. One had to learn to live with both kinds of authority and constraint.

In his own house, the twenty-five-year-old Amar Singh obeyed grandfather Zora-war Singh and father Narain Singh, the former an eighty-year-old widower, growing blind, but alive to all the affairs of the household. His permission had to be obtained to employ a servant or clip the trees in the mango grove or give five (rather than three) horses in a granddaughter's dowry. His leave had to be obtained for any travel plans. If Amar Singh wished to go to Jodhpur to visit his wife, who had gone to her home there to bear their first child, grandfather's permission had to be obtained under the complex conditions imposed by an etiquette which forbade juniors from showing interest in those nearest to them before their elders. (Amar Singh became adept in providing good reasons in family terms to justify trips that would take him to his wife.)

Because Amar Singh's much admired and respected father was away in service, there was little occasion for him to exercise authority in the big house. He would, in any case, defer to Zorawar Singh if he could not gain his objective by diplomacy or strategic maneuvers. On occasional home visits, Narain Singh tried to explain away grandfather's ever more penurious directives by referring to his increasing age, and he counseled patience and obedience. Much to Narain Singh's and Amar Singh's chagrin, the estate house at Kanota fort had to remain dusty and in disrepair, the arms rusty, the mango grove decaying, so long as Zorawar Singh's regime of thrift held sway.

Although confined to its particular ambience, the authority of older women was no less formidable and irksome than that of older men. With the death of his grand-mother, Amar Singh's mother, as the wife of the Kanwar, Thakur Zorawar Singh's eldest son and heir, became the senior woman in the house, empowered to command her daughters-in-law and, through them, rule her sons.[25] If Amar Singh took pleasure in dining often with his wife in the *zenana*, he was coming under her power and less under his mother's. Snide or cutting remarks from aunties and servants were deployed until his wife, harried and cowed, herself barred him from the *zenana* at the dinner hour, forcing Amar Singh back out into the men's society of the *mardana*.

The authority of elders remained for many years, well into Amar Singh's adult-hood. He was thirty when his grandfather died, and forty-six when his father died. While he spent many years of his army career (1901–1921) away from the elders' authority in the big house, his wife and children remained in the family *haveli* at Jai-pur. At his father's death when Amar Singh was forty-six, he became the Thakur of Kanota, the leading figure in the household. In gaining this position he had, of course, unique advantages as the eldest son in a primogeniture system of inheritance. Had he been a younger son, he would have remained—as four of his brothers did remain—subject to some measure of restraint by the eldest brother.

Gerontocratic familial authority is sometimes pictured as an apolitical utopia of omnipotence, operated with untroubled effectiveness because those below willingly adhere to the social roles and rules prescribed by cultural norms.[26] Like lower partici-pants in formal organizations, family members had many ways of escaping, evading, circumventing, and manipulating the master of the house, Zorawar Singh. He was invariably offered respect and overt compliance; but to imagine that his will, not theirs, dominated all outcomes is to confuse authority with power. The wiles of infiltration and resistance from below, the capacity to organize coalitions and alliances around common values and interests or in the pursuit of shared objectives, and political skill in winning consensus from above demonstrated the incongruence of authority and power in the big house and belied the image of gerontocratic omnipotence.[27]

The larger corporate unit, composed of the three related households, also limited gerontocratic authority in the big house. When Zorawar Singh ruled that elephants and emeralds should not be part of a granddaughter's dowry, Thakur Roop Singh of Naila held that not giving them reflected on the standing of all three houses, and he threatened not to attend the wedding if the dowry was not improved. Zorawar Singh relented. He in turn implored the related branches to observe the rule of propinquity to the main stem in adoptions where there was a failure of direct heirs. When a childless relative threatened to adopt a favorite cousin, contravening the claims of nearer ones and undermining the rule, he intervened effectively. The common interest of the related families limited the sway of the elders in the big house. The crosscutting influence of other elements in the larger corporate unit also gave a clever young man opportunities to affect policy and decisions at home. Amar Singh, unable to challenge Zorawar Singh's penuriousness directly, encouraged uncle Roop Singh of Naila in his complaints against it.

Common purposes were more important in family decisions and actions than were the desires of individuals, although the latter were by no means ignored, particularly when pursued with skill and with the help of others. Contracting a marriage involved questions of economics and status and their improvement. Being married also involved questions of family interest. It is unlikely that the durable Western romance of the Oriental seraglio, where husbands enjoy the pleasures of several wives, would survive a reading of the diary. Cousin Bhoj Raj Singh, heir apparent at Gondher, is Amar Singh's close friend and companion. He has been married for thirteen years and is devoted to his wife. Because they have not had a son, Mukend Singh, Bhoj Raj's father, has no heir. If no son is born, the estate will go to a nephew. Bhoj Raj Singh is told he must marry again. When he resists, a long and arduous campaign is launched to convince him and his wife that it is prudent to agree. Her diet is systematically reduced; her clothes are not replaced; she is given burdensome work; the door of her bedroom is locked against her husband; her mother-in-law and the maid servants abuse her. After some two years, when she is reduced to a shadow of herself, she and Bhoj Raj implore the elders to find him a new wife. Now the elders refuse, unless both husband and wife give guarantees that the new wife will be as well cared for and loved by her husband as the old. To insure compliance, maid servants are placed at the keyhole of the new bridal chamber and report all that they hear—or don't.

Although cousin Pratap, a widower afflicted with a nervous stomach, has had two wives, he is given a third. With only one son, Naila's fortunes are not secure. Pratap is irresolute, finding it difficult to begin the relationship. His behavior is observed and reported with close and ardent interest by the maid servants and by relatives. Pratap's stomach trouble becomes worse. When he tries to escape his dilemma by not visiting his wife, his father upbraids him for lack of virility: today's sons can not even go to their wives. Amar Singh, who watches with sympathy and concern as the stomach condition worsens, observes with pre-Freudian insight that it will not go away until Pratap ceases to live with his father and his father's close companion, cousin-uncle Mehtab Singh.

The corporate structure portrayed here articulated and enforced the values and interests of an extended family, often at considerable psychic and physical cost to particular members. But there were benefits, too, and they were individual as well as collective. The extended family created a sense of being a meaningful presence in society and history, a self, and a somebody in the past and the future as well as in the present. And it provided the material and moral support to create or enhance life chances: supplied a tradition for those who could live by it, shaped some not in its own image, financed and encouraged individual opportunities because they benefited the person involved even while they expanded family influence and resources. These elements—coercions, pains, and penalties, support for new men and careers as well as old, material security, and psychic enhancement—capture some of the cost-benefit valuation of "embeddedness."

IV

The nuclear family, out of which most notions of adulthood have arisen, seems less expansive and substantial than the extended family depicted here. The psychological model of the nuclear family is a triad: mother, father, child. A model of the extended family of feudal Rajasthan would more closely approximate a polyhedron—polycentric, multifaceted, and three-dimensional. The familial polycentrism of the extended family has several consequences. Possible and actual affective relationships are more numerous than in the nuclear family: the objects of affection are less likely to be stereotyped (mother, father), and the bonds of affection more apt to be diluted. The intense relationships expected and encouraged in the nuclear family are distributed over a larger, more variable population. Mother, uncle, aunt, grandmother, and maid or manservant are all possible candidates for affective ties or emulation on the part of the growing child.

Amar Singh does not live with or get to know his father well until he is in his twenties. Father was an inspector general of the Jaipur police and, later, guardian to the Maharaja of Alwar; he therefore lived away from home much of his life. At ten, Amar Singh was sent to Jodhpur to be brought up by the regent, Sir Pratap Singh, his father's close friend. The experience was not unusual. When famine struck Jodhpur, cousins from Peelva, the stem family in Jodhpur, came to live at Naila house in Jaipur; several of Amar Singh's brothers lived away from the big house with their father, Narain Singh, and less prosperous cousins lived in Kanota house.

Amar Singh's "education" at Jodhpur, his brothers' stay with their father at the court of the Maharaja of Alwar, and the Peelva cousins' transfer to Naila house approximate the pragmatic family arrangements Philippe Ariès describes in medieval society. When, in twelfth-century Macon, a knight called Guignet entrusted his two young sons to the eldest of his three brothers, he was supplying service to the brother and apprenticeship to the sons. The child entrusted to a master was to serve him truly and well and to learn from his new situation.[28] Although mothers and fathers did have special standing, there was no stereotyped notion concerning which relative was most appropriate to raise a child. As Ariès puts it, speaking of his reality:

> Thus the family at that time was unable to nourish a profound existential attitude between parents and children. This did not mean that the parents did not love their children, but they cared about them less for themselves, for the affection they felt for them, than for the contribution those children could make to the common task. The family was a moral and social, rather than sentimental, reality.[29]

Lines of affect are more dilute and more apt to diverge from the lines of authority than is commonly the case in nuclear families. Grandfather Zorawar Singh and father Narain Singh were the most important authority figures in the family, yet neither of them was a significant object of affection for the young Amar Singh, the one because of his generational distance, the other because of his geographic distance. For ten years, from age ten to twenty, Amar Singh's principal sources of affective support were his peers, the nephews of Sir Pratap sent to live with the regent to benefit from his ascetic discipline and social and political influence. Sir Pratap himself figured, too, but distantly, as did Amar Singh's teacher and friend, the Charan Ram Nath jee.

The divergence between the lines of affect and of authority creates a different mix from that of the nuclear family. Socialization is less intimately tied to relations with fathers and mothers; cultural norms are learned without exclusive emulation of them. The nuclear family scenario for adulthood, which calls for accomplishing the double task of becoming like "father" even while separating one's self from him, has to be carried out with fathers who unite affect and authority, an explosive amalgam whose elements the extended family tends to keep separate.

The diffusion of affect in the extended family and its polycentric and multifaceted structure reenforce the coalitional nature of family conflicts. In the nuclear family, conflicts typically take dyadic form, father or mother against son or daughter, father against mother. Conflicts are asymmetrical in terms of the distribution and capacity to use economic and social resources, although perhaps more symmetrical with respect to deployment of affective resources. In the extended family, conflicts are apt to mobilize overt or convert coalitions; grandmothers, cousins, uncles, and aunts may explicitly support cherished nieces, grandchildren, age mates, or, by joining in a psychological chorus from behind the arras, weaken the legitimacy and will of an opponent. Under these circumstances family struggles cannot be easily contained, may spread, drawing the family into factional groupings that make life miserable for all those who dwell in the big house. The young Amar Singh, confronted with conflicts between one or another aunt and his mother, periodically maneuvered unsuccessfully to partition the family into its nuclear components. But with all its potential for factional or coalitional conflict, the extended family offered its men (its women much less) room for maneuver and withdrawal, even escape. Its size and complexity kept the psychological temperature relatively low and its interstices offered ways out in times of trouble.

One result of the diffusion of affect in the extended family seems to be that oedipal objects are less important and powerful and the foils of a new identity less obvious than in a nuclear family. The "problem" for the would-be adult is detachment not from one or two but from a plethora of significant others. Differentiation, too, although complicated by less clear articulation of those from whom one wishes to distinguish oneself, may be easier than in a nuclear family because none of the putative parental objects is invested with the psychic charge they readily acquire there.

For Amar Singh, in any case, establishing an autonomous manhood was eased by the contingent and shifting nature of the parental models he experienced. The regent of Jodhpur, Sir Pratap Singh, loomed large in Amar Singh's formative years; from age eight to twenty-three, he recognized him as his "master."[30] An ascetic disciplinarian devoted to cold baths, sparse food, and hard beds, he imposed a Spartan regime on his young charges. Possessed of great prowess as a soldier, ruler, sportsman, and socialite, he was an all-India figure, a favorite of viceroys and perhaps the most influential statesman of princely India. He was, in a sense, awesome—Amar Singh never read and rarely sat in his presence, although he was with him a great deal[31]—yet he had feet of clay, weaknesses that Amar Singh recognizes early in the diary and that loom ever larger over the years.[32] Sir Pratap trained Amar Singh to be a soldier and sportsman, patronized his career, and arranged and financed his marriage.

Although without doubt a parental object in Amar Singh's psychic development, as an oedipal figure, Sir Pratap was diluted by others, such as the teacher Ram Nath jee, from whom Amar Singh learned so much and to whom he was devoted and respectful. Their relationship survived the crisis that attends the passage from inequality to equality; they became something akin to peers and close friends. The young men with whom he lived in his adolescent years also served as models (sometimes negative) and occupied considerable psychic space. So, too, did the wardens of the boys' school where he boarded. In his late teens and early twenties, two Englishmen, Major Turner, with whom he fought in China during the Boxer Rebellion, and Captain Cameron, the adjutant at the imperial cadet corps, who encouraged and sponsored him, became models and foils for his psychic and cultural development. Throughout, his parents in Jaipur, whom he saw only rarely, provided a significant if invisible presence, constant reminders of his place in Rajput society and history.

When his father reenters his life in 1901, Amar Singh is twenty-three. It is as though father had been there all along. Amar Singh respects him greatly, pleased to share the general approbation and great esteem he finds his father attracts from the society around him. He is not disappointed as he comes to know him. Amar Singh expects his father to be wise, skillful, and good, and he constantly finds that he is. He is twenty-three, his father fifty-two. It is a good relationship, not surcharged by struggles over mother, independence, or identity.

Some students of Indian socialization argue that the diffuse nature of affect and authority and the absence of unique, single-minded guidance in the Indian extended family leads to weak superegos and indifference to obligations. This interpretation is reinforced by the observation that the omnipresence of the diffuse socializing authorities ready to shame undesirable behavior makes incorporation of moral guides and their rules of conduct less necessary and thus less likely. As Mannoni would have it, "the individual is held together by his collective shell much more than by his moral skeleton."[33]

There is little in the behavior and what we know of the inner life of leading figures in the Kanota *haveli*, Amar Singh, his father, his grandfather, his cousins—many of whom live away from home, some in European contexts—to support this view. Their internal monitors not only operate at home but also adjust to new, sometimes cultural-ly alien environments. Like successful Indian business communities abroad, the Guja-rati joint families of West India who colonized East Africa, or the merchant castes of Madras who settled in Burma, Ceylon, and Southeast Asia, the upbringing of Kanota-house offspring among a variety of parental figures does not appear to have dis-advantaged them in the development of initiative.

Finally, the extended family patterns life stages in very different ways from those arising out of the world of the nuclear family in industrial societies. We have come to consider "natural" the expectations and behavior that are deeply conditioned by cul-ture and social context. Just at the time when young adults in our society "move out," Amar Singh "moves in." After thirteen years with Sir Pratap in Jodhpur he returns home to Jaipur married and enters, with his bride, the big house with its intricate web of rules and relationships. His particular circumstances—the years with Sir Pratap— are somewhat special, but the pattern is not. Brides leave their families to live in the households of their mothers-in-law, a condition that enmeshes them and their hus-bands in the extended family at a moment when conjugal units in industrial societies are expected to establish independent households and life trajectories. Amar Singh serves away from home in the Indian army from 1905 to 1921, when he returns to Jaipur to become in a few years the Thakur of Kanota and the senior military officer in the Jaipur state. Throughout his Indian army career his wife and children live in the Kanota *haveli*. That part of his life that is familial remains rooted in the big house and the extended family. His brothers also bring their wives to live in the big house or, to shape the language more faithfully to the context, their parents send them.

It is the presence of Amar Singh's bride in Jaipur that gives his mother greatly increased influence and authority over him. For thirteen years she had no direct hold; now he moves into her ambit, and that of other family members and the servants. Their expectations and sanctions cannot be ignored; they shape his behavior as hus-band, son, father, nephew, and master-to-be.[34] His mother, by comparison with moth-ers—and mothers-in-law—in the three related households, offers relatively few difficulties. They clash over what she regards as his excessive attendance on his wife. The conflict is more over power than love—who is to have predominant influence over the master-to-be of the household. However much easier his mother is than others in his circle, he finds adjusting to her demands and expectations—and those of uncles, aunts, and maid servants—most irksome. "It is now gradually dawning upon me," he observes in the diary, "as to what real difficulties there are in a Hindoo and specially a Rajput family life."[35]

But while his wife is the occasion for the restraints the family is able to exercise over him, there is much more to the relationship than this aspect alone would suggest. It is often held that in the affective structure of the Indian family, the mother-son tie counts much more than that of the husband-wife. Yet it is plain in Amar Singh's life as a young man that he "owes" love to his mother but that he loves his wife. The relationship with her is warm and intimate, a source of great happiness and pleasure. When he goes up the stairs from his room on the second floor of *bichli haveli* to her quarters on the third, often after midnight lest he be seen by seniors who should not witness his going to his wife, they close themselves into a private, very special world in which mother and others in the big house have for the moment no place. While she cannot fully respond to his zealous efforts to interest her in books and ideas, sometimes becoming apprehensive that the few precious hours they have alone together will be dissipated in reading, she brings him happiness in all other matters.

Amar Singh's first moments alone with his wife during the maelstrom of marriage ceremonies capture the tone and spirit of their relationship in the early years:

> I was made to sit in [the *rath*, a bullock-drawn caparisoned carriage] for a couple of minutes and even in that short time I managed to see my wife's face in spite of her resistance. I am glad to write here that her features are as mild, beautiful and as much to my taste and liking as I could have wished. In the whole circle of my family . . . there is none to surpass her in nobleness and mildness of features. . . . I was quite satisfied with her looks at that time and her manners and temper by now. She is exactly what I thought she would be by the look of her features.[36]

Eighteen months later, while instructing the seventeen-year-old Maharaja of Kishengarh on love and marriage, Amar Singh presents the virtues and benefits of monogamy:

> Marrying more than one wife would be very troublesome and would prove the ruination of one's enjoyment in life. In a house where there are two wives, the result can never be any other than quarreling. Besides this, it is not right by the laws of nature; . . . one can never satisfy more than one woman . . . he must be content with her in order that he not wander out in quest of debaucheries . . . if a man is not satisfied with one, he will never be with two, three or any number. He will always be hungering for new ones.[37]

Still, temptations can come in one's way; the correct path may not be so easily known or, if known, so easily followed. In August, 1904, on his way to Jaipur on home leave from the imperial cadet corps, Amar Singh encounters a lady in his railway carriage. Daughter of a Rajput mother and Christian father, the second of a Mohammedan gentleman's three wives but living apart from him, she is not in purdah. They talk late into the night. "I was quite tempted by this woman . . . ." "She did not object" to his advances. "God only knows what would have happened if the other pair [an English couple] had not been with us. . . ." Amar Singh then ruminates about the problems of being a faithful husband:

> I have a sort of vow never to go to another woman, but I do not know whether I shall be able to carry it out to the end of my life . . . it is all right while you don't have the temptation. But it is quite a different thing when you get the chance. I am sure I would never do such a thing so long as I have my wife near, but I may be tempted while away from [her] and especially if the separation has been of long duration.[38]

He identifies with the suffering of his cousin, Bhoj Raj Singh, whose parents pressure and coerce him into accepting a second wife. When Amar Singh's father hints to Bhoj Raj Singh "that he would not mind marrying Amar Singh a second time," he writes:

> I do not in the least want to marry, because I know what the troubles will be in the end. Besides this, I sincerely love my wife and do not want to hurt her feelings. A second marriage will . . . hurt her happiness as well as mine . . . the will of the parents will be obeyed but at what cost?[39]

When "the real difficulties" of "a Hindoo and specially a Rajput family life" dawn on Amar Singh, he confronts the central issue for Rajput adulthood: how to fit into the family while preserving a sense of self and purpose compatible with collective obligations and goals. It must be done in an unhelpful physical setting. The big house's large, multiple courtyards surrounded by smaller rooms organize the life and relationships of its nuclear units. Unlike the big houses of the aristocracy or bourgoisie in eighteenth- or nineteenth-century Europe, Rajasthani big houses provide very little privacy. Reflecting on the fact that some of his then seven brothers will marry soon, Amar Singh observes, "there are only four doors" but already four married men. One cannot escape the omnipresent relatives and servants. It is difficult even to have private thoughts. Amar Singh tells us that in Naila house cousin Pratap Singh's elders

> . . . take care to appoint [as his servants] those who are sort of spies . . . thus he can not tell what he feels to anyone. . . . As an instance . . . we began to talk at polo. We were sitting rather away from the others. As soon as my cousin noticed this he said that we had better go and sit with the others because he was afraid Mehtab Singh [his father's favorite and estate agent] might think we were having some private talk. . . .[40]

Obedience and compliance are stressed. Amar Singh and his father, Narain Singh, discuss the fact that cousin Bhoj Raj Singh has been forced to marry a second wife against his wishes. Bjoh Raj Singh has already agreed, but his family, sensing his inner resistance, is dissatisfied with the formal compliance, and Bhoj Raj Singh finds it difficult to exhibit the appropriate attitude: "My cousin told me that he was [so sorry] because he tries to please his family but does not know how to do so." Narain Singh conveys the culturally indicated advice: "I told all this to my father who told me to tell Bhoj Raj Singh jee that this can not be helped and he advised him to bear as much as he could and never let his parents know that he can bear no more."[41] Amar Singh, who frequently sighs with relief because he lives in happier circumstances than his cousin ("I am the happiest in the three houses"), yet recognizes the stresses: "People say the peace of the house must be kept at any cost. Is it possible to keep the peace under these conditions?"[42]

Over the four years from 1901, when he marries at twenty-three and enters the big house, to 1905, when he has learned from four years' experience, he conveys in the diary an increasing sense of being at ease and of mastery. The situation is inherently complex, continuously fraught with the possibility of conflict simply because so many different individuals must be accommodated. As the Marwari proverb, which he often cites, would have it: "Where there are many brass vessels in the cupboard, they will often knock together."

As he learns what living in an extended family entails and becomes more knowledgeable and skillful at it, its interactions become opportunities as well as constraints and irritants. He continues to complain about the quarrels among the women: "These quarrels are a great source of trouble to me. . . . I am absolutely tired of living with my aunts. My grandfather ought really to separate them now. . . ."[43] And the women's realm is especially difficult for him to reach and influence: "[My mother] said that the [male] cousin is in your hands and you can make him do whatever you like, but it is different dealing with women. . . ."[44] Yet he begins to discover the means by which he can influence even this most difficult realm. He busies himself helping a distant aunt deal more effectively with the agent who handles her estate affairs; he concerns himself with the marriage arrangements of his cousins and in-laws. These activities give him a handle on more immediate affairs: the aunt has nephews and nieces in the related households who may now adhere more to Amar Singh's interest in intrafamilial affairs; aiding successful matches creates allies within the household. The household is a complex institution whose alliances, factions, and divergent interests can yield concord as well as disharmony. Maturity involves among other things knowing how to manage its internal politics in ways that advance its interests or welfare along with one's own.[45]

V

The literature on the extended family, for the most part structural and functional in its theoretical orientation, depicts it as maximizing security, control by elders, and conformity to tradition and community values. It follows by logical deduction or inference that the extended family either causes or is associated with a lack of individual autonomy, initiative, and entrepreneurship with the consequence that it inhibits innovation and change. Under such circumstances adulthood is, at best, a flawed state, crippled by the exigencies of extended family living, at worst the expression of man's potential at a lower stage of human evolution. Such a view of adulthood in the extended family is too aprioristic and deductive. The evidence of the Amar Singh diary, from which we have constructed an interpretation of Rajput adulthood, belies its characterizations in a variety of ways and for a variety of reasons.

We have found that the interdependence characteristic of the extended family often calls for initiative, individuality, and autonomy. The extended family's corporate interests and values are best protected and pursued if some of its members can adapt and innovate in response to historical and environmental change. Becoming an adult involves detachment and differentiation from a diverse set of parental models and a distinct sense of self. In arguing this way, we do not mean to suggest that becoming an adult in an extended family is just like becoming an adult in a nuclear family, but we do find that it is not so different, not so dichotomous, not so mirror-like, as much of the literature dealing with it depicts it to be.

This is because cultural rules and social roles do not make so much difference at the individual and behavioral level as they do at the collective and normative. Members of extended families, like participants in formal organizations, are not the social objects that the rules and roles of family or organization expect them to be. Their motives and inner states, and some of their behavior, are only contingently related to rules and roles. The "detachment" that Freud emphasized as a prerequisite to adulthood is found more at the level of motives and inner states than at the level of rules and roles. Because this is so, the contrast between the two types of family exaggerates in the nuclear family and understates in the extended family the capacity for adulthood.

The distinction between role and rule, on the one hand, and motive and behavior, on the other, is not a bad beginning for a definition of adulthood in the setting of the extended family. Adulthood involves, among other things, both the internalization of roles and rules and the capacity to bear a sufficiently contingent relationship to them that one can use them, shape them, and exploit their parameters, instead of being merely their embodiment. The two sides of the oedipal relationship, which dictate (to the boy) both incorporation of the father and detachment from him, state affectively what we have above stated more socially and culturally. Living in the big house, one must construct one's identity in the midst of others and among their monitoring of one's emerging self. Adulthood involves, particularly for those who will be the most visible and significant members of the extended family, a strong capacity for differentiation. The task, however, is to create the proper balance between differentiation and detachment, on the one hand, and compliance and conformity, on the other. An adult man or woman must obey the rules as they are enforced by elders to an extent sufficient to fit into common purposes. Within the extended family, one must first define one's own purposes in order to serve them and enhance them. But the strategies of these two norms remain related.

The object of differentiation for an eldest son, such as Amar Singh, is to distance himself sufficiently from the many around him so that he can take a strategic view of their and his interests and devise means on behalf of his own purposes and growth that include the needs and demands of the family. This is a political and moral skill that requires at once a sense of oneself and of the collective unit. This suggests what may be general in the Freudian paradigm: for individuals to be effective in the complex organization of the extended family, "detachment" is as much a requisite of adulthood as it is in the nuclear family, but the tasks of detachment and their problematics are differently structured.

Erik Erikson, whose psychology encompasses the later as much as the earlier stages of life, emphasizes that in adulthood "you learn to know what and whom you can take care of."[46] In his exploration of adulthood, he suggests it is more communitarian than other stages of life. It stresses skills and concerns directed to others, rather than those designed to perfect and protect independence. Nineteenth-century men affirmed that in the adulthood of man and species individualism was exceptionally important. In the twentieth century, having explored the limits of that insight, men are less confident about it. They may be more inclined to credit the communitarian elements in adulthood and give a more sympathetic understanding to the extended family and to the adulthood it fosters.

REFERENCES

[1]We are indebted to the National Science Foundation, the American Institute for Indian Studies, the Guggenheim Foundation, the Committee on Southern Asian Studies and the Social Sciences Research Committee of the University of Chicago, the American Council of Learned Societies, the American Philosophical Society, and the Bureau of Educational and Cultural Affairs, Department of State, for their support at various times over the past six years of our research on the diary.

[2]The Amar Singh diary fills eighty-seven volumes and covers the years 1898 to 1942. The manuscript copy is in the possession of the family at Kanota house, Jaipur, Rajasthan; microfilm copies are in the Nehru Memorial Museum and Library, New Delhi, and the Joseph Regenstein Library, University of Chicago.

[3]The family we discuss here does not have the characteristics of the ideal type of Hindu joint family, "a group of adult coparceners [joint heirs] and their dependents." M. S. Gore, "The Impact of Industrialization and Urbanization on the Aggarwal Family in Delhi Area," unpublished Ph.D. dissertation, Columbia University, 1961, p. 8. Rajput families, except in Barmer and Shekhawati, base inheritance on primogeniture, though younger brothers are entitled to maintenance. For two different, important accounts of the joint family, see S. J. Tambiah and Jack Goody, *Bridewealth and Dowry* (Cambridge, England, 1973), and Irawati Karve, *Kinship Organization in India* (Bombay, 1968). For a comparative view, see A. J. Coale, L. A. Fallers, Marion J. Levy, David M. Schneider, and Silvan M. Tomkins, *Aspects of the Analysis of Family Structure* (Princeton, 1965), p. 9.

[4]For an account of Rajput history and polity, see Susanne Hoeber Rudolph, Lloyd I. Rudolph, with Mohan Singh, "A Bureaucratic Lineage in Princely India: Elite Formation and Conflict in a Patrimonial System," *Journal of Asian Studies*, XXXIV: 3 (May, 1975), pp. 717-54.

[5]See Joanne Waghorne's discussion of Kathakar Brahmans in her "Images of Dharma; The Epic World of C. Rajagopalachari," unpublished Ph.D. dissertation, University of Chicago, 1975. For the place of Charans in Rajput society, culture, and history, see K. R. Qanungo, *Studies in Rajput History* (Delhi, 1960), Chapter III, "The Role of Non-Rajputs in the History of Rajputana," especially pp. 39-50; Kaviraj Shymaldas, *Vir Vinod* (Hindi; *Heroes' Entertainment*), (Udaipur, privately printed by Maharana Fateh Singh, 1886), I, pp. 168-84; Rani Lakshmi Kumari Chundawat, *Gir Ooncha Ooncha Gadhan* (Rajasthani; *High the Mountains, Higher Still the Forts*), (Jaipur, 1966), a collection of folklore tales, three of which are by or about Charans.

[6]"The Amar Singh Diary," "Notes About My Seventh Term in the Cadet Corps," June 1-12, 1905, *XIV: The Mess*.

[7]For an influential account of a sharply contrasting rule, see Margaret Mead, *And Keep Your Powder Dry* (New York, 1942), Chapter VI.

[8]Sigmund Freud, *General Introduction to Psychoanalysis* (New York, 1960), p. 295.

[9]O. Mannoni, *Prospero and Caliban: A Study of the Psychology of Colonisation* (London, 1956).

[10]*Ibid.*, p. 41.

[11]*Ibid.*

[12]*Ibid.*, p. 52.

[13]*World Revolution and Family Patterns* (New York, 1963), pp. 1, 19, and 22. See also Neil Smelser, *Social Change in the Industrial Revolution* (Chicago, 1959), which is responsive to Talcott Parsons' similar conclusions in *The Social System* (New York, 1949), Chapter 5.

[14]"A Cross-Cultural Perspective on Adult Life in the Extended Family," mimeographed, 1975, p. 9.

[15]Erik H. Erikson, *Gandhi's Truth; On the Origins of Militant Non-Violence* (New York, 1969), p. 42.

[16]*Ibid.*, p. 43.

[17]*Ibid.*

[18]*Centuries of Childhood: A Social History of Family Life* (New York, 1962), p. 411.

[19]*Ibid.*, p. 413.

[20]*Ibid.*, p. 414.

[21]*Ibid.*, p. 375.

[22]*Ibid.*

[23]*Ibid.*, p. 376.

[24]The population of Aix-en-Provence at the end of the seventeenth century showed the poor in small houses with few people, the rich in large houses with many; this is believed by Ariès to be characteristic. *Ibid.*, p. 391. The Indian census of 1911, which claims a distribution of joint and nuclear families in the population similar to what might be expected in a European context, including a 4.5-person average family size, notes that "except among the higher castes, who form but a small fraction of the total population, the joint family is not nearly so common as so frequently supposed." Government of India, *Census of India*, I, Part I: *Report*, p. 46. For similar findings in China, see F. L. K. Hsu, "The Myth of Chinese Family Size," *American Journal of Sociology*, 48:5 (March, 1943).

[25]A large part of Indian family literature stresses the dominance of the affective tie between mother and son. In the diary, that tie was less important than Amar Singh's mother's authority over him, which to a considerable extent she exercised indirectly through control of her daughter-in-law. The triadic relationship was colored more by power than by love.

[26]Comparing the old man to one who can live out the omnipotence fantasies of the young child, David Guttman pictures members of the extended family offering "automatic, unquestioned respect to the older man; and by so doing [helping] revive childhood memories of total and unconditional acceptance," *op. cit.*, p. 13.

[27]For a discussion of the behavior of "lower participants" and of the role of authority and power in modern organization, both of which can be found in extended families also, see Lloyd I. Rudolph and Susanne Hoeber Rudolph, "Authority and Power in Bureaucratic and Patrimonial Administration: A Revisionist Interpretation of Weber on Bureaucracy," paper delivered at the annual meeting of the American Political Science Association, Chicago, September, 1974.

[28]Ariès, *op. cit.*, p. 66.

[29]*Ibid.*, p. 368.

[30]An example suggests the importance of "Sarkar": "It was a grand race indeed [Horse Steeple Chase of two miles, the fourth race of which Amar Singh wins]. There was a thunder of cheers and even Sarkar himself said, 'well done, my boy' which is the first time he has done so since the day we left Jodhpore in August 1900, though I think I deserved it more than once without the slightest doubt." "The Amar Singh Diary," April 25, 1901.

[31]"While Sarkar [Sir Pratap] is present, no matter where, either in or out, we are not supposed to speak, even among us. He would not say anything about it, but will never like it." "The Amar Singh Diary," January 9, 1901.

[32]"According to my mind he lives a most miserable life though he considers it enjoyable. He is the laughing stock of Major Turner and the other Englishmen," *ibid.*, January 9, 1901.

[33]Mannoni, *op. cit.*, p. 40.

[34]"Thus it is a short sketch of the way and mode in which I spent my honeymoon. I was always quite free and at liberty to do nearly anything that I wanted to do. I enjoyed myself thoroughly. *Still*, if I had been sent away to Kanota for this short time, I would have been much more freer. Our etiquette is too strict and puts a strain on us to move freely about. So long as my uncle [Bhim Singh] was in the *haveli*, I was unable to go in. A little more freedom would be much more preferable." "The Amar Singh Diary," November 9, 1901.

[35]"The Amar Singh Diary," "Notes About My Last Summer Vacation," May 21-23, 1903, *XXXII. My Experiences.*

[36]"The Amar Singh Diary," "Notes About My Marriage," *VII. The Marriage Ceremonies*, September 17, 1901. The moment of first seeing the wife's face can be traumatic. We know of one case in which the groom left the marriage party in a distraught state and subsequently refused the marriage. We have no comparable evidence for women's reactions to the first viewing, but do not doubt this is at least as fraught with possibilities of trauma, perhaps even more so, because women in such societies are less able than are men to defend their interests.

[37]*Ibid.*, February 2, 1903.

[38]*Ibid.*, "Notes About My Sixth Term in the Cadet Corps," *XXIX. The Return Journey*, August 25, 1904.

[39]*Ibid.*, "Notes About My Last Vacations," *XI. My Father*, October 21, 1904.

[40]*Ibid.*, "Notes About My Christmas Vacation," *XIV. Pratap Singh*, January 6-8, 1905.

[41]*Idem.*, *XIII. Bhoj Raj Singh jee.*

[42]*Idem.*

[43]*Ibid.*, June 10, 1905.

[44]*Ibid.*

[45]"The main thing," Ariès writes of a similar setting, "was to maintain social relations with the whole of the group into which one had been born, and to better one's position by skillful use of this network of relations . . . [and] to win a more honorable standing in a society whose members all saw one another, heard one another and met one another nearly every day." *Op. cit.*, p. 376.

[46]*Dimensions of a New Identity* (New York, 1974), p. 124.

Ch w/memory :

MARTIN E. MALIA

Adulthood Refracted: Russia and Leo Tolstoi

> All happy families are happy in the same way,
> each unhappy family is unhappy in its own way.
> —The opening phrase of *Anna Karenina*

I

THE TOPIC SET FOR THIS ESSAY implicitly assumes that there exists a national dimension to both the concept and the phenomenon of adulthood. In other words, one is, or becomes, an adult in differing ways depending on the country and the culture in which one is reared, and adulthood is, in some measure, relative to nationality. *A priori* this appears to be a very sensible proposition: since nationality molds everything in the modern world, why should it not also affect the process and the end result of growing up?

Yet when one attempts to spell out just what this national dimension of adulthood is—for Russia or for any other country—major methodological difficulties arise, particularly for the historian. Outside the crucial area of individual biography, the historian deals with fairly large-scale problems of political, social, or cultural explanation, for which the individual life cycle and even the family are not very significant "variables." In addition, the body of evidence for delineating patterns of adulthood in a given country is so vast and yet so fragmented that as a practical matter the task of investigation becomes virtually unmanageable. This difficulty is further augmented when one considers that a nation is not a homogeneous unit: its character changes over time and varies from one segment of the population to another. It is thus impossible to generalize about "adulthood in Russia." An anthropologist or a psychologist can do this for a given segment of the population at a precise moment in time, usually on the basis of data he has generated himself. But it would be meaningless to attempt such a task for a nation as an aggregate and in a long-term historical perspective. It need hardly be added that generating survey-research data for Soviet Russia is not a feasible enterprise.

A further cautionary word is in order. Although the fact of adulthood is certainly universal, explicit and self-conscious concern with "what it means to be an adult" is a specifically American phenomenon, and a rather recent American phenomenon at that. Indeed, no precise equivalent of the Anglo-American term "adulthood"—i.e., denoting a distinct stage in the life cycle—exists in any other European language. Instead, the French say *maturité*, the Germans *Mündigkeit*, and the Russians *zrelost*, all of which mean "maturity," in the sense of "ripeness" as applied to any living thing. All these languages, to be sure, have in addition the terms "grown up" and "major" (i.e., of legal age)—in Russian, *vzrosly* and *sovershennoletnii*—and all these terms further carry the connotation of "adult" or "responsible" as applied to behavior. But none of these languages singles out adulthood as a special stage of human development. It would thus be an error to extrapolate from specifically American forms of concern for the place of adulthood in the life cycle to the culture of a country so different from ours as Russia is. The best one can hope for is to find some parallels that filter through the distinctive features of Russian life.

Given these various limitations, then, what is feasible to attempt here is an indication, in broad outline, of the cultural context for "maturity," the social matrix molding the life cycle, in modern Russia. The observations that follow, moreover, will be divided into two unequal and asymmetrical parts: first, a sketch of this cultural context taken as a whole and, second, a more closely focused case study of the impact of this context on the personal destiny and the literary evolution of Leo Tolstoi. This case has not been chosen because it is in any sense typical or paradigmatic for all Russians. Rather it has been chosen, first, because one of Tolstoi's main artistic themes is exactly that of this volume: the meaning of the human life cycle. In addition, his own life cycle is one of the most minutely documented in history (thirteen volumes of diary alone, not to mention correspondence and the heavily biographical literary works). Finally, his personal destiny intersects with the larger context of modern Russian life in such a manner as to bring into particularly sharp focus some of the basic peculiarities of that context.

Now to all this it might well be objected that such heavy use of literary "evidence" —and writers other than Tolstoi will be exploited—does not constitute proper historical procedure. Yet, to this it may plausibly be answered that the literary materials used will all be drawn from the "classics," that is, from works chosen to be read in class, and that it is fair to assume for any culture that such works in fact represent a significant consensus as to national values and the profounder communal perceptions.

One final methodological excursus is in order: namely, delineation of the concept of "maturity" employed in this essay. Here it is convenient to distinguish a number of concentric circles of meaning. There is first biological maturity, which presumably does not differ notably from one society to another; this core meaning signifies that the individual, from being a child, gradually becomes able to procreate children and to provide in turn for their growth to maturity. This process, moreover, also obviously entails psychological maturation, which makes possible the successful adaptation to each stage of this *relève des générations*.

But beyond this basic circle of physical and psychological maturity there are clearly other dimensions of the term. First of all, it is recognized in the format of this volume that modes of adulthood can be expected to differ not only from one nationality to another, but also from one religious tradition to another. But these two differences overlap with many others. For example, is adulthood socially the same for a man and a woman? In the European context, at least, the Roman concept of the *paterfamilias* held that a wife was subject to her husband in the same manner and degree as were his children; though this radical inequality of sexual roles was attenuated over the centuries, notably by Christianity, a great deal of the ancient attitude survived into the early twentieth century in such institutions as the *Code Napoléon*—and, as we shall see, in the attitude of Tolstoi as well.

Other differences suggest themselves: Is maturity the same from one social class to another? Or from one profession to another within the same socioeconomic grouping? For example, is maturity the same for a peasant and a lord in an old-regime, agrarian society? Is it the same for a manual worker, a white-collar worker, and a liberal professional specialist in an industrial society? Is maturity, in any society, the same for the literate and the illiterate? The answer to all of these questions must clearly be "no." Since all of the contrasting situations just listed imply very different skills, social roles, and cultural horizons, "mature" adaptation to these different situations must lead to the development, in some measure, of differing psychological characteristics and values. Thus, stretching out beyond the basic biological and psychological meanings of maturity, a series of other circles of meaning, referring to sex, social class, functional role, and cultural level presents itself. It is with these outer meanings of adulthood, its social and cultural dimensions, that this essay will primarily be concerned; for it is only in this way that the problem can be given a historical dimension.

Within this general perspective, moreover, we shall concentrate on the last century of the Russian old regime, with only passing reference to conditions since 1917. The reason for this choice is that that period represents the most creative age of Russian culture and the high point of national reflectiveness and articulateness; the literature of "social command" of the Soviet period simply cannot yield comparable insights into the national character, and the literature of Soviet dissent is not abundant and varied enough to make up for this lack.

II

In the last century of the Russian old regime, then, what constituted Russia's national distinctiveness within the general pattern of European life? Although all European societies were at best imperfectly democratic, mobile, and "open" before 1914, Russian society was by far the most rigid and authoritarian, and the overwhelming majority of the population—the peasantry—lived in a situation of radical subordination to superior authorities in a manner which struck everyone, natives and foreigners alike, as the distinctive feature of the national life. Surely, social arrangements of this sort can only have had major consequences for achieving maturity.

Just what these consequences were is aptly indicated by a famous statement of Kant at the opening of *What Is Enlightenment?*, composed in 1784. This work, to be sure, was not written with reference to Russia, but it highlights a central dilemma in an old-regime society of the sort that Russia preeminently remained in the nineteenth century and even into the twentieth:

> Enlightenment means leaving man's self-caused immaturity. *Immaturity* [Unmündig-
> keit] *is the incapacity to use one's intelligence without the guidance of another* [italics

added]. Such immaturity is self-caused if it is not caused by lack of intelligence, but by lack of determination and courage to use one's intelligence without being guided by another. *Sapere aude*!

For Kant, of course, the forces that sought to perpetuate immaturity and to "guide" society like a troupe of children were the forces of princely absolutism and established, dogmatic religion. Maturity, therefore, meant the development of critical intelligence and the use of this intelligence to change society.

Thus, in social and political terms, the fullness of adulthood must mean intellectual and ethical self-determination and ultimately the freedom of civic action. In short, in the modern world, in secularized society since the Enlightenment, there can be no full maturity without *citizenship*, without some measure of informed participation as a free agent in the *res publica*. But any old-regime society, which is by nature paternalistic, a society of "guardians," systematically denies such self-determination and participation to most of its members, thereby inevitably creating enormous unresolved tensions. And throughout the history of modern Russia this denial has been particularly thorough, brutal, and prolonged, and the tensions have been correspondingly magnified.

Let us recall the elementary facts of the modern Russian situation. Until 1861, some forty-five per cent of the population was enserfed to gentry landowners and another forty-five per cent to the state, leaving only ten per cent of the population in a free status. Then, after 1929, a new form of agrarian servitude was introduced in the form of the *kolkhoz* (until 1974, Soviet peasants did not have internal passports and hence could not leave their village), a regime which it is not unreasonable to call state serfdom, while at the same time industrial regimentation introduced an only slightly less oppressive order in the cities. In the political sphere, a significant measure of public participation in government at the local level and modern civil liberties were not introduced until the *zemstvo* and judicial reforms of 1864; while, on the national level, the country remained an integral autocracy until the concession of a Legislative Duma in 1905. Then, in 1917, a new and far more severe form of autocracy was established, and all popular participation in local government and all civil liberties were rapidly suppressed. Thus Russia has known the full fruits of citizenship, an "adult" freedom of intellectual and civic life, only between 1905 and 1917, or for a mere twelve years of her modern history.

At the same time, however, from the end of the eighteenth century onward, Russian society was increasingly penetrated by the forces of European Enlightenment, and throughout the last century of the old regime the demand constantly grew stronger for an end to the national "immaturity" imposed by archaic institutions and maintained by fearful "guardians." Moreover, after 1820, Russia began to produce an extraordinarily dynamic and creative literary culture that expressed with most compelling effect the national aspiration to a fuller life, for under the old regime, unlike the new, society enjoyed a large measure of artistic freedom. (After 1917, even aesthetic energies were curbed or driven underground, to reemerge into the light of day only belatedly, in the nineteen-fifties, in the *samizdat* literature of dissent.) Under such contradictory circumstances, the level of ideological tension could not fail to be exceptionally high. And amidst such tension one would naturally expect that the aspiration to civic maturity could only express itself in refracted and often distorted fashion.

In this perspective, it is not surprising that the majority of Russian subjects, the peasants, should generally have felt themselves to be the wards, almost the collective children, of social authorities viewed as protective, or domineering, or in some way parental. For the bulk of the population, then, the fullness of adulthood was beyond the realm of possibility. Not surprisingly, Russian folk language is replete with terms that convey such an attitude. To take only one example, we may examine the uses of the word *batiushka* (usually translated as "little father"). This term was used among the peasantry to address, or to refer to, one's biological father. It was also used to address a priest—but for God, the more formal term *otets* ("father") was employed. It was used, in addition, to address all persons above oneself in the social hierarchy: for example, a white-bearded, seventy-year-old village elder would address his eighteen-year-old master (*barin*) as *batiushka*. Finally, the peasant would refer to the tsar as *batiushka-tsar* and would conceive of him as ruling over something—or rather someone—called *matushka Rossiia* ("little mother Russia"). Thus Russian peasant soldiers would sing as they went into battle: *Idem my na vraga za matushku Rossiiu, za batiushku tsaria* ("We go against the foe for mother Russia, for father tsar"). And in the twentieth century Soviet soldiers were instructed to go into battle to the cry of *za Stalina, za rodinu* ("For Stalin, for the motherland"). But all this is quite familiar to attentive readers of Russian novels of whatever period.

III

Quite different, and more interesting, is the case of the Europeanized, "enlightened" elite, whether among the gentry or the intelligentsia. The simple people, after all, as its vocabulary suggests, lacked the cultural horizon to desire active participation in the wider *res publica*; it wished only that the inevitable authority of superior social and political power should be a benevolent rather than an oppressive one. The gentry and the intelligentsia, on the other hand, had acquired the cultural horizon, the sophisticated skills, and the sense of personal dignity for which modern citizenship was the logical and fully mature social expression. Yet, as we have seen, the existing structure of Russian society made it impossible to accommodate this desire in direct political fashion. One inevitable result of this situation was the emergence of a revolutionary movement, beginning tentatively with the Decembrist revolt in 1825 and reappearing as a permanent force with the "nihilism" and Populism of the eighteen-sixties and -seventies, a movement which, in its naive utopianism and impatient maximalism, displayed a political immaturity that reflected quite exactly that of the order it sought to combat.

But more significant for our purposes is that the enlightened elite's aspiration to civic maturity expressed itself above all in refracted form, by sublimation into the one domain of true freedom in Russia—the realm of art and literature. Once the full power of the "Russian Word" had first been revealed by Pushkin in the eighteen-twenties and Gogol in the eighteen-forties the means were at hand for the intelligentsia to effect a substitution of aesthetic self-fulfillment for civic emancipation, to embark on a quest for self-determination through art and literature to make up for the lack of self-realization in politics and society. It was the critic Belinsky who in the forties, taking Pushkin and Gogol as his texts, first spelled out the full implications of this situation: he proclaimed that the Russian writer had an inescapable moral mission to use the power of his art to work for the "humanization" and "enlightenment" of Russian life. With this he launched a tradition that has endured in one or another guise, and through all the vicissitudes of Russian politics and letters to the present day. As the matter was put recently by the widow of the Soviet poet, Mandelshtam: "The work of a poet . . . has a *social* character . . . concerned with the doings of the poet's fellow men . . . whose fate he shares. He does not speak 'for them,' but 'with them,' . . . otherwise he would not be the source of truth."

The general tradition established by Belinsky, however, could lead to at least two distinct, indeed quite antithetical, practical approaches to the role of art as a vehicle for enlightenment. It could lead, first, to the notion, perhaps best exemplified by Turgenev (and echoed by Mme. Mandelshtam), that art as a free creative endeavor, as the spontaneous expression of the writer's conscience, would automatically bear witness to truths capable of humanizing Russian life. It is this view that underlies most of the great creative accomplishments of Russian letters since the eighteen-forties. Or the idea of the social responsibility of art could lead to a literature of direct exhortation, seeking to unmask present evils and to urge the rising generation to immediate action on behalf of the "people." This is the tradition of "civic" or utilitarian art, first developed to its logical extreme by Chernyshevsky, Dobroliubov, and Pisarev in the eighteen-sixties, and continued by Gorky into the twentieth century, a tradition which has always stood in close relation to the active revolutionary movement. Its aesthetic accomplishments have at best been meager, and more often than not it has degenerated into crass propaganda—as in the radicals' breviary, Chernyshevsky's *What Is to Be Done?*

We are thus confronted with a paradoxical situation: the ideal of the social responsibility of art was first advanced, and was most relentlessly pursued, by the left of the Russian intelligentsia; yet almost all the great Russian literature of social import has in fact been produced by men of the center and, above all, the right. This was so because only outside the doctrinaire confines of the "civic" school was it possible to place creative freedom above immediate social utility and thereby to preserve the full power and authenticity of the "Russian Word." Yet, on another level, both traditions converged to produce a single result and one unique to the Russian situation: namely, to confer on the successful man of letters the role of surrogate civic leader and national moral authority—indeed, to hold out to the true creative genius the temptation of becoming a secular prophet.

The first major figure to assume some of these roles was the moderate liberal Turgenev. Although genuinely committed to his political position, he was above all committed to his art, and his preferred theme was the private world of the emotion of love. Still, responding to the pressures of the age, he always recognized that his gift as an artist also placed upon him the moral duty to be a surrogate civic leader. Thus, from the *Sportsman's Sketches* in the eighteen-forties, to *Fathers and Sons* in 1862, to *Virgin*

Soil in the late eighteen-seventies, he regularly commented on the unfolding of the national destiny and discreetly conveyed to his readers an ethic of social concern—too discreetly, as it turned out, for the theorists of "civic art," who, rightly sensing his lack of total commitment to the "cause," attacked him so vehemently after 1862 that he found it more comfortable to move to Western Europe. Still, his stature as aesthetic-civic spokesman had become such that the government, deeply fearing demonstrations at his funeral in 1883, called out the police. Nonetheless, Turgenev, because of his very moderation, never chose to go beyond pragmatic civic commentary to assume the mantle of living writer-prophet with a quasi-charismatic national role. This status has been reserved to only four major figures, all on the right, and all with pretensions to some form of religious inspiration. These are Dostoevsky and Tolstoi under the old regime and Pasternak and Solzhenitsyn under the new.

Of these four cases, that of Tolstoi is undoubtedly the most striking. His contemporary, Dostoevsky, did not live long enough to acquire full prophetic stature until his very last years, and his message was too antagonistic to the dominant melioristic strain of Russian letters to achieve the mass following of Tolstoi, who appropriated enough of the values of the left to create the illusion of an ecumenical national appeal. As for Pasternak, his career as prophet was too brief and too effectively stifled to put him in the very first rank among his fellows. The nearest competitor to Tolstoi is Solzhenitsyn, but even though his career has not yet run its course, it is already clear that in purely literary terms he is not Tolstoi's equal. The latter thus remains the acme of this peculiarly Russian tradition.

IV

But before becoming a prophet, Tolstoi had first to become a writer, and it is in his role as writer that his example is, in the first instance, relevant to the problem of adulthood.

It has often been remarked that every author has basically only one book to write and that he produces this volume over and over, in multiple variants. In the case of Tolstoi, the central theme to which he constantly returned was the couple and the family. (Or to put the matter more broadly, and as he himself came to see it fully only toward the end of his career, his central theme was the elemental cycle of human growth and decay, the process of maturation from childhood, to the formation of the married couple, to the nurturing of a new family, to the anticipation of dissolution and death—and beyond this, to the quest for some moral absolute that would give meaning to the whole.

There are, to be sure, other major themes in Tolstoi as well. There is always the theme of Russia, its various social classes, and its national destiny. Related to this is the theme of the corruption bred by the sophistication of civilization and of high society. And stemming from this, finally, is the theme that man's moral quest can be completed only in a rediscovery of natural simplicity. Yet all of these ancillary themes are always explored in the context of a grand design of movement from "childhood" to a hoped-for "resurrection." And it is in this concern with the grand design of life that Tolstoi ultimately found his role as prophet.

In order to account for this evolution, it should first be noted that, although Tolstoi sprang from a closely knit, extended "gentry nest" of old nobility—a circumstance that gave him a deep sense of rootedness in the most secure stratum of Russian society—he did not grow up with any significant direct experience of an immediate, nuclear family. His mother died when he was two and his father, when he was six, with the result that he and his brothers were brought up by a disparate collection of grandmothers, aunts, nannies, foreign tutors, and serf "uncles." Moreover, although very conscious of his status as grand gentry, he grew up in unusual closeness to the rough-and-ready mores of peasant life, a form of "socialization" that made him ever after ambivalent toward both groups. Finally, it is significant that he came to literary maturity during the Crimean War and its reforming aftermath under Alexander II, when gentry-serf Russia, the world of his ancestors and his childhood village memories, began to give way to a more Westernized and rationalized order, as demanded by the newly emerged left.

Tolstoi responded to this series of pressures by setting himself resolutely against the new Russia (even though he was sensitive to the issue of social justice for the peasants) and by idealizing the old Russia of village and manor house. At the same time he began to explore the meaning of his own unfolding destiny in its relation to the family and society. The result was the trilogy of the eighteen-fifties, *Childhood, Boyhood,* and *Youth*, the work of Tolstoi's twenties. In these short novels, by a deft transposition of real circumstances and individuals, Tolstoi gave to himself, in the person of the young Irteniev, an immediate family he had never in fact possessed, and he lent to serf-gentry Russia an aura of wholesomeness and perenniality that its impending demise clearly belied. The entire enterprise was carried out with a power of realistic presentation that makes of Tolstoi the supreme illusionist in convincingly imposing on life the moral vision he needed to find there.

All Tolstoi's subsequent major works of fiction represent the development of the quest for the fullness of maturity begun with *Childhood*. His three great novels—*War and Peace, Anna Karenina,* and *Resurrection* (which take us from 1864 to 1899)—go beyond the story of the young man still striving to grow up, to take as their central theme the adult couple, marriage, and the family. It should be noted, however, that these three works describe a descending curve of faith on Tolstoi's part in the possibility of achieving true maturity through conjugal and family love. In *War and Peace* his faith is almost total; with *Anna Karenina* the couple is called into fundamental doubt; and in *Resurrection* mere human love is declared to be a dead end, and the fullness of life is proclaimed to lie in an asexual potential beyond all flesh.

It should be noted that this descending curve of Tolstoi's faith in the family parallels exactly the descending curve of the fortunes of his own married life. Moreover, at the same time as the conjugal couple faded as the central value in Tolstoi's work and life, the role of moral prophet to the nation came to dominate his activities as man and writer. Thus, in the last thirty years of his life, by exploiting the celebrity and authority conferred by the literary accomplishments of the previous thirty years, Tolstoi became a national moral authority on a scale that Russia had never before seen.

To return to the beginning of this odyssey, the successfully maturing young male presented in the closing pages of *Youth* had been notably lacking in one quality of adulthood: the ability to master and direct his sexual appetites. This was, of course, the problem of Tolstoi himself, who, as his diaries amply illustrate, was endowed with what Viktor Shklovsky has called a "bull-like peasant eroticism." Since Tolstoi also possessed the power of the Russian village landowner, the peasant girls of Yasnaia Poliana were always readily available to satisfy his desires—a combination of ethical and social circumstances that filled Tolstoi with immense guilt and periodically called into question the meaning of his life. The solution was to find a pure and virginal woman of the genteel upper classes, who would direct this degrading lust toward the founding and the nurturing of a family. In 1862, at the "advanced" age of thirty-four, Tolstoi married Sophia Andreevna Behrs, aged eighteen, whose mission was to redeem and civilize her master. And this redemption of the flesh in marriage gives us the idyllic picture of the couple and the family presented in *War and Peace*.

If we leave aside the larger public world of "war," the world of Alexander I, Napoleon, and Kutuzov, the smaller, private world of "peace" is basically structured around three existing families and two new couples formed from these families. To this basic structure are ajoined a few outsiders, notably the illegitimate aristocrat, Pierre Bezukhov and the sage peasant Platon Karataev. The three families, all aristocratic, are the complex, restless, and reflective Bolkonskys, the simple, spontaneous, and unintellectual Rostovs, and the sophisticated yet shallow and corrupt representatives of high society, the Kuragins. Pierre, on the other hand, clumsy and confused yet basically good, represents the unattached individual seeker after roots and the meaning of life, and Karataev figures as the serene, elemental wisdom of the suffering peasantry, which alone can give a social and ethical purpose to the questing aristocracy and intelligentsia.

The action of the novel is this: the young heroes and heroines from the two "good" families along with Pierre are almost destroyed by their counterparts in the "bad" family (for there is evil and temptation in every destiny). Yet in the end, all of the positive characters find salvation, though in a complex pattern none of them had originally foreseen. The ideal man, both active and contemplative, Andrei Bolkonsky, initially betrothed to the ideal woman, Natasha Rostov, finds his chances for terrestrial happiness destroyed when the exuberant Natasha, almost succumbing to blind carnality, attempts to run off with the cynical Anatole Kuragin—an episode which almost destroys her. But Andrei finds a higher salvation in a patriotic death illuminated by discovery of the primordial meaning of life as communicated to him by Karataev. Pierre is almost destroyed by marriage to the faithless Hélène Kuragin, before finding his true "identity" in wedlock with a now chastened and mature Natasha. At the same time, Nicholas Rostov, the ideal active man, after refusing the love of his adoring cousin, Sonia—admirable in herself, but simply not for him—finds his destiny in the arms of the plain yet morally deep and intelligent Maria Bolkonsky—who herself had almost been lost through her father's efforts to betroth her to the ubiquitous cynic, Kuragin. Thus opposites are unexpectedly yet successfully paired in the two "good" families, though not without the sacrifice of some of the best in each clan. The two new couples end by presiding over expanding broods so as to ensure the succession of the generations and the continuation of society.

This was Tolstoi's paean to the stable equilibrium of his life in his thirties, to the

first decade of happiness with Sophia Andreevna, who devotedly bore him children almost annually, while at the same time copying out in longhand seven times the crabbed
drafts of *War and Peace*.

Anna Karenina, the work of Tolstoi's forties, presents a distinctly less optimistic
picture of the human condition. The novel is, again, the story of two couples and of interlocking families, with good and bad in both. The secondary couple, Kitty and Levin,
is largely a replay of Pierre and Natasha, though in more mediocre form, and it is this
very quality, plus the rural life, that assures their salvation. In the primary couple,
Vronsky, though without real depth, represents the most attractive type of male produced by high society, a "stallion" of breeding. His partner, Anna, represents the acme
of womanhood in every respect: beauty, grace, depth, and, above all, capacity for true
love. Yet she is doomed, and precisely because of her great qualities. Since she truly
loves Vronsky, she refuses to compromise and to hide her relationship with him by becoming his mistress while remaining with her husband for appearances' sake. But this
honesty founded on love places her in a situation of social ostracism. Vronsky is unable
to bear this isolation or to sustain love, at least at Anna's level, in a situation entirely *à
deux*. When Anna realizes that their world of love is crumbling, life loses all meaning
and she destroys herself under an onrushing train.

Thus the fullness of human love expressed by the most superb of creatures now
leads as easily, indeed, more easily to death than to the generative fulfillment formerly
attained by Natasha Rostov. For such procreative, vegetative felicity, the mediocrity of
Kitty and Levin is far more satisfactory than is the vitality of the ideal woman. *Anna
Karenina* ends on a note of profound ambiguity about the goal and meaning of the life
cycle. And it is this carefully balanced ambiguity that makes the novel the most perfect
of all Tolstoi's works.

Then, in 1880-81, just over the age of fifty, Tolstoi went through an agonizing
crisis leading to his "conversion" and to a completely new mode of life. Expanding his
insight in *Anna*, he concluded that death was the end of *all* human fulfillment: the
couple, the family, the creative accomplishments of art. These false idols, therefore,
must be renounced in favor of God, who alone could overcome death. But God could
not be found through the rituals of the Church or the reasons of philosophy; He could
only be found by accepting the pure, unquestioning faith of the peasant in a pre-
ternatural moral order of life. This faith, for Tolstoi, led directly to the Gospels, which
he understood, moreover, as a simple, rationally demonstrable code of ethics (in five
crystal-clear points), centering on love, non-violence, and service to one's fellow men,
especially the common people.

Over the years Tolstoi elaborated a pseudo-religion around these principles, and
the new creed acquired a nucleus of active disciples and a broad national, indeed international, audience that soon made of Yasnaia Poliana a veritable center of pilgrimage.
This "Tolstoian religion" condemned the state, war, the official Church, social inequality, and private property, and it advanced a crude utilitarian theory of art akin to
that of the "civic" school—a collection of tenets Boris Eikhenbaum has called an "an-
archism of the Right." In addition, sex, even in marriage, was denounced as simply another form of aggression and violence, the source of hate rather than love. Sophia An-

dreevna obviously could not adapt to this creed, which denied all that she had so long and so devotedly lived for. As the spouses aged, the marriage degenerated into a running war of acrimonious and often hysterical scenes, with threats of suicide and mutual accusations of betrayal, followed by fits of remorse and reconciliation. In the midst of this hell, Tolstoi fell back increasingly on his favorite daughter, Sasha, to assume the mother's former role of secretary and "guiding star," a situation of rivalry that only made family life still more infernal.

This new condemnation of the carnal couple as the source of mutual destruction was expressed with the profoundest pessimism in *The Death of Ivan Ilich* and *The Kreutzer Sonata*, the major works of Tolstoi's fifties. In *Ivan Ilich*, a sterile and loveless marriage and the empty pomps of worldly success are portrayed as the logical prelude to the lonely dissolution of death. In the much more violent and directly autobiographical *Kreutzer Sonata*, marriage itself is presented as a kind of living death, a dialectic of hate falsely masquerading as an exchange of love. For man desires woman solely to assuage his porcine sensuality, and woman avenges herself by enslaving man through the artful exploitation of his sensual needs. As a solution, Tolstoi advocated total continence, despite the fact that this might lead to the extinction of the species, for death was the destiny of mankind in any event.

But Tolstoi's final word on the theme of the couple and the meaning of the life cycle was the more complex message of *Resurrection*, the work of his late sixties. The hero, Prince Nekhliudov, had seduced and then abandoned a peasant girl, Maslova, thus driving her to prostitution—much as the young Tolstoi himself had once done to a serf mistress. Some years later, Maslova, falsely accused of poisoning a client, is brought to trial, and Nehkliudov finds himself in the morally untenable position of being on her jury. Thus, when Maslova is condemned to Siberia, Nekhliudov renounces his life of pleasure in order to follow his victim into exile. In this action, however, he is moved not by a revival of his old and purely carnal love, but by compassion and the spiritual need to atone for his sin through working for Maslova's redemption. And, in fact, through shared suffering the two are redeemed and recover their moral innocence. Nekhliudov then proposes marriage, but Maslova refuses, preferring instead another prisoner whom she does not love, but whom she can serve in a practical way. Thus the true union of the once carnal couple of Nekhliudov and Maslova can only be spiritual. And this, to the aged Tolstoi, was the only authentic adulthood, the true crown of the life cycle, for all selfish, sinful, and suffering mankind.

Ten years after delivering this message, in 1910 at the age of eighty-three, the now hallowed national prophet at last decided to act in full accord with his own advice. Following a final, bitter scene with Sophia Andreevna, he fled Yasnaia Poliana with Sasha to live as a homeless, propertyless peasant—in a senescent caricature of Nekhliudov's pilgrimage into Siberia. His health, however, immediately broke down, and at the railway station of Astapovo, after a protracted agony, he died in his daughter's arms (for Sasha had refused to let her mother into the room). At the same time, the authorities, fearing demonstrations from the crowds that had gathered for the deathwatch, mobilized the gendarmes throughout the province.

V

It is obvious that no single, simple conclusion can be drawn from so extraordinary a life; yet, for purposes of the present inquiry, a number of generalizations rather clearly suggest themselves.

In his twenties, thirties, and forties, Tolstoi gave the most powerful and convincing depiction of the process of human maturation existing in Russian and, no doubt, in world literature in the series of portrayals that take us from the young Irteniev, to Pierre and Natasha, to Kitty and Levin. Moreover, he lived life in all the fullness with which he described it in fiction. Though not without problems to overcome and trials to undergo, Tolstoi at each step in his development during these years adapted with extraordinary success, in both the private and the public spheres, to the challenges of growing up: as young-man-in-search-of-himself, as husband, as father, as manager of a great estate, and finally as the supreme creative artist—which in Russia was also the supreme civic role. His whole career until 1880 exudes health, balance, and "maturity." And so, too, does his art.

Then, at the age of fifty, everything went awry, at least in terms of a "normal" life cycle. Suddenly Tolstoi proceeded to denigrate and destroy all that he had previously built: his marriage, his family, his art. Even his gentry conservatism, which had always been directed against the encroachments of the modern world, once that world had thoroughly undermined old Russia and the gentry's cause was lost, became transformed into an anarchistic populism that sought to level everything in sight. In place of these immolated values, Tolstoi put a God in which he could not really believe and which he vainly tried to "know" by purely rational means; he devised an ostensible ethic of love, which, in its imperious intolerance, only fostered hatred among those nearest and hitherto dearest to him; and he pathetically strove to resolve these dilemmas by acting the humble peasant, which for a Count Tolstoi and world-renowned author was an intrinsically impossible enterprise.

Several explanations for this amazing *volte-face* suggest themselves; all are plausible, though none is conclusive. And the most plausible is also the most elusive: namely, to seek the deeper cause of Tolstoi's crisis not in the immediate "triggering" circumstances of late maturity, but in some fundamental maladaptation of early life, in some warped phase in the basic formation of the personality.

Yet here we can only speculate, by noting, for example, that Tolstoi never really knew his mother and hence always boundlessly idealized her faceless image. To this childhood deprivation, we may plausibly relate his later obsession with defining the ideal woman and his propensity always to characterize her not as a love object, but as a vessel of "generativity." For this was the role of Natasha, of Kitty, and, indeed, of the young Sophia Andreevna, whereas the pure love object, Anna, was destined only for death. Even in Tolstoi's most eloquent encomia to womankind, and long before his "conversion," there was always a strain of doubt about the ultimate sanctification of sex.

Similarly, though with greater certainty, we may note that the philosophical serenity, the "realistic" mastery of life exhibited in the great novels, only imperfectly masked an undercurrent of deep moral disquiet and an impatient aspiration to total truth. Indeed, these impulses yielded the first adumbrations of the "Tolstoian religion" in the metaphysical questings of Prince Andrei, Pierre, and Levin, and in the person of that peasant icon, Karataev. If one rereads Tolstoi's earlier, "healthy" works in the light of his later conversion, both the psychological and the ideological germs of that event are present from the time of his first "confession," *Childhood*.

Then, on the downward slope of fifty, new circumstances suddenly brought this long-germinating crisis of moral identity to the surface. Fear of the approaching chill of death, as expressed in *Ivan Ilich*, is clearly the most obvious of these "triggering" circumstances. Fear of the loss of sexual potency—itself the harbinger of death—was perhaps more immediately important. For, as Tolstoi now fully realized, since youth his virility had been both the glory and the scourge of his existence and hence the crux of the moral dilemma of his life: on the one hand, it was the supreme manifestation, indeed the very source, of being, on the other, it was an expression of wild, exploitative aggression against another being. The loving submission of Sophia Andreevna for twenty creative years permitted him to elude (if not to resolve this dilemma; after fifty, he could first foresee that in some relatively finite future the problem would no longer exist. Hence, as potency began to wane, he fell back increasingly on an ethic of pure incorporeal love, and at the same time he projected onto Sophia Andreevna his resentment at having only a dwindling margin of choice.

These suppositions lead to still another, and related, explanation of the great "conversion": after fifty, Tolstoi feared that he would never again be able to duplicate the titanic feats of *War and Peace* and *Anna Karenina*, and his pride would settle for no less. For he was quite aware that artistic creativity was related to generative potency; as Turgenev confided to him in 1881: when one can no longer love, one can no longer write.

One final explanation may be adduced: perhaps Tolstoi should be taken at face value, and his "conversion" should be interpreted as genuine. For, whatever self-seeking personal motives led to his decision, in the last analysis he was basically repeating, though in aberrant and simplistic fashion, an intuition as old as Job, St. Paul, and St. Augustine: that the highest accomplishments of human creativity are ultimately as ashes and that only an Absolute beyond all earthly contingency can give moral meaning to the unfathomable turns of the terrestrial "life cycle." An illusion, perhaps. But without it, the crowds would not have stood in such silent awe around the station at Astapovo, as if some latter-day apostle had really descended into their midst.

Tolstoi's "mature" solution to the enigma of life may therefore be interpreted either as a neurotic regression into infantilism or as a true transcendence of carnal contingency, depending on one's point of view. (The majority would no doubt side with Sophia Andreevna in favor of common-sense "adjustment" to the process of aging.)

Yet in either case one fact remains inescapable: Tolstoi's solution was made possible only by the unique position of the writer-as-prophet in Russian life. Without this potential role his religio-moral lucubrations would not have found a "market," and without the stimulation of this market he could not have pursued them to the ruthlessly logical extremes that he did. (Just try to imagine Victor Hugo, Zola, or G. B. Shaw, all of whom were not without prophetic pretensions, waxing so blatantly apostolic in Paris or London—it simply would not have "gone over" with the public.) And—let it be repeated—Tolstoi's ostentatious prophetism and his market were both made possible in turn only by the denial of civic and social maturity to the Russian elites by the "guardians" of the crumbling old-regime structure of the nation.

These facts, however, suggest a somewhat ambiguous conclusion. On the one hand, the Russian formula of the writer-as-prophet generated pressures that have produced literary accomplishments which no other modern European nation can boast; on the other, this formula represents an intrinsically "immature" state, for it pretends that the moral power of art can adequately replace real participatory politics—which is simply not so.

Thus the aesthetic-political tradition of Russian letters has led to paradoxical results. It has led to the tyranny of pseudoscientific ideology over life on the left, as in the case of Chernyshevsky or Gorky. And, on the right, it has led to the tyranny of pseudo-religion over life, which in the last analysis is the most plausible interpretation of Tolstoi's pretensions in his post-"conversion" phase. For the pressures of old-regime Russian life were such that both the narrowly committed revolutionary writer and the independent writer of moral conscience felt that they must offer a solution to *all* problems, or they had failed. But the result has been that this ethical-ideological megalomania, on both sides, has simply served to perpetuate the civic immaturity from which it was first born.

It is certainly no easy matter to win through to the self-determination of "adulthood" and maturity in any age or any society. And it has clearly been more difficult to do so in modern Russia than anywhere else in the European world. Yet it is perhaps also true that, outside of *felix America*, adulthood cannot be considered as a fixed and finite goal, but that it can only be seen as an ever receding approximation to the fullness of the human potential. In this perspective, might not even the most outlandish of "prophets" have a relevant word to say? For on the treadmill of the human "life cycle" who really knows: *quo vadimus?*

BIBLIOGRAPHICAL NOTE

For an essay of this sort, which deals essentially in general impressions gathered from a wide range of literary and historical works, detailed annotation would be a futile enterprise. The more extended treatment of Tolstoi, however, is in a different category, and some of the relevant works are listed here. A general bibliography of Tolstoi can be found in Esfir' Efimovna Zaidenshnur, *Bibliografiia proizvedenii L. N. Tolstogo: Izdaniia na russkom iazyke (1928–1953); Izdaniia na iazykakh i narechiiakh narodov SSSR (1917–1953)*, (Moscow, 1955). Among the more important biographies of Tolstoi are V. Shklovskii, *Lev Tolstoi* (Moscow, 1967), Ernest J. Simmons, *Leo Tolstoi* (Boston, 1946), and Henri Troyat, *Tolstoi* (Paris, 1965), English translation, *Tolstoy* [New York, 1967]). Some of the more important critical discussions of Tolstoi are Isaiah Berlin, "Tolstoi and Enlightenment," in *Mightier Than the Sword* (London, 1964); *idem, The Hedgehog and the Fox* (London, 1953); R. P. Blackmur, "The Dialectics of Incarnation: Tolstoy's *Anna Karenina*," in *Eleven Essays in the European Novel* (New York, 1964); Albert Cook, "The Moral Vision: Tolstoy," in *The Meaning of Fiction* (Detroit, 1960); B. M. Eikhenbaum, *Lev Tolstoi*, 2 vols. (Leningrad, 1929-31); Kathryn B. Feuer, "Solzhenitsyn and the Legacy of Tolstoy," in John B. Dunlop *et al.*, eds., *Aleksandr Solzhenitsyn: Critical Essays and Documentary Materials* (Belmont, 1973); Henry Gifford, comp., *Leo Tolstoy, A Critical Anthology* (Harmondsworth, 1971); Konstantin Leont'ev, *Analiz, stil', i veianie; o romanakh* gr. *L. N. Tolstogo. Kriticheskii etiud* (Providence, 1965); Dmitri Merezhkovsky, *Tolstoy as Man and Artist, With an Essay on Dostoevski* (London, 1902); Renato Poggioli, "Tolstoy as Man and Artist," *Oxford Slavonic Papers*, X (1962); Leon Shestov, *In Job's Balance* (London, 1932); Viktor Borisovich Shklovskii, *Material i stil' v romane L'va Tolstogo 'Voina i mir'* (Moscow, 1928); and Ralph E. Matlaw, ed., *Tolstoy, A Collection of Critical Essays* (Englewood Cliffs, 1967). The quotation from Nadezhda Mandelshtam is in her *Hope Against Hope* (New York, 1970), p. 188. To my knowledge, there exists no study of the theme of the couple and the family in Tolstoi.

WINTHROP D. JORDAN

Searching for Adulthood in America

IT IS AN INTERESTING COMMENTARY ON OUR CULTURE that we find ourselves asking: What does adulthood mean? As with so many human affairs, the meaning lies in the question. From a historian's vantage point, what is arresting is that we should be asking a question that would have made so little sense to our forebears.

A word of caution is in order: my present assignment is to trace the history of the concept of adulthood in one country—the United States. It is immediately obvious that there are difficulties in treating the concept within a single national unit, particularly the United States, where one is dealing with a multiplicity of cultural traditions. One could argue that the United States is merely one segment of Western culture or, today, of technological world culture. On the other hand, one could stress the diversity of the nation and discuss concepts that have prevailed among various American ethnic and religious groups. To do so would entail entering a fascinating arena, but one so thicketed with complexities as to require a very lengthy disquisition. We would have to deal, for example, with such phenomena as ten-year-old black youths calling each other "man," as well as with their fathers who are called—or at least used to be—"boys." We would have to deal, too, with Irish Catholic families in which sons become "Fathers" to their parents. There are myriad similar problems. Rather than plunge into this briarpatch, I will confine myself to prevailing ideas in America—most evident and predominant in the non-ethnic middle class—trusting that it will be borne in mind that many of these ideas were not, and are not, confined to this country and, indeed, that the concept of adulthood constitutes a most inappropriate vehicle for any attempt to define America's uniqueness. Indeed "adulthood," as we ordinarily think of it today, is largely an artifact of twentieth-century American culture. Historically that concept emerged by a process of exclusion, as a final product resulting from prior definitions of other stages in the human life cycle.

I

If one ransacks the cultural baggage of the early English settlers of this nation, one searches in vain for any well defined concept of adulthood. Perhaps one might at least expect to find some vague outlines of such a concept in the extensive Puritan literature on the family, but one does not. In early seventeenth-century England, the Reverend William Gouge's *Of Domestical Duties* managed to offer more than six hundred pages on the family without saying anything about the life cycle of families or of individuals.[1] Gouge's approach was typical of the day: he discussed the duties of the husband, of the wife, of children, and of servants. The roles played by each are entirely static; growth and even change are totally absent.

It would be a mistake to see Gouge's portrayal as a reflection of an entirely static society. His England was just the opposite: dynamic and in the throes of social and economic change—a restless, voyaging, trafficking, discovering nation whose accomplishments were so eloquently trumpeted by Richard Hakluyt. Rather, it makes much more sense to view the rigidities of Gouge's description as reflecting concern about increasing fluidity in the social and perhaps even familial structures of Tudor-Stuart England. While Hakluyt called upon the English to plant themselves in America, Gouge cautioned the godly to perform their domestic duties—each according to his appointed familial station. The duties—not the development—of the roles were what counted.

If one turns to the theology of the early English settlers in America, which was predominantly Puritan or at least Low-Church Protestant, one finds an analogous situation. A predestinarian theology, no matter how much modified by covenants that restrained God's arbitrary power, was scarcely the body of thought to encourage notions of personal growth, maturing, or becoming psychologically adult. No matter how dynamic in the long run, Puritanism spoke for stasis, for striving to know one's existing condition rather than becoming something one was not. To some extent the conversion experience implied change, but it was a limited one since no matter how diligently the individual nurtured the seed of grace, in the end God did all. It is striking that the prevailing imagery of conversion was not one of maturation (despite the seed) but of rebirth. In the long run, indeed, the Arminianization of this theology was required before a fully developed psychological concept of adulthood could emerge. I use the ungainly term "Arminianization" as shorthand for that lengthy process by which Calvinist predestinarianism gave way to a theology that emphasized the individual's ability to gain salvation by means of his own efforts, often aided by revivalistic preaching. Only when the individual's own struggles were given far greater weight in the process of conversion would there be room for a process of reaching psychological maturity. In mid-nineteenth-century America, creeping Arminianization had rusted the bolts of the one-hoss shay pretty badly; it was then that one of the most popular religious books on the family could be entitled *Christian Nurture*.

It would be absurd to contend that our forebears in the nineteenth century—or in the seventeenth century—had absolutely no realization that human beings are born pretty helpless and irresponsible and that their capacities for dealing with the world gradually enlarge. They knew perfectly well that some people were grown-ups and others were children. Though they were not inclined to articulate their recognition of biological and psychological maturity, at times they were forced to draw distinctions based on the reality of human maturation.

In this connection it is instructive to turn to the realm of the law, which embodies a society's ground rules for social rights and responsibilities. Given the rigidities and formalism of Anglo-American written law, one would expect to find some chronological definition of when infant irresponsibility was judged to have ended and adult rights and duties were said to have been acquired. For centuries the common law, and until very recently American statutory and constitutional law, placed that age at 21. Twenty-one has traditionally been the end of nonage. This is not to say, however, that the law has been decisive and unambiguous in plumping for 21 (or 18), since there have always been considerable confusion and inconsistency on the matter. Indeed, the law has reflected a strong sense that individuals acquire capacities gradually, as well as the fact that, in this culture at least, males and females acquire them at different ages. In the seventeen-sixties, for example, Blackstone, the English common-law jurist who was so influential in America, summarized the situation as follows:

> The ages of male and female are different for different purposes. A male at *twelve* years old may take the oath of allegiance; at *fourteen* is at years of discretion, and therefore may consent or disagree to marriage, may choose his guardian, and, if his discretion be actually proved, may make his testament of his personal estate; at *seventeen* may be an executor; and at *twenty-one* is at his own disposal, and may alien his lands, goods, and chattels. A female also at *seven* years of age may be betrothed or given in marriage; at *nine* is entitled to dower; at *twelve* is at years of maturity, and therefore may consent or disagree to marriage, and, if proved to have sufficient discretion, may bequeath her personal estate; at *fourteen* is at years of legal discretion, and may choose a guardian; at seventeen may be executrix; and at *twenty-one* may dispose of herself and her lands.

Still more revealing of uncertainty concerning chronological age was Blackstone's discussion of the ages of criminal responsibility. From age 14 a person could be punished capitally; under the age of 7, he could not. But, Blackstone wrote, "the period between *seven* and *fourteen* is subject of much uncertainty," and he went on to cite "two instances, one of a girl thirteen, who was burned for killing her mistress; another of a boy still younger, that had killed his companion, and hid himself, who was hanged; for it appeared by his hiding that he knew he had done wrong, and could discern between good and evil."[2]   A similar lack of certainty has prevailed in this country to this day, exacerbated by a federal system of government. Not only have the various states set various ages at various times for various purposes, but the national government has wavered on the matter. In general, marriage has tended to confer certain rights regardless of age, which is one reason why the states have regulated the age of marriage, with what consistency may be judged from the following:

MINIMUM AGE FOR MARRIAGE, SELECTED STATES, 1971[3]

	WITH PARENTAL CONSENT		WITHOUT PARENTAL CONSENT	
	Male	*Female*	*Male*	*Female*
Alabama	17	14	21	18
Florida	18	16	21	21
Maine	16	16	20	18
Michigan	No provision	16	18	18
North Dakota	18	15	21	18
Texas	16	14	19	18

That females have earlier rights probably reflects assumptions about their customary subordination in marriage rather than about their earlier maturation. As for males, their age of suitability for military service has been judged at various times to be as low as 16 years or as high as 21, with no clear trend through time nor correlation with wartime exigencies.[4]

And the relationship of these data with the concept of adulthood? It would be possible, of course, to argue that these various ages reflect a consciousness of maturation as a process, of adulthood as something people grow into. On the other hand, it may well be that the real importance of these figures lies in their imprecision, especially in a society so given to quantitative preciseness. Indeed, if there had existed a clearer concept of adulthood, there might well have been greater consistency regarding the age at which the society's members were deemed to have attained that status. It is in this light, perhaps, that we may view the very recent tendency to settle upon the single age of 18 for legal maturity for most or all purposes and for—the point is of some importance—both men and women. It is only in the nineteen-seventies that we are approaching a consensus as to the proper legal age of majority.

As another means of assessing the early shape of the concept of adulthood, one can turn to the term itself. If the *Oxford English Dictionary* is correct, the word "adulthood" came into use only a century ago: the *OED* gives 1870, though "adultness" appears a century earlier. The term "adult" itself is, of course, considerably older, but nonetheless a relatively recent acquisition. It derives from the past participle of the Latin *adolescere*, "to grow up," but it may have been adopted directly from the French *adulte*, itself a sixteenth-century adaptation of the Latin. It was used in English once in 1531 but, says the *OED*, was "not really naturalized till the middle of the seventeenth century." Even then it seems not to have firmly acquired its modern meaning(s), for in 1726 one author announced that "an adult Age is above the age of Puberty and under that of twenty-five years." At least in my experience, the word was not frequently used in eighteenth- or even nineteenth-century America. And of course it has only been in recent years that the term has taken on the burden of freight it carries in such phrases as "adult education" and "adult films" for "adults only."

II

All this is to argue the negative proposition that, to put the matter baldly, the concept of adulthood, in the psychological sense we ordinarily use today, did not appear in America at all until after the Civil War and not really until the early twentieth century. One reason for this absence, already suggested, was theological: American Christianity had to be Arminianized. Another necessary precondition for the emergence of a concept of adulthood was, once again to state the case bluntly, that the family had to be de-politicized—that is to say, notions about maturity and immaturity, mastery and dependence originally had pronouncedly political overtones in which we can detect the potentiality of a shift toward emphasizing these qualities in individuals.

The analogy between the family and the state has its own long history. It was very commonly drawn in seventeenth-century England and America. The family was, as the equation went, "a little commonwealth" whose head was its "governor." And of course familial imagery was very commonly used to describe the state. Amid all the contractualism of the seventeenth and eighteenth centuries, the king remained the "father" of his people. John Locke's instinct was perfectly sound when he advanced his political contract in the form of an attack upon Sir Robert Filmer's patriarchal theory of monarchy.

Although historians have not chosen to pay much attention to it, there was a crescendo of familial-political imagery at the time of the American Revolution. As he was so repeatedly denominated, George III was the "father" of his people and they properly owed him "filial" obedience and respect until he transformed that "natural" relationship by becoming a "tyrant." While George III was the "father," Great Britain was the "parent" or the "mother" country of the Colonies. It was precisely these natural relationships that Thomas Paine so successfully assailed in *Common Sense* when he denounced the king as "the royal brute of Great-Britain" (i.e., standing in an *un*natural relationship to the colonists) and declared that Europe, not England, was the "parent" of America.

These terms were common currency, and it is scarcely any wonder that many writers extended the analogy by incorporating an image of maturation to describe what was happening. It was not a new image. In the seventeenth century, James Harrington had described the colonies in America as being "yet Babes that cannot live without sucking the Breasts of their Mother Citys," but they will "wean themselves," he warned, "when they come of age."[5] In August, 1776, one English friend of the American cause, Richard Price, undertook to refute the common assertion that the "infant" colonies owed obedience to the "parent state":

> Children having no property, and being incapable of guiding themselves, the author of nature has committed the care of them to their parents, and subjected them to their absolute authority. But there is a period when having acquired property, and a capacity of judging for themselves, they become independent agents; and when, for this reason, the authority of their parents ceases, and becomes nothing but the respect and influence due to benefactors. Supposing, therefore, that the order of nature in establishing the relation between parents and children, ought to have been the rule of our conduct to the Colonies, we should have been gradually relaxing our authority as they grew up. But like mad parents, we have done the contrary; and, at the very time when our authority should have been most relaxed, we have carried it to the greatest extent, and exercised it with the greatest rigour. No wonder then, that they have turned upon us; and obliged us to remember that they are not children.[6]

More pithily than Price, Thomas Paine announced airily, "To know whether it be the interest of the continent to be independent, we need only ask this easy, simple question: Is it the interest of a man to be a boy all his life?"[7]

This mode of political discourse became less common after the Revolution, but it did not dissipate entirely until after the Civil War. In the antebellum era, Americans declaimed on the virtues of "the founding fathers" and made George Washington "the Father of his country." At the time of the War of 1812, it was still possible to utilize (and to mix) the metaphor of maturation: "We can watch them better than our fathers were able to do. In 1776, the vessel of state was launched into an unknown sea . . . and we were as children. . . . In 1812, we have a stable and solid government . . . we are abundantly supplied with weapons of defence, we are in a state of comparative manhood. . . ."[8] At the time of the "fratricidal" Civil War, after Lincoln refused to let the "erring sisters depart in peace," he was hailed as "Father Abra'am."[9] But the first president to be assassinated was the last to be assigned such paternity. We have only to try "Father Woodrow" or "Father Franklin" for sound to realize the inappropriateness of the concept in the twentieth century.

A major reason for the demise of this imagery in the political arena was growing concern about actual parents and children. Very briefly, that concern seems to have arisen almost immediately after the American Revolution. At first it manifested itself in discussions about what sort of education would be most proper for the new "infant" Republic and in attempts to produce a suitable literature for the little republicans who would all be becoming "citizens." By 1830, Americans were more than concerned about their children; they were downright worried. At the same time, in the eighteen-thirties, Americans began to worry about adults in a novel way, but not, emphatically, as adults. Rather, the concern was with men and women, with sex roles. This was, of course, the period of the beginnings of the women's rights movement—and of very widespread opposition to it. Much more energy, however, went into concern with parental roles, especially as to their proper sexual differentiation. American Victorians placed the woman on a pedestal, but that pillar was located specifically at the hearthside of the home. The wife was now more the mother, the husband the father. When he was not busy at the counting house he, too, belonged at home. The famous temperance poem caught the spirit exactly: "Father, dear father, come home with me now. . . ."

What this meant was that the antebellum process of depoliticization of the family was *pari passu* the development of an ideology of domesticity. Antebellum America was not concerned with any bimodality between childhood and maturity, but rather with proper roles within the home. As is well known, this ideology was at least in some measure a response to rapidly changing social and economic conditions. In a commercializing, urbanizing, expanding economy, more and more men and women were working, traveling, and buying and selling away from home, and it is scarcely any wonder that the family home came to be a focus of concern.

This concern for domesticity interacted in a novel way with political discourse. A defensive South attempted to transform its commercial slavery into a domestic institution—domestic in the sense of being "peculiar" to the South, but domestic also in the sense that the plantation was increasingly thought of as a family. The master became a patriarch and his slaves, children. Northern critics cried out that the master was frequently the literal father of his slaves and that slavery was a brothel house—an anti-home. Southerners retorted that it was Northern wage slavery which threatened the family and that Northern women were "unsexing" themselves by leaving their hearthsides in order to attend the "promiscuous assemblies" so characteristic of Northern "fanaticism."

At the same time, the egalitarianism of the Jacksonian era was helping to lay the groundwork for later changes in the way in which domestic roles would be conceived. Partly, the homogenizing of ranks and stations in life tended to reduce the citizenry to an undifferentiated mass. The widening of the suffrage, which was accomplished easily and noiselessly compared to the analogous process in Europe, produced a novel situation.

It is perhaps more profitable to think of the suffrage as being limited along new lines. If almost all white adult males could vote (as they could by the time of the Civil War) the suffrage was, in effect, no longer defined by property but by three other criteria—race, age, and sex.[10] In one sense, then, political democracy made the distinction between the political adult and the political child *more* important. At the same time, however, the sexual criterion effectively countered this tendency by drawing together members of each sex. Tocqueville was describing this process when he wrote that, as the laws and manners become more egalitarian in America, "the realm of father and son become more intimate and more affectionate; rules and authority are less talked of; confidence and tenderness are often-times increased."[11] It was no accident that Tocqueville picked the male "realm of father and son."

The Jacksonian concern with proper sex roles was so strong as virtually to preclude, in and of itself, any interest in a concept of adulthood as such. A pronounced emphasis on the distinction between women and men tended to override any perception of commonality; manhood and womanhood perceptually overrode adulthood. What room was there for adulthood when a physician could write that after menopause a woman was "degraded to the level of a being who has no further duty to perform in this world"?[12] What mattered was the distinction between the male and the female parent. "The father may instruct," declared another writer, "but the mother instils; the father may command our reason, but the mother compels our instinct; the father may finish, but the mother must begin. The empire of the father is over the head; of the mother, over the heart."[13]

That such remarks were part of a very basic social change is suggested by the fact that in the mid nineteenth century there seems to have been less premarital sexual intercourse in America than at any time before or since. Even sex was only for parents (not to mention only for men and women). The modern "sexual revolution" (including more premarital pregnancies) seems to have begun in the United States in the very early twentieth century.[14] This was also the approximate time of two other demographic developments which may well have helped engender the development of an explicitly articulated concept of adulthood. Throughout the nineteenth century the fertility rate in the United States fell quite markedly. At the same time, particularly at the end of the century, the mortality rate declined. The combined result was that grown persons no longer spent such a large portion of their lives in the parental role; the "empty nest" syndrome is a relatively recent one.[15] What was to be done with this new period in the life cycle?

This development was accompanied, not by the discovery of adulthood, but by the discovery of adolescence and of old age. Both the term and the concept of "adolescence" were first widely popularized by G. Stanley Hall's book of that title in 1904, though the term itself is much older—considerably older, indeed, than the term "adult." There had been discussion of "youth," as distinct from "childhood," in the nineteenth century, but Hall's work placed "adolescence" firmly as a distinct phase of life and as a description of inner and outer behavior. It is suggestive that Hall placed considerable emphasis on adolescence as that period of life when religious conversion was most likely to be expected; in doing so he was drawing upon an emphasis which in the nineteenth century had accompanied the Arminianization of American Protestantism.

It is less well known that Hall later wrote another book entitled—not "Adulthood"—but *Senescence* (1922). In that book, Hall described "adolescence" as lasting until age 25 or 30, "maturity" from 25 or 30 to 40 or 45 (which left ten or, at best, twenty years for adulthood); "senescence," which he lumped with "old age," was, as announced by the subtitle, "The Last Half of Life." The difficulty that the concept of adulthood was having in getting off the ground is suggested by Hall's conclusion in a previous article (1921) that "leaving out of consideration here the initial prepubertal stage and the terminal one of the post-climacteric or old age proper, all the rest of life which lies between these is divided into two parts, adolescence and senescence, that the latter begins where the former ends [at about forty-five years of age], and that all we have thought characteristic of middle life consists of only the phenomena which are connected with the turn of the tide."[16]

Hall's work on adolescence was heavily influenced by post-Darwinian evolutionary biology. Mankind (particularly the much esteemed Teutonic and Anglo-Saxon portion thereof) was seen as evolving through stages into higher and higher forms. Hall himself thought individual development recapitulated the development of the species. Evolutionary biology worked to pave the way for various developmental psychologies. It was no accident that Hall was attracted by a far more powerful developmental model then being shaped in Europe; his interest and admiration were evident at the famous psychological conference at Clark University in 1909 at which he hosted Dr. Sigmund Freud.

The general tendency in various schools of psychology in the early twentieth century was to segment the life cycle into increasingly discrete and well defined units. An accompanying tendency was fully as important: the various segments of the life cycle were seen not merely as temporal stages but as *descriptions* of inner life and external behavior. Thus the "oral stage" was not merely a temporal segment of the life cycle but a psychological syndrome. Thus, too, "adolescence" was far more descriptive of a mode of behavior than was "youth" in the nineteenth century. The earlier, less content-laden segmenting of the life cycle in the nineteenth century was best typified by the popular prints showing "the stages of man," usually four or six stages such as childhood, youth, maturity, and old age.

A parallel process occurred in American schools and colleges. It was not merely the slow demise of the one-room schoolhouse which caused increasingly precise age-grading in the schools; it was a growing sense that age differences among young people really mattered. This same sense somewhat later permitted the development of the concept of "mental age" in connection with the I.Q. test. To speak of "the college years" as typifying any sort of behavior would have been difficult in the nineteenth century when those years ran from the early teens to the late twenties. In the nineteenth century, grown-ups attended lyceums; in the twentieth, they undertook "adult education."

Finally (and there is scarcely need to belabor the point) this same first quarter of the twentieth century saw the gradual extension of the suffrage to (mostly white) adult women. The body politic was no longer defined in sexual terms: only race and age remained. Politically, only adulthood mattered. Even within the family a parallel process occurred: by the nineteen-twenties, the Victorian mother and father were becoming good modern *parents*, self-consciously "raising" their children according to certain diffuse notions indirectly derived from Dr. Freud. The new medical specialty of pediatrics was by now respectably established. The twin streams were shortly to be united in one of the most popular books ever written for American adults—*Baby and Child Care* by Dr. Benjamin Spock. Despite the Doctor's emphasis on parenting, there remained in his book strong traces of sex differentiation in the parental roles. But it is also true that the book signaled which way the wind was blowing. Spock has, in the nineteen-seventies, been self-consciously revising his text with an eye to meeting, even eliminating, sex differences in parental duties.

III

Given these developments, the concept of adulthood was bound to flower. What is surprising, perhaps, is that it took until 1975 for a symposium on adulthood to materialize, and that, as of 1968, the *International Encyclopedia of the Social Sciences* has articles on "Aging" and "Adolescence," but none on adulthood. The concept was fully evident in popular magazines in the nineteen-twenties. By 1952, the bellwether magazine of popular taste was offering a quiz, "condensed from *McCall's*," entitled

"So You Think You're Grown-Up!" "How old," the introduction asks, "do you have to be before you're an adult? By psychological standards you can be grown-up at 20 or a child at 50." After fifteen questions ("1. Would you ever, by choice, spend an evening alone?"), "to see how 'mature' you are, turn to page 91."[17] From this sort of thing it has been no step at all to the spate of selfhood books of the nineteen-sixties and seventies. Since 1930 there have, of course, been interesting changes in the concept: Dale Carnegie could scarcely have written a book entitled *I'm O.K.—You're O.K.*

Americans had discovered in "adulthood" a novel and ambiguous guide to the maze of an unusually fluid, mobile society which offered a dazzling array of career lines. They were no longer told to labor diligently in an appointed worldly calling. As a guide to life they were now enjoined, as one magazine put it, to "Act Your Age."[18] William Gouge would have greeted such an injunction with towering incomprehension.

Always the current emphasis is on growth and change. At the popular level the approach is to provide a smorgasbord of "psychologies." A new magazine entitled *Personal Growth* offers as "some of the areas we cover": "Self-Actualization Techniques"; "Gestalt Therapy"; "Encounter Groups"; "Meditation"; "Bio-Energetic Analysis"; "Hypnotherapy"; "Relaxation Techniques"; "Self-Analysis"; "Transpersonal Psychology"; "Peak Experiences"; "Creativity Training"; "Depth Imagery & Dream Work"; "Primal Therapy"; "Psychoanalysis"; "Biofeedback Training"; "Transactional Analysis"; "Psychosynthesis"; and "Altered States of Consciousness."[19] One wants instantly to reach for the Alka-Selzer. At a slightly more serious level, the *New York Times* offers such articles as (in characteristic voice): "Three Phases of Adulthood: Transitions Termed as Difficult as Adolescence."[20]

What we seem to be involved in now is a synergistic interaction between a newly dynamic concept and a new social reality. Take, for example, the opening paragraph of a recent newspaper article entitled "Transition: How Adults Cope with Change":

> Adults don't stay put the way they used to. Everywhere you look, people are moving around, changing jobs, going back to school, getting divorced. Starting over, in short. At age 30, 40, 50, 60—there's no end to it.[21]

In such remarks we sense not only a description of real events but an endorsement of them. We also sense that without such endorsements the events would not be taking place.

What we are up against here is a very traditional problem in historical causation—the relationship between social and ideological change. We can see the two factors dynamically interacting in the case of legislation concerning children during the early years of the twentieth century. During the nineteenth century, a large proportion of children went to school until age 12 or 13, and then went to work. About 1900, as part of the process of industrialization, new machinery began displacing children in many jobs in agriculture, factories, and commercial establishments. What has been called "the first stringent" child-labor law was passed by Illinois in 1903.[22] Child-labor laws went hand in hand with compulsory-schooling laws which raised the age at which children were allowed to leave school. Increasingly, extended schooling was seen as necessary preparation for a life of work in a highly complex society. At the same time, women were coming to constitute a rapidly growing proportion of the total labor force. In other words, work, or "career," began to lose its linkage with sex just at the time when the age of "getting a job" was rising considerably. There was an increasingly solid social base for thinking of the late teens as an age when people of both sexes entered a distinct new phase of their lives, one which would last until it came to an abrupt halt, not so frequently as before by death, but by mandatory retirement. The junior citizens of the young Republic, trained by the schools for their adult careers, would eventually become "senior citizens," drawing retirement benefits with a number that had been assigned them when they first entered the work force. Accompanying these changes was widespread discussion of childhood and adolescence as periods of growth, learning, expanding horizons and capacities. There was much talk about children's play, no longer seen as reprehensible "idle pastimes," but as necessary to an expanding, exploring personality. Schooling and play became preparative for—and the moral equivalent of—work, the "business" of adults.

If one had to plump for any single factor as being of central importance in this process, it might well be the actuality and expectation of rapid social change—not limited to the United States, of course, but probably of longer standing there than in most other countries. Technology, geographical and social mobility, and social pluralism have worked to speed up life so that we not only expect our children to lead different lives from ourselves, but we expect our own lives to change, perhaps drastically, through time. In the more static world of our ancestors it would scarcely have been possible to conceive of time in the way which permitted Henri Bergson to write, at about the turn of the twentieth century, "To exist is to change; to change is to mature; to mature is to create oneself endlessly."[23] We have moved, over the years, from condition to process. In our culture, adulthood as a condition used to be simply assumed; as a process, it now seems to demand explanation.

REFERENCES

[1]William Gouge, *Of Domestical Duties* (London, 1622).

[2]William Blackstone, *Commentaries on the Laws of England*, book 1, chap. 17, sec. 629-630.

[3]Virginia G. Cook, *The Age of Majority* (Lexington, Kentucky, 1972), p. 19.

[4]Commonwealth of Massachusetts, *Report of the Legislative Research Council Relative to Lowering the Age of Majority* ([Boston], 1971), pp. 25-30.

[5]Quoted in Christopher Hill, *Puritanism and Revolution* (New York, 1964), p. 311.

[6]Richard Price, "Observations on the Nature of Civil Liberty, etc.," section 1, quoted in *Connecticut Courant*, August 19, 1776.

[7]Philip S. Foner, ed., *The Complete Works of Thomas Paine*, 2 vols. (New York, 1945), I, p. 79.

[8]*Niles' Weekly Register*, II (July 27, 1812), pp. 284-85.

[9]Benjamin P. Thomas, *Abraham Lincoln* (London, 1953), pp. 325-40; David Donald, *Lincoln Reconsidered* (New York, 1959), p. 153; Willard A. and Porter W. Heaps, *The Singing Sixties: The Spirit of Civil War Days Drawn from the Music of the Times* (Norman, Oklahoma, 1960), pp. 89-90.

[10]In many Northern states, conventions which broadened white male suffrage at the same time specifically disfranchised black voters.

[11]Alexis de Tocqueville, *Democracy in America*, 2 vols. (New York, 1961), II, p. 233.

[12]Augustus Kinsley Gardiner, *Conjugal Sins* (New York, 1870), p. 150.

[13]Artemus Bowers Muzzey, *The Fireside: An Aid to Parents* (Boston, 1854), p. 9.

[14]Daniel Scott Smith, "The Dating of the American Sexual Revolution: Evidence and Interpretation," in Michael Gordon, ed., *The American Family in Social-Historical Perspective* (New York, 1973), pp. 321-35.

[15]Robert V. Wells, "Demographic Change and the Life Cycle of American Families," in Theodore K. Rabb and Robert I. Rotberg, eds., *The Family in History: Interdisciplinary Essays* (New York, 1971), pp. 85-94.

[16]Quoted in Dorothy Ross, *G. Stanley Hall: The Psychologist as Prophet* (Chicago and London, 1972), p. 431. The bracketed interpolation is Ross's.

[17]*Reader's Digest*, LXI (July, 1952), pp. 78, 92.

[18]*Vital Speeches of the Day*, XIV (Sept. 15, 1948), pp. 731-34.

[19]Advertising flyer for *Personal Growth* magazine received by the author, May, 1975.

[20]*New York Times*, July 11, 1971, p. 41.

[21]*San Francisco Chronicle*, June 4, 1975, p. 36.

[22]Ross M. Robertson, *History of the American Economy*, (3rd ed., New York, 1973), pp. 382-83. On the matter of child labor and schooling, I have greatly benefited from the counsel of Stuart Bruchey and David Tyack at the Center for Advanced Study in the Behavioral Sciences.

[23]Quoted in Sylvia Anthony, *The Discovery of Death in Childhood and After* (New York, 1972), p. 182.

TAMARA K. HAREVEN

The Last Stage: Historical Adulthood and Old Age

"To learn that one is old is a long, complex, and painful experience. Each decade the circle of the Great Fatigue narrows around us, restricting the intensity and endurance of our activities." It was probably no coincidence that G. Stanley Hall, who had developed the concept of "adolescence" in the eighteen-eighties, offered a synthesis of "senescence" as his last creative opus in 1920, when he himself was eighty years old. While his contemporaries focused on the deterioration of old age, or sought the secrets of longevity, Hall emphasized the unique psychological processes connected with aging and their societal significance. Rather than viewing old age as a period of decline and decay, he saw it as a stage of development in which the passions of youth and the efforts of a life career had reached fruition and consolidation: "There is a certain maturity of judgment about men, things, causes and life generally, that nothing in the world but years can bring, a real wisdom that only age can teach."[1]

The interest in the meaning of aging in the early part of the twentieth century had not grown merely from idle curiosity. It was related to questions about the limits of usefulness and efficiency on the job that had arisen with industrialization and to the movement for providing social insurance for the aged. In 1874, psychologist George Beard had already begun to ask questions about the limitations of old age: "What is the average effect of old age on the mental faculties?"; "to what extent is the average responsibility of men impaired by the change that the mental faculties undergo in old age?" Analyzing the record of "human achievements," he considered at what age the "best work of the world" had been done and found that 70 per cent of creative works had been achieved by age 45 and 80 per cent by age 50. Within this range, he identified 30 to 45 as the optimal period of life. Although he was emphatic about the need for setting a retirement age for judges, he did not recommend an automatic retirement age for laborers.[2] Beard's investigation represented the first attempt at a scientific inquiry into the relationship between aging and efficiency, and it set the stage for the concept of the "superannuated man" that was to come.

In the late nineteenth century, American society passed from an acceptance of aging as a natural process to a view of it as a distinct period of life characterized by decline, weakness, and obsolescence. Advanced old age, which had earlier been regarded as a manifestation of the survival of the fittest, was now denigrated as a condition of dependence and deterioration: "We are marked by time's defacing fingers with the ugliness of age."[3] Writers began to identify advancing years with physical decline and mental deterioration. Beginning in the eighteen-sixties, the popular magazines shifted their emphasis from attaining longevity to discussing the medical symptoms of senescence. In 1910, I. L. Nascher, a New York physician, became the first to formulate the biological characteristics and medical needs of senescence as a life-cycle process. He drew on the work of his predecessors to conceptualize its medical treatment and thus laid the foundation for geriatrics as a medical discipline.[4]

In the beginning of the twentieth century, public concern for, and interest in, old age converged from various directions. In addition to physicians, psychologists, and popular writers, efficiency experts and social reformers were especially instrumental in attracting public attention to old age as a social problem. A variety of medical and psychological studies by industrial-efficiency experts focused on the physical and mental limitations of old age. At the same time, social reformers began to expose the poverty and dependency suffered by many old people, as part of a general investigation of "how the other half lives," and to agitate for social security and social insurance.

Government recognition of old age evolved more gradually and began on the state level; by 1920, only ten states had instituted some form of old-age legislation; all programs were limited in scope, and most of them were declared unconstitutional by the Supreme Court. Nevertheless, agitation for old-age security continued and finally culminated in the Social Security Act of 1935. It was not until the nineteen-forties, however, that gerontology was recognized as a new medical field and even more recently that social scientists identified old age as constituting a new and pressing problem for mankind. Social definitions of age limits and public treatment through institutional reform, retirement legislation, and welfare measures represent the most recent societal recognition of this stage of life.[5]

How does one examine an age group and a stage of life when their experiences, social definitions, and public treatment change over time? How does one conceptualize "old age" and "aging" as social and cultural phenomena in relation to historical change? How does one correlate individual time and historical time—that is, the synchronization of individual development with historical change? Social scientists and popular writers have long been accustomed to examining categories such as class, ethnicity, and race; more recently, they have begun to use gender as a category as well. But they have been less systematic in their use of age because maintaining a distinction between an "age group" and "aging" as a process is difficult. Adolescents, for example, are an "age group." At the same time, adolescence, however bounded by sociopsychological conditions, is a process, subject to change and redefinition. Age and aging are related to biological phenomena, but the meanings of age and aging are socially and culturally determined. "Social age" is a relative concept and varies in different cultural contexts. In trying to understand the societal conditions affecting adulthood and old age, it is important to realize that the definitions of aging, as well as the social conditions and functions of every age group, have not only changed significantly over time but have also varied among cultures.

Gerontological literature approaches the problems of aging from several directions: the developmental perspective has focused on biological and psychological changes connected with aging; the institutional approach has stressed socioeconomic status and the roles of old people; and the cultural perspective has concentrated on stereotypes and perceptions of the elderly. Some of these approaches have also tended to confuse the "aged" as an age group or as a social class with aging as a process.[6] Little effort has been made to integrate these views or interpret them as interrelated processes over the life course.

The emergence of "old age" as a social, cultural, and biological phenomenon can best be understood in the context of other stages of life. The social conditions of children and adolescents in a given society are related to the way in which adulthood is perceived in that society, and, conversely, the role and position of adults and the aged are related to the treatment of children and youths. The formidable task of investigating the synchronization of individual development with social change requires an approach that would take into account the entire life course and differing historical conditions, rather than simply concentrating on a specific age group.

The "discovery" of a new stage of life is itself a complex process. First, individuals become aware of the specific characteristics of a given stage of life as a distinct condition. This discovery is then passed on to society in popularized versions. If it appears to be associated with a major social problem, it attracts the attention of agencies of welfare and social control. Finally it is institutionalized: legislation is passed and agencies are created to deal with its special needs and problems.

The articulation of new stages of life and their recognition in American society in the past generally came as a response to external pressures and to a fear of the disorganization that, it was thought, might otherwise ensue from societal neglect of some particular age group. In the nineteenth century, this apprehension was particularly dramatic as it was manifested in attitudes toward treatment of children and adolescents, where undisciplined and unsocialized young people were compared to the *proletaire* of Paris and were regarded as the "dangerous classes." At that time, the elderly received comparatively little attention, because they were not considered dangerous to the social order. The physical weaknesses and inevitable end associated with old age did not present an imminent danger to society and did not, therefore, evoke the anxiety produced by problems among the youth. The argument against the neglect of children was that they would grow up into dangerous, socially destructive adults. No parallel argument applied to the aged. In a society which had lost its fear of the afterlife, and in which awareness of and contact with death were not integrated into everyday life (for death no longer held a mythical power over the living), there was no reason to fear any potentiality of revenge from among the old people. Consequently, the first demonstration of organized political power on the part of the aged was not manifested until the Townshend movement in the nineteen-thirties, which succeeded in pressing the federal government into instituting social security.

As early as the late eighteenth century, however, American society had gradually begun at least to acknowledge the existence of various stages in life and to develop a corresponding series of institutions to deal with them. As we have seen, it "discovered" childhood in the first half of the nineteenth century and "invented" adolescence toward the end of it, both emerging into public consciousness as a result of social crises associated with those age groups in a manner similar to the emergence of old age later on.[7] However, despite the growing awareness of childhood, adolescence, and youth as pre-adult stages, no clear boundaries for adulthood in America emerged until much later, when interest in the "middle years" as a distinct segment of adult life arose out of the need to differentiate the social and psychological problems of "middle" from "old" age. The psychological, social, and cultural conditions of the past half century have since contributed to the sharpening of the boundaries between those two stages. Several social scientists have tried to distinguish additional categories in adult life, such as the "young old" and the "old old," but it is too early to tell whether these will develop into useful concepts.[8]

It is clear, however, that in American society "old age" is now recognized as a specific period of adulthood. Unlike the other stages, it has a formal beginning—age 65—at least so far as an individual's working life is concerned, and it is institutionalized by a rite of passage—retirement and the commencement of social security. Since so much of adult life in American society is contingent on work, especially for men, retirement also often involves migration and changes in living arrangements.

Popular social-science literature has recently devoted a great deal of attention to the social and economic plight of older people and to their isolation as a result of urbanization and industrialization. The major developments that have been cited as explanations for these problems are: demographic changes arising from increases in life expectancy in childhood and early adulthood and, to some degree, from prolongation of life in old age due to advances in medical technology; the increasing proportion of older people in the population resulting from the decline in fertility and increase in life expectancy; the decrease in productive roles that older people are allowed to play as the result of the shift from a rural to an industrial economy; the technological revolution; and, finally, the denigration of old age, which is thought to be explained by the "cult of youth." Without denying the importance of these explanations, problems of old age and aging in American society can be more fully understood by examining them in terms of more fundamental historical discontinuities in the life course. These changes are rooted in three interrelated areas, all of which are essential for the achievement of what Erikson calls "integrity": location in historical time, work life and productivity, and family orientation and functions. This essay will discuss briefly the historical developments in each of these aspects of adult life and their effects on the conditions of old people in American society.

Location in Historical Time

Because age boundaries and criteria for adulthood vary significantly across cultures, classes, and historical periods, the meaning of adulthood cannot be defined merely in terms of a specific age span, and unlike adolescence, which represents a person's passage through puberty, it cannot be clearly defined in biological terms. Even within the same age group, the social meaning of adulthood and the functions associated with it vary among cultures and according to psychological conditions. For these reasons, it is difficult to determine to what extent and in what ways individuals have in the past perceived their entry into adulthood and transitions to old age under varying historical conditions.

How did individuals pass through their life course?[9] How did they time their transitions from one role to another, and how was this timing related to their family experience and to external social conditions? In what ways did such experiences vary within the same age cohorts?[10] How did these processes vary over time, and how did they differ from the same processes now? Answers to questions such as these would help explain the position of individuals and age groups at different times in the past and would illuminate their interaction with contemporary conditions.

Reuben Hill has noted that in periods of rapid social change, each cohort "encounters at marriage a unique set of historical constraints and incentives which influence the timing of its crucial life decisions, making for marked generational dissimilarities in life-cycle career patterns."[11] This means that the social experience of each cohort is influenced not only by the external conditions of its own time but also by the cumulative experience of its earlier stages in life. Consequently, the position of the elderly in modern American society has been shaped in part by social and economic conditions which have combined to isolate them from family and productive life when they enter their sixties, and in part by their previous cumulative experience along their life course. For example, individuals who reached the age of sixty in the eighteen-nineties and were still working had commenced work at an earlier age and would continue to work until the end of life, or so long as they were able. Having grown up in periods when transitions in the life course were less rigidly marked, they would have found imposed retirement at a set age far more traumatic than a cohort which had come of age in the early twentieth century, when both entry into and exit from the labor force were more clearly timed according to age. The response of an older cohort to changing social and economic conditions is therefore significantly different from that of a younger one, because it is based on very different individual and social experiences. In trying to understand those differences, it is necessary to view both the contemporary social milieu in which they reach that age and the cumulative experience of that cohort over its entire life.

In preindustrial society, demographic, social, and cultural factors combined to produce only a minimal differentiation in the stages of life. Childhood and adolescence were not regarded as distinct stages; children were considered miniature adults, gradually assuming adult roles in their early teens and entering adult life without a moratorium in their youth. Adulthood flowed into old age without institutionalized disruptions. The two major adult roles—parenthood and work—generally stretched over an entire lifetime without an "empty nest" and compulsory retirement. In various rural societies, the insistence of older people on self-sufficiency and their continued control over family estates delayed the assumption of economic independence by their children and afforded aging parents a bargaining position for support in old age.

The integration of economic activities with family life also provided continuity in the usefulness of older people, particularly for widows, even when their capacity to work was waning. One should not, however, idealize the condition of the elderly in preindustrial society. John Demos has pointed out that publicly they were venerated, but they were insecure in private life. Some of the symptoms of insecurity and uncertainty are reflected, for example, in contemporary wills where support for a widowed mother was made a condition for the inheritance of family estates. Nevertheless, old people experienced economic and social segregation far less frequently than they do today, and they retained their familial and economic positions until the end of their lives. If they became "dependent" because of illness or poverty, they were supported by their children or other kin or were placed by the town authorities in the households of neighbors, or even strangers, but not in institutions.[12]

Under the impact of industrialization and the demographic changes of the nineteenth century, however, a gradual differentiation in age groups and specialization in functions began to emerge, although it was by no means complete by the end of that century. Discontinuities in the individual life course were still not marked, and age groups were still not completely segregated in accordance with their functions. While today parents generally complete their child-rearing functions with one third of their lives still ahead, nineteenth-century parenthood was a lifelong career: the combination of relatively late marriage, short life expectancy, and high fertility rarely allowed for an "empty nest" stage. In addition, marriage was frequently broken by death of a spouse before the end of the child-rearing period.[13] Because they married earlier and lived longer than men, this pattern was more common among women.

Widowed or not, however, the extension of motherhood over most of the life course continued to engage women in active familial roles into old age. Peter Uhlenberg has shown that what is today considered a normal life-course sequence for women—marriage, motherhood, survival with husband through parenthood, the launching of children, and widowhood—was experienced by only 44 per cent of females born in 1870 who survived beyond age 15. The remaining 56 per cent never achieved the "normal" life-course pattern, either because they died young, or never married, or were childless, or because their marriage was broken by the death of their husbands or by divorce.[14] As one moves into the twentieth century, the percentage of women conforming to this "normal" life-course pattern gradually increased.

Under conditions in which the life course was compressed into a shorter and more homogeneous span, major transitions into adulthood, such as leaving school, entering the labor force, leaving home, marrying, and having children were not so clearly structured as they are today. Except for marriage and the formation of households, they did not even necessarily represent moves toward independent adulthood. The order in which they occurred varied significantly, rather than following a customary sequence. Children and youth shuttled back and forth from school to work, depending on the seasons, the availability of jobs, and the economic needs of the family. Departure from school did not mark a definite turning point, nor, at a time when child labor was an established practice, did entry into the labor force necessarily imply the onset of adulthood: leaving home, a phenomenon typically associated with the commencement of adulthood today, had no such significance in the preindustrial and early industrial period.[15] Some children left home in their early teens to become servants or apprentices, others continued to live on the family farm and to postpone marriage and the assumption of adult responsibilities until much later. In nineteenth-century urban working-class families, sons and daughters often continued to live at home until well into their twenties and to contribute their income to the common family budget. Irish immigrant families in Massachusetts, for example, customarily kept the youngest son at home through his late twenties. Among other immigrant industrial workers in New England, the last remaining daughter was expected to remain single and continue living in the family household to care for her parents so long as they lived. When unmarried children did leave home, they often spent transitional periods as boarders or lodgers with the families of strangers, rather than setting up their own households.[16]

Even marriage, which is usually regarded as an "adult" act in twentieth-century society, much less often marked the transition to autonomous adult life in the nineteenth. In urban communities, where immigration produced both scarcity in housing and unemployment, it was difficult to set up an independent household, and newlyweds often brought their spouses to live in their parents' households for a transitional period. Even when they lived separately, it was usually nearby, often in the same neighborhood. In the early years of marriage and especially after the birth of the first child, young couples were willing to sacrifice privacy for the luxury of parental assistance and support, a willingness that increased during periods of economic crisis and depression or during family crises brought on by unemployment, sickness, or death.[17]

The absence of dramatic transitions to adult life allowed a more intensive interaction among different age groups within the family and the community, thus providing a greater sense of continuity and interdependence among people at various stages in the life course. But, as greater differentiation in stages of life began to develop and as social and economic functions became more closely related to age, a greater segregation between age groups emerged. Child-labor laws and compulsory education to age 14 (or 16) tended to segregate the young, increasingly so from around the middle of the nineteenth century. Similarly, the gradual ousting of older people from the labor force toward the end of the nineteenth century and the decline in their parental functions in the later years of life tended to disengage them from their offspring and from active social functions. One of the most important changes affecting the elderly, therefore, was the increasing association of functions with age and formation of segregated, age-based peer groups. This segregation by age occurred first among the middle class, and was only later extended into the rest of society.

Work Life and Productivity

The growing specialization of work and the demand for industrial efficiency under the impact of advanced industrial development resulted in the imposition of age-related standards of usefulness and productivity in American society beginning around the turn of the century, but retirement at a specific age was an invention of the twentieth; it represents the most drastic development in the emergence of old age as a separate stage of life. The almost universal practice of arbitrary retirement has imposed a uniformity which is related to age rather than to the nature of the tasks involved. By contrast, during the second half of the nineteenth century and into the early twentieth, when there was no institutionalized retirement, how old one was often depended on the kind of job one held as well as on social class. Members of the working class experienced signs of advancing age earlier than white-collar workers or professionals. Industrial workers in physically demanding jobs were "old" in their middle years, while others continued to work until the end of their lives. As the system of production advanced technologically and intensified in pace, performance on the job became even more closely related to age.

Prior to the institutionalization of formal retirement, work in the nineteenth and in the early twentieth century extended over one's entire life. Although careers were frequently punctuated by long periods of unemployment, they were terminated only by severe illness or death. The nature of the employment varied, however, as men reached their forties: "The great majority of the men who do the world's work are comparatively young men," concluded a 1900-census analyst. Nearly half the total number of gainfully employed males in 1900 were between the ages of 16 and 34; the proportion increased to two thirds when the category was expended to 44.[18] Yet 90 per cent of males between the ages of 55 and 65 were still employed, a percentage not significantly different from that of employed men in their thirties and forties. By comparison, only 68.4 per cent of men older than 65 were still working. To understand these figures, it must be emphasized that the kind of job that was held was closely related to age: industrial work commanded the years between 20 and 40. Workers younger than 20 or older than 45 were primarily employed in agriculture or in unskilled service jobs. In addition, while work careers have generally been viewed as linear progressions, either upward, or downward, or continuing on a relatively even keel, in reality late-nineteenth-century work careers meandered about. Permanence on a job was rare among the majority of the working population; what we would regard today as a "disorderly" career was then often the norm.

Industrial workers experienced their first "retirement" or career change in their middle or late forties, as years of exhausting industrial labor started at an early age began to render them "useless." (Mule spinners—skilled textile operators—for example, walked around thirty-five miles a day on the job.) Consequently, in the last third of their lives, even highly skilled workers were forced into temporary jobs in unskilled occupations, after having spent the better part of their lives in efforts to move up the ladder. "I started out as a sweeper, I worked my way up to overseer, and here I am a sweeper again," said a 65-year-old former textile worker who found himself dependent on occasional jobs in the last years of his life. "The age deadline is creeping down on these men. I'd say that by forty-five, they are through," was a recurrent verdict of superintendents of major factories in "Middletown" in the nineteen-twenties.[19] One of the advocates of old-age compensation described this spreading phenomenon: "It is notorious that the insatiable factory wears out its workers with great rapidity. As it scraps its machinery, so it scraps human beings. . . . Middle age is old age, and the worn-out worker, if he has no children and if he has no savings, becomes an item in the aggregate of the unemployed."[20]

Contemplating the "industrial scrap heap" in one's middle years became one of the nightmares of industrial society. The Amoskeag Corporation, the world's largest textile manufacturer, began to lay off, rather than reassign, its slow workers beginning about 1920. When a middle-aged woman weaver protested her dismissal, after twenty years of work, before the union's grievance committee, the management upheld the overseer's rule: "In deciding who we should keep and who we should lay off, we follow the simple rule of the 'survival of the fittest.' " This same overseer, who had risen from bobbin boy to that much coveted position, himself ended up as a sweeper.[21]

The major transition in the work life was, therefore, not necessarily the complete termination of the individual's work career, but often the move to a temporary, semi-skilled or unskilled job while still in his forties or early fifties. As workers grew older, they tried to hold on to their jobs by trading their skills and expertise for physical assistance from young apprentices, who were often relatives as well. It was not uncommon for young workers in the shop to share the work load of "Old Spence" or "Old Joe" in order to keep him going. By the nineteen-twenties, however, the efficiency movement had won out in most industrial concerns, and tasks were assigned according to age.

The labor unions tried to solve the problems of the aging worker by establishing the principle of seniority, a principle that caused considerable conflict with corporations. Because management saw seniority as being inconsistent with the requirements of efficiency and individual initiative, the unions were unsuccessful, at least in the beginning. Thus, insecurity in old age, particularly among the working classes, came to culminate a career that had already included exhausting labor, unemployment, especially in middle age, and insecurity at every age through the constant threat of frequent industrial accidents and other illnesses. The 1900 census reported 28.3 per cent of all workers in manufacturing and mercantile occupations as having been unemployed for from three to six months of that year. A study of the Massachusetts Commission on Old Age Pensions in 1909 found that approximately 24 per cent of the population of that state who were 65 years or older were dependent on charity. Robert Hunter, an early social investigator of poverty in the United States, following E. S. Rowntree's studies of poverty in England, showed in 1904 that working-class families generally slipped in and out of poverty throughout life, but were most likely to fall below the margin at two particular stages: as young parents, burdened with numerous children too young to work, and in their middle or later years, after the children had left home and the parents remained without a steady income.[22]

The insecurities and vagaries of old age, intensified by unstable employment and recurrent poverty at earlier ages, made collective economic strategies imperative for the family unit. The functions of old people in the late nineteenth and early twentieth century can be better understood within the framework of the family economy. Work careers and family organization were clearly intertwined, and reciprocity among family members along the life course was essential for survival in old age. Exchanges across generations were critical for the survival of old people, particularly in the working class, as an intensifying industrial system was gradually ousting them from their jobs without providing public-welfare mechanisms for their support.[23]

Family Orientation and Functions

The family organization and ideology of nineteenth-century society and, in particular, the strong interaction of family and kin enabled older people to maintain active familial roles as they gradually withdrew from the labor force, even if they were not living with their adult children. Research has clearly established that families in the past tended to reside in nuclear units and that the co-residence of three generations was even then extremely rare. This rejection of the myth of the extended multi-generational family should not be misconstrued, however, as meaning that old people lived in isolation. Solitary residence was most uncommon throughout the nineteenth century in all age groups. Except for Western frontier communities and mining towns, only about 3 to 5 per cent of the population were found to be living alone.[24] Old people strove to remain in charge of their own households. Rather than moving in with their adult children or other kin, they took relatives or strangers into their own homes. In 1850, only about one in ten persons over the age of 65 was not the head of a household or the spouse of a head. By 1880, the proportion had risen to about one in eight. The trend accelerated in the United States into the twentieth century: in 1953, the ratio was about one in six, and, in the late nineteen-sixties, it approached one in four,[25] reflecting the present large percentage of old people who live alone or share accommodations with non-relatives.

The supposed isolation of the nuclear family in urban, industrial society has frequently been cited as the explanation for the present plight of the elderly. Talcott Parsons has provided us with the classic formulation of this view: "In the first phase, the most important single distinctive feature of our family structure is the isolation of the individual conjugal family. . . ." Mathilda Riley and her associates have pointed out that the trend has not been so much toward the isolation of the nuclear family as toward a subdivision into two nuclear families: the young couple with their dependent children and the middle-aged or aged parents. Parsons's generalization has been further revised by a number of sociologists who have documented the existence of elaborate patterns of assistance and social interaction among members of the nuclear family and other kin in contemporary society.[26]

The relationships of mutual support and exchange of services that old people had earlier entered into with their kin carried greater significance before the introduction of social security and other forms of public old-age assistance. Except in cases of infirmity or extreme poverty, they engaged in reciprocal support relationships with their kin which simultaneously allowed them to maintain their autonomy. Close contact and mutual exchanges among parents, their adult children, and other kin persisted throughout the nineteenth century and survived to a large degree in the lives of the working-class families into the twentieth. In the later years of life, parents expected their grown children to support them in exchange for a variety of services which they themselves had rendered earlier in life. Such exchanges among parents, their children, and other relatives were based on calculated needs and expectations, particularly insofar as parents relied on future support from their sons and daughters as a source of social insurance. Societal values and norms governing children's obligations for parental aid provided an ideological reinforcement for these reciprocal relationships.[27]

Migration did not contribute to the isolation of old people to the extent that was previously assumed: the argument that geographic mobility during the nineteenth century tended to separate grown children from their parents and from available kin is gradually being disproved. When people moved, they tended to migrate into areas where other relatives had already settled, and after sons and daughters had established themselves, they often sent for their parents.[28] Even if migration did separate parents from their children, or brothers from sisters, surrogate familial arrangements were developed by taking strangers into the household. About one third of the men and women in their twenties and thirties in nineteenth-century American urban communities boarded with other families, suggesting the pervasiveness of these surrogate relationships. For young men and women in a transitional stage between their departure from their parents' homes and the establishment of their own families, boarding offered familial settings without parental pressures. For older people, particularly for widows, it provided the extra income needed to maintain their own residence and it also helped to stave off loneliness after the children had left home. These arrangements helped balance and distribute resources, and they often fulfilled the function of what Irene Taeuber calls "the social equalization of the family."[29]

The separation of the work place from the home wrought by the industrial revolution was by no means complete by the end of the nineteenth century. Among the urban working classes as well as the rural populations, work and family roles continued to be mutually reinforcing. For these groups, work entailed a contribution to the collective effort of the family unit. This meant that family members functioned as interchangeable components of a larger work unit. For example, the work of wives in the textile industry helped stabilize the family's income while husbands risked taking higher paying, but less permanent, jobs. During slack periods, the men who were laid off took care of the house while their wives continued to work: housework and child care were not regarded as demeaning; they were valued as important contributions to the family's resources. During periods of economic constraint, families thus balanced their resources through the allocation of tasks and responsibilities among their members. In this setting, old people could also continue to perform valuable services. After they were too old to work, they took care of the children of working mothers, helped with the housekeeping, and, if necessary, shared housing space with younger family members in exchange for economic support.[30]

This integration of work with family life in the nineteenth century should not be construed as an ideal situation from a lost past. The system often placed considerable constraint on individual careers and generated tension and conflict between aging parents and their children. Nevertheless, in the absence of institutional buttresses, instrumental relationships were a pervasive and realistic response to the pressures that economic exigencies imposed on individuals and families. They prevented familial fragmentation and segregation by providing a basis for interaction among individuals in different age groups and at different stages in life by exchanging services, even as they were pursuing individual careers. Such interdependence also exposed children and youth to greater responsibility toward older people and to a fuller view of life and a broader range of experience than is common among them today.

The major changes that have led to the isolation of older people in society today were rooted not so much in changes in family structure or residential arrangements, as has generally been argued, as in the transformation and redefinition of family functions. Changes in functions and values—especially the erosion of the instrumental view of family relationships—and the resulting shift to sentimentality and intimacy as the major cohesive forces in the family have led to the weakening of the role and function of extended-family members. Affective relationships have gradually replaced instrumental relationships in middle-class families in particular.

This shift first occurred in the middle class, around the mid-nineteenth century, but it soon affected the working class and its various ethnic groups, as growing conformity introduced middle-class values into working-class lives. Since then, the emphasis on domesticity and child rearing as the major preoccupations of the middle-class family—and especially on the role of women as custodians of domestic intimacy—has tended to insulate middle-class urban families from the influence and participation of aging parents and other relatives.[31] From the eighteen-thirties on, middle-class urban families became avid consumers of popular child-rearing and advice-to-parents literature, not because older relatives were not present to offer such advice, but because guidance based on personal experience and tradition was gradually rejected in favor of "packaged" information. This transition added to the loss of power and influence of the old people in the family.

The ideology of domesticity that emerged during the first half of the nineteenth century also enshrined privacy as a major value in family life. The home was glorified as a retreat from the world and, at the same time, as a specialized child-nurturing center. Philippe Ariès succinctly summarized these changes for Western European society: "The modern family . . . cuts itself off from the world and opposes to society the isolated groups of parents and children. All the energy of the group is expended in helping the children to rise in the world, individually and without any collective ambition: The children rather than the family."[32]

Through a process of differentiation, the traditional family surrendered many of the functions previously concentrated within it to other social institutions. The retreat and growing privatism of the modern middle-class family drew sharper boundaries between family and community and intensified the segregation of different age groups within the family, leading to the elimination of the older people from viable family roles. The transfer of social-welfare functions, once concentrated in the family, to institutions in the larger society further contributed to the segregation of older people. The care of the dependent, the sick, the delinquent, and the aging, which had been considered part of the family's obligation in the preindustrial period, was gradually transferred to specialized institutions such as asylums and reformatories. The family ceased to be the only available source of support for its dependent members, and the community ceased to rely on the family as the major agency of welfare and social control.[33] In the nineteenth century, some childless old people, especially widows, were already expecting to end up in institutions in their later life. Mrs. Kelleham, for example, a widow in Westcote, New York, in the eighteen-fifties, had had ten children, several of whom had died in childhood, and "in those who remain the poor woman seems to take little comfort." The woman for whom she worked as a domestic servant reported in her diary: "She says, the mother's joy has never measured with the mother's care. She will not be a burden to her children. She will work while she can work, and when she can no longer she will go to the old ladies' asylum near New York."[34]

But these early institutions and asylums—although they were to become more specialized in the second half of the nineteenth century—segregated people because of poverty, not because of age. "Poor farms," houses of refuge, and mental hospitals were not differentiated by the age of their inmates. The old were simply treated as a variety of dependent poor. The first to be institutionalized by age (during the second half of the nineteenth century) were children, a reflection of the recognition of childhood as a life stage, but special institutions for the elderly based on age rather than on destitution did not appear until later.[35] They began toward the end of the nineteenth century, with the segregation of the infirm, the destitute, the mentally ill, and the retarded from the "respectable" old who needed help only because of their age. At that time, the intent was not so much to segregate age groups as to separate "deserving" dependents from paupers, and it involved the institutionalization only of those unable to take care of themselves and to obtain assistance from their relatives. Many homes for the aged in the second half of the nineteenth century were depicted by reformers in terms similar to the description of the "death camps" which social investigators find in nursing homes today. One inspector of a state institution in Pennsylvania reported in 1920:

> There was no genuine homelike spirit. Most of the inmates looked sullen and wore depressed and downcast mien. Practically all were eager to get out of the place. . . . This feeling of depression is augmented by the fact that in no homes is an attempt made to segregate the old people—who have been compelled to go to the almshouse through no fault of their own—from the feeble-minded, and in some cases even the partially insane. In many places they are compelled to eat at the same table and sleep in the same dormitories with the latter groups.[36]

This practice of institutionalizing the old people of the lower classes was subsequently extended to the "warehousing" of old people from the middle and upper classes as well. By the end of the nineteenth century, there were some institutions for middle- and upper-class people that were more respectable and inhabitable replicas of the asylums for the aged poor. The stigma attached to institutionalization persisted, however, as a carry-over from the earlier institutions even with respect to these middle-class "retirement homes."[37]

The difficulties for the aged in modern American society have been compounded by contradictions inherent in the welfare system. The process of differentiation by which institutions in society assumed functions of social welfare and old-age support previously held by the family has never been fully rationalized in the United States.

Even in Great Britain, where the public-welfare system is broader, old people have generally tended to rely on familial support along with their public assistance. In the United States, the level of public support for the aged under the social-security system has been so minimal that it only provides basic subsistence. Old people have to fall back on their own resources or to rely on their families for assistance, for services, and particularly for sociability. At the same time, however, the state has not provided the kind of support that would enable families to carry out these obligations. The American public-welfare system has been designed to support individuals rather than families. As was the case with the nineteenth-century poor laws, it tends to disrupt families in need of assistance rather than to support the family as a unit.[38] Nor has the welfare system provided substitutes for the sociability and social integration that kinship ties offered to old people in the past.

In trying to understand the problems of old age in modern American society, it is important to remember that, while the poor are most vulnerable, some of these problems are no less persistent among the middle class. The growing privatism of the modern middle-class family has tended to diminish the kin network as a viable framework for economic and social interaction. Geographic segregation has been compounded by suburbanization, which has drawn young and middle-aged couples into the suburbs and led the elderly into retirement communities or left them behind in the central city. These changes have been accompanied by the development of what Erving Goffman has called the "spoiled identity" or what others have referred to as the "mystique of the aged." The characterization of the aged as "useless," "inefficient," "unattractive," "temperamental," and "senile" accompanied the gradual ousting of people from the labor force at age 65 and barred them from a variety of occupations even earlier.[39] Such negative stereotypes had already begun to appear in popular literature in the United States during the later part of the nineteenth century. Their emergence should not be misconstrued as causing an immediate decline in the status of older people, but it did reflect the beginnings of an increasing tendency to denigrate the aged in society.

Some people have attributed the emergence of a negative image of old age to a "cult of youth" in American society, but while there is undeniably a connection, one cannot be construed as an explanation of the other. The glorification of youth and the denigration of old age are both aspects of far more complicated processes. They are results of the growing segregation of different stages of life—and of their corresponding age groups—in modern American society. The socioeconomic changes of the past century have gradually led to a segregation of work from other aspects of life and to a shift from the predominance of familial values to an emphasis on individualism and privacy. These changes have affected each stage of life: they have resulted in the segmentation of the life course into more formal stages, in more uniform and rigid transitions from one stage to the next, and in the separation of the various age groups from one another. The problems of older people in American society are in some respects unique to this age group, but in others they reflect in its most acute form problems experienced by other age groups and other stages of life as well. They illustrate the personal and social discontinuities that Erik Erikson sees as being major problems in modern American society:

> As we come to the last stage [old age], we become aware of the fact that our civilization really does not harbor a concept of the whole of life. . . . Any span of the cycle lived without vigorous meaning, at the beginning, in the middle, or at the end,

endangers the sense of life and the meaning of death in all those whose life stages are intertwined.[40]

REFERENCES

Note: An earlier version of this paper was presented at the Conference on Human Values and Aging: New Challenges in the Research to Humanities, which was funded by the National Endowment for the Humanities. I am grateful to Professor David Van Tassel, Director of the Conference for permission to publish. I am also indebted to John Modell, John Demos, and Randolph Langenbach for their valuable comments on earlier versions of this essay and to Howard Litwak for valuable editorial assistance. Support from the Rockefeller Foundation for the History of the Family Project under which this paper was written is gratefully acknowledged.

[1]G. Stanley Hall, *Senescence: The Last Half of Life* (New York, 1922), p. 366.

[2]George Beard, *Legal Responsibility in Old Age, Based on Researches into the Relationship of Age to Work* (New York, 1874).

[3]"Apology from Age to Youth," *Living Age*, CXCIII (January 14, 1893), p. 170. For a discussion of the popular and medical literature on aging in the late nineteenth century, see W. Andrew Achenbaum, "The Obsolescence of Old Age in America, 1865-1914," *Journal of Social History*, Winter, 1974, pp. 47–62.

[4]I. L. Nascher, *Geriatrics* (Philadelphia, 1914).

[5]Hall, *Senescence*. See also Abraham Epstein, *Facing Old Age: A Study of Old Age Dependency in the United States and Old Age Pensions* (New York, 1922); Paul H. Douglas, *Social Security in the United States* (New York, 1936); Pennsylvania Commission on Old Age Pensions, *Report* (Philadelphia, 1919); Wisconsin Industrial Commission, *Report on Old Age Relief* (Madison, 1915).

[6]Clark Tibbitts, "Origin, Scope and Fields of Social Gerontology," *Handbook of Social Gerontology*, ed. Clark Tibbetts (Chicago, 1960); Michel A. J. Philbert, "The Emergence of Social Gerontology," *Journal of Social Issues*, XXI (October, 1965), pp. 4-13. On theoretical developments in gerontology, see Robert Kastenbaum, "Theories of Human Aging: The Search for a Conceptual Framework," *Journal of Social Issues*, XXI (October, 1955), pp. 13-37; Orville Brim, Jr., and Ronald P. Abeles, "Work and Personality in the Middle Years,". *Items*, XXIX: 3 (September, 1975). An exception to this is Mathilda White Riley and Anne Foner, *Aging and Society*, Vol. I: *An Inventory of Research Findings* (New York, 1968), which integrates the various aspects of aging.

[7]The historical discovery of stages of the life cycle was first conceptualized by Philippe Ariès in *Centuries of Childhood: A Social History of Family Life*, trans. Robert Baldick (New York, 1962). John Demos has explored this question in *A Little Commonwealth: Family Life in Colonial Plymouth* (New York, 1971). See also Kenneth Keniston, "Youth as a New Stage of Life," *Journal of Interdisciplinary History*, 2 (Fall, 1971), pp. 329-45; Tamara K. Hareven, "The Discovery of Childhood in American History," paper presented at the meeting of the Organization of American Historians, April, 1969; Robert H. Bremner, John Barnard, Tamara K. Hareven, and Robert Mennell, eds., *Children and Youth in America*, Vols. I-III (Cambridge, Mass., 1970-74), particularly Vol. I; John and Virginia Demos, "Adolescence in Historical Perspective," *Journal of Marriage and the Family*, September, 1969; Joseph Kett, "Growing Up in Rural New England," in Tamara K. Hareven, ed., *Anonymous Americans* (Englewood Cliffs, New Jersey, 1971).

[8]On the middle years, see Bernice L. Neugarten and Nancy Daton, "Sociological Perspectives on the Life Cycle," in Paul B. Baltes and K. Warner Schale, eds., *Life Span Developmental Psychology: Personality and Socialization* (New York, 1973).

[9]The term "life course" is used here, rather than "life cycle," because I shall consider not only the stages of the individual life cycle such as those formulated by Erik Erikson and his followers, but the synchronizations of individual development with the collective experience of the family as it moves through its life course. The "life course" is more encompassing than the individual development and the collective organization of the family as individuals move through life.

[10]The term "cohort," rather than "generation," will be used throughout this paper because it refers to a specific age group with a common experience; "generation " is less precise and can also have connotations of kinship. See Riley and Foner, *Aging and Society*, I, pp. 8-10.

[11]Reuben Hill, *Family Development in Three Generations* (Cambridge, Mass., 1970), p. 322. The most important formulation of the life course as it changes over time is in Glen Elder, Jr., "Historical Changes and the Life Course," forthcoming in the *Journal of Family History*.

[12]See Kett, "Growing up in Rural New England," and John Modell, Frank Furstenberg, and Theodore Hershberg, "Social Change and Transitions to Adulthood in Historical Perspective," *Journal of Family History*, I:1 (September, 1976).

[13]Philip Greven, Jr., *Four Generations of Population, Land and Family in Colonial Andover, Mass.* (Ithaca, 1970); Daniel Scott Smith, "Parental Power and Marriage Patterns: An Analysis of Historical Trends in Hingham, Massachusetts," *Journal of Marriage and the Family*, 35 (August, 1973), pp. 419-29.

[14]Peter Uhlenberg, "Cohort Variations in Family Life Cycle Experiences of U.S. Females," *Journal of Marriage and the Family*, 36 (1974), pp. 284-92, and "Changing Configurations of the Life Course," in

Tamara K. Hareven, ed., *The Family Cycle and the Life Course in Historical Perspective* (forthcoming). See also Paul Glick, "The Family Cycle," *American Sociological Review*, XII (April, 1947), pp. 164-74; Alice Rossi, "Family Development in a Changing World," *American Journal of Psychiatry*, March, 1972, pp. 1057-66.

[15]Modell, Furstenberg, and Hershberg, "Social Change and Transitions to Adulthood in Historical Perspective."

[16]Tamara K. Hareven, "Family Time and Industrial Time: The Interaction between Family and Work in a Planned Industrial Town," *Journal of Urban History*, I (Spring, 1975); John Modell and Tamara K. Hareven, "Urbanization and the Malleable Household: An Examination of Boarding and Lodging in American Families," *Journal of Marriage and the Family*, XXXV (August, 1973), pp. 467-78.

[17]Howard P. Chudacoff, "Newly Weds and Familial Extension: First Stages of the Family Cycle in Providence, R.I., 1864-1880," forthcoming in Tamara K. Hareven and Maris Vinovskis, eds., *Demographic Processes and Family Organization in Nineteenth-Century American Society*.

[18]U.S. Bureau of the Census, *Twelfth Census of the United States, Occupations* (Washington, D.C.), pp. cxix-cxx.

[19]Robert and Helen Lynd, *Middletown* (New York, 1929), p. 34.

[20]Edward T. Devine, *Misery and Its Causes* (New York, 1907), p. 125.

[21]Amoskeag Co., Grievance Files.

[22]Robert Hunter, *Poverty* (New York, 1904).

[23]Tamara K. Hareven, "Family Time and Industrial Time." For an analysis of economic strategies of the family, see John Modell, "The Fruits of Their Toil," forthcoming in Hareven and Vinovskis, eds., *Demographic Process and Family Organization*.

[24]A cumulative body of historical research on the family has documented the continuity of nuclear households from preindustrial to industrial times in Europe and America. See Peter Laslett and Richard Wall, eds., *Household and Family in Past Time* (Cambridge, England, 1971) and Tamara K. Hareven, "The Family as Process: The Historical Study of the Family Cycle," *Journal of Social History*, Spring, 1974.

[25]Talcott Parsons, "Changing Family Relationships of Older People in the United States During the Last Fifty Years," in Clark Tibbitts and Wilma Donahue, *Social and Psychological Aspects of Aging* (New York, 1962).

[26]Riley and Foner, *Aging and Society*, pp. 167-68. Talcott Parsons, "Age and Sex in the Social Structure," *American Sociological Review*, VII (1942), pp. 604-16. For a sociological critique, see Marvin Sussman, "The Isolated Nuclear Family: Fact or Fiction," *Social Problems*, VI (1959), pp. 333-47.

[27]For a formulation of instrumentalism as an important theory of kin relations, see Michael Anderson, *Family Structure in Nineteenth-Century Lancashire* (Cambridge, England, 1971).

[28]Robert E. Bieder, "Kinship as a Factor in Migration," *Journal of Marriage and the Family*, XXXV (August, 1973), pp. 429-39.

[29]Irene Taeuber, "Change and Transition in Family Structure," in *The Family in Transition, Proceedings of the Fogarty International Center* (Washington, D.C., 1969); Modell and Hareven, "Urbanization and the Malleable Household."

[30]Tamara K. Hareven, "Family Time and Industrial Time"; Modell, "The Fruits of Their Toil."

[31]Demos, *A Little Commonwealth*; Greven, *Four Generations*.

[32]Ariès, *Centuries of Childhood*, p. 404.

[33]Robert H. Bremner, *From the Depths: The Discovery of Poverty in the United States* (New York, 1956); David Rothman, *The Discovery of the Asylum* (Boston, 1971).

[34]Diary, 1850, Cornell University Archives.

[35]Bremner, *From the Depths*.

[36]Pennsylvania Commission on Old Age Pensions, *Report* (Philadelphia, 1919).

[37]James Leiby, *Charities and Corrections in New Jersey* (New Brunswick, N.J., 1967); Epstein, *Facing Old Age*; Walter K. Vivrett, "Housing and Community Settings for Older People," in Tibbitts, ed., *Handbook of Social Gerontology*.

[38]On this point, see Frances Fox Piven and Richard Cloward, *Regulating the Poor* (New York, 1971) and Richard Elman, *The Poorhouse State* (New York, 1966).

[39]Rosalie Rosenfelt, "The Elderly Mystique," *Journal of Social Issues*, XXI (1965), pp. 37-43.

[40]Erik Erikson, *Insight and Responsibility* (New York, 1964), pp. 132-33.

ROBERT COLES

Work and Self-Respect

I begin with a prelude to acquaint the reader with the nature of my own work, which, in turn, enables this essay on the way "work" affects the lives of others, and the self-regard those others struggle to get for themselves. I spend every weekday afternoon going to certain homes, talking with grown-up men and women and with their children. I have described the work at length in chapters on "method" in the three volumes of Children of Crisis *so far published. Essentially, I get to know families of various social, cultural, economic, racial, and regional backgrounds, and I try, through weekly or twice weekly visits, to learn from them about how they think and feel—what they believe in, hope for, fear, hate, and envy in others. The conversations are sometimes tape-recorded, sometimes not. I spend years with a limited number of people, and make no claims to statistical significance for my "findings"—that is, the portraits I try to write of particular human beings. All I have is eyes, ears, the clinical training of a child psychiatrist, and, one hopes, whatever good judgment and skill as a writer fate has happened to provide. When I bring the reader quotations from people, those quotations have, of course, been edited, and often, for the purpose of narration, directness, emphasis, pulled together from remarks made over time.*

I am a "fieldworker," I suppose, "out there," one hopes and prays, not to "treat" people, or make caricatures of them, but to convey something of their often exceedingly complex lives. I am sure that in so doing I miss things. I am sure that I fail to ask valuable questions out of various subjective blind-spots or personal inadequacies; and conversely, and for the same reasons, tend to stress certain other matters. I am sure, too, that I risk or succumb to a number of hazards: over-identification with the people I come to know as friends as well as "informants"; a romantic unwillingness to dwell on warts and worse—outright crudities, banalities, meanness; a failure to make personal or ethical judgments about the words I hear, the people I hear speaking those words—and, instead, an almost desperate effort to "appreciate" and "understand" anyone and everyone; and not least, a combative, arrogant anti-intellectualism, in which the observer turns instead on the university, on intellectuals, rather than on those he or she works with everyday. In that last regard, one plaintively, self-protectively summons a "tradition," mentions the writing of George Orwell, James Agee, Simone Weil, Georges Bernanos, and others who have, it can be said, stood between two worlds, and in so doing, have taken chances, hoping thereby to learn a little, but failing occasionally to learn as much as might have been possible, and sometimes, failing utterly to do justice to the lives of people met, visited, and later evoked in articles and books.

LIVES, ANYWAY, RESIST AS WELL AS YIELD to the social or psychological observer's interest in approximation, never mind definition. No one is all that typical or

217

representative; the closer the outsider's look, the more inconsistencies or outright contradictions come out in the wash of visits and more visits. A few conversations with a factory worker and he seems like Mr. Average White American Worker. With a few more conversations, the man with the questions, and in the back of his mind (not too far there, either) the various articles or books that await writing, is ready to say good-bye, forget what he's been hearing lately. If a lingering moral impulse (not to mention professional need) questions such an inclination, there is always the justification that comes with the knowledge that appearances deceive, that the whole point of doing psychologically sophisticated "interviews" over an extended stretch of time is to find out who really is what he or she seems to be, and who is one person to all appearances, but quite another when a close look is taken.

Seventy-five years after *The Interpretation of Dreams* was published it is no secret that every person's various surfaces cover up any number of psychological idiosyncrasies (to say the least). It is true, the polls and various "surveys" tell us that there are generalizations that can be made by social scientists and substantiated rather quickly, or decisively refuted, by asking people to answer a series of questions. And sometimes the most outrageously blunt or naive or simple-minded or rude or vague question can strike any number of people as not one of those—but merely something to be answered, an occasion for reflection and a comment or two. Nevertheless, subjects like "work" (what does one *think* of it, what is one's *attitude* toward it, what kind would one do *ideally*, if one had the choice?) or like "adulthood" (how would you characterize it, define it, describe it, talk about it with your wife, or husband, or children?) ought with good reason to strike terror in the minds, if not the hearts, of those of us who make a living, do *our* work, by appealing to other people for words and more words. Presumably we make sense of those words, use them to help substantiate our various theories, along with an occasional ideological disposition, and thereby give others and ourselves the impression of seriousness, reliability, thoughtfulness, good judgment. Ours is the work, we believe, of dedicated and sensible individuals, of *adults*, rather than the product of an erratic or exploitative or hysterical or fatuous mentality—the kind that belongs to a grown-up child, or an immature youth, psychologically speaking, who only pretends to live up to his or her accumulation of years.

But many factory workers, blue-collar workers, so-called working-class men and women are not likely to agree with that judgment of us. They distrust intellectuals, and they have no faith in the value of endless self-scrutiny; rather, an aversion to it. And then there is the matter of time and money. Who, they wonder, has the luxury of hours to spend talking about himself or herself, and his or her ideas—and for pay? The result, during an "interview" not so cleverly as one thinks disguised as a casual conversation, is steadfast silence; and when an assault, subtle or not so subtle, is made on that silence, the result is perplexity, annoyance, frustration, contempt, or, often, a mixture of all of them. On the other hand, in some instances—that is, with a particular person—there may be another outcome; a question acts as the cause of an explosion and water pours over a suddenly weakened dam. And the analogy is not inappropriate, and sometimes exactly right, because afterwards the same person who has talked and talked feels violated, betrayed, upset by the outpouring of words, no matter what their message, and upset, too, with what has been said, or more precisely, told. It is at such moments, of course, that the visitor with his or her further questions decides to turn elsewhere for "information"; and there is no great literature, certainly, that tells us, in an honest-to-God, soul-searching way, what happens then—between the person interviewed and the person asking questions and, later, between the man or woman who is "doing research" and himself or herself as a writer. Do troublesome ambiguities get set aside? Do the objections, or worse, expressed by people who get called, of all things, "subjects" become soft-pedaled, or silently explained away as necessary "hazards" of "research," and of no real consequence? (It is astonishing, by the way, how much has been written about "transference," how little about "counter-transference," though one would think there is a certain existential parity between the two.)

All this is not perhaps an overly long prelude to a discussion of the "meaning" of work in the lives of grown-up American men and women who are not by any means embarrassed (but only sometimes proud) to give themselves titles like "a working man," or "a plain housewife" (meaning "a very hard-working woman, let me tell you"), or "an ordinary person" (meaning "just someone who works for a living, I guess that's all"). The last qualification, "that's all," is not meant to denigrate the amount or worth of the labor, but to indicate the speaker's lack of interest in self-enhancing heroics, or in talking about, as the currently faddish expression goes, "belonging to a community," namely one that contains millions of fellow working men and women. Nor is any account, however tentative, of what words like "adult" or "adulthood" mean to those same Americans best begun without a similar prefatory remark—that is, some qualification that expresses, really, an observer's quite difficult experiences with men and women who haven't, at times, known what to say (or think, or, more specifically, think of the stranger in their midst) when faced with his latest and odd line of questioning. The demurrers have been, for the most part, immediate and strong—as if, for example, a man who works in a General Electric plant in Lynn, Massachusetts, felt himself privy to the knowledge Wittgenstein and Heidegger both came upon, slowly and painfully, whereupon they used words more sparingly, if at all. Here is that man distinctly echoing those two philosophers: "I don't know about growing up—the time you're supposed to be an adult, and not a child any more. I tell my kids they'd better grow up when I think they're acting like fools, or behaving spoiled. They get the message. If they don't, I remind them again! But I'd be crazy if I tried to sit down and explain to them what's 'grown up' and what isn't—in the way you act. Some things—you either know them or you don't. If you don't, let me tell you, you're in real bad trouble. Like I say to my wife: when the kids get to a certain age, no lectures will make any difference. It's not what you say, a lot of times, anyway; it's what you mean in your heart. It's what your life is about—or isn't about. I tell my kids to be good to each other, and I think they get the message. But if someone asked me to sit down and explain why they should, and what I mean—well, I'd have to leave and get a beer and go cut the grass!"

No one had confronted him arbitrarily with questions about the "meaning of adulthood"; he and his wife had slipped quite naturally into a discussion of their children, and, specifically, their fourteen-year-old boy, who was, as they described it, "really growing up," an expression which had for them psychological and moral as well as physical implications. The expression is also comparative, depending for its meaning upon a contrast. But as that "meaning" becomes a subject for discussion, if not interpretation, the speaker begs off; he moves initially into an abstract vein, talks of an "adult" as against a "child," tries to spell out a particular psychological and philosophical position, then begins to feel and give expression to a certain futility, and with it a sense of what some might call "existential resignation": either one knows, and so there is no point in saying anything more, or one doesn't, in which case there is no point even in using words, never mind trying self-consciously and earnestly to spell things out precisely. Anyway, he is sure that an effort to define "adulthood" ought not to stand or fall on what he and his wife or others like them say or think. He has often made that point: "Everyone to his own work! I don't know how to answer the questions I read in the paper—the Gallup poll questions. I'm glad Mr. Gallup and his people don't come around here! I'd probably say yes or no a lot, but I'd be holding back a lot; or, I'd say to myself that I'm not telling all I have to say on the subject! Once I had a long talk with my brother; he's the one in our family who went to college, and he became a priest. I asked him if there's any way he can find out, during confession, if he's hearing the whole story. He said he doesn't want to. He said it's enough to hear what he does hear! He said people are all mixed up; they have a lot of different ideas cross their minds, and he tells them he doesn't want to hear everything. Sometimes there'll be someone, and she'll want to go on and on in confession."

He has without any ostentatiousness made a statement: "someone" becomes "she'll," and it is women who talk more about their thoughts or feelings than men do. Not that he will at that time, and in the context of that conversation, elaborate any further. Nor would anyone be wise to start pointing out to him his verbal "slip" or his "assumptions." He knows about the latter, actually; at another moment, upset enough to "give a speech," as he put it, some of those assumptions come forth quite candidly, in a rather forceful and, arguably, well organized and coherent fashion: "My wife used to have more time for thinking; she was home all day. She's religious, and when she was upset—one of the kids sick, or her mother and father still fighting, old as they are—she would go to church and talk with the priest. Now she has a job. She comes home as tired as I am. Work takes it out of you; no energy left for a lot of talk. There's barely enough energy to finish the day: supper, television, and to bed. Half the time we're both dozing in front of the set.

—>"I wouldn't mind being rich. I wouldn't mind having a lot of days off. But it would take me a year or two of decompression; you can't get used to the pace I'm used to, and then suddenly know what to do with yourself when you're not working. I never really stop working; even on weekends, even on holidays and vacations, I have work to do here around the house. I heard on television someone say that everyone should have a hobby, and there's a big future for the three-day week. My wife and I thought at first we'd like that a lot: time to unwind. But we don't have a weekend yacht to go sailing on! We stay here and there's one thing that needs fixing, and another. Who has the money to pay for someone else to come and do it? I've become a jack-of-all-trades. Then, there are the kids. I try to take them where they have to go; there's baseball and football and basketball—that's the nearest I come to relaxing, at those games. But you want your own kid to do better than someone else's, so you're not just sitting there having a coke and cracking open the peanuts! There are days that I say to my wife I wish *I* was the priest in the family. I'd never give her up, though, or our boys and girls. Never! I'm not made to be a priest! I'd go nuts!"

He goes on to spell out, a bit shyly but unmistakably, why: he couldn't take celibacy. But there are other reasons, too. His brother does "a lot of thinking," asks "a lot of questions," and that is not for everyone—certainly not, he adds, for "people who work all day, every day, including Sunday." For him Sunday's supposed "rest" is a fiction, the product of television stories, he pointedly mentions. He is sick and tired of them, even as he watches them in the evening. For him the Nielsen ratings are as suspect as political polls. In any event, if he were ever called, unlikely he knows, he would not be home. But his mind would not be a blank: "All day I stand there at work, and I talk to myself. I say, an hour on the assembly line for the groceries, and an hour for the mortgage, and then another hour for the groceries and another hour for the mortgage. Every once in a while, I add something else—clothes for the kids. None for me, though; I haven't bought myself a piece of clothing in seven years, since my kid sister got married, and I don't care if I even buy myself a shirt. A suit—forget it! Who has the money for a suit? I don't see why my kids like clothes so much. But we try to give them what we can. That's why my wife is working. That's why I do odd jobs on Saturday. When you grow up and take on responsibilities, that's your life. What else is there?"

He hastens immediately to insist that he is not complaining. Nor is he *only* coming up with one of those "denials" or "reaction-formations" some of us have come to notice rather often, especially when a disclaimer becomes a little too strongly spoken. Unquestionably he does upon occasion feel moody, bitter, resentful—and envious. Others may have a rather easy time, whereas for him there is an apparently endless succession of long, hard, exhausting days. His own children, for that matter, have a more interesting life than he has, or had when he was their age; and they may well, he hopes, continue to live more comfortably, because they may get better jobs, "live better" he puts it. But in addition to self-pity and a touch of regret, there is pride and a sense of satisfaction. He considers himself a hard-working man, and is looked up to as such by his wife and children. He is ingenious at saving money by learning how to fix things himself, and is applauded by his family and their neighbors as someone who can learn to do anything around the house—a plumber, steamfitter, electrician, carpenter, painter, paperhanger, or, in sum, "an all-around handy man." And he is admired for his apparently endless reservoir of energy. No one has ever seen him tired; everyone says that he is tireless. His youngest daughter for a long while called him Superman, and he never really showed any annoyance or incredulity at the accolade. In fact, he took to telling his wife that there are moments, or indeed days, when he has to agree: he has found it within himself to do the apparently impossible, or at the very least, the enormously demanding.

At night he dreams of work. The dreams are not pleasant, not unpleasant. He has his own footnote for *The Interpretation of Dreams*: "When you stand there, all day, doing your job, you can close your eyes or work blindfolded. That's not actually true; I tried to do it once, and got everything wrong. But it seems like you've become a part of the machinery, and at night your mind is still going strong. Why should it stop? Why shouldn't it keep the old motor going? I come to work early in the morning and I'm all ready; my mind is humming from the night before. When I wake up I tell my wife I wish I got paid for all I've done at night! She laughs; she says she'll wake up in a cold sweat, because she's been dreaming that she was supposed to be doing something, and she'd forgot to do it, or she didn't have the time."

So it goes—the intersection, during the long night, of what some would refer to as a "technological culture" and the "psychodynamics of human personality." Neither the man nor his wife has any use for such talk; they have heard a glimmer of it at home from their oldest daughter, who is taking a course on "child development." Some parents who want "the best" for their children shudder at what they hear when "the best" makes its appearance! But the demands of "time," of "life," work against confrontations; this is not a home where people sit about, hour after hour, "talking things out." This is not a home where "goals" are discussed, "commitments" regarded carefully and analytically. Goals are there; they are part of a father's constant dedication, a mother's unceasing labor. Commitments are also there—worked into the grain of lives that are lived, rather than talked about, examined, fitted into theories. And always, there is sacrifice—though not mentioned as such. That is to say, a mother and a father assume, rather than say to themselves or to each other, that to be their age, and married, and the parents of children, and of their circumstances or station in life, means to work long, hard, and unstintingly, in the hope that one's children will have a little easier time.

It is put like that—tentatively, guardedly, with a carefully weighed amount of optimism; and when it is put that way, a touch of philosophy and a limited measure of psychological introspection also are permitted: "We do the best we can. What more can you do? I'm sure my kids will have a better time than I've had; they'll get more education, and get better jobs. At least, I hope they will. You can't tell these days, the way it's going in this country. If my kids turn out okay, then I'll be a success. That's the only thing that counts—how your kids are when they're grown up. Our neighbors tell us the kids aren't spoiled. I could dance when I hear them say that! But the kids have their own ideas. I don't want them to obey me, as if I'm a sergeant in the Marines, and their mother is some witch. The other day my youngest boy asked me what I'd like to be, if I had a wish. I said no one but myself! I have a good wife, and good children. What more can a man ask for? I have a job, and I manage to keep my head above water. If I can do that until my last kid is out of high school and has a job, then I'll be ready to go, whenever He wants me up there. I'll have done my work, all of it. I'd be able to die with some self-respect. I only hope they keep me busy where I go next. I wouldn't mind going to Hell, if I could only keep busy."

He sounds more driven, more anxiously on the go, than he is. He doesn't have to push himself. He is supposed to be at work about ten minutes before eight, and that means leaving the house, allowing for the unpredictability of traffic, about seven in the morning. He is up a little before six and, as he puts it, "glad to be up then." His wife is up a half-hour earlier, preparing for him, for their children. She is a neat, orderly woman—who knows, however, when to relax and enjoy a certain anarchy: "I try to keep everything running smooth. I miss having a baby, but there has to be a last child! I used to keep the house spotless; then I'd watch the kids mess things up; then I'd go to work again, picking everything up. I didn't mind, though! It's harder now; the kids are growing up, and I have to get *them* to clean up, and it's a lot of work, reminding them over and over again. On some days I'm plain tired; I say to myself: forget it—let them make the biggest mess this house has ever seen! I go make myself a coffee soda. I remember my mother; she'd get more and more upset, and finally she'd tell us that she didn t care *what* we did, and *what* we said, because she was going to make herself a coffee soda. And she did, and we always knew that mother was going to sit there and enjoy us! I try to do the same. I read the newspaper, or I watch television. If I had a million dollars I'd get a bigger house, and I'd buy myself a car, but then I'd still have the kids to bring up, and I'd still want to make sure they're not spoiled. I go and work, so they can get that extra dress or go to the hockey rink and the baseball game. If I had a lot of money I'd worry; the children would take too much for granted. That's the worst thing that can happen in life. We should be grateful to the Lord for putting us here in the United States, and for giving us the health to keep going all day. I'm lucky, actually; I work at a switchboard, so I sit on the job. And my poor husband, he's on his feet all day. But that's life. Don't ask *why* in this life; just try to get through it so you end up having some respect for yourself. That's important."

She speaks about the importance of self-respect to her children rather often—once a month, she estimates, when things aren't going "exactly well," and she senses the need, *theirs* as well as hers, "for a good explosion." It is on those occasions, actually, that she speaks her "philosophy of life." She tells her children what she, what life, expects of them—"the best that's in them." And why? And for what purpose? If they ask, or if she has any nagging doubts that make her ask on behalf of them, there is soon enough an answer. She recalls the gist of what she has said on various occasions: "I'm more excitable than my husband. He says there's no point getting angry about a lot of things, because there's nothing you can do to change them. I'm different. I get heated up about something; I simmer along for a while; and soon I'm boiling, and the pot overflows, and the children just have to listen! I tell them that when they grow up, they'll know more about what I mean, but even now they should stop and remind themselves that life is no bowl of cherries, and you've got to help keep the house clean, and pay attention, and go get a summer job—everything that kids have to be told and told and told. I have one boy who asks *why* a lot; he always did when he was six or seven, and he still does, now that he's fourteen. I tell him why; I tell him that it's not for us to know the answers to a lot of questions; if his father and I started thinking *why* all the time, we'd soon be thrown out of the house, because the bank would call us on the mortgage, because we had no money for the payments; and we'd be without food, too.

"We're here to be tested, like the priest says. It's a trial. You do the best you can. We're lucky to be in America. Think of how bad it is in other countries. I tell my children that in this life you have to do the best you can—work hard, bring up your children to believe in God and love their country and be good citizens, and obey the law. Then they'll get married and they'll have children, and then they'll know what their mother was shouting about! Of course, I want them to have some fun for themselves. That's part of life, too. Once a month their father and I go out. I don't care how good the movies are on television, it's not the same as leaving all your worries and cares at the doorstep and going out to a movie. We'll grab a hamburg before. I feel better for days and days afterward—a change, a break in the rhythm. You get out of life what you put into it. If you're halfway good—and we all make mistakes, I know—then you'll do all right, provided you have luck, and the country doesn't get into bad trouble and start falling apart. So long as you keep your chin up, and do what you have to do. That's what it means to be a grown-up; you don't feel sorry for yourself all the time, and you don't go asking a lot from others, and you don't expect the world to be served you on a silver platter, and like the priest says, you know the difference between Heaven and Earth, and you try to live up to the Bible, and what you believe, and if you stumble, or if things go against you for a while, then that's just part of the story, and you pick yourself up and keep going. How do the young people say it: keep trucking?"

For her, for her husband, for their relatives, friends, neighbors, and co-workers, and no doubt for millions whose social and economic situation is similar, such moments reveal about all there is to reveal, so far as a subject like "adulthood" goes. The word itself is not used, though "adult" comes up sometimes—as a synonym for "grown-up," which is indeed used from time to time. To be "grown up" is to be responsible, hard-working, dedicated, and, not least, self-sacrificing without demon-strations of self-pity. To be "grown up" is also to be busy, to have found a mission in life, a purpose: the bills to be paid, the children to be brought up, and so on. Occasionally the mother just quoted makes it quite clear that she sees beyond her own condition or fate, recognizes the different obligations of others—those of a priest, an unmarried schoolteacher of one of the children, a childless couple who live nearby. But mostly, she sees her sons and daughters as the center of her life, and by extension, she regards children as the *raison d'être* of life in general: one labors over the years so that they will "turn out good," even as one's parents did likewise.

All in all a mixture of Christian fatalism and acquiescence to the prevailing economic and social system (accompanied by brief outbursts of protest, behind the closed doors of the home, usually in connection with a specific complaint or burden—such as yet another rise in the cost of food, or the threat of busing for one of the younger children). For that man and woman, and for others like them, at least in one observer's experience, a host of religious or metaphysical (or metapsychological) questions get expressed in a few phrases or sayings which may strike some of us as hollow, trite, or banal, as evidence of "brain-washing" or bondage of various kinds, but which have for those who call upon them a strong and continuing significance. When a man says that he has "no time for problems," or that he takes his problems to work, and they "get dissolved there"; when a woman tells her children that they will learn something "in the college of hard knocks" if they don't learn that something from her, then and there; when they both say, "a million times" by their count, that "hard work never killed anyone," and that one ought to "do the best possible, and that's all anyone can ask of you"—then, arguably, at least one "definition of adulthood" is being earnestly and sincerely attempted.

There are other moments, more explicitly religious in nature. A husband prays to God that somehow, in some way, He might deign to "change everything around." Yet, the reason such hope is expressed turns out to be personal, rather than an outcome of social or economic criticism: "On some days I don't think I can make it. I'm tired, and I begin to feel myself getting angrier and angrier. I even question God. I ask him, when I'm driving, why He still lets the world be so unfair, so rotten unfair, for most of the people, while a few lucky ones pick up all the pieces. If He got angry when He was here—and the priest keeps telling us that Jesus did get plenty angry—then why shouldn't I, and a lot of other people I know? Then, I stop myself. I get scared. What can I do? What can anyone do? What's the point of trying to figure anything out? It's all in His hands, up there, and He's not telling us. But I tell the priest sometimes in confession, when he tells me about 'the sin of pride,' that I've got even more 'pride' than I confess to! There are times when I'd like to be able to change the whole world; there are times when I catch myself saying—God forgive me: If only I was Jesus Christ, then I'd take care of the fat-cat crooks and liars in the world, and try to give the little guy and his wife and kids a break.

"Most of the time, though, I try to keep my mind on my work—on what I'm doing at the moment. The trouble with going to church—I told the priest once—is that you get to thinking, and thinking, and thinking afterwards. But what can you *do*? Nothing, I'll tell you. That's what you learn in this life. That's what you know your kids will learn, and you watch them learning it. If you're a plain working man like me, you take it, take it, and who knows if it's God who means for life to be like that, or whether someday the world will be different because us human beings finally figure out how to behave better toward each other, like Christ said we should. Meanwhile, I'll tell you, there's nothing to do but go along with the way things are and try to get the most you can out of life, even if it's not much you're getting."

For others, from a different class or "background," such remarks only seem to confirm pre-existing notions, if not outright prejudices: the "alienation" of the working class, or the influence of "the Protestant ethic and the spirit of Capitalism" on working men and women. Even Simone Weil, who struggled so hard to remove herself from the snobbish excesses of the intellectuals, and from the ignorance they have with respect to the lives of others different from themselves, could say this about France's factory workers: "From one day to the next, he finds himself an extra cog in a machine, rather less than a thing, and nobody cares any more whether he obeys from the lowest motives or not, provided he obeys." She had herself worked in the Renault plant outside Paris, and she had become appalled, saddened, moved to expressions of concern and outrage. Yet, one wonders whether even then, when the conditions of work were surely much worse than those that obtain today in the General Electric factories of this country, the workers she saw and for a while (but, inevitably, *only* for a while—as with the rest of "us" who go to be with, observe, get to know, and struggle alongside "them") stood with in solidarity, actually regarded their fate as she did. Now, of course, we have Herbert Marcuse's permission to go much further—he is one in a substantial tradition: to go after those Parisian workers, or at the two Americans called upon here, relentlessly and with an air of unabashed authority. They are "one dimensional"; they are blind to their "real" situation, and their efforts to describe their lives, to affirm themselves, are mere (and pitiable, crude) slogans, or vague and undiscerning pieties.

Maybe so; no one can "prove" the contrary. There does, however, come a point at which repeated and sincerely stated statements deserve not only to be "interpreted," or regarded as "defensive" in nature, or considered to be, underneath, the opposite in meaning, but also at least in possession of a glimmer of the truth—the deeply held convictions of men and women who are capable of fierce pride, shrewd realism, and insistent rejection of self-pity, or the pity of others, which can, of course, mask condescension or contempt. In home after home of ordinary working-class Americans one hears work described as a measure, as *the* measure, of a person's "grown-up" status. However critical those individuals are of a particular company or, at times, of the whole society, they find it almost impossible to talk about themselves without reference to the work they do—at home or in a factory, an office, a store; and, indeed, in dozens of ways they feel that they *are* what they do: "I am a policeman," or "I am a machinist"—definitions that are quite intimately tied to a sense of one's maturity, one's arrival, so to speak, in the "grown-up world," as many put it, when they are talking about their own time, as responsible workers and parents. (Freud's emphasis upon "love and work" as criteria for a person's relative normality and maturity is quite in keeping with the stress put on both by these not especially psychologically minded men and women, who almost never gauge their own "success" as persons without reference to their jobs and to their family life: does he or she work well and hard, no matter what the job's pay, status, or demands, and does he or she "have a good family to come home to"?

It is against such a background that one must evaluate the meaning of unemployment for the young, or the sudden loss of jobs experienced by the elderly, or, for that matter, the judgment by our various social critics that for many millions in, say,

America, work is largely felt to be meaningless or exploitative. For youths who can find no jobs life is often "lousy," as one of them who lives not far from the factory worker quoted above puts it repeatedly. His elaboration of just *how* lousy is forceful, touching, revealing (some of us would certainly say), and quite like the comments others in a similar dilemma come up with: "The worst time is when I'm looking at myself and I feel lousy, so lousy I want to smash the window. If I had a job, I wouldn't be standing there, staring at myself in the first place! Who wants to have that kind of time on his hands? I hate myself; then I hate everyone else. I guess I wish I'd been one of those brainy ones who got a scholarship to college. But college graduates are having their troubles, too. It's a rotten deal when you can't find a job and don't earn your own money. Who wants to draw unemployment money, then borrow from the parents? I feel myself getting younger by the day—becoming a kid, feeling sorry for myself, and getting lazier by the minute. No good. After a while you're ready to return to elementary school!"

Maybe he is "regressing," as old people similarly do when faced with long hours of time and no work to fill them up. But maybe he is also speaking the plain truth, as he sees it. He is, perhaps, like many who do have work that others might consider "unattractive" or not "fulfilling" or "menial" or "rote, pure rote in nature," yet do indeed have quite another view of the matter—not a view that has themselves "duped" or "hoodwinked," but one that declares themselves to be psychological realists: aware of the world millions of working men and women live in, desirous often enough that it will some day be changed (though not necessarily in all the ways some of "us" who write about "them" would like), but also anxious "to live an ordinary life," to "be a 'grown-up,' " to "hold a job and take care of a family," "to pay the bills and see the kids grow up to be good people," if one may draw upon certain "definitions of adulthood" used by a number of American citizens.

WALLACE STEGNER

The Writer and the Concept of Adulthood

IF THE TERM "ADULT" MEANS ANYTHING, its meaning must be social. One does not declare oneself adult; one is perceived to be. Unavoidably, the qualities we call adult are on the side of "sanity," "normality," rationality, continuity, sobriety, responsibility, wisdom, conduct as opposed to mere behavior, the good of the family or group or species as distinct from the desires of the individual. It is unthinkable that we should call "adult" anyone who is unstable, extreme, or even idiosyncratic. In its purest form, adulthood is expressed in the characters of saints, sages, and culture heroes.

But in our pluralistic society, saints and sages are of many kinds, not always fully reconcilable. They derive from Christian, Jewish, Greek, and many other traditions. They have their roots in religion, law, humanistic ethics, art, in piety or skepticism, faith or stoicism or doubt, the agricultural or pastoral or industrial life, the tribe or the horde or the *civis*, wars or folk-wanderings or myths. To those brought up in a tribal or ethnic or religious tradition which retains its integrity, the accepted saints and sages provide satisfying models of adulthood. A Hopi Indian knows pretty precisely what growing up to manhood or womanhood means. But if tradition is broken or unformed—if one is a black American, say—all guides may be unacceptable. To a black man who is fatherless, jobless, status-less, and without authority figures except those who have humiliated his race and him, the only attractive adult image may be that of avenger, an image of violence such as that embraced by Eldridge Cleaver. And even so limited and essentially perverse a version of adulthood is subject to change as American society evolves. After another few centuries of the melting pot one might expect a gradual reconciliation of our various notions of what it means to be grown up. On the other hand, if the present tendency toward accentuated ethnicity continues, there may never be a recognizably American adult, but instead the continuation and hardening of diverse and possibly hostile patterns within many sub-cultures.

One instrument of both preservation and change is obviously the artist, especially the writer. Even in an age of anti-heroes and competing sub-cultures he continues to create or report models for emulation or repudiation. Yet to examine the concept of adulthood as it relates to the concept of the artist—and to do it without an adequate definition of either—may seem an undertaking of dubious utility. For one thing, artists and writers are as various, and reflect as many competing traditions, as the rest of us. For another, artists are banned from the Republic and the company of the philospher-kings precisely because, in their lives or their works or both, they are said not to demonstrate the sobriety and responsibility which the good of the state requires and which are basic to most of our tentative definitions of adulthood. Indeed, the Romantics from Blake and Wordsworth to D. H. Lawrence have insisted that the writer ought to be a child, or a primitive, and that acceptance of social obligations and duties, far from being a sign of maturity, is the saddest sort of surrender. Egocentrism, bohemianism, rebelliousness, lack of self-control and of that "developed strength" that Erik Erikson suspects is central to maturity—these are qualities we expect to find in writers and often do. We especially fear the artist in politics, but we rather fear him everywhere. He is an unsound man; and though he is a sort of anticoagulant in society, and hence indispensable, he has no clear social role. Not even the Internal Revenue Service allows for him on its forms. Not even our habit of nomenclature, which produces millions of Carpenters, Wheelwrights, Farmers, Fishers, Hunters, and Shepherds, has any family name such as Writer. The closest it comes is perhaps Clark, which is not the same thing by quite a margin.

The artist is as hard to define as the adult. There can be, and have been, Apollonian artists whose gifts of insight and wisdom ally them with that *vir* who is the vessel of *virtu*. But in our time the artist is likely to be Dionysian, marked not by the essentially conservative wisdom of the old chiefs, but by the passion and recklessness of the young warriors. As he is generally perceived, and as he more often than not perceives himself, the writer has only the obligation to be open to experience, even to personally and socially destructive experience. He may even commit experience as field work for his writing. He is the priest of human possibility, not of any limited system, and his fate is sometimes to be a sacrifice to his openness: sometimes we destroy him or ignore him to death because he threatens us, and later immortalize him because he has enlarged our vision. According to that pattern, Socrates was an "artist" done in by "adults." It is ironic that that interpretation was given to us by Plato, an artist who feared artists, an authoritarian adult uneasy about the coercive power of society.

Yet we should not, I think, dismiss artists from any consideration of adulthood. They are not quite gifted but irresponsible children; they are mixtures and approximations like other concepts—like adults, for instance. And from the time of the invention of the alphabet, writers have helped to shape our ideas of adulthood. On occasion writers have themselves achieved status as saints and sages. Moreover, writers are not static: they grow and change, and perhaps they grow toward greater wisdom and responsibility; perhaps there are stages in their lives that correspond to the stages of childhood, adolescence, adulthood, and senility in the life of Everyman. Perhaps, furthermore, the very qualities that self-protective societies find dangerous are the proofs of a higher adulthood, beyond and above the prescriptive and limited adulthood that limited societies feel comfortable with. Writers would like to think so. "What is Chaos?" asks Stanislaw Lec. "It is the Order destroyed during Creation."

There are writers of every stature. We are talking, I presume, only about the serious and gifted. And I have never known a serious writer who wasn't as responsible, in his way, as any priest or professor or public servant. The difference is that a writer is responsible not to a tradition or a church or any sort of social stability and conformity, but to his personal vision of truth and social justice, to his gift. That often sets him at odds with the "adults" of his system, but it also makes him indispensable. His vision and the integrity with which he pursues and promotes it are elements needed for a larger and more humane synthesis, which in the nature of things will again harden and will need once more the services of iconoclasts.

Iconoclasts, moreover, who *work*—whose work is never done, whose work is coterminous with consciousness and energy, who are diligent, self-disciplined, independent, and endlessly patient. Work is the means through which a writer puts into communicable and evocative and perhaps memorable form what he wants to say. If any quality seems to entitle him to be called adult, it is his capacity for work. Unfortunately, this society's attitudes toward work are so ambiguous that they call for some preliminary discussion.

There is hardly an activity of man so consistently bad-mouthed as work. It has had a hostile press ever since Genesis 3:19. Children are warned that all work and no play make Jack a dull boy. At least in some moods, we associate work with discomfort, imprisonment, fatigue, boredom, indignity, exploitation, everything that hangs like chains around the ankles of our pleasures. Those who affect to like work we call victims of the puritan work ethic; we tell them that if they don't relax and let the pleasure principle in, they will suffer consequences compared to which cholera would seem benign.

Work is what almost everybody says he would rather be doing anything else than. Fantasies of work's unpleasantness are matched by counter-fantasies of idyllic laziness and liberation. In keeping with some Huckleberry Finn wishfulness that inhabits our mental cupboards next to memories of Poor Richard, a hundred million non-fishing American men, asked what they would do if work were abolished tomorrow, reply that they would find a grassy bank, lay in a good supply of beer, and lie down with a fishline tied around their toe to watch a cork bob in lazy water forever.

We all partially subscribe to the stereotype that puts work and pleasure at opposite ends of the scale. Children, who do not have to work, are envied by adults, who do. Five days, the script goes, we grudgingly labor, and on the sixth and seventh we renew ourselves. Vacations are all that keep us from being pulverized by the Old Grind. We work at our recreation very hard, and when we limp exhausted back to factory or office we are greeted by groans of sardonic sympathy. Back to the salt mines, ha ha. Hello, sucker.

Thus the folklore of industrial and corporate man. Recovery from work is the excuse for many diversions, from managerial alcoholism and call girls to blue-collar taverns with topless waitresses and Saturday-night brawls. Yet most of us, even those of us who work at routine jobs, don't dislike work as much as we say we do. Not too rebelliously, we accept the fact that work is what we build our lives around, and many of us discover it to be a satisfaction, even a pleasure. It not only gets us what we need and want, it proves to us that we are grown up.

We are at least as industrious a species as the ants, even while we disparage the work ethic. If our play is sometimes work so is our work sometimes play. We think we get more fun out of life than the people we vaguely call puritans. But nobody ever accused Ben Franklin of being dour, even if he did write *Poor Richard's Almanack*; and who is to say that John Cotton, rising at three to study Greek and Hebrew scriptures for three hours before his day's work properly began, and closing out his eighteen-hour work day by sweetening his mouth with a bit of Calvin before sleeping, was not enjoying himself? Joy in work is largely a matter of motivation, and Cotton's urge to walk piously with God was perhaps as effective a motivation as that of Dr. Freud, another man who worked himself very hard.

Even parents who habitually pursue the pleasure principle from Las Vegas to Puerto Vallarta may have a disconcerting and not entirely consistent way of urging, driving, and bribing their children to work hard in school. When children become adolescents, moreover, and begin to yearn for the independence and presumed freedom of adulthood, few, even in these days of the counter-culture, question the law that ties their maturity to self-supporting labor. As it said on the gate at Auschwitz, *Arbeit macht frei*. And pleasure-prone American parents are likely to consider their child's first serious job a rite of passage comparable to graduation from high school. The fathers of the sixteen-year-old boys I sometimes hire as handymen consult me anxiously in private. How's the kid doing? Has he learned to work? Can he do a job?

If he has, if he can, he has begun to "grow up." Work is perhaps the ultimate measure of adulthood. Pleasure in work is another and more debatable matter, for even those who accept work willingly may pretend to dislike it. Yet the pleasure principle which is supposedly incompatible with work has a way of entering quietly by the employees' entrance. Many an individual finds, on retirement, that during his life he has got more fun out of his work than out of his fun. Thrown into total leisure and unproductiveness, he invents jobs in order to have them to do. The companion-ship of fellow workers and the satisfactions of a shared function turn out to be more valuable than we ever thought while we had them. That goes for workers whose jobs have been routine as well as for those who have enjoyed a certain professional autonomy. As the retired executive may yearn for the sense of power and usefulness that his desk once gave him, the ex-postman's feet wistfully remember the comfort-able turnings and re-turnings of his old route.

In short, more people than would probably admit it find in work the scaffolding that holds up the adult life. Of course it can be a compulsion, a neurotic symptom: like almost any human activity it can be carried to that excess that constitutes sin. But even when it is compulsive and neurotic it may be the only thing that holds a life together; for what is a neurosis but an adaptation, perhaps desperate but an adaptation, designed to keep disintegration and panic at arm's length? And sometimes work is more than a satisfaction, a comfort, a habit, or a sanctuary. It is a joy.

Levin reaping his fields with a crowd of peasants in *Anna Karenina* is exalted beyond thought or fatigue. His anxious self-questioning is lulled, his sensuous perceptions are heightened by the delight of rhythmical muscular exercise and by association with men whose physical competence is a challenge and whose integrity as workmen he respects. I have seen executives on vacation, playing at bringing in wood from a woodlot, experience the same intense pleasure. I have experienced it myself with a crew of Vermont farmers cooperating around a drag saw. Women preparing a church supper, students organizing a bonfire or a confrontation, even a detail of soldiers digging a latrine will experience it if health and morale are good. I suppose some optimum of work-pleasure is achieved by a string quartet either practicing or performing. The joy of joint effort is at the heart of all team sports. Alexis de Tocqueville, observing quilting and husking bees and neighborhood barn raisings, thought their communal labor one of the most attractive as well as one of the most democratic aspects of American life. In an odd way, moreover, this shared work that effaces the individual also enhances him. Even more than competition, it makes him do his best, and better than his best.

Unfortunately communal work-joy is incompatible with industrial capitalism, so that our feelings about it are mixed. It is too easily exploited. It weakens the hand of collective bargaining. Also, it has bad political associations. Dictators both left and right are students of the symbols, slogans, songs, parades, and eurhythmics that help produce this productive form of group hysteria. We hear from recent travelers that China is full of smiling people in blue blouses happily carrying out the directives of Chairman Mao, and we ask why we hear of no such unanimity among artists and intellectuals, why the cultural revolution was thought necessary. We answer ourselves with the assurance that Mao has the same view of artists that Plato did. Artists and intellectuals don't relish the role of Pavlov's dog or the worker bee. They are unsound, dangerous to the system, and hence (it could be argued) un-adult.

So communal work-joy does not seem to have much of a future in America, outside the activities of musical groups, sports teams, certain academic and research organizations, and spontaneous associations of farmers, vacationers, and eleemosynary volunteers. Our aspiration is in the opposite direction, toward maximum self-realization as individuals. When Edwin Land, the founder and president of the Polaroid Corporation, tells us that the worker is entitled to more than an eight-hour day with a martini at the end, the "more" that he has in mind is not Chinese enthusiasm and unanimity, but the individual pleasures of creativity and problem-solving. When Mr. Land himself is on a problem he is at the lab at all hours of the day and night, because nothing else he could be doing could possibly interest him so much or give him so much pleasure. He would like to give Polaroid employees a chance at the sort of work-pleasure he himself enjoys. When we come down to it, that isn't greatly different, except in its objectives, from the dedicated strenuousness of a John Cotton.

Work folklore to the contrary notwithstanding, that is what many kinds of Americans hunger for. They try to evade or supplant the system, not cooperate with it. The young people who flee industrial civilization and build their log cabins, yurts, or geodesic domes in the woods, there to live off their subsistence gardens while their children grow up as part of the wildlife, are following a fad, certainly, and repeating the perennial American fantasy of a return to innocence, and sometimes paradoxically submerging themselves in an alternative group. But they are not running from work. They are only trying to restore to work the elective freedom, the meaningfulness and joy, that industrialism has taken out of it. Instead of tightening individual nuts, they want to handle the whole product. They want to pursue their own ends, not those of a corporation. They prefer the human (sometimes the tribal) to the industrial scale. Neither the collectively-bargained-for reluctances of the assembly line nor the singing unison of the hive satisfies them. Significantly, a lot of them yearn to be artists or writers or craftsmen; they take up leather-working or wood sculpture or black-smithing, they make miles of macramé. Papered-over puritans, they aspire to a working autonomy that in our society is now enjoyed principally by experimental scientists, intellectuals on fellowships, hermits, free craftsmen, and hippies with trust funds. The artist's relation to his work—autonomous, independent, creative, free, joyful, and presumably easy because uncoerced—is the relation many of us entangled in the world's drudgery yearn toward. We pay our writers the compliment of envy and emulation, even while, as a society, we disparage their easy and irresponsible life, or try to sterilize them with celebrity.

I suppose that creation—the creation, say, of a novel—is one of the highest pleasures available to us, pleasure at a godlike level. But the novelist's life is not quite the carefree matter that popular condescension and envy assume. As De Lawd said in *The Green Pastures*, "Bein' God ain't no bed of roses." The more independent work is, the more solitary it is likely to be. It rarely involves enough of the stimulation of human warmth and contact. Its sharing is more often done after the fact than during the act. It breeds no songs, chanteys, dances, or any of the spontaneous folklore which, once created, adds enthusiasm and delight to the work it sprang from. Writers, especially, work with an austerity that is close to puritan, and with a dedication that approaches, and often becomes, compulsion.

The self-starting, self-directed, self-disciplined writer is commonly a harsher boss to himself than any external boss could be. He is his own victim. Unlike a compulsive moneymaker or tycoon, he cannot at a certain age divest himself of his monomania and turn his life to enjoyment of his gains by becoming a gourmand or a collector of paintings. He can no more be relieved of his creative curse than Hawthorne's Georgiana could be relieved of her birthmark: it is entangled with the very roots of his life. Hundreds of writers, ancient and modern, have testified that a day without work is a day lost, and some of the saddest people in the long sad history of mankind have been creators whose creativity wore out before they did. One such, as his *Life in Letters* makes clear, was John Steinbeck. In considering the ways in which a writer's life may be given its shape and meaning by his management of or by his gift, I have Steinbeck frequently in mind.

It is all but standard for serious writers to coerce their creative activity into a frame of habit. Except for amateurs and dilettantes, writing is not a part-time occupation, nor is it the automatic spilling-over of genius. It is the hardest kind of work, the making of something from nothing. No one but a dedicated, disciplined, even bull-headed individual is going to go on, day after day, sweating for five or six hours to make a page that may have to be thrown away tomorrow. If, as Henry Adams said, chaos is the law of nature and order the dream of man, and if the imposition of order on a corner of chaos is the function—or the illusion—of art, then the writer feels obliged to begin by imposing order on himself, at least during working hours. "The getting to work is a purely mechanical thing, as you well know—a conscious and self-imposed schoolroom," Steinbeck wrote to a friend. "After that, other things happen, but the beginning is straight pushing."

The establishment of a working routine is more than a means of making oneself toe the line. It is also a protection from interruption by friends, acquaintances, and strangers who assume that since you are at home you are not working, and who further assume that even if you are, your work is like other work and may be lightened and sweetened by interruption. The writer at work is submerged, and every intrusion that draws him to the surface costs him his concentration. More than that, his routine is part of a mystique. His time is braced on every side by habits and propitiations. The writing is not only done during certain regular hours, it is likely to involve a foreplay as essential as that of sex. We sharpen pencils, clear the desk, change the ribbon, warm up the finger by writing a letter or two. We fritter and putter, we read over yesterday's pages and perhaps rewrite them, perhaps throw them away. We work closer and closer, not being too obvious about where we are headed, until all at once we are there, and writing. That is when we need a wife who will answer the telephone or the doorbell and swear we are not at home. As a matter of fact, we're not.

Furthermore, no writer I ever knew wants to examine too closely what goes on when he is writing well. (I exempt Arthur Koestler, who had already given up writing novels before he took up the study of creativity.) The creativity studies conducted at Berkeley over a good many years found writers their least cooperative subjects. Asked to demonstrate with blocks how he organized a short story, Frank O'Connor said disgustedly that he had quit playing with blocks when he was three. I have seen a pair of distinguished psychologists meet only stony suspicion and refusal when they asked members of my advanced-fiction seminar to volunteer as hypnotic subjects. The idea was to sneak up on their creativity when it wasn't looking. Those young writers did not want their creativity sneaked up on. They felt it to be not only intensely personal, but fragile. Instead of exposing or analyzing it, they surrounded it with a camouflage of routine and casualness. They kept it in its hideout where it was safe; only at *their* will, not at that of some investigator, did they turn it loose to make its raids on human experience.

Ordinarily, the establishment of working habits goes on simultaneously with a writer's exploration of his talent, discovery of his themes and subject matters, and finding and polishing of techniques. The habit of work is perfected in a time of promise, ambition, hope, and often crazy energy. It is a time of great happiness for many, for they are both discovering themselves and putting themselves to use. They are exemplars of the examined life; and their examination is not isolated and analytic, but synthetic and in context. They are constructing, in stories, novels, poems, or plays, scale models of their insights and beliefs. They know the joy of creating a world.

Many writers, perhaps most, have found their workrooms places of sanctuary, and work a magic that exorcises demons. "By God I envy you people," a psychologist told me once. "You can write your lives instead of having to live them." He was not quite accurate: one does both, and simultaneously. I helped my mother die, and I was writing with some part of my mind much of the time. When I received word of my father's death I said, without premeditation and to my own dismay, "Now I know how that novel ends." The writing habit can be a carefully prepared schizophrenic closet into which one retires to make intolerable reality into something bearable.

Such experiences mark the first and most exhilarating stage of the characteristic novelist's career. The second has arrived when subject matters and themes have been found, techniques learned, audience achieved. It is not a stage that happens to everyone: fledgling writers make it to safety about as infrequently as newly-hatched turtles or salmon fry. But for those who do, this is the stage of self-confident achievement, emancipated from too much self-scrutiny.

So what was at first spontaneous, absorbing, full of discovery and delight is disciplined into a habit rich in satisfactions, and then becomes a refuge whose pleasures are more rueful, to be accepted with gratitude. And if personal troubles threaten to get out of hand, or if new themes come harder or not at all, if creation comes hard, or stops entirely, then there is a third stage marked by desperation and compulsion. Instead of enjoying his work habit, or finding safety in it, the writer may become imprisoned in it, and work may become a self-made hell. Like a dwindling oil well, the novelist has to pump ever harder for what little he produces. Or like a beaver whose teeth grow constantly, he must chew incessantly, not to eat, not to build dams, but simply to keep his jaws from being locked shut.

There is such a thing as writer's block, there is such a thing as being written out. A writer who lasts through several decades can hardly avoid experiencing both in some degree. I remember Walter D. Edmonds, once a dazzling success story among the writers of Cambridge, Mass. About 1941 he ran into a total block. The harder he tried, the less anything worked. He never succeeded in writing again, except for children, but I know he went through all the circles of hell clear to the ninth, which, as if to accommodate writers, is lonely and cold, before he adjusted himself to silence. I remember Bernard DeVoto after he had written the trilogy of Western histories which were so clearly what he had been born to write; he suddenly found himself without book. Art, he had said, was man determined to die sane. Art was the instrument and proof of self-control. For a long time he carried on the professional hackwork and the essays on public affairs that he had always done as a second full-time job. They didn't satisfy. The desk which had been both a sanctuary and the place of deepest satisfaction became a prison and an excuse. The creative excitement dried off like mist off a windowpane and let him look through to what he didn't want to see. The compulsive worker who for years had held off dread and panic could no longer hold them off, and he died desperate.

Happiness in work? Satisfaction in work? I know they exist, for I have experienced them. But I am sobered by the many writers who in order to pacify their demon turned work into a compulsive habit and found themselves at the end enclosed in it, as empty as the shell of a dead tortoise. What does the novelist do when the awareness that this has happened comes on him? Sometimes he works all the harder, a machine that at least for the time being cannot do anything but run. Often he projects great plans to persuade himself of something—that this will be the biggest thing in his whole career. Eventually he might have to admit that he is "written out." One of the special anguishes of a writer in this condition is the fact that writers, by definition and profession, are *aware*. Often they also have an over-developed sense of mission. It is very hard to accept the end of their specialness.

And what does this tell us about adulthood? Nothing very coherent, I fear. It raises more questions than it provides answers. Is the novelist, threatening though he often is to our conventions and assumptions and socially protective inhibitions, dangerous child or prophet? Was Steinbeck, for example—exposing the exploitation and social injustices of California's factories in the fields—the hateful radical the growers thought him, or the prophet he seemed to the Americans with a developed social conscience? I suppose he was both, for the growers had to move over and make room for reforms that *The Grapes of Wrath* made inevitable. By his choice of subject matter and the direction of his sympathies and the expression of his anger, he established himself as a milestone on the road to Cesar Chavez and the United Farm Workers, and so as a kind of champion of justice. By speaking from within the democratic mass, he offended the literary intellectuals, who dismissed, and still dismiss, his work as middlebrow. Where does adulthood lie among such contradictions?

There are other questions raised by the decline of a writer's creative powers. Is adulthood only a stage, the stage of full vigor and confidence, in the life of a writer? Is an author "adult" only during his middle years when he is full of things to say, has developed the means to say them, and perhaps has a vast audience to say them to? Does his growing anxiety and eventual silence represent a decline from adulthood, a diminishment toward impotence and senility, or should we take them as a maturing into sad but acceptant wisdom, a fully matured stage when personal desires, ambition, and the other vanities have been worn out and the writer's mind is clear, passionless, only faintly regretful? How much does personal serenity, that state so seldom observed among men and women of any profession, define adulthood?

I do not know, for our notions of adulthood are various and contradictory, but I do know that many writers display those ambiguous symptoms and suggest the same questions. Was the Sinclair Lewis of *Main Street* and *Babbitt*, during the years when he was in full vigor and capable of the most acid commentary on mid-American life, more or less mature than the chastened Sinclair Lewis of *It Can't Happen Here* and *The Prodigal Parents*, books whose theme was the unspectacular but utterly essential goodnesses and stabilities of middle-class life threatened by fascism or by youthful intransigence? Young warriors do sometimes become old chiefs, even among artists. They seem to go through stages like the rest of us, and at different stages they embody and celebrate different aspects of our social aspiration, different versions of good. What may begin as a determination to remake the world in the image of perfection, or express only its highest ideals or its most civilized aspects, may subside into the tired perception that the ideal is an impossible dream and that the best anyone can do is to help hold things together with sticking plaster. Is it more "adult" to aspire to the impossible, or to accept imperfection?

Moreover, the stages that sometimes seem to be apparent in the lives and works of writers may be less precise than they appear to be. The fact is that literature is helplessly culture-bound, which means that in a pluralistic society it reflects the wildest variety of norms, and that variety itself changes with time, with the changing proportions and dominances among the populations, and much else. As the mordant Stanislaw Lec remarks, every stink that fights the ventilator thinks it is Don Quixote. But it does not follow that every such stink can be ignored: sometimes it *is* Don Quixote. Not every child who plays with fire can be ignored, either: sometimes he turns out to be Prometheus. So it is impossible to say that youthful rebellion against law, convention, custom, and prevailing literary practice is necessarily immature and that more conservative responses are more adult.

We grow up unevenly, into a world which puts uneven values on our qualities. By a kind of consensus, the dedication and self-discipline that artists quite commonly display in their work entitle them to be called, at least in that respect, mature. But what is written in those disciplined hours may be absurd, jejune, unreal, dead wrong. Work discipline may serve illusion and self-deception and, occasionally (at least in the view of some readers), downright evil. On the other hand, if adulthood is held to be the hard-won product of age, thought, and experience, it is almost inevitably allied with resignation, and its strongest counsel will be caution. Nestor, not Odysseus and certainly not either Achilles or Agamemnon, becomes the adult model—and we have no counsel which could lead either to the fighting or the writing of the Trojan War, a testing ground for heroes.

We grow up unevenly. It is unlikely that we will see, among writers or among the population at large, any individual who is clearly and unambiguously culture hero, saint, or sage. What we are more likely to find is that collection of contradictory qualities, that *homme moyen sensuel*, whom by a process of averaging we agree to call adult. He will have in him some element of the man who sets out to change what he cannot bear and some element of the man who makes up his mind to bear what he cannot change. He may be wise, he may in fact be a true sage, as Robert Frost was one; yet, along with his profundity and wisdom, Frost displayed both in private and in public an unbecoming malice, and he was given to childish tantrums. Or he may be strictly controlled and disciplined, as in his writing Ernest Hemingway was, and never grow up beyond envy and spite, never write a line, however disciplined, that is uncorrupted by his own egomania.

I do not believe that adulthood is definable as a stage in the life either of artists or of less self-conscious mortals. I do not believe that it is even a precise cluster of qualities, for qualities are different depending on the point of view and the time and the circumstances. Adulthood, I should say, is always an approximation—a failed approximation. Among the saints it may be justified by faith; more generally it is shaped by indecision and doubt. And I think it does not necessarily last from the time when it is approximately achieved to the time when the coffin lid is closed upon the serene and upward-staring face. It is a stage on the way to senility—or, in the case of many writers, a tentative, half-scared, half-hopeful, nearly-compulsive time for the exploitation of a gift that at any time may be cruelly withdrawn.

KENNETH S. LYNN

Adulthood in American Literature

IN 1922, WHEN THE CRITICAL REEVALUATION of nineteenth-century American literature was just getting under way, D. H. Lawrence wrote: "We like to think of the old-
fashioned American classics as children's books. Just childishness on our part."[1]
Lawrence was only half right: the childishness is in the books as well as in ourselves.

It is, of course, true that Cooper, Irving, Melville, Hawthorne, and Poe created
characters of all ages. Yet, for the most part, they were curiously insensitive to the
dramatic possibilities of the human life cycle and made only the crudest effort to
distinguish between the fascinatingly different stages of its later half. If, for example,
a historian with a particular interest in the family and in problems of early maturity
should try to find out how young married couples in the early nineteenth century
responded to the sudden onset of familial responsibilities, he would gain nothing from
reading the best American writers of the period. For, while the books they wrote
were intensely psychological, the fears and anxieties that grip their characters rarely
serve to illuminate the dilemmas of particular age groups. The terrors experienced by
Roderick Usher, Clifford Pyncheon, and Ichabod Crane are states of feeling that
anyone, young or old, can understand. Thus it was not just the thrilling action and
detective-story suspense of the old-fashioned American books that caused them to be
appropriated by an audience that was much younger than the authors had in mind;
their reductionist renditions of grown-up life also made it easy for juvenile readers to
regard these books as belonging to them. By the end of the nineteenth century, the
masterworks of an earlier era—an entire literature!—could be found in the closets and
cupboards of children's bedrooms.[2]

Cooper's *Prairie* (1827) is a good example of the sort of childishness I am talking
about. The novel was composed by a thirty-eight-year-old man, but its portrayal of
Natty Bumppo as an octogenarian could as well be the work of a boy of twelve. A
juvenile perspective is established in the very first appearance of the trapper. Coming
to a halt at the top of a rise, Natty compels us to look up at him in the manner of
awestruck children gazing at a strange adult:

> The sun had fallen below the crest of the nearest wave of the prairie, leaving the
> usual rich and glowing train on its track. In the centre of this flood of fiery light a human
> form appeared, drawn against the gilded background as distinctly, and seemingly as
> palpable, as though it would come within the grasp of any extended hand. The figure
> was colossal; the attitude musing and melancholy . . . . But imbedded, as it was, in its
> setting of garish light, it was impossible to distinguish its just proportions or true
> character.

Coming closer to the man against the sky, we see that he is very old. His "withered" form and "look of emaciation, if not of suffering" clearly show that he has endured the hardships of an outdoor life for "more than eighty seasons." Yet as soon as he moves, his decrepitude drops away from him as if by magic: "With a facility a little remarkable for his years and appearance," he shoulders his "heavy rifle" and plunges down the hillside in order to show an emigrant family where to pitch camp for the night.

The episode launches a systematic evasion of the painful problem of being an old man in a young country. In all likelihood, Cooper created the hero of his novel in the image of the grizzled pioneers whom he remembered from his youth in Cooperstown, New York, in the seventeen-nineties, but who by the canal-building eighteen-twenties had long since disappeared. Cooper's re-creation, however, is not really old; he is a young man in a gray wig, an elegiac symbol ungrounded in human truth and possessed of only a fraction of the poignant meaning he might have had. At an age at which most pioneers would have been content to sit near the stove in country stores, Natty has found a new life as a beaver trapper in the high plains country of western Nebraska and eastern Wyoming. He traverses this huge territory alone and on foot ("horses have I never craved, nor even used"), sleeping at night on brush piles under the open sky and killing animals for food as he goes. Despite his periodic protestations that his prowess with a rifle is not what it used to be, the novel demonstrates that Natty is no bleary-eyed relic, but the Hawkeye of old. Not only can he still take "a leaping buck atwixt the antlers" and make short shrift of grizzlies and panthers, but when several younger people are in danger of being run over by a herd of stampeding buffaloes, he singlehandedly saves their lives:

> The old man, who had stood all this while leaning on his rifle, and regarding the movements of the herd with a steady eye, now deemed it time to strike his blow. Levelling his piece at the foremost bull, *with an agility that would have done credit to his youth* [italics mine], he fired. The animal received the bullet on the matted hair between his horns, and fell to his knees . . . .

There is also nothing wrong with his sense of hearing. Although a man less than half his age interprets a distant sound in the night as the pounding footsteps of a herd of terrified buffaloes being driven by a panther, Natty knows better: "Your ears are cheats," cries the old man, "the leaps are too long for the buffalo, and too regular for terror." A short time later, the appearance of a band of Sioux Indians riding horseback proves him right—as always.

Eight pages from the end of a long novel, this gerontic marvel finally lies down and dies. At long last, his eyes are "glazed." Even on his deathbed, however, Natty denies the realities of adulthood. He experiences no more pain or fear than the sunset which is simultaneously occurring, and as he speaks his valedictory the old trapper's force of voice has "the same startling effect upon his hearers as is produced by the trumpet, when its blast rises suddenly and freely on the air." As he himself says, "I die as I have lived."[3]

Leslie Fiedler has claimed that American storytellers are pathologically incapable of dealing with adult sexuality and have been driven as a result toward an obsession with death.[4] But the classic American writers had very little to say on a lot of subjects, including factory work, railroad construction, banking, farming, newspaper-editing, running for political office, school-teaching, child-rearing, house-clean-ing, bill-paying, and the systematic exploitation of Negro slaves. As for their alleged substitution of death for sex, they skirted the agonies of terminal illness as carefully as they did the excitements of love-making. Their inability to deal with adult sexuality, in other words, was only a symptom of a larger, more encompassing failure.

In lieu of all the life they left out of their books, the classic American writers told stories of self-discovery and self-preservation. Some of these narratives are distinguished by a charming humor, others by a calculated sensationalism, still others by an obviously genuine despair. But beneath their vast differences they have one characteristic in common: psychic immaturity. I say psychic immaturity because one of the signs of an underdeveloped personality is the failure to recognize that serious personal and social problems cannot be solved by running away from them. Over and over again, however, the leading characters of classic American literature react to the crises in their lives by taking to the sea or withdrawing into gloomy mansions or high-walled castles or disappearing into the forest. One of the first, and undoubtedly the most celebrated, of these escape artists was created by Washington Irving. In the character of Rip Van Winkle, Irving established the archetype of the adult hero who is a child at heart.

Easygoing Rip has spent his entire life evading responsibilities. When his shrewish but practical wife reminds him for the thousandth time that his laziness has brought them to the brink of financial ruin, Rip responds by going off into the woods, instead of back to work. Falling into his famous sleep, he enters the sort of dream world a child might conjure up, wherein Henry Hudson and his shipmates eternally play at nine pins. Forty winks last for twenty years, at which point Rip wakes up and returns home. The American Revolution has taken place in his absence, and a quiet Dutch village is now a noisy American town. Rip is terrified by its unfamiliarity. "Everything's changed," he shouts, "and I'm changed, and I can't tell what's my name, or who I am!" Most terrifying of all to a lazy man is the realization that Dutch somnolence has given way to Yankee hustle. Thus the wide-spreading tree that had formerly shadowed the courtyard of Nicholas Vedder's inn has been replaced by a tall, skinny flagpole, and the inn is in the hands of a bustling entrepreneur named Jonathan Doolittle. Even in this alien world, however, escape is still possible, because by sleeping for twenty years Rip has successfully bypassed the remaining years of his active adulthood. His wife, moreover, who symbolized the hateful responsibilities of work and marriage, has long since died. Taking his place on the bench at the inn door, he idles away his days with an impunity that is usually reserved for infants. By becoming old, Rip in effect has become a child again. He no longer needs to worry about behaving like a man.[5]

Within a generation of its appearance in *The Sketch Book* (1820), "Rip Van Winkle" transcended the realm of fiction and became a part of American folklore. Its childish vision had obviously touched a national nerve. Younger authors, including Richard Henry Dana, Herman Melville, and Ik Marvel, the author of *Reveries of a Bachelor*, now began to act out escapist fantasies as well as to write about them. When Henry Thoreau went to live on the banks of a pond outside Concord, Massachusetts, he, too, was seeking an alternative to the quietly desperate world of work and marriage. In the book he wrote about his experiment, he calls upon us to take him seriously, but almost every episode in *Walden* reveals an astonishing immaturity. His seemingly meticulous budget, for instance, which makes such a fuss about half-penny and quarter-penny expenditures for food and lumber, fails to make any provision for the payment of poll taxes, the possibility of catastrophic illness, the cost of a coffin, and other annoyances of adult life.

Thoreau is simply playing house at Walden Pond, yet when he encounters the Irishman John Field, who lives in a leaky shanty with his greasy-faced, bare-breasted wife and their several children, and who ekes out a cruelly marginal existence hoeing the boggy meadows for a neighboring farmer at the rate of ten dollars an acre, he has the nerve to tell the hard-pressed immigrant how to reorder his priorities. In this appalling passage, Thoreau reveals more than just a bachelor's vagueness about the sort of worries that a husband and father would have on his mind; he shows himself to be as innocent as a child:

> I tried to help him with my experience, telling him that he was one of my nearest neighbors, and that I too, who came a-fishing here, and looked like a loafer, was getting my living like himself; that I lived in a tight, light, and clean house, which hardly cost more than the annual rent of such a ruin as his commonly amounts to; and how, if he chose, he might in a month or two build a palace of his own; that I did not use tea, nor coffee, nor butter, nor milk, nor fresh meat, and so did not have to work to get them; again, as I did not work hard, I did not have to eat hard, and it cost me but a trifle for my food. . . . I told him, that as he worked so hard at bogging, he required thick boots and stout clothing, which yet were soon soiled and worn out, but I wore light shoes and thin clothing, which cost not half so much, though he might think that I was dressed like a gentleman (which, however, was not the case), and in an hour or two, without labor, but as recreation, I could, if I wished, catch as many fish as I should want for two days, or earn enough money to support me a week. *If he and his family would live simply, they might all go a-huckleberrying in the summer for their amusement* [italics mine].

One hopes for Thoreau's sake that he was not entirely serious in his advice to Field and that his carefully detailed pseudo-budget was mainly intended as a joke on Benjamin Franklin. There can be no doubt, however, that he meant every word of what he wrote about the correspondences between man and nature. Unfortunately, the correspondences are inexact, and his failure to acknowledge that fact is another sign of his incorrigible puerility. The seasonal metamorphoses described in *Walden* are a means of talking about the triumphant renewal of a human consciousness. What is left unsaid is that the course of the year has also made Thoreau's body twelve months older. Physically speaking, there is a terrifying lack of correspondence between nature's life cycle and man's: one is a circle, the other is an arc. The flesh and blood of an adult human being constitute a decaying, non-renewable organism, but the only sort of physical corruption that Thoreau is prepared to talk about is the mulch on the forest floor out of which slender saplings spring. The miracle of nature's rebirth is his constant substitute for thinking about the tenuousness of his own triumph.

When Thoreau decides to leave the Pond, it is for the announced reason that he has other lives to lead—and for the unannounced reason that if he stays any longer his sense of wonder will begin to fade and his aging body will grow unresponsive. "The sun is but a morning-star"—and novelty is a hypodermic needle. For the narrator of *Walden*, as for other escape artists of his time, life is an endless series of get-aways. Even the cataclysmic saga of *Moby Dick* ends with an "Epilogue" about Ishmael and a coffin life buoy.[6]

The classic American writers in their flight seldom turned back to the society in which their fellow citizens lived. Cooper sometimes did, and so did Melville in

"Bartleby the Scrivener." But the most important exception to the prevailing escapism was Hawthorne's *Scarlet Letter*. A penetrating study of human relationships, the story not only involves the adulterous principals, but a wronged and eventually vengeance-seeking husband and a disturbingly neurotic child. The novel's setting is social, its perspective is historical, and the moral victory of which it speaks at the end is achieved only through the abandonment of the sort of childish self-love that Thoreau celebrated: "In the lapse of the toilsome, thoughtful, and self-devoted years that made up Hester's life, the scarlet letter ceased to be a stigma which attracted the world's scorn and bitterness, and became a type of something to be sorrowed over, and looked upon with awe, yet with reverence too."[7]

In the later decades of the nineteenth century, the number of writers who were interested in the moral drama of adult relationships increased. The disastrous marriage of Bartley and Marcia Hubbard in Howells's *Modern Instance* climaxes in desertion and culminates in divorce. Mrs. Todd in Sarah Orne Jewett's *Country of the Pointed Firs* remains involved in the life of her community, despite anguishing personal losses. In Kate Chopin's *Awakening*, Edna Pontellier finally rebels against the traditional female role of the dutiful wife.

Even more striking, though, than the psychic maturity of certain books in late-nineteenth-century American literature is the blatant immaturity of many others. For in the wake of the Civil War, the hero who was a child at heart became a child in fact. The process of transformation began with Louisa May Alcott's *Little Men* and *Little Women*, Horatio Alger, Jr.'s *Ragged Dick*, and Thomas Bailey Aldrich's *Story of a Bad Boy*; but it was not until the enormous success of Mark Twain's *Adventures of Tom Sawyer* (1876) that the child hero really came into his own. In the fiction of the eighteen-eighties, twelve-year-olds were difficult to avoid, especially in the weekly and monthly magazines. A decade later, Henry James and Stephen Crane also became interested in child characters. Although *Whilomville Stories* and *What Maisie Knew* are notable books, *The Adventures of Huckleberry Finn* is unquestionably the greatest achievement in this literature—and the most childish. In *Tom Sawyer*, Mark Twain had told the story of a boy in the third-person, literary language of an adult. In *Huckleberry Finn*, however, the author closed the gap between himself and his hero. Man and boy became one, as Mark Twain merged his own viewpoint with Huck's and abandoned literary language in favor of a waif's vernacular.

If the child hero had a rival in popularity in post-Civil War writing, it was the morally spontaneous, intellectually vivacious American girl whom Howells and James delighted in writing about in their early novels and stories. Although half again as old as Mark Twain's heroes, she was by no means an adult. An innocent abroad, she invaded Europe with the intrepidity of Natty Bumppo blazing a wilderness trail or of Tom Sawyer attending his own funeral. Only rarely did Howells and James follow her into marriage, for encumbrances were not her style. She, too, was an escape artist who wanted no limits to be placed upon her. She, too, symbolized the remarkable reluctance of nineteenth-century American writers to implicate their characters in the confining circumstances of adult life.

How can we account for their reluctance? What were the sources of the psychic immaturity that inspired so many childish themes, childish characters, childish points of view? The fact that most of the front-rank writers of nineteenth-century America grew up in families in which the father was either dead, missing, physically crippled, or financially inept suggests the possibility that fears about growing up affected their literary imaginations. Yet their perception that their fathers were weak and had somehow let them down was not the only source, or even the main source, of the immaturity of their art. Public events were also in the writers' minds, and their effects were decisive. The childish qualities of nineteenth-century American literature had their origins in the historical circumstances that fostered childishness in an entire civilization.

In the seventeenth and eighteenth centuries, colonial America had been deeply involved in transoceanic affairs. At the same time, the colonists had persevered in the effort to build a society of their own. The paradox of being a part of a world order and yet separate from it proved politically fruitful. The literature of the pre-Revolutionary period expresses the proud realization of the colonists that they had come of age with extraordinary speed. Psychopolitical fables such as Francis Hopkinson's "Pretty Story" recount the history of the British-American relationship in terms of parents and rapidly maturing children; the point of these stories is always that the new imperial policies of George III represented a monstrous attempt to reverse the course of the human life cycle.

After achieving political independence, however, America sought isolation, and an unprecedented innocence settled upon the national mind. We seemed to think that we had seceded from history. International relations were for other people, not for morally immaculate Americans.

Within this secluded mini-world, the frontier beckoned, the economy burgeoned, and the fluidity of American society soon became the envy of the world. Unfortunately, spectacular opportunities also made for anxiety and alienation, especially among the middle-class white males who had the best chances to get ahead. Indeed, for many such men the endless process of competing became a waking nightmare. It took them away from their wives and children, set them in opposition to other men, and stunted their emotional growth. The fluidity of American life also beguiled its psychological victims into thinking that some day they would deal with their unhappiness by pulling up stakes and moving their families to a new location; in a more drastic version, they thought of going alone. Why should they continue to carry intolerable burdens, when they could so easily walk out the door and start life all over again somewhere else? The number of men who actually dropped out of sight in this way will never be known, but statistics are not really the point. It was the example set by the runaways, not their precise number, that counted. For these disappearances lent plausibility to the daydreams of men who stayed home, thereby diminishing their involvement in the only reality they would ever know. On the international level, the secessionist fantasies of nineteenth-century Americans blocked the development of meaningful relations with other nations; on an individual level, they were similarly inhibiting. In both instances, psychic immaturity was the result of an inability to make contact.

Men who were strangers to one another practiced a politics of evasion. From one end of the nineteenth century to the other, Americans relied on the expansion of their society to provide painless solutions to social problems. There was no need to formulate a coherent policy to alleviate the lot of the poor, because upward mobility would automatically take care of most of them and society would be better off if the rest died. The Negro question would go away as soon as the last black buck was shipped off to the Caribbean—or would Africa be better, as Lincoln insisted? The superficiality of such ideas was breathtaking, but surely the most jejeune of them all was the claim of Northern abolitionists and Southern secessionists alike that the question of sectional antagonism could be answered by dissolving the Union.

To a degree—but only to a degree—the best writers of the century stood apart from their countrymen and from the characters in their own books. Melville, for instance, was keenly conscious of the unformed quality of the national character. At the end of his career, he presented an unforgettable portrait of American innocence in the person of Billy Budd—handsome as a baby, stutteringly inarticulate, and unable to express his anger except with a mortal blow. The author of *Typee* also knew that the dream of escaping one's own past was unattainable inasmuch as one can never escape from oneself. Other writers contributed other insights into the national enthusiasm for avoiding problems rather than confronting them. The symbolic Americans in Poe's stories have not found security in their withdrawal from the world; on the contrary, they are men at bay, who are scared to death of the nameless horrors that have breached their sanctuaries. Even the sanctuary of childhood was vulnerable, as Mark Twain showed. For the mood of recaptured delight never lasts in his stories: Huck's raft gets smashed, Nigger Jim disappears, and the trip down the river turns into a nightmare. As for painless solutions to social questions, Hawthorne's satirical account of the utopian community at Blithedale effectively punctured at least one secessionist bubble.

Yet the leading writers of nineteenth-century America were not so much the critics as the creatures of their civilization. From the yearnings of Washington Irving to lose himself in a land of dreams to Henry James's expatriation, their secessionist fantasies were only variations on a national theme, and emotional detachment from the world around them had as crippling an effect on their personalities as on their countrymen's. To discover as much meaning in family life as Tolstoi did, or to implicate their characters in social settings to the extent that Balzac and Zola did, was simply beyond the psychic capacity of the American writer. Henry James, for instance, not only failed in his Balzacian ambition to become the secretary of American society, but he experienced extreme difficulty in dramatizing relationships between individuals. Thus in *The Portrait of a Lady* he reduced the married life of Gilbert Osmond and Isabel Archer to a series of frozen postures that are even more devoid of human reality than Cooper's portrait of Natty Bumppo as an old man, and his attempt to persuade us that Isabel really cares for Osmond's young daughter is literary fakery, nothing more.

Working within a narrow range of experience, a half-dozen minor writers of the period showed a much more consistent willingness to confront the ordinary problems of adulthood than the major writers did. The fact that most of these writers were women is striking, but not hard to understand. It was, after all, much more difficult for women than for men in nineteenth-century America to convince themselves that some day they would throw over their responsibilities and walk out, slamming the door behind them. Women had fewer rights, fewer opportunities, fewer choices of any sort than men did. Family life and community life enveloped them; perforce, they stayed put, while the whole world celebrated the freedom and openness of American society. Their situation may have been frustrating and often depressing, but it seems to have saved many of them from the prevailing immaturity of their times. If literature is a reflection of life, then nineteenth-century American women were markedly more "adult" than their men, as Hawthorne suggested when he contrasted Hester Prynne's behavior with the Reverend Mr. Dimmesdale's.

The serious female writers who emerged in the middle and later decades of the century—I am thinking not only of Kate Chopin and Sarah Orne Jewett, whom I have already mentioned, but of Harriet Beecher Stowe and Mary Wilkins Freeman—did not traffic in the disappearing acts that are a childish literature's stock in trade. Instead, they involved their characters in webs of social circumstance and watched them struggle. In bits and pieces, a drastically incomplete, but nevertheless significant, picture of adult life emerged from their books. Eventually Willa Cather would model her pioneer heroines on the indomitable women whom Stowe and Jewett had portrayed, and Edith Wharton would amplify the theme of female entrapment that Chopin had adumbrated in *The Awakening*.

At the end of the eighteen-nineties, Theodore Dreiser also began to deal with adult themes. The first American novelist of any significance who had neither a middle-class nor an "old American" background, Dreiser looked at life from a much more skeptical perspective than his predecessors had. But *Sister Carrie* (1900) was not merely a personal testament. It also reflected the disillusioning events of the decade in which it was conceived. For a hundred years, citizens of the United States had cherished assumptions about the opportunities their society provided, but in the nineties those assumptions were suddenly called into question by a number of stunning developments, the most notable of which were the disappearance of the frontier, the rise of the trusts, and the outbreak of a series of bloody industrial strikes. The publication of *Sister Carrie* marked the beginning of a new theme in American literature—modern society was a trap from which no one, male or female, could possibly escape. Through the bitter story of George Hurstwood, the Chicago saloon manager, who at the outset of the novel dazzles the inexperienced Carrie Meeber with his suavity and his success, but whose life ends in suicide in a Bowery flophouse, Dreiser provided a vision of modern American adulthood that Saul Bellow's Herzog might very well have had in mind when he was musing about the subject some sixty years later:

> Well, for instance, what it means to be a man. In a city. In transition. In a mass. Transformed by science. Under organized power. Subject to tremendous controls. In a condition caused by mechanization. . . . In a society that was no community and devalued the person. Owing to the multiplied power of numbers which made the self negligible.[8]

Nevertheless, the immaturity of American literature did not end with Dreiser's massive assault upon it. The child hero, to be sure, did not last much beyond Booth Tarkington's *Penrod* (1914), but his place was soon taken by the sad-faced post-adolescents of *The Sun Also Rises* and *The Great Gatsby*. The concept of adolescence had been formalized by G. Stanley Hall in 1904, and Hemingway and Fitzgerald had come of age (which is different from growing up) in an America that had fallen in love with a new view of the human life cycle. The Census Bureau may have announced in 1890 that the nation no longer had a frontier, but the old American dream of escaping from reality was not dead, after all. The escape routes that "nature's nation" no longer offered would now be supplied through human nature. By the nineteen-twenties, Stanley Hall's soberly scientific insistence that we pay attention to the "storm and stress" of adolescence had been transmogrified in the popular mind into a cult of youth.

Hall had warned that adolescence was a waiting period that must not be arbitrarily foreshortened; it should be allowed, he said, to run its full natural course.

But Hemingway and Fitzgerald carried this further: in their early work they revealed that the waiting period could be prolonged more or less indefinitely. This revelation appealed not only to readers of their own age, but to somewhat younger readers as well. Just as the emotionally childish works of Cooper's generation were appropriated by twelve-year-olds, so the emotionally adolescent stories of Hemingway and Fitzgerald were quickly picked up by high-school and college students; since the paperback revolution of the early nineteen-fifties, in fact, youthful readers have almost surely been their most important constituency.

For teen-age Americans, reading Hemingway has become a kind of initiation rite. How to make out in a sleeping bag or a gondola or simply under the trees by a Michigan lake; what to order when you go to the Brasserie Lipp (try the *pommes à l'huile*), and where you should try to get seated; why a twenty-to-one martini is called a Montgomery, and who used to make the best daiquiris in Havana: his books contain the answers to all sorts of questions like these, and the more money the neophyte reader has in his pocket, the more helpful Hemingway becomes. What salesman at Abercrombie's, after all, can tell you that you not only want a .256 Mannlicher Shoenauer, but you want the kind with the eighteen-inch barrel that the stores are not allowed to sell any more? There is, alas, a certain justice in the fact that a hot-dog skier from Sun Valley has been able to parlay her grandfather's name into a million-dollar advertising deal and a well-publicized liaison with a hamburger king. In the age of consumership, and of the youth culture that dominates it, a Hemingway endorsement sells the product.

The recent film version of *The Great Gatsby* led to tie-in sales of "Gatsby white" men's suits and kitchenware. Yet Fitzgerald's adolescent fantasies were far less tangible than Hemingway's. Like the hero of his novel, he did not believe in fancy shirts so much as he did in the masturbatory dreams they symbolized. It is Daisy's voice, not Daisy herself, that holds the dreamer. The song she sings is sad, though, for at three o'clock in the morning the party is almost over and the magic of youth is fading. Gatsby, Nick Carraway, and Tom Buchanan have all turned thirty, and *it is a terrible thing*. A youth-worshiping civilization had already decided that thirty was not a particularly happy birthday, but Fitzgerald elevated it into a major crisis. All the insistent power of his romanticism was brought to bear on the subject, until an utterly sophomoric idea became a national obsession. We shall never be able to count the times that psychoanalysts have had to listen to the anguished confession, "I am no longer in my twenties!," but we do know that in the nineteen-sixties a generation of college students who had been raised on paperback copies of *The Great Gatsby* made their refusal to trust anyone over thirty a battle cry. How many novelists, in any age in any country, can claim to have influenced an entire nation's perception of the life cycle?

The Fitzgerald hero's conception of himself as not only beautiful but damned has become an idea that many college students entertain about themselves. Making a separate peace in the manner of Frederic Henry in *A Farewell to Arms* is the recurrent dream of prep-school boys, as J. D. Salinger and other witnesses have testified. While the appeal to youth of Hemingway and Fitzgerald is perennial, they themselves eventually discovered that their fantasies were unlivable. At some point in their work, consequently, the mood suddenly shifts, and we come upon a different sort of hero. He has gangrene in his leg, a hangover that will not go away, and an oppressive sense that he has wasted time. Although he talks a lot about himself, there is a significant vacancy at the center of his story, for he has moved directly from over-aged adolescence to middle-aged crack-up without ever having been mature. Despite its flashbacks, *Tender is the Night* gives us no real sense of why Dick Diver decided to go to medical school, or of the long effort that presumably went into the making of his professional reputation; the only thing the novel makes us believe in is Dick's disintegration, the principal symbol of which is the loss of his youthful ability to perform athletic tricks.

Hemingway tells us even less about the background of Thomas Hudson. Near the end of *Islands in the Stream*, Hudson nostalgically recalls his "time of innocence" in Paris, when he was starting out as a painter, but the story of how a young man actually fulfilled his artistic promise is a subject about which we learn nothing first-hand. Dreiser could portray a man at the height of his powers, and he did so again and again in the early chapters of *Sister Carrie*, in *Jennie Gerhardt*, in *The Financier*, and in *The Titan*, but Hemingway could not. In *Islands in the Stream*, all he can show us is a death-haunted alcoholic who likes boats and guns and who finally is hit in the crotch with "three chickenshit bullets" that "fuck good painting and prove nothing.[9]

Dreiser, on the one hand, versus Hemingway and Fitzgerald, on the other: American literature in the early twentieth century was torn between a willingness to confront "what it means to be a man" and a desire to postpone that confrontation as long as possible. This tension continues. It is as if an adult principle and an adolescent principle were locked in a Manichaean struggle for possession of our literary souls. The struggle vacillates back and forth, with some authors even divided against themselves—Saul Bellow, for example, who scorns "the cheap mental stimulants of Alienation, the cant and rant of pipsqueaks about Inauthenticity and Forlornness," but can't break free of them in his own books for more than two chapters at a time.[10] Yet, for all its inconclusiveness, the struggle has a pattern. The adult principle certainly seems to have had the upper hand in the nineteen-thirties, when Faulkner and Steinbeck were doing their finest work, whereas in the nineteen-sixties, when Kurt Vonnegut, Jr., was presiding over the greening of America and Norman Mailer was substituting unzipped exposures of himself for the novels he could not write, the adolescent principle was once more in the ascendancy. These psychic shifts are not accidental, but are related to historical events. Just as *Sister Carrie* emerged out of a socially upsetting decade, so *Absalom, Absalom!* and *The Grapes of Wrath* were products of the Great Depression; conversely, Vonnegut became a cult figure, as Fitzgerald had before him, in an age of unprecedented prosperity.

In the mid-nineteen-seventies, the mood of the nation has darkened again. One has the sense that the United States—indeed, the whole world—is waiting, waiting, waiting for catastrophe. As our fear deepens, we turn to history and to family life, as Faulkner and Steinbeck did, and watch *Upstairs, Downstairs* on the tube. Even Jerry Rubin has published a book called *Growing (Up) at Thirty-Seven*. But, as his parentheses indicate, the erstwhile clown-prince of the sixties is still not sure whether he is joking or not. In any event, American literature is not likely to become completely serious until, in Kierkegaard's words, we have known hell through and through.

REFERENCES

[1]D. H. Lawrence, "Studies in Classic American Literature," in *The Shock of Recognition*, ed. Edmund Wilson (Garden City, New York, 1943), p. 907.

[2]A good many authors in early-nineteenth-century Great Britain, most notably Dickens and Scott, also appealed to readers of all ages. But many other writers, for example, Jane Austen, were completely lost

on young children. A similarly mixed situation existed on the Continent. Only in America did all the major writers of fiction command the attention of juvenile as well as adult readers.

[3]James Fenimore Cooper, *The Prairie*, ed. Henry Nash Smith (New York, 1955), pp. 8, 9, 11, 22-23, 26, 33, 63, 67, 85, 224, 231, 445-47.

[4]Leslie A. Fiedler, *Love and Death in the American Novel* (New York, 1960).

[5]Washington Irving, *The Sketch Book*, with an afterword by Perry Miller (New York, 1961), pp. 41-53.

[6]Henry David Thoreau, *Walden*, ed. Sherman Paul (Boston, 1957), pp. 40-41, 141-42, 227.

[7]Nathaniel Hawthorne, *The Scarlet Letter*, Introduction by Austin Warren (New York, 1954), p. 250.

[8]Saul Bellow, *Herzog* (New York, 1964), p. 201.

[9]Ernest Hemingway, *Islands in the Stream* (New York, 1970), p. 464.

[10]Bellow, *Herzog*, p. 75.

JOSEPH GOLDSTEIN

On Being Adult and Being An Adult in Secular Law

"ADULT," UNLIKE "CHILD," IS A WORD infrequently used in secular law. This may be because laws, after all, are written by adults with adults in mind. The law initially establishes for all persons—adult and child—general rights, obligations, and prohibitions. It then carves out for children certain disabilities and privileges, including the special responsibility of those adults who are parents to care for their children and to safeguard the right of each child to become an adult. Thus, law defines an adult primarily by implication: its meaning is determined by the general exceptions provided for the non-adult—the infant, the minor, the juvenile, and the unemancipated person.

Unlike the biological and psychological sciences and the "legal" systems of the great religions discussed in a previous issue of this journal, a secular legal system does not establish an ideal model for being or becoming adult. Secular law does not define "adult," rather it makes a general determination of who is to be recognized by the state as "an adult" as opposed to "a child" person. In its pure form, secular law limits itself— limits the state—to fixing minimum standards for acquiring and maintaining the status of an adult. A secular legal system, for example, does not establish rules for child-rearing to accord with some particular religious or scientific ideal. It presumes the capacity and recognizes the authority of adults to act as parents for their children in accordance with their own individual beliefs, preferences, and values. It requires only that parents meet minimal standards of child care that are negatively set in neglect, abuse, and abandonment statutes and affirmatively set in such provisions as those obligating parents to send their children to school, to keep them out of the labor market, and to have them vaccinated against smallpox. Similarly, a secular system's code of crimes holds all adult persons to minimal standards of conduct and thereby establishes wide boundaries within which each adult in law can give meaning to his own notions of being and becoming adult. The criminal law does not hold persons to the highest ethical or moral standards, nor does it compel them to be generous, kind, completely honest, or, as some might say, "adult," in their relationships with others. Rather a secular criminal law limits itself to setting standards below which no person can go without jeopardizing the free and peaceful pursuit of private and public interests which government, through law, is designed to safeguard.

To be "an adult" in the eyes of secular law, then, is not to be confused or equated with "being adult" in one's own eyes or in the eyes of one's family, teachers, friends, or of some religion, culture, science, ethic, philosophy or any combination of these or other sources of what to be adult "should" mean. With this distinction between "an adult" and "being adult," this essay examines the interrelated processes in secular law for determining what persons are to be recognized as adults and within what boundaries such persons are to be free of coercive state intervention to pursue their own individual notions of adulthood.

The Secularity of Law

Bound by a Constitution that separates church and, less clearly, science from the state, secular law is precluded from proscribing or prescribing the theories of adulthood of any particular religious, scientific, or other school. With a fundamental law that protects the right of all persons to freedom of belief, of speech, and of inquiry comes a tradition of governmental protection for each person to determine in his own way, whether it be religious, cultural, scientific, or otherwise, how to become and be adult. But secular law is never purely secular. Law, particularly that related to crime and marriage, for example, is not yet free of the vestiges of the colonial period when the settlers "equated crime with sin and thought of the state as the arm of God on earth."[1]

The notion of the separation of state and science or any other possible source of dogma does not have, as does the separation of state and church, explicit roots in the Constitution. Yet it is not implausible to suggest that the freedom of speech and religion clauses of the First Amendment would prohibit establishment by the state, in Lysenko-like fashion, of any single scientific theory, doctrine, or dogma as to what it means to be "adult," "mature," "wise," or "ethical." In *Epperson v. Arkansas*, the Supreme Court declared unconstitutional a statute which prohibited (because of a conflict with a particular religious interpretation of the Book of Genesis) the teaching in public schools and universities of Darwin's theory of evolution.[2] If the words "science" and "scientific" are substituted for, or added to, the italicized words "religion" and "religious" in the following paragraph from the Court's opinion, it becomes apparent that the notion of the separation of science and state is compatible with the purposes of the First Amendment:

> Government in our democracy, state and national, must be neutral in matters of *religious* theory, doctrine, and practice. It may not be hostile to any *religion* or to the advocacy of no-*religion*; and it may not aid, foster, or promote one *religion* or *religious* theory against another or even against the militant opposite. The First Amendment mandates governmental neutrality between *religion* and *religion*, and between *religion* and non-*religion*.[3]

It is not far-fetched to read "non-religion" and "militant opposite" to include the sciences and thus to entitle them to the neutrality that secular law guarantees to the religions.[4] Indeed, science may be less different from religion than most would care to acknowledge. In any event, the First Amendment is essential to the life of science which must always remain free of official orthodoxies and thus able to challenge and to modify the scientific truths of the moment.[5] While the notion that science and state are separate raises constitutional issues too complex to unravel in this essay, it is introduced to elaborate the distinction between the task of secular law to acknowledge the status of a person as "an adult" and the task of non-secular law to define what it means to be "adult."

Whether required by the Constitution or not, secular law is meant to protect individuals and groups, religious and non-religious, scientific and non-scientific, in their independent pursuits by word and deed freely to define and redefine the term "adult." Unlike all other dogma, the dogma which underlies a secular legal system requires the state to tolerate any dogma unless its implementation would harm another who does not share it. But in that freedom of belief and liberty to act lies an inherent threat from those who come to perceive their beliefs as the only truths. The success of a secular legal system can be measured, then, by its capacity to safeguard each person or group from the tyranny of having another's truths about what it means to be adult dictated by the state.[6] The processes for qualifying and disqualifying a person as "an adult"—free to determine for oneself what it means to be "adult"—will thus be considered with special regard for the manner and extent of the law's deviations from pure secularity.

Qualification by Chronological Age

To be an adult in law is to be not a child. To be a child in law is to be below the age of majority and thus to be dependent upon at least one adult called "parent." The rite of passage in secular law from childhood to adulthood is simple, certain, and easy to establish. A person need only reach the magic statutory age of majority to be "independent" of parental control and protection and to be presumed competent by the state to take care of himself—to make and to be responsible for his own acts and decisions.

The statutory age of majority is an age which has varied over time, which varies between states, and which, despite its generally common significance, may even vary within a state for different purposes. The traditional age of 21 seems to have its origins in, and to be linked to a time when, bearing arms meant having the physical strength "to hold up a heavy suit of armour and lift a lance or a sword at the same time."[7] Partially in response to different concerns about the capacity to bear arms, the trend since World War II has been toward lowering the age—a trend which was given great impetus with ratification in 1971 of the Twenty-sixth Amendment to the Constitution which reduces the federal voting age from 21 to 18.[8]

While still avoiding individual judgments about the capacities of specific individuals, the law also sets certain specific ages of qualification and disqualification outside and within the general age of majority. For example, economic considerations and less clearly other societal reasons based on common perceptions of maturity or expectations about risk of injury have led the law to set a lower age than majority in order to obtain a driver's license, to purchase alcoholic beverages, or to enter the job market. For reasons of assuring responsible government and out of a societal perception of an increasing capacity for "mature" judgment, the United States Constitution, for example, sets higher ages than the age of majority to be eligible for membership in the House of Representatives (25), for membership in the Senate (30), and to serve as President (35).[9] Finally, reflecting economic concerns about ensuring employment opportunities for the young and a degree of financial security for the old, the law sets ages higher than majority to receive social security and medicare benefits or to be retired from certain jobs. Such exceptions aside, when persons reach majority, whether the legislature selects 18, 19, 20, or the still more common 21, they are no longer entitled by law to depend upon their parents to provide or decide for them.[10] Nor are they subject to the parental control and the disabilities associated with being a child. They are presumed to have the capacity, *inter alia*, to make binding contracts, to hold and to dispose of property, to marry, to vote, to hold public office, to consent to, or reject, medical care, to commit crime, to make testamentary dispositions—that is, to engage in any activity and to be held responsible for it.[11] Thus, in its presumption of general competence, the law distinguishes by chronological age the person who is "an adult," though not necessarily "adult," from the person who is a child.[12]

Whatever a person's sex, creed, and color, he need only reach the chronological age of majority to be entitled to the state's basic trust in his or her capacity to decide how to exercise the rights, privileges, and obligations afforded by law, that is, to determine for himself a meaning for "adult." Such age-qualified persons need not prove to the satisfaction of parents or of some official body of "wisepersons" that they qualify for a license to be an adult; they need not pass a test for maturation or for making sound judgments or for managing their frustrations and their finances; nor need they submit themselves to any other examination designed and scaled by for-the-moment-officially-recognized experts on what it means or should mean to reach a given stage of the life cycle and to be adult. They need only, and only if their adult status is questioned, present their birth certificates or other evidence of age.

Secular law's general policy of open and automatic enrollment for adult status holds in check pressures from "expert groups" toward official orthodoxies. It safeguards each individual from the deprivations and discriminations that stem *not only* from the prejudices of the evil-meaning, who, for example, may wish to deny some the right to vote, *but also* from the rescue fantasies of the well-intentioned, who, for example, may wish to protect others from themselves by denying them the right to determine what, if any, medical care they should have. Thus, through qualification by chronological age, secular law seeks to ensure that its authority is administered with relative restraint from abuse.

In using chronological age as the mark of adulthood, secular law provides an impersonal process for acknowledging the right of all persons to become adult and to define and redefine for themselves what it means to be adult. But in so doing, it does not take a simplistic view of adulthood or of human beings. Rather it recognizes how varied is the range, both in kind and intensity, of man's religious, cultural, scientific and ethical beliefs and how overlapping and ever changing are the modes of their expression within and between generations and at all stages of the life cycle. In thus implementing its basic commitment to man's autonomy—his freedom to and his freedom from—the law not only acknowledges how complex man is, but also how limited is its own capacity for making more than gross distinctions about man's needs, his natures, and his routes of development.

However, the law's restraints on man's tendency to deny to others the right to determine for themselves their own meanings of "adult" have never been, and are not now, absolute. The law fixes limits on the ambit of choice for all age-qualified persons. It also provides procedures both for determining whether a particular individual "should" lose (or have restored) his or her status as an adult and for determining whether a particular individual "should" be entitled to choose to do something outside the generally established boundaries within which adults in general may exercise a choice. The remainder of this essay focuses first on such general restraints and then on individual case-by-case proceedings of exemption and disqualification.

General Limitations on Being Adult

The freedom of age-qualified persons to determine what they will do and what may be done to them is not unlimited. In the making and the administration of law, there is a constant tension between serving compelling state interests and safeguarding the autonomy of each person to pursue his interests as he sees them—that is, to give his own meaning to being adult without coming into conflict with the law. To the extent laws are justified less on meeting societal needs and more on a legislative, judicial, or administrative perception of a general incapacity of persons to act for themselves, the state, as *parens patriae*, treats its "adults" like children.[13]

This tension in law between expanding and contracting the ambit of choice for adults is to be found, for example, in Justice Stewart's opinion for the United States Supreme Court in the case of *Faretta v. California*.[14] The decision is concerned with whether the constitutional right of an accused to be assisted by counsel in a criminal trial includes the right of an accused to choose to represent himself. The nature of the tension is reflected dramatically in the two different ways in which Justice Stewart describes the question before the Court:

> *The question* . . . is whether a defendant . . . has a constitutional right to proceed without counsel when he voluntarily and intelligently elects to do so. *Stated another way, the question is* whether a State may constitutionally . . . force a lawyer upon him, even when he insists that he wants to conduct his own defense.[15]

Justice Stewart immediately adds: "It is not an easy question, but we have concluded that a State may not constitutionally do so."[16]

What does Justice Stewart's conclusion mean? Is it an answer to his first or second version of the question before the Court? Does it mean that the trial-court judge must presume that an accused adult who is competent to stand trial is capable of deciding what is "best" for himself and thus must honor the defendant's wish to represent himself? Or does it mean that the trial-court judge is *not* to presume that an accused who is competent to stand trial is capable of deciding what is best for himself and thus should honor such a request only if the judge, like a beneficent and knowing parent, thinks that the "child-like" defendant is making an intelligent choice? Justice Stewart's conclusion apparently applies to his second question:

> We confront here a nearly universal conviction on the part of our people as well as our courts, that forcing a lawyer upon an unwilling defendant is contrary to his basic right to defend himself if he truly wants to do so. . . . The right to defend is personal. The defendant, and not his lawyer or the State, will bear the personal consequences of a conviction. It is the defendant, therefore, who must be free personally to decide whether in his particular case counsel is to his advantage. And *although he may conduct his own defense ultimately to his own detriment, his choice must be honored out of "that respect for the individual which is the lifeblood of the law."*[17]

Giving this construction to Justice Stewart's opinion, Justice Blackmun's dissent assumes a *parens patriae* posture: "If there is any truth to the old proverb that 'one who is his own lawyer has a fool for a client,' the Court by its opinion today now bestows a *constitutional* right on one to make a fool of himself."[18]

Justice Blackmun, however, may have misread the degree of Justice Stewart's commitment to a legal process that recognizes the right of an adult "to make a fool of himself." Justice Stewart appears to qualify his commitment by adding at the close of the Court's opinion: "In order to represent himself, the accused must 'knowingly and intelligently' forego [the traditional benefits associated with the right to counsel]."[19] With the word "knowingly," Justice Stewart stresses the importance of protecting the state's interest in preserving, in fact and in appearance, the integrity of the trial process. The accused must be told of his constitutional right to counsel. He is not to be deprived by agents of the state of an opportunity to be "made aware of the 'dangers and disadvantages' of self-representation." Thus, the Court with the word "knowingly" fulfills its supervisory function over the administration of criminal justice by forcing focus on the conduct of state authorities in order to assure that they neither deny an accused access to counsel nor force him to waive counsel.

However, Justice Stewart in adding the word "intelligently" must have intended to introduce a meaning other than "knowingly." If "intelligently" means "rightly" or "wisely" as common usage would have it, then Justice Stewart appears to be inviting trial judges, as *parens patriae*, to focus on the accused and to determine the "wisdom" of his choice. Therefore, judges would not be precluded from forcing counsel upon an accused if they believed that he was not acting "intelligently," even if "knowingly." If the accused is to be treated as an adult person, if his "right" of self-decision is to be acknowledged, all that the law may require is that the trial judge provide him with an opportunity to know of his constitutional right to counsel. It may not require that the accused's choice be an intelligent, informed, and an unemotionally determined decision, but only that it be *his* choice. Out of regard for his adult status, authorities must honor that choice, even if it is a foolish one in the eyes of the state.

Minimally, the *Faretta* decision tends toward greater secularity in criminal procedure. It can be read to have a strong restraining influence on judges who are tempted to protect an accused, as if a child, from himself. The Blackmun dissent and the possible qualification of the majority opinion on the unqualified right of an accused to waive counsel reflect the constant tension in law between safeguarding an adult's freedom to manage his own affairs and yielding to parental inclinations to protect him from himself, often under the guise of a compelling state interest. The case also demonstrates the process by which courts may enlarge or reduce the area in which adult persons may work out their own meanings of being adult.

Further, in declaring the right of an accused adult to self-representation, the Court refrains from extending that right to children charged with offenses. By implication, the *Faretta* decision thus reenforces the distinction between adult and child persons in law. As persons, both adult and child are entitled to "due process" under the Constitution, one in a criminal proceeding, the other in a juvenile delinquency proceeding. But, unlike an adult, a child would be required to "accept" counsel against his wishes. Even if the child is "knowing," he is not presumed capable of "intelligently" making such a choice or of representing himself. What is not clear is whether counsel could be imposed on a child against the wishes of his parents. *In re Gault*, in which the Supreme Court extended the right to counsel to juvenile delinquency proceedings, can be read to mean that parents are not to "be relied upon to protect the infant's interests" in such proceedings.[20] Alternatively it can be read to mean only that a child in a juvenile proceeding will not be deprived of representation solely because his parents are financially unable to afford counsel. *Gault* held that: "The child and his parents must be notified of the child's right to be represented by counsel retained by them, or if they are unable to afford counsel, that counsel will be appointed to represent the child."[21]

Under either interpretation of *Gault*, the Court is reenforcing, not blurring, the distinction in law between an adult person and a child person. In expanding the rights of a child to include rights accorded an adult, *Gault* and other children's rights decisions (both legislative and administrative) acknowledge the personhood, not the adulthood, of a child. Accordingly, a child is not to be perceived as a chattel but as a person, albeit a dependent one, with civil rights to be specially safeguarded by adults. To enforce a child's rights generally entails the substitution of the state's "adult" judgment, as *parens patriae*, for the "adult" judgment of parents who are declared incompetent to protect the rights of a child as a person.

For example, Judge Murphy, for the Superior Court of the District of Columbia, authorized blood transfusions for an infant over the objections of his parents, and at the same time declined to order blood transfusions for the infant's mother, who in the face of death, refused to consent to such a medical intervention.[22] Over the objection of the "adult" parents' wishes and without regard, of course, to the infant's "wishes," Judge Murphy, as a substitute parent, decided to protect the child's right as a person to reach the age of majority, at which point he too would become entitled to make life and death decisions for himself. By implication, the Judge had found the infant's parents temporarily incompetent to care for the child, but simultaneously had acknowledged the adult status of the mother by declining to use her refusal of blood as a basis for declaring her a danger to herself and thus as incompetent as a child person to decide for herself.

The scientific "fact" that death was inevitable without transfusion was not in dispute. The issue was whether the judge and doctors, as adults with an unqualified value preference for life, could use the power of the state to impose their "adult" judgment on an adult in law whose own "adult" judgment gave greater weight to another preference. On behalf of the adult person the answer was "no"; on behalf of the child person the answer was "yes." The court avoided mistaking as a scientific fact the doctor's preference for life. It recognized that the law cannot find in any science the moral, political, or social values upon which to base its decision.[23] It honored the mother's refusal to consent because the refusal rested on her constitutionally protected religious beliefs. Full respect for any age-qualified person as an adult would entitle such a person in a purely secular legal system to refuse medical assistance without explanation or for reasons not tied to a religious belief or for reasons incomprehensible or personally unacceptable to judge or doctor. But even secular law will not allow such adults as parents to exercise their religious freedom to choose not to protect the right of their children to life. Because they are presumed incompetent to care for themselves, children cannot be denied their right as persons to an opportunity to become adult persons; they will then be presumed competent and entitled to accept or reject death, at least for religious reasons, as an alternative to proven medical care.

The goals of the children's rights movement are not to be confused with those of the civil rights movements. The "minority" movements seek to achieve, for example, equal protection and rights for black and female *child* persons, on the one hand, and for black and female *adult* persons, on the other. In their efforts to gain further recognition for the personhood of both adults and children, those movements buttress, rather than undercut, distinctions in law between an adult and a child.[24]

However, the state, as *parens patriae*, often blurs the distinction between a child and an adult by limiting the range of opportunities for self-determination associated with adulthood. For example, the law has denied "consent" to age-qualified adults to form or join organizations for negotiating their terms of employment; to marry more than one person at the same time or to marry a person of the same sex; to divorce a spouse without "good" (acceptable-to-the-state) cause; to use contraceptives, alcohol, or drugs; to declare certain sexual preferences and remain in the armed services; to gamble; to contribute unlimited amounts to finance political campaigns; to possess obscene material; to perform or have an abortion; and to choose to die. The purpose of the list is not solely to illustrate the law's potential for deviating from secularity nor to identify areas of human activity which may be beyond the actual capacity of law to control. It is introduced primarily to demonstrate the nature of boundaries which law has often set to restrict the area in which age-qualified persons may determine, without fear of reprisal by the state, their own individual expressions of being or becoming adult. Conversely in repealing or declaring unconstitutional such restrictions, the law enlarges the area of individual expression and hence becomes more secular.[25]

Individual Modification of Adult Status

In its struggle to meet not necessarily separate or equal commitments to protecting societal interests and safeguarding each adult's freedom to be autonomous, secular law tends to be ambivalent. That ambivalence remains operative even after the law has fixed, at least for the moment, the boundaries to free expression. Not only does the state, as *parens patriae*, find it difficult "to really let go" (as do many parents), but it also has second thoughts about the wisdom of its own decisions. In part out of recognition of the inherent conflict in its dual mandate, secular law seeks to avoid the brittleness that comes with absolutes by establishing processes for either exempting or disqualifying age-qualified persons from certain legal duties or rights. This section considers first the processes of *exemption*, that is, procedures for allowing certain adults because of some compelling personal justification to choose to act outside the lawful boundaries set for all adults. Next it discusses briefly the processes of *disqualification*, that is, procedures for denying adults because of "incompetence" their right to pursue activities within the lawful boundaries set for all adults.

PERSONAL EXEMPTION

Recognition of conscientious objection as a basis for exempting an individual from combat illustrates one way of expanding the limits in law to being adult in the eyes of one's self. As Harlan Fiske Stone observed in 1919:

> Both morals and sound policy require that the state should not violate the conscience of the individual. All our history gives confirmation to the view that liberty of conscience has a moral and social value which makes it worthy of preservation at the hands of the state. So deep in its significance and vital, indeed, is it to the integrity of man's moral and spiritual nature that nothing short of the self-preservation of the state should warrant its violation; and it may well be questioned whether the state which preserves its life by a settled policy of violation of the conscience of the individual will not in fact ultimately lose it by the process.[26]

In 1965, in *United States v. Seeger*,[27] the Supreme Court adopted the Stone position. The Court rejected government efforts to restrict conscientious exemptions to those based upon the tenets of an organized religion. *Seeger* extended the secularity of the draft law by virtually obliterating the previously critical distinction between a "religious" and a "merely personal moral" belief in pacifism. Thus agents of the state are precluded from substituting their personal meaning of "religious belief" for that of an individual objector:

> We recognize the difficulties that have always faced the trier of fact in these cases. . . . While the applicant's words may differ, the test is simple of application. It is essentially an objective one, namely, does the claimed belief occupy the same place in the life of the objector as an orthodox belief in God holds in the life of one clearly qualified for exemption?
>
> Moreover, it must be remembered that in resolving these exemption problems one deals with the beliefs of different individuals who will articulate them in a multitude of ways. In such an intensely personal area, of course, the claim of the registrant that his belief is an essential part of a religious faith must be given great weight. . . . *The validity of what he believes cannot be questioned.* Some theologians, and indeed some examiners, might be tempted to question the existence of the registrant's "Supreme Being" or the truth of his concepts. But these are inquiries foreclosed to Government. . . . Local boards and courts in this sense are not free to reject beliefs because they consider them "incomprehensible." Their task is to decide whether the beliefs professed by a registrant are sincerely held and whether they are, in his own scheme of things, religious.[28]

Subsequently, in *United States v. Sisson*,[29] Federal District Court Judge Wyzanski elaborated the *Seeger* Court's expansive construction of a conscientious objector's right to exemption:

> Some suppose that the only reliable conscience is one responsive to a formal religious community of memory and hope. But in *Religion in the Making*, Alfred North Whitehead taught us that "religion is what the individual does with his own solitariness."
>
> Others fear that recognition of individual conscience will make it too easy for the individual to perpetrate a fraud. . . .
>
> *Seeger* cut the ground from under that argument. So does experience. Often it is harder to detect a fraudulent adherent to a religious creed than to recognize a sincere moral protestant. . . . We all can discern Thoreau's integrity more quickly than we might detect some churchman's hypocrisy.
>
> There have been suggestions that to read the Constitution as granting an exemption from combat duty in a foreign campaign will immunize from public regulation all acts or refusals to act dictated by religious or conscientious scruple. Such suggestions fail to note that there is no need to treat, and this court does not treat, religious liberty as an absolute. The most sincere religious or conscientious believer may be validly punished even if in strict pursuance of his creed or principles, he fanatically assassinates an opponent, or practices polygamy, . . . or employs child labor. . . . Religious liberty and liberty of conscience have limits in the face of social demands of a community of fellow citizens. There are, for example, important rival claims of safety, order, health, and decency.[30]

In this way Judge Wyzanski resisted the temptation to assume a *parens patriae* stance and avoided the nonsecular pressures which subsequently were fully undercut by Congress's decision to make service in the armed forces voluntary.

The private-school exemption in the compulsory-education law offers another illustration of the law's effort to preserve for adults an opportunity for self expression. This concern for secularity was extended, though with a more restrictive definition of religion than it had adopted in *Seeger*, by the Supreme Court in *Wisconsin v. Yoder*.[31] The Court, in effect, exempted Amish parents from a general obligation, imposed by Wisconsin law, to send their children to public or private school until age 16. The

Yoders and other members of the Amish Church refused to send their 14- and 15-year-old children to public school after the eighth grade. Further, they would not enroll them in a private school so as to qualify for an exemption under the compulsory-education law. They claimed that the criminal provision compelling attendance violated their religious rights under the First and Fourteenth Amendments. The Court sought to balance what appear to be two competing goals—one, a compelling state interest to assure for all children an educational opportunity essential to becoming "self-reliant and self-sufficient" adults; the other, to preserve "doctrinal flexibility" at the boundaries by protecting the right of "self-reliant and self-sufficient" parents, as adults, to determine in accord with their religious beliefs how to educate their children to become adult in the eyes of their church. The dynamic tension in this conflict, the complexity of maintaining the secular quality of the legal system, the distinctions between persons in law as adults and as children, as well as being adult or child-like in the eyes of one's self or one's church, and the way in which the state as *parens patriae*, may impinge upon self-expression by age-qualified persons are encapsulated in excerpts from the opinion by Chief Justice Burger for the Court:

"Old Order Amish communities today are characterized by a fundamental belief that salvation requires life in a church community separate and apart from the world and worldly influence. This concept of life aloof from the world and its values is central to their faith.

"A related feature of Old Order Amish communities is their devotion to a life in harmony with nature and the soil, as exemplified by the simple life of the early Christian era that continued in America during much of our early national life. Amish beliefs require members of the community to make their living by farming or closely related activities. Broadly speaking, the Old Order Amish religion pervades and determines the entire mode of life of its adherents. Their conduct is regulated in great detail by the *Ordnung*, or rules, of the church community. Adult baptism, which occurs in late adolescence, is the time at which Amish young people voluntarily undertake heavy obligations, not unlike the Bar Mitzvah of the Jews, to abide by the rules of the church community.

"Amish objection to formal education beyond the eighth grade is firmly grounded in these central religious concepts. They object to the high school and higher education generally because the values it teaches are in marked variance with Amish values and the Amish way of life; they view secondary school education as an impermissible exposure of their children to a 'worldy' influence in conflict with their beliefs. The high school tends to emphasize intellectual and scientific accomplishments, self-distinction, competitiveness, worldly success, and social life with other students. Amish society emphasizes informal learning-through-doing, a life of 'goodness,' rather than a life of intellect, wisdom, rather than technical knowledge, community welfare rather than competition, and separation, rather than integration with contemporary worldly society.

"Formal high school education beyond the eighth grade is contrary to Amish beliefs not only because it places Amish children in an environment hostile to Amish beliefs but also because it takes them away from their community, physically and emotionally, during the crucial and formative adolescent period of life. During this period, the children must acquire Amish attitudes favoring manual work and self-reliance and the specific skills needed to perform the adult role of an Amish farmer or housewife. They must learn to enjoy physical labor. Once a child has learned basic reading, writing, and elementary mathematics, these traits, skills, and attitudes admittedly fall within the category of those best learned through example and 'doing' rather than in a classroom. And, at this time in life, the Amish child must also grow in his faith and his relationship to the Amish community if he is to be prepared to accept the heavy obligations imposed by adult baptism. . . .

"There is no doubt as to the power of a State, having a high responsibility for education of its citizens, to impose reasonable regulations for the control and duration of basic education. . . . Providing public schools ranks at the very apex of the function of a State. Yet even this paramount responsibility . . . yield[s] to the right of parents to provide an equivalent education in a privately operated system. . . . [A] State's interest in universal education, however highly we rank it, is not totally free from a balancing process when it impinges on other fundamental rights and interests, such as those specifically protected by the Free Exercise Clause of the First Amendment and the traditional interest of parents with respect to the religious upbringing of their children so long as they . . . 'prepare [them] for additional obligations'. . . .

"It follows that in order for Wisconsin to compel school attendance beyond the eighth grade against a claim that such attendance interferes with the practice of a legitimate religious belief, it must appear either that the State does not deny the free exercise of religious belief by its requirement, or that there is a state interest of sufficient magnitude to override the interest claiming protection under the Free Exercise Clause.

"A way of life, however virtuous and admirable, may not be interposed as a barrier to reasonable state regulation of education if it is based on purely secular considerations; to have the protection of the Religion Clauses, the claims must be rooted in religious belief. Although a determination of what is a 'religious' belief or practice entitled to constitutional protection may present a most delicate question, the very concept of ordered liberty precludes allowing every person to make his own standards on matters of conduct in which society as a whole has important interests. Thus, if the Amish asserted their claims because of their subjective evaluation and rejection of the contemporary secular values accepted by the majority, much as Thoreau rejected the social values of his time and isolated himself at Walden Pond, their claim would not rest on a religious basis. Thoreau's choice was philosophical and personal rather than religious, and such belief does not rise to the demands of the Religion Clauses.

"Giving no weight to such secular considerations, however, we see that the record in this case abundantly supports the claim that the traditional way of life of the Amish is not merely a matter of personal preference, but one of deep religious conviction, shared by an organized group, and intimately related to daily living. . . .

"The impact of the compulsory-attendance law on respondents' practice of the Amish religion is not only severe, but inescapable, for the Wisconsin law affirmatively compels them, under threat of criminal sanction, to perform acts undeniably at odds with fundamental tenets of their religious beliefs. . . . It carries with it precisely the kind of objective danger to the free exercise of religion that the First Amendment was designed to prevent. [The Amish] must either abandon belief and be assimilated into society at large, or be forced to migrate to some other and more tolerant religion. . . .

"The court must not ignore the danger that an exception from a general obligation of citizenship on religious grounds may run afoul of the Establishment Clause, but that danger cannot be allowed to prevent any exception no matter how vital it may be to the protection of values promoted by the right of free exercise. By preserving doctrinal flexibility and recognizing the need for a sensible and realistic application of the Religion Clauses

> . . . we have been able to chart a course that preserved the autonomy and freedom of religious bodies while avoiding any semblance of established religion. This is a "tight rope" and one we have successfully traversed. Walz v. Tax Commission, supra, at 672. . . .

"We must not forget that in the Middle Ages important values of the civilization of the Western World were preserved by members of religious orders who isolated themselves from all worldly influences against great obstacles. There can be no assumption that today's majority is 'right' and the Amish and others like them are 'wrong.' A way of life that is odd or even erratic but interferes with no rights or interests of others is not to be condemned because it is different. . . .

"Indeed, the Amish communities singularly parallel and reflect many of the virtues of Jefferson's ideal of the 'sturdy yeoman' who would form the basis of what he considered as the ideal of a democratic society. Even [the] idiosyncratic separateness [of the Amish] exemplifies the diversity we profess to admire and encourage.

"[While Jefferson recognized that education was essential to the welfare and liberty of the people, he was reluctant to directly force instruction of children 'in opposition to the will of the parent.' Instead he proposed that state citizenship be conditioned on the ability to 'read readily in some tongue, native or acquired.']

". . . the State . . . argues that a decision exempting Amish children from the State's requirement fails to recognize the substantive right of the Amish child to a secondary education, and fails to give due regard to the power of the State as *parens patriae* to extend the benefit of secondary education to children regardless of the wishes of their parents. . . .

"Contrary to the suggestion of the dissenting opinion of Mr. Justice Douglas, our holding today in no degree depends on the assertion of the religious interest of the child as contrasted with that of the parents. It is the parents who are subject to prosecution here for failing to cause their children to attend school, and it is their right of free exercise, not that of their children, that must determine Wisconsin's power to impose criminal penalties on the parent. The dissent argues that a child who expresses a desire to attend public high school in conflict with the wishes of his parents should not be prevented from doing so. There is no reason for the Court to consider that point since it is not an issue in the case. The children are not parties to this litigation. The State has at no point tried this case on the theory that [parents] were preventing their chidren from attending school against their expressed desires, and indeed the record is to the contrary. The State's position from the outset has been that it is empowered to apply its compulsory-attendance law to Amish parents in the same manner as to other parents—that is, without regard to the wishes of the child. That is the claim we reject today.

"Our holding in no way determines the proper resolution of possible competing interests of parents, children and the State in an appropriate state court proceeding in which the power of the State is asserted on the theory that Amish parents are preventing their minor children from attending high school despite their expressed desires to the contrary. Recognition of the claim of the State in such a proceeding would, of course, call into question traditional concepts of parental control over the religious upbringing and education of their minor children recognized in this Court's past decisions. It is clear that such an intrusion by a State into family decisions in the area of religious training would give rise to grave questions of religious freedom comparable to those raised here. . . .

"The State's argument . . . appears to rest on the potential that exemption of Amish parents from the requirements of the compulsory-education law might allow some parents to act contrary to the best interests of their children by foreclosing their opportunity to make an intelligent choice between the Amish way of life and that of the outside world. The same argument could, of course, be made with respect to all church schools short of college. . . .

"Indeed, it seems clear that if the State is empowered, as *parens patriae*, to 'save' a child from himself or his Amish parents by requiring an additional two years of compulsory formal high school education, the State will in large measure influence, if not determine, the religious future of the child. . . . This case involves the fundamental interest of parents, as contrasted with that of the State, to guide the religious future and education of their children. That the history and culture of Western civilization reflect a strong tradition of parental concern for the nurture and upbringing of their children is now established beyond debate as an enduring American tradition. . . .

"To be sure, the power of the parent, even when linked to a free exercise claim, may be subject to limitation . . . if it appears that parental decisions will jeopardize the health or safety of the child, or have a potential for significant social burdens. But in this case, the Amish have introduced persuasive evidence undermining the arguments the State has advanced to support its claims in terms of the welfare of the child and society as a whole. . . .

"In the face of our consistent emphasis on the central values underlying the Religion Clauses in our constitutional scheme of government, we cannot accept a *parens patriae* claim of such all-encompassing scope and with such sweeping potential for broad and unforeseeable application as that urged by the State.

"For the reasons stated we hold, with the Supreme Court of Wisconsin, that the First and Fourteenth Amendments prevent the State from compelling respondents to cause their children to attend formal high school to age 16. Our disposition of this case, however, in no way alters our recognition of the obvious fact that courts are not school boards or legislatures, and are ill-equipped to determine the 'necessity' of discrete aspects of a State's program of compulsory education. This should suggest that courts must move with great circumspection in performing the sensitive and delicate task of weighing a State's legitimate social concern when faced with religious claims for exemption from generally applicable educational requirements. It cannot be overemphasized that we are not dealing with a way of life and mode of education by a group claiming to have recently discovered some 'progressive' or more enlightened process for rearing children for modern life."[32]

In *Yoder*, the Court appears to have increased slightly, but only slightly, the secularity of the law of compulsory education. In extending to Amish parents the right to a religious claim of exemption, it held the rope tight. Unlike the conscientious-objector decisions, *Yoder* limited the exemption to members of long-recognized organized religions. The Court did not construe protected religious beliefs to include beliefs which "occupy the same place in the life of the [claimant] as an orthodox belief in God holds in the life of one clearly qualified for exemption." In explicitly excluding the likes of a Thoreau from an exemption, the Court refused to secularize compulsory-education laws to the degree it had secularized the draft law. As Kurland has observed: "The Court [in Yoder] holds no truck with contemporaries who would also aspire to return to an agrarian democracy without interference by the states. It matters not how conscientious the belief of the moderns may be, only an established church can lend support to a claim of religious freedom."[33]

For the Court to extend its exemption to the sincerely held belief of any parent— or, as Justice Douglas might have it in his dissent, to the belief of the adolescent student—would put too great a strain on the compelling interest of the state in the education of children. Consequently, responding to such tension—which after all is the source of all exemptions—the Court could not (as the Chief Justice has claimed) have successfully "traversed the tightrope" between *promoting* the Amish religion in violation of the First Amendment's establishment clause and *preserving* the rights of Amish adults to the exercise of their religious beliefs in accord with the First Amendment's freedom clause. To protect the freedom of the Amish to give their own meaning to becoming and being adult, without extending the exemption to others whose beliefs cannot be attributed to, and justified by, membership in an ancient organized group, is to give preference, *to establish*, one religion over others. But not to give even such limited exemptions would be to assert the power of the state over the autonomy of some individuals to whom the compelling state interest need not apply.

Despite, then, the difference in the breadth of the exemptions for the draft and for compulsory education, the function of exemptions is the same. The exemption minimizes intrusions on individual autonomy which by definition must be sacrificed for some compelling state interest. Thus secular law responds to tensions which can never be fully eliminated by placing the burden of establishing entitlement to an exemption from a legal obligation or prohibition upon the adult or group of adults who challenge the too confining boundary to their being adult.

PERSONAL DISQUALIFICATION

In proceedings of disqualification, however, the burden properly shifts to the state or to some private challenger to overcome the general presumption of capacity and authority of a particular age-qualified person to determine his own course within the bounds set by law. These proceedings are in essence non-secular. They rest not upon scientific "fact," but primarily upon vague and ambiguous psychiatric models of normality and abnormality.[34] In effect the state has *established* psychiatry. Its teach- ings are used to justify declaring an adult no longer competent to give his own expression to being adult. He is classified incompetent to care for himself, to manage property, to contract to marry, to divorce, to be a parent, to stand trial, to serve on a jury, to vote, to hold public office, to commit a crime, to be executed, or to make a valid will. The population of adults, or the ambit of choice for some of them, is thereby reduced under statutes which entitle the state as *parens patriae* to adjudge age- qualified persons "incompetent by reason of mental illness, sickness, drunkenness, excessive use of drugs, insanity, or other mental or physical condition."[35]

The "harmless incompetent" may be placed, like a child, in the custody, care, and control of an adult guardian. Moreover, those "adults" whom the state declares, in accord with the established science, to be either "dangerous to self" (undefined) or "dangerous to others" (undefined) may be incarcerated indefinitely "to prevent self-injury or violence to others."[36] These processes for disqualification, including provisions for restoring an adult's "competence," are inherently offensive to individual autonomy. Such procedures deviate from the goals of a purely secular system in the same way, but not as massively, as would a procedure for individually qualifying each person for adult status, rather than automatically admitting him to that status at a statutorily fixed chronological age.

In *O'Connor v. Donaldson*, the Supreme Court accepted the claim of an involuntarily incarcerated age-qualified person against a hospital staff for "having intentionally and maliciously deprived him of his constitutional right to liberty."[37] The case illustrates not only the inherent dangers of individualized disqualification and requalification procedures, but also the extent to which the Court has begun to recognize violations of constitutional rights in the administration of such "nonsecular" laws. On the initiation of his father, who believed his 49-year-old son was suffering from "delusions," Kenneth Donaldson was found by a county judge to be suffering from "paranoid schizophrenia" and was indefinitely committed to confinement in a state mental hospital in 1957. He was held against his will for fifteen years, even though he had posed no danger to others during his long confinement or at any other time in his life. Donaldson's confinement was a simple regime of enforced custodial care, not a program designed to alleviate or cure his supposed illness. The jury returned a verdict for Donaldson and awarded compensatory as well as punitive damages. The Court of Appeals affirmed the judgment. It held that a person who is confined against his will at a state mental institution has "a constitutional right to receive such individual treatment as will give him a reasonable opportunity to be cured or to improve his mental condition."[38] Conversely, the Court of Appeals implied that it is constitutionally permissible for a state to confine a mentally ill person against his will in order to treat his illness, even if his illness only renders him dangerous to himself, not others.

In his opinion for the Supreme Court, Justice Stewart concluded that the *Donaldson* case did not raise "the difficult issues of constitutional law" decided by the Court of Appeals. He wrote:

> Specifically, there is no reason now to decide whether mentally ill persons dangerous to themselves or to others have a right to treatment. . . . As we view it, this case raises a single, relatively simple, but nonetheless important question concerning every man's constitutional right to liberty. . . .
> A finding of "mental illness" alone cannot justify a State's locking a person up against his will and keeping him indefinitely in simple custodial confinement. Assuming that that term can be given a reasonably precise content and that the "mentally ill" can be identified with reasonable accuracy, there is still no constitutional basis for confining such persons involuntarily if they are dangerous to no one and can live safely in freedom.
> May the State confine the mentally ill merely to ensure them a living standard superior to what they enjoy in the private community? That the State has a proper interest in providing care and assistance to the unfortunate goes without saying. But the mere presence of mental illness does not disqualify a person from preferring his home to the comforts of an institution. Moreover, while the State may arguably confine a person to save him from harm, incarceration is rarely if ever a necessary condition for raising the living standards of those capable of surviving safely in freedom, on their own or with the help of family or friends.
> May the State fence in the harmless mentally ill solely to save its citizens from

exposure to those whose ways are different? One might as well ask if the State, to avoid public unease, could incarcerate all who are physically unattractive or socially eccentric. Mere public intolerance or animosity cannot constitutionally justify the deprivation of a person's physical liberty. . . .

In short, a State cannot constitutionally confine without more a nondangerous individual *who is capable of surviving safely in freedom by himself or with the help of willing and responsible family members or friends.* Since the jury found, upon ample evidence, that O'Connor, as an agent of the State, knowingly did so confine Donaldson, it properly concluded that O'Connor violated Donaldson's constitutional right to freedom.[39]

In *Donaldson* the Court questions the constitutionality of only a small part of the mental-health law's processes for disqualification. The state may continue to deprive an adult of his right to determine for himself whether he can "survive safely in freedom," whether he needs "the help of . . . family members or friends," or whether he should enter a mental hospital. Adopting the myth of mental illness and using the official science for predicting an undefined harm to self or others, the state may continue to make a dependent out of an adult who, by definition, is an independent. Under mental-health law the state is thus left with authority, despite Justice Stewart's observations, to impose its will on "unattractive" or "eccentric" adults whom it cannot disqualify under the criminal law which establishes the bounds to lawful conduct. To protect the adult status of all age-qualified persons, criminal law, unlike mental-health law, requires the state to presume an individual's innocence, his entitlement to adult status, until it has established beyond a reasonable doubt that the individual accused caused a statutorily defined harm. Unlike mental-health law, the criminal law cannot disqualify an adult simply because of his status and a prediction of the likelihood of his causing harm which has not been defined and, even if it were, which has not occurred.[40]

Thus *Donaldson* leaves standing processes for disqualification which subvert the secular supports of criminal law and which violate individual autonomy and affront human dignity. Yet, in terms of secularity, processes of *disqualification* which deny adult status to those whom the established science declares to be sick, dangerous, abnormal, or otherwise unacceptable are to be preferred to processes of *qualification* which deny adult status to each person until the established science certifies that he is normal and competent to manage his own affairs.

Conclusion

From the start, this examination of the relationship between being "an adult" in secular law and being "adult" in one's own eyes was destined to be less than complete and to be easily misunderstood. The law is too big and too various and the notion of adult is too vague and too subject to the independent fantasies of the writer and the reader to reduce their relationships—if any—to the dimension of a single essay.

The misunderstanding to be avoided is the attribution to the legal system of a magic it does not have. Many distinguished dissenters and civil disobedients have demonstrated that law, no matter how restrictive and demeaning, is limited in its capacity to destroy or bend to its will a person's sense of self. Moreover, no matter how tolerant and respectful law may be of the "deviant," "sick," or "strange," it is not capable of giving to each person an adult sense of self. To be an adult in law is not necessarily to be adult. And to be a child or dependent in law is not necessarily not to be adult. But to acknowledge this is not to suggest that law makes no difference or that legal systems cannot be distinguished in terms of the extent of their secularity. Rather such an observation should serve to emphasize the importance of recognizing how complex and frail are the processes in secular law for both safeguarding societal needs and preventing one person's truth from becoming another person's tyranny.*

*I wish to acknowledge the research assistance of Donn Pickett and the substantive and editorial assistance of Mr. Pickett and Lon Babby, both students at the Yale Law School. I am also indebted to Bruce A. Ackerman, Meir Cohen, Owen M. Fiss, Sonja Goldstein and Burke Marshall for their assistance.

REFERENCES

[1]Nelson, "Emerging Notions of Modern Criminal Law in the Revolutionary Era," *New York University Law Review*, 42 (1967), pp. 450-51. Cf. "Vatican Statements on Sexual Ethics," *New York Times*, January 16, 1976, p. 11, col. 1: "Christian doctrine . . . states that every genital act must be within the framework of marriage. Experience teaches us that love must find its safeguard in the stability of marriage if sexual intercourse is truly to respond to the requirements of its own finality and to those of human dignity. These requirements call for a conjugal contract sanctioned and guaranteed by society."

[2]393 U.S. 97 (1968). *Accord* Daniel v. Waters, 515 F.2d 485 (6th Cir. 1975), holding unconstitutional a 1973 Arkansas statute requiring textbooks relating to the origin of man to include a disclaimer that its explanation is a theory and "is not represented to be scientific fact," to include equal accounts of the Genesis theory, and to exclude "the teaching of all occult or satanical beliefs of human origin."

[3]*Ibid.*, at 103-04. Cf. Meek v. Pittenger, 421 U.S. 349, 358 (1975). The Court described the first part of a three-part test to judge the constitutionality of state aid to non-public schools as "First, the statute must have a *secular* [emphasis added] legislative purpose."

[4]This view would appear to be buttressed by the Supreme Court in Turner v. Department of Employment Security, U.S. 96 S. Ct. 249 (1975), (*per Curiam*). The Court rejected the State's claim of authority to refuse unemployment benefits to women during the last three months of pregnancy and first six weeks following delivery simply because it presumed that all such women are unable to work. In holding that the presumption violated the Fourteenth Amendment, the Court overturned a Utah court's ruling in which the pregnant applicant was advised that: "What she should do is work for the repeal of the biological law of nature. She should get it amended so that men shared equally with women in bearing children. If she could prevail upon the Great Creator to so order things, she would be guilty of violating the equal protection of the law unless she saw to it that man could also share in the thrill and glory of Motherhood. . . . In the matter of pregnancy there is no way to find equality between men and women. The Great Creator ordained the difference, and there are few women who would wish to change the situation" (531 P.2d 870-71 [Utah 1975]).

[5]This construction of the First Amendment is reflected in the Court's strong support for academic freedom. See, e.g., Keyishian v. Board of Regents, 385 U.S. 589, 603 (1967): "Our Nation is deeply committed to safeguarding academic freedom which is of transcendant value to all of us . . ."; Sweezy v. New Hampshire, 354 U.S. 234, 250 (1957): "To impose any strait jacket upon the intellectual leaders in our colleges and universities would imperil the future of our Nation." Indeed, the protection afforded by the First Amendment against government efforts to "homogenize" either by political or other dogma is far-reaching. Note, "Alien's Right to Teach: Political Socialization and the Public Schools," *Yale Law Journal*, 85 (1975), p. 90. See also T. Emerson, *The System of Freedom of Expression* (1970), p. 7: "[The principle of freedom of expression] carries beyond the political realm. It embraces the right to participate in the building of the whole culture, and includes freedom of expression in religion, literature, art, *science*, and all of the areas of human learning and knowledge [emphasis supplied]."

[6]A. Bickel, *The Morality of Consent* (New Haven, 1975), p. 141: "In the end perhaps the revolutionaries will unmask themselves. The faith embodied in the First Amendment is not only that in a free society few will want to make a revolution, but that where the revolutionary idea may be freely ventilated it will defeat itself. The answers are obvious: those of us who insist on striving and on swilling beer don't really know what we want, and the revolution would enable us freely to want what we should. And we would not be dancing in the streets all the time but fulfilling ourselves at play and at work. Those of us who play too much would be told gently, persuasively, but in the end firmly by our new leaders (positioned not above us, but side-by-side with us) that for our own and the common good we ought to work more and play less. And we would do it gladly, for the society would be ours, not the CIA's, as it is now. When we work, we will do the work that fulfills us, not some task to which we have been arbitrarily assigned, and if we fall into some individual error about what work really does fulfill us, we will be shown our mistake, we will see it, and proceed to do what we ought to do. It all rings true. Such a system can surely be built. It is only that there is a name for the means that must be employed to create that system and maintain it. That name is tyranny. . . ."

[7]*Report of the Committee on the Age of Majority*, #38, p. 21 (Cmd. 3342), (1965), (hereinafter *Report*).

[8]See generally, Council of State Governments, *The Age of Majority* (1972).

[9]Art. I, Sec. 2; Art. I, Sec. 3; Art. II, Sec. 1. Interestingly the Constitution sets no special qualifying age for justices of the Supreme Court.

[10]In some jurisdictions the population of adults also may include persons who marry below the statutory age. And in some jurisdictions partial emancipation may be accorded children who become pregnant and wish to determine without regard to parental wishes whether or not to obtain an abortion. See, e.g., Ballard v. Anderson, 4 Cal 3d 873, 484 P.2d 1345, 95 Cal R. 1 (1971).

[11]*Report*, Appendix 7 (and 3344).

[12]The British Committee adopted the following guides to the selection of an age of majority. "The law should . . . be amended to ensure that: (1) no child or young person is in any way restricted in his or her capacity or independence as a citizen solely for the benefit of any other person or persons, and (2) young persons should be protected, by legal incapacity to act independently, from having attributed to them legal responsibility likely to be unduly burdensome to a person of that age. . . ," *Report*.

[13]"The concept of *parens patriae* is derived from the English constitutional system. As the system developed from its feudal beginnings, the king retained certain duties and powers, which were referred to as the "royal prerogative." Malina and Blechman, "Parens Patriae Suits for Treble Damages Under the Antitrust Laws," *Northwestern University Law Review*, 65 (1970), pp. 193, 197; "Parens Patriae Suits for Damages," *Columbia Journal of Legal and Social Problems*, 6 (1970), pp. 411, 412. These powers and duties were said to be exercised by the king in his capacity as "father of the country." Traditionally, the term was used to refer to the king's power as guardian of persons under legal disabilities to act for themselves" (Hawaii v. Standard Oil Co., 405 U.S. 251, 257 [1971]). "This prerogative of *parens patriae* is inherent in the supreme power of every State, whether that power is lodged in a royal person or in the legislature, and has no affinity to those arbitrary powers which are sometimes exerted by irresponsible monarchs to the great detriment of the people and the destruction of their liberties. On the contrary, it is a most beneficient function, and often necessary to be exercised in the interests of humanity, and for the prevention of injury to those who cannot protect themselves. . . . This beneficient function has not ceased to exist under the change of government from a monarchy to a republic; . . . it now resides in the legislative department, ready to be called into exercise whenever required for the purposes of justice and right . . ." (Mormon Church v. United States, 136 U.S. 1, 57-58 [1889]).

[14]422 U.S. 806 (1975).

[15]*Ibid.*, at 807 (emphasis added).

[16]*Ibid.*

[17]*Ibid.*, 817, 834 (emphasis added). Cf. United States v. Denno, 348 F.2d 12, 15, (2d Cir. 1965): "Even in cases where the accused is harming himself by insisting on conducting his own defense, respect for individual autonomy requires that he be allowed to go to jail under his own banner if he so desires and if he makes the choice 'with his eyes open.' "

[18]422 U.S. at 852 (emphasis in original).

[19]*Ibid.*, at 835.

[20]387 U.S. 1, 35 (1967).

[21]*Ibid.*, at 41.

[22]In re Pogue (D. C. Super. Ct., Nov. 12, 1974), in *Washington Post*, November 14, 1974, at Cl. col. 1. See Erickson v. Dilgard, 44 Misc. 2d 27, 28, 252 N.Y.S. 2d 705, 706 (Sup. Ct. 1962), refusing to order blood transfusion over patient's objection: "The court concludes that it is the individual who is the subject of a medical decision who has the final say and that this must necessarily be so in a system of government which gives the greatest possible protection to the individual in the furtherance of his own desires". But see Application of President and Directors of Georgetown College, 331 F.2d 1000 (D.C. Cir., 1964), *cert. den.* 377 U.S. 978 (1964) and State ex rel Swann v. Pack, 527 S.W. 2d 99 (Tenn. Sup. Ct. 1975) cert. den., 44 U.S.L.W. 3501 (March 9, 1976), in which the court, after holding that the Holiness Church of God in Jesus' Name "is a constitutionally protected religious group" (*ibid.*, at 107), held that the state could prohibit a ritual which called for the handling of poisonous snakes and the drinking of strychnine poison. It observed: "Yes, the state has a right to protect a person from himself and to demand that he protect his own life . . ." (*ibid.*, at 113).

[23]J. Goldstein, "Psychoanalysis and Jurisprudence," *Yale Law Journal*, 77 (1968), pp. 1053, 1059. The expansion of the opportunity for individual choice is often accompanied by restrictions which reflect nonsecular resistances to the loosening of legal boundaries. In declaring unconstitutional laws making abortion a crime, the Supreme Court, for example, enlarged the range of lawful choices for pregnant women and their physicians. At the same time, the Court authorized states to limit such free choice to the first trimester of a pregnancy in the light of currently acceptable medical "fact." Roe v. Wade, 410 U.S. 113 (1973). Justice Blackmun, in his opinion for the Court, limits, but does not eliminate, the authority of states to treat pregnant women (and their attending physicians) as children who are incompetent to determine for themselves as adults what course to pursue with regard to the pregnancy. He cloaks in science his personal preference and thus obscures that law cannot find in science the values upon which to base its decisions:

"With respect to the State's important and legitimate interest in the health of the mother, the 'compelling' point, in the light of present medical knowledge, is at approximately the end of the first trimester. This is so because of the now established medical fact . . . that until the end of the first trimester mortality in abortion is less than mortality in normal childbirth. It follows that, from and after this point, a State may regulate the abortion procedure to the extent that the regulation reasonably relates to the preservation and protection of maternal health. . . .

"This means, on the other hand, that, for the period of pregnancy prior to this 'compelling' point, the attending physician, in consultation with his patient, is free to determine, without regulation by the State, that in his medical judgment the patient's pregnancy should be terminated. If that decision is reached, the judgment may be effectuated by an abortion free of interference by the State." *Id.* at 163.

Thus a state, except during the first three months of pregnancy, continues to have the authority, in effect, to substitute what it thinks is best for a particular potential mother's well being for what she and her physician as age-qualified persons, as adults, prefer. Only to an extremely limited extent, then, does the Court enlarge in its abortion decision the area of an adult's choice to give meaning to being adult.

[24]Exceptions are now being acknowledged to the presumed incompetence of children in the form of medical emancipation, especially in late adolescence. See, e.g., Ballard v. Anderson, *supra*, note 10, construing the California abortion statute to permit minors to obtain therapeutic abortions without parental consent; Melville v. Sabbatino, 313 A.2d 886, 30 Conn. Supp. 320 (Super. Ct. 1973), construing Conn. Gen. Stat. Ann. 17-187 (1963) to permit minors sixteen and over, despite parental objection, to exercise the rights of voluntary adult patients to demand release from a mental hospital. For our purposes, then, the child is perceived as an adult in these legislative and judicial decisions.

[25]Starting from another point of inquiry, law may be viewed "as a concrete and continuous process for meeting both man's need for stability by providing authority, rule, and precedent, and his need for flexibility by providing for each authority a counter-authority, for each rule a counter-rule and for each precedent a counter-precedent. . . . To the extent law provides a proper mix of continuity and flexibility it provides the basis for a stable, vital and viable society capable of keeping its resolutions peaceful." J. Goldstein, "Psychoanalysis and Jurisprudence," *Yale Law Journal*, 77 (1968), pp. 1053, 1056.

[26]Stone, "The Conscientious Objector," *Columbia University Quarterly*, 21 (1919), pp. 253, 269.

[27]380 U.S. 163 (1965) (emphasis added). See also Welsh v. United States, U.S. 333, 356 (1970), Justice Harlan concurring: "The constitutional question that must be faced in this case is whether a statute that defers to the individual's conscience only when his views emanate from adherence to theistic religious beliefs is within the power of Congress. . . . Having chosen to exempt, [Congress] cannot draw the line between theistic or nontheistic religious beliefs on the one hand and secular beliefs on the other. Any such distinctions are not, in my view, compatible with the Establishment Clause of the First Amendment." The majority reached its decision on a statutory interpretation of the draft law. Cf. Gillette v. United States, 401 U.S. 437 (1971), upholding section 6(j) of the Military Selective Service Act which exempts persons who oppose participation in all war, but not those who object only to participation in a particular war.

[28]380 U.S. at 183-85 (emphasis added).

[29]297 F. Supp. 902 (D. Mass. 1969) *appeal dismissed* 399 U.S. 267 (1970).

[30]*Ibid.*, at 909-10.

[31]406 U.S. 205 (1972).

[32]*Ibid.*, at 210-35.

[33]P. Kurland, "The Supreme Court, Compulsory Education, and the First Amendment's Religion Clauses," *West Virginia Law Review*, 75 (1973), pp. 213, 236-37.

[34]See D. L. Rosenhan, "On Being Sane in Insane Places," *Science*, 179 (January 19, 1973), p. 250; J. Katz, J. Goldstein, A. Dershowitz, *Psychoanalysis, Psychiatry and Law: Part Two* (New York, 1967); and J. Goldstein and J. Katz, "Dangerousness and Mental Illness—Some Observations on the Decision to Release Persons Acquitted by Reason of Insanity," *Yale Law Journal*, 70 (1960), p. 225.

[35]Fla. Stat. Ann. §394.22 (1) (1969). This statute was applicable in O'Connor v. Donaldson, 422 U.S. 563 (1975) and was repealed by Fla. Stat. Ann. §394.459 (1973). See S. Brakel and R. Rock, eds., *The Mentally Disabled and the Law* (1971).

[36]Fla. Stat. Ann. §394.22 (11) (1969), repealed by Fla. Stat. Ann. §394.459, 394.467 (1973): "A person may be involuntarily hospitalized if he is mentally ill and because of his illness is: (1) likely to injure himself or others if allowed to remain at liberty or (2) in need of care or treatment and lacks sufficient capacity to make a responsible application on his own behalf."

[37]422 U.S. 563, 565 (1975).

[38]*Ibid.*, at 572 (quoting Donaldson v. O'Connor, 493 F.2d 507, 520 [5th Cir. 1974]).

[39]*Ibid.*, at 573, 575-76.

[40]There are, of course, in the inchoate crimes of attempt, solicitation, and conspiracy, and in procedures of preventative detention before conviction and parole denial after conviction, opportunities for violation of this general principle of criminal law.

Notes on Contributors

ROBERT N. BELLAH, born in 1927 in Altus, Oklahoma, is Ford Professor of Sociology and Comparative Studies at the University of California, Berkeley. He is the author of *Beyond Belief* (1970), *Émile Durkheim on Morality and Society* (1973), *The Broken Covenant* (1975), and is co-author (with Charles Y. Glock) of the forthcoming *The New Religious Consciousness*. He is preparing a larger study on the development of religion in human history.

WILLIAM J. BOUWSMA, born in 1923 in Ann Arbor, Michigan, is Sather Professor of History at the University of California, Berkeley. He is the author of *Venice and the Defense of Republican Liberty* (1968).

ROBERT COLES, born in 1929 in Boston, is research psychiatrist for the Harvard University Health Services. He has written numerous articles on the problems of desegregation and on the lives of migrant farm workers and sharecroppers which have appeared in medical, psychiatric, and general publications.

ERIK H. ERIKSON, born in Frankfurt-am-Main, Germany, of Danish parentage, in 1902, is professor emeritus of human development at Harvard University, and has been senior consultant in psychiatry for the Mount Zion Hospital in San Francisco since 1972. His many publications include *Childhood and Society* (1950), *Young Man Luther: A Study in Psychoanalysis and History* (1958), *Gandhi's Truth* (1969), and *Dimensions of a New Identity* (the Jefferson Lectures, 1973) (1974).

JOSEPH GOLDSTEIN, born in 1923 in Springfield, Massachusetts, is Walton Hale Hamilton Professor of Law Science and Social Policy at the Yale University Law School. His published works include *The Family and the Law* (with Jay Katz) (1965); *Crime, Law and Society* (with A. S. Goldstein) (1971), and *Beyond the Best Interests of the Child* (with Anna Freud and A. J. Solnit) (1973).

TAMARA K. HAREVEN, born in 1937 in Czernautz, Romania, is professor of history at Clark University, director of the History of the Family Program, and editor of the *Journal of Family History*. She is the author of *Eleanor Roosevelt: An American Conscience* (1968), and *Anonymous Americans: Explorations in American Social History* (1971).

WINTHROP D. JORDAN, born in 1931 in Worcester, Massachusetts, is professor of history at the University of California, Berkeley, and the author of *White Over Black: American Attitudes Toward the Negro, 1550-1812* (1968).

HERANT A. KATCHADOURIAN, born in 1933 in Iskenderun, Turkey, is associate professor of psychiatry and behavioral sciences and a member of the faculty for the program in human biology at Stanford University. Among his publications are *Transition to Adulthood* (in press) and, as co-author, *Fundamentals of Human Sexuality* (2nd edition, 1975).

IRA M. LAPIDUS, born in 1937 in New York City, is professor of history at the University of California, Berkeley. He is the author of several studies on the social history of the Near East, including *Muslim Cities in the Later Middle Ages* (1967), and is the editor of *Middle Eastern Cities* (1970).

KENNETH S. LYNN, born in 1923 in Cleveland, Ohio, is professor of history at the Johns Hopkins University. His most recent books include *William Dean Howells: An American Life* (1971), *Visions of America* (1973), and the forthcoming *A Divided People*.

MARTIN E. MALIA, born in 1924 in Springfield, Massachusetts, is professor of history at the University of California, Berkeley, and the author of *Alexander Herzen and the Birth of Russian Socialism* (1961), and the forthcoming *Russia Under Western Eyes: From Peter the Great to Khrushchev*.

THOMAS P. ROHLEN, born in 1940 in Evanston, Illinois, is associate professor of anthropology and fellow of Cowell College at the University of California, Santa Cruz. He has written *For Harmony and Strength: Japanese White-Collar Organization in Anthropological Perspective* (1974).

Notes on Contributors

LLOYD I. RUDOLPH, born in 1927 in Chicago, is professor of political science and the social sciences at the University of Chicago. He has published, with Susanne Hoeber Rudolph, *The Modernity of Tradition: Political Development in India* (1967), *Education and Politics in India: Studies in Organization, Society and Policy* (1972), and *The Coordination of Complexity in South Asia* (1975).

SUSANNE HOEBER RUDOLPH, born in 1930 in Mannheim, Germany, is professor of political science and the social sciences at the University of Chicago. She is the co-author of several books with Lloyd I. Rudolph (see above).

TU WEI-MING, born in 1940 in Kunming (Yünnan), China, is associate professor of history at the University of California, Berkeley. He is the author of *Neo-Confucian Thought in Action: Wang Yang-ming's Youth (1472-1509)* and *Centrality and Commonality—An Exploratory Essay on Chung-yung*, both to appear in 1976.

WALLACE STEGNER, born in 1909 in Lake Mills, Iowa, is a writer and professor emeritus of English at Stanford University. He is the author of many books, including *The Big Rock Candy Mountain* (1943), *Beyond the Hundredth Meridian* (1954), *Angle of Repose* (1971), and *The Uneasy Chair: A Biography of Bernard De Voto* (1974).

Index